THINKING IN TIME

THINKING IN TIME

The Uses of History for Decision-Makers

Richard E. Neustadt
Ernest R. May

FP
THE FREE PRESS

The Free Press
A Division of Simon & Schuster Inc.
1230 Avenue of the Americas
New York, N.Y. 10020

First Free Press Paperback Edition 1988

Printed in the United States of America

printing number

30 29 28 27 26 25 24

Library of Congress Cataloging-in-Publication Data

Neustadt, Richard E.
Thinking in time.

Bibliography: p.
Includes index.
1. United States—Politics and government—1945—Decision making—Case studies. 2. United States—Foreign relations—1945—Decision making—Case studies. 3. Decision making—Case studies. 4. Historical models. I. May, Ernest R. II. Title. III. Title: The uses of history for decision-makers.
E743.N378 1986 350.007'2 85-29169
ISBN 0-02-922790-9
ISBN 0-02-922791-7 pbk.

TO BERT

who critiqued the first draft

Contents

Preface

This book is addressed to those who govern—or hope to do so. It is for men and women elected or appointed to public office. It is also for those who assist them, as aides or "bureaucrats," and those who report on them or study them or try to influence them. The purpose of this preface is to make plain what we undertake—and why.

For most of our lives history and governance have fascinated us. We have spent a lot of time wondering how the first might help the second. Since the 1970s we have jointly taught a professional school course labeled "Uses of History." Of those who studied with us, only a few were "students" in the usual sense of the term. Most were men and women sent back to school in midcareer to train for higher assignments. A number were senior officials—legislators, bureau chiefs, colonels, generals, ambassadors, and the like—enrolled in executive programs.

We started the course in part because we sensed around us—in our classes, in the media, in Washington—a host of people who did not know any history to speak of and were unaware of suffering any lack, who thought the world was new and all its problems fresh (all made since Hiroshima or Vietnam or Watergate or the latest election) and that decisions in the public realm required only reason or emotion, as preferred. Yet we also saw that despite themselves Washington decision-makers actually used history in their decisions, at least for advocacy or for comfort, whether they knew any or not. We began our course in hope that, with help from government officials doubling as students, we could develop workaday procedures to get more history used better on the job by busy people preoccupied with daily decisions and other aspects of management.

Who taught whom is a nice question. Much of what we say in this book we learned from students, especially ones who called or wrote to tell us how some use of history "really worked!" Nearly all those who took the course tell us they enjoyed it. More important, they tell us it has helped them do what they are paid to do, namely to make decisions and manage programs.[1] Their testimony gives us hope that this book too can be enjoyed *and* put to use—both at once.

In every sense of the term the book is co-authored. We taught together, class by class, and have written together, chapter by chapter. It has been a long process. We each wrote half the chapters in our first draft, then swapped them for redrafting with the rule that anything could be changed. Almost everything was. We had a further rule that any changes could be argued. Some were, some not. We carried on the argument by means of successive drafts, with new material subject to the same rules. There were so many swaps that each of us would change something only to be surprised by the other's "O.K. with me, you wrote it." We debated sources and have argued out interpretations. Not only can we no longer recall who first wrote what, we cannot now remember who first thought what—or even who first found what when we jointly researched something. We are of one mind and (we hope) one voice.

Though the book is about *uses* of history, not history *per se,* the uses are illustrated by examples taken from history. Some of our readers may be surprised to find that most of the examples come from the 1950s and later, some even from the 1970s and 1980s. Like many of our practitioner-students, they may have been taught to think of "history" as ending around the time their parents were born, certainly long before they were. Our definition is more literal and catholic, comprehending any happenings of record, down to and including today's headlines.

Our chosen illustrations, being mostly American and mostly from the last four decades, fall within the remembered past for the majority of people now at senior levels in our government. For the successor generation, born in the decade after World War II, some of the events lie in dead spots—too recent to have been talked about in school but already too distant to have often come up around the home. For still younger men and women just entering professional life, our illustrations are nearly all of that sort. Twenty-two-year-olds have only dim associations, if any, with words or phrases pungent for men or women a decade older. "Tet" and "Watergate" are examples; "hostages" as in "Teheran" and "marines" as in "Beirut" will soon be others. We focus on cases from probable dead spots in part because, as we argue in later chapters, one of history's uses is to understand people whose age, sex, race, nationality, or beliefs are different from one's own. We focus on those cases also because, at our ages, they are meaningful for us, a point to which we shall return.

Most of our illustrations qualify as horror stories. That is not because life is necessarily so. It is partly because reporters prefer to record trouble and discord, partly because memoir writers provide more convincing detail when puzzling out why they did something wrong than when bragging that they did something right. It is also, however, because fully certified horror stories serve our purposes best.

In the majority of our cases participants themselves feel something went wrong. Among such instances are the Bay of Pigs affair, the Americanization of the Vietnam War, Gerald Ford's effort to protect the country from a swine flu epidemic that never came, various episodes from the Carter Administration, and the Reagan regime's early misadventure with social security cuts. The individuals who made the key decisions, or at least some of them, looked back and asked, "How in God's name did we come to do *that?*"

Given that opening, we can ask of each case: If routine staff work had brought into view historical evidence overlooked or not sought, might *"that"* not have occurred? Of course we use hindsight. What else? But our use of hindsight is professional rather than political, at least in the common sense of "political," intended more to identify pointers for future performance than to render a verdict on anyone or any group. Omitted here are any number of stories which we regard as awful but which participants think were pretty good—the 1970 invasion of Cambodia, for example. Our preference is to second-guess only people who have already second-guessed themselves.

Some readers are apt to think us unduly hard on the Carter Administration. We go back and back to the Carter years like someone tonguing a sensitive tooth. There are at least three reasons for that. The Carter presidency came and went while we were working hardest on our course. It offered something for discussion almost every time the class met. Second, as we wrote this book, Carter, his Chief of Staff, his National Security Assistant, and his Secretary of State all published memoirs. Those measurably improved our ability to document hunches. Third, the memoirists all agreed that many things had gone wrong. While no two joined on just what had gone awry or who was to blame, all implied that what happened ought to have been preventable. Memoirs from the Eisenhower and Nixon administrations had accorded us few such points of entry. The memoirists ascribed misfortune to the stars or at least to Congress or the Constitution, not to possible shortcomings in their own thinking or procedure. The literature of the Carter Administration by contrast invited our question: What staff work by whom, and when, might have made outcome match intention better?

There may be a fourth reason. James Fallows, once a speechwriter for Carter, wrote in the *Atlantic Monthly* of "Carter's cast of mind: his view of problems as technical, not historical, his lack of curiosity about how the story turned out before."[2] We may find in the Carter Administration so many illustrations for our points because the staff work inspired by Carter was markedly ahistorical.

Had we started this book later, and were there now more memoirs from Ronald Reagan's time than former Secretary of State Alexander Haig's not very revealing *Caveat,* we would surely seem more up to date in criticism. What, after all, were U.S. Marines doing in Beirut in 1983? As it is, we see no choice but to ride Carter, complementing tales about his time with others going back to John F. Kennedy (another President exposed by memoirists) and on back to Franklin D. Roosevelt. All we can do is repeat that we are not trying to blame anyone but only to suggest how, at the margin, the public's business might be better done in future.

Of each illustration, we ask whether the decision-makers,

within the limits of their circumstances, could have done a bit better. If so, how? And what generalizations could practitioners extract for their own—or anyone else's—workaday use? To ask those questions involves imagining how the story might have worked out if some characters had played their roles differently. For scholars trained to think of history as a seamless fabric, impenetrably complex, not to be changed by a stitch here or a tuck there, such imagining is intellectually painful. How much so, only other scholars, similarly trained, can fully appreciate. But, given our purpose, no alternative approach suggested itself.

We are concerned with practice in government service, and the government that concerns us is primarily our own. That is not for lack of interest in others. Rather, it acknowledges our debt to our students, most of them American, and our recognition that institutional arrangements in the United States have a very special character, even as against those of other technologically advanced countries. If what we find turns out to fit conditions in other regimes, or in private firms, well and good. But we make no claim to that effect. We hope this book facilitates comparisons; making them, however, is not our present purpose.

Our aim has strict limits. We offer suggestions as to *how* officials and their aides might do their work. We say little about *what* they have done or ought to do. That our suggestions about procedure stress question-asking and presumption-probing mitigates, we think, any charge of Machiavellian indifference to the morality of governmental action. If our approach prompts an alternative charge of encouraging conservatism in expectation, caution in conduct, so be it. We argue at various places in the book that use of history can stimulate imagination: Seeing the past can help one envision alternative futures. But we concede that analysis can also be an enemy of vision. Columbus probably would never have sailed had he been more aware of the flimsiness of his premises. Still, our own experiences, vicarious through reading as well as direct, tell us that caution is a virtue, never more than now in the third decade of the missile age. To this extent, we plead guilty.

Also, we make no pretense of organizing a capital-M Methodology. Our stories are accompanied by thoughts about what then had to be analyzed or advocated, and how actual performances might have been improved upon (or in successful cases reproduced) by busy people comparably placed. For them we derive and define a set of guidelines we label "mini-" or "small-m" methods, intended to be easily remembered and applied for short times on short notice, as befits men and women at work.

After horror stories survivors usually see questions they should have asked. Those questions fall into general categories: Why did we believe *that?* Why did we expect *that?* What made us believe he or she (or they) would do *that?* Taken in sequence, our mini-methods provide a checklist of questions to be asked early instead of late. Other checklists may work equally well. All we can claim for ours is that it has been repeatedly revised, reworded, and trimmed, partly as a result of rethinking examples, partly as a result of reports of trial and error on the job. The mini-methods have no magic, but most people who try them find that they work.

Lest encouragement from our practitioner-students go too much to our heads, we invited several senior figures in our stories to read and react. One of them was Dean Rusk. Offering us comment on this book in manuscript, he observed (among other things):

> Let me begin by teasing you a bit. During my Pentagon service in portions of World War II, I was familiar with the template for staff memoranda. . . . Many, many times those who wrote such staff memoranda started with [recommendations] and then wrote the memorandum backwards. Sometimes the most strenuous arguments occurred over how to state the problem to fit what had already been written. I have the impression that at times you . . . began with your own conclusions as to what ought to have been done on certain problems and then constructed your argument to come out at that point. If I mention this, it is simply to remind you that you are human beings like the rest of us.
>
> A more important comment is that the written record reflects only a portion of the thoughts in the minds of those who are making decisions and of the content of discussions among themselves which do not appear in the written record. Any foreign policy question of any significance has within it dozens upon dozens of secondary and tertiary questions and the minds of policy officers run through a very extensive checklist of such elements—regardless of what the written record shows. These checklists faintly resemble that which an airplane pilot uses before taking off in the plane. My impression is that you have somewhat underestimated the complexities of some of these issues and have underestimated the processes through which decision makers go before they reach a decision.

With regard to his first point we argue only, in our own defense, that within human limits we have tried, consistently, *not* to let our hindsight run away with us. We think, in any case, that what *we* wish had been done (when we do have wishes) actually was advocated, or at least conceived, contemporaneously, by at least some participants. As for Rusk's second point, we hope we have not simplified unnecessarily; where it is willful we have done it solely in deference to the reader's attention span. Our stories are intended but to illustrate *our* points, not to provide a substitute for other historical records. We try, accordingly, by note, to give the reader access to fuller accounts elsewhere.

For nearly all illustrations, it is true, we also draw on what has been said or written to us privately by participants, and not all of that additional testimony has been footnoted or even formally recorded. We have been guided by their wishes. This is not to imply that readers should take on trust our version of these stories; it is simply to give warning that the notes do not identify all our sources. Some of what we have written qualifies, we hope, as journalism.

Throughout we make three assumptions, all implicit in our hope that usual practice can be improved. They are at the heart of our teaching and at the heart of this book:

- In employment of government power, particulars matter. Ideology, *Zeitgeist,* or general forces in society or the economy express themselves through given minds employing given means on given days in given places, and results for given people will not be the same when any of those variables change.
- Marginal improvement in performance is worth seeking. Indeed, we doubt that there is any other kind. Decisions come one at a time, and we would be satisfied, taking each on its own terms, to see a slight upturn in the average. This might produce much more improvement measured by results.
- A little thought can help. No decision-maker may be altogether rational. Rational or not, most are bound to miss cues some of the time. Still, like teachers everywhere within the reach of Western science, we take rationality as a convention of and standard for performance. Yet simultaneously we are aware that busy people in authority, when faced with complicated governmental problems and compelled to act under uncertainty, will not—cannot—escape an almost irresistible temptation to think first of what to do and only second, if

at all, of whether to do anything. But how much thought, how long, can practitioners spare for history? How much can they stand while that temptation to act tugs so at them and everyone around them? Prudence cautions against sweeping answers. Ours are modest.

Before getting to our stories themselves, we have to add three further prefatory points. The first is that this book mirrors, in a way, the history we have lived through. How can it not? Naturally, so do our illustrations. In choosing instances to illustrate our points we have been guided not alone by the availability of other people's memoirs and records but by the extent of our own feel for situations, our own memories. We introduce, for instance, Frances Perkins, the first woman Cabinet member at the Federal level, and also sketch aspects of social security since Franklin Roosevelt's early presidency. One of us—Neustadt—was in Washington at high school then; his father, a New Deal official, had been friendly with Perkins for twenty years and played a part in the establishment of social security. Things heard at the dinner table can lodge in young minds, especially when there was so much of interest, color, uplift, and amusement to be heard during FDR's first term. No doubt our choice of illustrations was affected by some fragments Neustadt stored up young.

Our choice of other stories was still more affected by some facets of his subsequent career. At the start of the Korean War he was a junior aide to Harry Truman, working mostly on the legislative side of White House business (including, incidentally, the expansion of social security); Neustadt saw and felt the consequences of the war politically from that perspective. A decade later, as a consultant to President Kennedy, Neustadt, among other things, made a detailed study for him of the so-called Skybolt crisis with the British. That led to some assignments early in the Johnson years on other issues with our NATO allies. It also led, much later, to a comparable study for Joseph Califano, Carter's first Secretary of Health, Education, and Welfare (now Health and Human Services), who had been an assistant at the Pentagon in Kennedy's time. Califano recalled the Skybolt study, and wanted an equivalent to point up the administrative problems he had just inherited in the immediate aftermath of the swine flu scare. Not surprisingly, we chose as illustrations for this book both Skybolt and swine flu, as well as the inception of hostilities in Korea. And in treating of Vietnam decisions, which affected us as teachers (to say nothing of our students, college, country) throughout so much of our academic careers—reasons enough to include them here—we utilized the insights into people Neustadt had acquired, incidentally, in the early and mid-1960s on the White House scene.

The other of us—May—a decade younger, first encountered Washington in uniform during the Korean War as a historian for the Joint Chiefs of Staff. His later work in diplomatic history led him to review the key decisions of that war, which dovetailed nicely, and in Johnson's time May surveyed for friends in the Pentagon, confidentially, the mixed bag of analogues with U.S. bombing meant to bring a change of heart at Hanoi. In the 1970s, under three successive Secretaries of Defense, May superintended a review in depth of the strategic arms race between Washington and Moscow since the Soviet atomic blast of 1949; SALT negotiations and their outcomes were within his purview. Like Neustadt's Skybolt study, May's work remains classified, but in the same way it served to guide our choice of illustrations, especially SALT II. In the 1970s May was also a consultant for the Senate committee investigating the Central Intelligence Agency. He occasionally looked over the shoulder of a former student, Anne Karalekas, as she prepared an official history of CIA. That history also figures in our illustrations.

Later in this book we write of "placement," a technique for arraying on a time-line both events in public history and known details in private life that may affect the outlook of a person with whom one deals. (This is where Perkins, among others, comes in.) Readers, as they deal with us, will note that our own histories have influenced our choice of illustrations and, moreover, that our many years in teaching, combined with the events through which we and our students lived—as well as those through which we lived as students—affect not alone the subject matter of this book but also its conclusions. Our stress is upon prudence; in our circumstances that can scarcely be surprising.

One of us was born immediately after World War I, the other at the onset of the Great Depression. We have shared adult awareness of historical events since World War II. We have done so as Americans and Westerners, Neustadt from California, May from there and Texas too. We both began university teaching—Neustadt at Cornell, Columbia, then Harvard, May at Harvard throughout—in the mid 1950s. May pursued diplomatic history, Neustadt political institutions, especially the American presidency, which brought our interests together. In the mid-1960s we developed and pursued a common interest in the question why so many results diverged so far from policy intentions. Vietnam and Great Society together sparked that question for us and for others of our colleagues whom we gathered in a research circle called the May Group, after its chairman. (Its formal title was a jawbreaker: Institute of Politics Faculty Study Group on Bureaucracy, Politics, and Policy.) It proved a productive circle; out of it came, among other things, seeds of a new management curriculum for the then emergent Kennedy School of Government. We have taught there ever since, often together.

In managerial terms prudence seems to turn, above all else, on canny judgments about feasibility—about the doability, that is to say, of contemplated courses of action. How to make such judgments or, more to the point, how to help decision-makers arm themselves to do so has concerned us in much of our previous writing. The search continues here. On the evidence of actual decision-making, those writings scarcely made a dent. That may be partly because we did not make our previous advice sufficiently persuasive or because we failed to get our previous formulations right. (Possibly the problem is impervious to anybody's writing, but we aren't ready to cry "uncle" yet!) Partly it may be because Americans in public life have been habituated by national history, at least until this generation, to "can do" beliefs. Anything we seek we can accomplish; implementation follows automatically from decision, assuming enough will. Twenty years ago, just at the start of Vietnam escalation, concerned that such beliefs were pushing it along, Neustadt testified to Senator Henry M. Jackson's Subcommittee on National Security Staffing and Operations;

> Government decisions, action decisions, the decisions which accrete into what we call public policy, always involve weighing the desirable against the feasible. The public officer at every action-level asks himself not only "what" but also "how," considering not only goals but also ways and means, and then he calculates his chances to secure the means. . . . [O]ur public officers have generally inclined to make the calculation without bothering their heads too much about their wherewithal in operating terms . . . have tended to assume that if they could assure political assent, they could invent, or improvise or somehow force the requisite responses from the men who actually would do the work in government and out. . . .

> That assumption probably has roots deep in our history: Americans have often improvised the means to do what nobody had done before. We invented federalism, won the West, conducted civil war on an unprecedented scale, coped with immigration, mastered mass production, built the Panama Canal—which was a great feat in its time. And since . . . we began to fashion our defense and our diplomacy in modern terms we frequently have followed the assumption in those spheres as well, with consequences which appear to bear it out. Witness Harry Truman's aid to Greece, the Marshall Plan, the Berlin airlift, NATO. . . .

In words that seem only mildly cautionary now but expressed a pessimism unfashionable then, Neustadt went on to say, "favoring conditions, I suspect, become prerequisites for an effective outcome of decisions which take management on faith. Unfortunately these conditions are not always present."[3]

The 1980s are not the 1960s. Hard happenings in the intervening years have contributed, relatively speaking, to cautiousness abroad and at home. Rhetoric about struggles with evil empires and a new national revolution accompanies shrinkage both in engagement internationally and in hopes held out domestically. Yet ebullient can-doism still persists. Witness what is said about how economic growth will somehow take care of all the disadvantaged people whom, it is presumed, government is now too poor or too ineffectual to aid. We like optimism and hope ebullience can be sustained. We yearn, however, to see can-doism disciplined a bit in ways uncharacteristic of the American past, and we hope this book can make a modest contribution to that end. By light of our experience, modesty is proper; the hope, however, is heartfelt.

Because decision-makers always draw on past experience, whether conscious of doing so or not, we sometimes tell students that our course has aims akin to those of junior high school sex education. Since they are bound to do what we talk about, later if not sooner, they ought to profit from a bit of forethought about ways and means. In this context a little knowledge, far from being bad, holds out the prospect of enhancing not alone safety but also enjoyment. Our second-to-last prefatory point stresses the fun.

Our book, like our course, has as a (not so) hidden agenda item: filling gaps in knowledge about important aspects of American history, at least that of the twentieth century, particularly in those dead spots which usually blanket the half-decade or so just before and after birth. Other longer, near-dead areas, encompassing almost all of human history before one's own, are commonplace. Filling in such gaps can be enjoyable indeed for intelligent, professionally educated ignoramuses. There are plenty of those, through little fault of their own, and American education makes for more each year. Our problem always is to keep our hidden agenda from swamping our avowed one. That is why we hold our illustrations tight in the chapters to follow. But in class we have to cope with students asking, almost regardless of age, "What happened next?" and "Why?" More often than not, alas, they do not know. Finding out strikes them as fun, if only somebody will tell them. Often the fun is in the spectacle.

We thus have always had in mind, as secondary objectives, the reasons most traditionally advanced for reading history. The reasons are aesthetic as well as informational and, in principle, encompass everybody. But our primary concern remains with those who try to govern, as they exercise authority through choices large or small. Our focus, to repeat, is on the uses they make of history, or fail to make but could, and how they might do better for themselves in their own terms.

Finally, as we have to say more than once to our practitioner-students: Ours is not a history course—and so to readers we repeat that this book is not a history book. It is, in fact, not even about the stories it tells. It is about how to *use* experience, whether remote or recent, in the process of deciding what to do today about the prospect for tomorrow.

REN ERM

Harvard University
Cambridge, Massachusetts
November 1985

1 Success Story

"They're too busy. Can't read what they get now. They'll glance at papers in the limousine, thumb them while someone is talking, or just wing it. If you do get their attention, you can't keep it. They will have to catch a plane or go to a press conference."

So an experienced diplomat responded to our argument that government officials should make better use of history. He was right. It may be easier to get a million dollars of public money than a minute from a president or a cabinet officer. The Bay of Pigs debacle (discussed later) occurred in part because President John F. Kennedy and his key advisers could never give it sustained attention for more than forty-five minutes at a time.[1] The same strains work on governors, mayors, and many officials much less exalted.

But we are not asking a lot. In government and outside, decision-makers use history now. They draw every day on the past experience of other people. They assign aides bits and pieces of historical research: going to the files or checking memories and comparing recollections. They look at a great many words on paper. A former high official wrote us, "Although the public impression is that Presidents and Secretaries of State have no time to read or think, the truth is that most of them spend an enormous amount of time reading material generated both in the government and outside."[2] We argue chiefly that uses now made of history can be more reflective and systematic, hence more helpful.

This book is about how to do it. With stories of success and failure we suggest practices which, if made routine, could at least protect against common mistakes. We have tried to make the stories entertaining. We think them also instructive, even for readers too young to vote. Our particular target audience, however, consists of decision-makers and the women and men who work for them (or hope to do so) as direct or personal staff. Almost every executive has a split personality. He or she wants to act and feels impatient with those who block action. Presidents feel so about Congress, the bureaucracy, foreign allies, and the press; cabinet officers feel so about Presidents; assistant secretaries feel so about cabinet officers; and so on down to the bottom rungs of management. At the same time, every executive fears being hustled into action by those impatient people down below. The same holds true for legislators; they also make decisions and have decisions thrust upon them. Good staff work consists of helping a boss with both sets of concerns—clearing obstacles on one side while setting them up on the other. This book is intended to be a manual for such staff work. We hope the bosses will read it and tell their aides to put its recommendations into practice. We hope the aides will use it and use it and use it.

We start with a pair of stories about successes: the Cuban missile crisis of 1962 and the social security reform of 1983. Not everyone will agree that those were successes, but the participants so regarded them, and the majority of journalists so label them. Knowing mostly tales with less happy endings, we are not inclined to apply more rigid criteria. In the one case the missiles were withdrawn and nuclear war didn't happen. In the other, the system didn't run out of cash and wage-earners weren't penalized. Both met immediate issues without ending longer-run concerns. Castro remains an unrepentant Communist; cost-of-living adjustments still give Budget Directors fits. The priorities, however, appeared sound to most contemporaries and appear so still, in retrospect. The results are enough for us. Besides, one case is foreign, one domestic, one occurred under Democrats, the other under Republicans. They thus argue that effective use of history is independent of policy area or party.

We turn now to the first of the two stories; the other follows in our second chapter. Then we sum up what both show about using history better.

For President Kennedy, the acute phase of the missile crisis started about 8:45 A.M. on Tuesday, October 16, 1962, when his National Security Assistant, McGeorge Bundy, came to his bedroom to report that a U-2, a high-flying reconnaissance airplane, had brought back photographs showing Russians at work in Cuba on launch sites for medium-range nuclear missiles.[3]

Kennedy reacted with a mixture of alarm and anger. Five years earlier the Russians had startled the world by sending "Sputnik" rockets into space. The Soviet leader, Nikita Khrushchev, said this showed Russia could destroy the United States with intercontinental nuclear missiles. Americans feared a "missile gap" opening in the Russians' favor. Elected in 1960 partly on a promise to close that gap, Kennedy as President gave high priority to a big defense buildup. By the time new intelligence had proved Khrushchev to be bluffing, the United States was on the way to creating a missile gap about two hundred to one in its own favor. Relations had been tense, especially when the Russians suddenly put up a wall between East and West Berlin. More recently tension had eased. Kennedy reached a few agreements with Khrushchev. He hoped for more. Now this!

And in *Cuba!* The revolution of 1959 putting in power Fidel Casto and a Communist regime had shocked Americans at least as much as Sputnik had. Kennedy in 1960 held out hope that he would also get Cuba back into Washington's orbit. His failure to do so gave Republicans an issue for 1962. Castro helped them by asking for—and getting—Soviet military aid. Republican Senator Kenneth Keating of New York charged that the Russians were going to base nuclear missiles in Cuba. Other Republicans echoed him. Senator Homer Capehart of Indiana, running for reelection, called for an invasion of the island. No one, however, produced solid evidence of anything but defensive, nonnuclear air defense missiles. CIA analysts pointed out to Kennedy that the Russians had never placed nuclear missiles even in Eastern Europe: Why would they put them in Cuba? (The answer probably was that a medium-range missile in Eastern Europe could reach the Soviet Union; one in Cuba could not. But that point was easier to see after the fact.)

By late August Kennedy felt worried. He began daily reviews of relevant intelligence. On September 4 he assured the public that the government had no evidence that any Soviet offensive weapons were going into Cuba. For Khrushchev's ears he added, "Were it to be otherwise, the gravest issues would arise." Afterward he received reassurances not only from his intelligence services but directly from Soviet Ambassador Anatoly Dobrynin. To Theodore Sorensen, the President's chief domestic policy adviser and speechwriter, Dobrynin said that everything the Russians were doing in Cuba was "defensive in nature." Dobrynin said the same to Robert F. Kennedy, the Attorney General (and the President's brother).

The news Bundy brought to the President's bedroom that Tuesday morning was thus not utterly unforeseen. It was none the less shocking. Kennedy's immediate response was to name a handful of men with whom he wanted to take counsel. The group would come to be called the Executive Committee of the National Security Council—ExComm for short. It included Bundy, Sorensen, Secretary of State Dean Rusk, Secretary of Defense Robert McNamara, and Secretary of the Treasury Douglas Dillon. Robert Kennedy took part continuously. Others were eventually asked in.

For a week, the President and ExComm managed to keep the matter secret. Kennedy preserved a noncommittal smile when Soviet Foreign Minister Andrei Gromyko repeated to his face assurances that Russia would do nothing provocative before November's congressional elections. By various ruses, Kennedy and the others kept the White House press corps ignorant of their day-and-night debates.

When Kennedy and his ExComm first went to work, they used history—and did not use it—in very standard ways. In cases of which we know, debate in serious decision situations starts at least nine times out of ten with the question: What do we *do?* Background and context get skipped. The past comes in, if at all, in the form of analogy, with someone speaking of the current situation as like some other. That may be to put a familiar face on something strange. It may be for advocacy—because the analogue's supposed lesson supports the speaker's preference as to what to do. Otherwise, all concern is for the present, with seldom a glance backward or, in any focused way, toward the future. Of such usual practice we shall offer many examples. Here, even in the missile crisis, one sees it at the outset.

Recordings of ExComm's first meetings are now publicly available. Anyone visiting the John F. Kennedy Library in Boston can hear excerpts. The group assembles in the Cabinet Room of the White House a little before noon. Experts from the Central Intelligence Agency explain the U-2 photographs. A few questions are asked about details. Then, in a measured Southern accent, part rural Georgian and part Rhodes Scholar, Secretary Rusk starts substantive discussion by setting forth two choices: give an ultimatum for withdrawal of the missiles or stage a quick surprise strike to destroy them. The crackling, confident voice of McNamara asserts that "any air strike must be directed not solely against the missile sites, but against the missile sites plus the airfields plus the aircraft . . . plus all potential nuclear storage sites." Joint Chiefs Chairman General Maxwell Taylor says clearly, "What we'd like to do is . . . take 'em out without any warning whatever," but he tallies other military options, including a naval blockade. After some back and forth, Kennedy himself, his famous Boston cadence soft-voiced and hesitating, sets the terms for the rest of the day's debate. He specifies three choices: "One would be just taking out these missiles. Number two would be to take out all the airplanes. Number three is to invade." His conclusion as the group recesses is, "We're certainly going to do Number One. We're going to take out these missiles."

During the initial meeting analogies make an appearance. Saying that the Russians may be trying to draw attention to Cuba because they plan a move elsewhere, perhaps against Berlin, Rusk speaks of the "Suez–Hungary combination," alluding to 1956, when Western preoccupation with Suez had made it easier for the Soviets to use tanks to crush a revolution in Hungary. Subsequently, "Suez" becomes shorthand for such a diagnosis.

For subsequent days' debates, we do not yet have verbatim transcripts. We have to reconstruct from contemporary memoranda and later reminiscence. Wednesday saw members of ExComm hold various meetings with Kennedy not present. He had concluded that second-level people such as Rusk's deputy, George Ball, or McNamara's, Roswell Gilpatric, were more likely to speak up with the President not in the room. The scene shifted too. An antiseptic conference room on the seventh floor of the new State Department building became from then on the principal meeting place.

From some early point Robert Kennedy had begun to feel queasy about an air strike. On Tuesday he spoke against going for both missiles and bombers. "I would say that, uh, you're dropping bombs all over Cuba if you do the second. . . . You're going to kill an awful lot of people, and, uh, you're going to take an awful lot of heat on it." Expressing similar doubts, George Ball invoked an analogy. "This, uh, come in there on Pearl Harbor just frightens the hell out of me." Robert Kennedy later recalled passing his brother a note which said, "I know now how Tojo felt when he was planning Pearl Harbor." On Wednesday Robert Kennedy emphasized this analogy. Arguing now against any surprise air strike at all he said that it would be "a Pearl Harbor in reverse, and it would blacken the name of the United States in the pages of history." Notes on the Wednesday meetings prepared for the President by Sorensen referred several times to "Pearl Harbor."[4]

All this parallels what we see as standard practice, far from any ideal. The records of the ExComm suggest myopic concentration on what to do tomorrow. Reference is made now and then, partly for word-saving, partly for advocacy, to analogies from recent history. Looking back now, one can see signs of practice contrary to the usual. If action had been taken either the first day or the second, however, those signs would be scarcely noticeable. The decision would almost surely have been for an air strike. Whether the President would have chosen to hit not only the missile sites but also bombers and air defenses, we cannot guess. Whatever his choice, and whatever happened in the longer term, historians looking back (assuming there were any) would see Kennedy's decision as a product of usual practice.

In fact, Kennedy was not to announce a decision until Monday, October 22—after more than six days of nearly continuous debate. Then, telling the world what the Russians were doing, he was to proclaim a naval "quarantine." That course of action, initially mentioned in passing by General Taylor, had found its first champion in Vice President Lyndon Johnson. By the evening of the first day it had also become McNamara's favorite option—"this alternative doesn't seem to be a very acceptable one," he said, "but wait until you work on the others."[5] At some point—probably early on—the President came to the same opinion. By the weekend there was near-consensus. The U.S. Navy would stop any new missiles from going to Cuba. Kennedy would thus buy time for trying to talk the Russians into removing the missiles already there. By the following weekend, however, having used the time to no avail, it seemed, Kennedy was back at his starting point. The question again was whether to bomb only the missile sites or to go also for airfields. But on the second Sunday Khrushchev announced that he would withdraw the missiles. The story thus became one of success.

It may be that the only decision-making that mattered was Moscow's. The main American contribution may have been delay that allowed the Soviets to collect themselves. We suspect that American decisions and nondecisions had some more independent influence on the outcome. Whatever the case, as we look back, it seems clear to us that deliberate prolonging of the crisis, together with various moves aimed at producing a peaceful settlement, originated in or were at least much influenced by resort to history in ways not ordinary for American government officials. If the happy outcome was due even in part to those choices by Kennedy and his ExComm, then *un*usual uses of history perhaps deserve part of the credit.

Kennedy and his ExComm departed from standard practice first of all in subjecting analogies to serious analysis. The President early invited into ExComm former Secretary of State Dean Acheson, at that time a lawyer in private practice. Acheson favored a quick air strike. Hearing the Pearl Harbor analogy, he judged it, as he was to write later, "silly" and "thoroughly false and pejorative." He told the President that there were no points of similarity and many points of difference, to wit:

> [A]t Pearl Harbor the Japanese without provocation or warning attacked our fleet thousands of miles from their shores. In the present situation the Soviet Union had installed missiles ninety miles from our coast—while denying they were doing so—offensive weapons that were capable of lethal injury to the United States. This they were doing a hundred and forty years after the warning given in [the Monroe Doctrine]. How much warning was necessary to avoid the stigma of "Pearl Harbor in reverse."[6]

For ExComm and perhaps for the President, the effect of Acheson's analysis was the reverse of that intended. By stripping away all the dissimilarities, Acheson exposed the analogy's relevant point. Robert Kennedy responded to Acheson by saying, "For 175 years we had not been that kind of country. A sneak attack was not in our traditions." Then—not earlier—Secretary of the Treasury Dillon was won over. "I felt that I was at a real turning point in history," he recalled later, "I knew then that we should not undertake a strike without warning."[7]

All in all, the proceedings of ExComm are distinguished by

the extent—unusual—to which analogies were invoked sparingly and, when invoked, were subjected to scrutiny. "Suez" did not last. A State Department lawyer referred to FDR's "Quarantine Address" of 1937 when suggesting that "quarantine" be substituted for "blockade," but no one represented the situations as analogous. Though Sorensen recalls talk of the Berlin blockade of 1948–49 and of the Bay of Pigs affair of 1961, possible points of comparison do not seemed to have gripped anyone's imagination.[8] When Kennedy went on television he referred to the "clear lesson" of the 1930s as one reason for demanding that the Russians back off. But that was rhetoric. The available records of ExComm debates are innocent of any allusion to "lessons" of the 1930s.

ExComm's second noteworthy departure from usual practice took the form of attention to the issue's history—to its sources and its context.

Kennedy himself had much to do with this, in part just by the choices he made in forming ExComm. He put a high premium on secrecy. "Maybe a lot of people know about what's there," he said at the initial meeting, "but what we're going to do about it ought to be, you know, the tightest of all, because otherwise we bitch it up." Nevertheless, he included in ExComm men who did not have to be there. Dillon is one example. The Treasury Department had no title to representation. Of course, Kennedy could see a partisan storm coming. "We've just elected Capehart . . . and Ken Keating will probably be the next President," he said to one aide soon after discovery of the missile sites. Since Dillon had been Under Secretary of State for Eisenhower and was the most conspicious Republican in the subsequent Administration, Kennedy may have wanted him for the sake of seeming bipartisan. The same could hold true for his inviting former Defense Secretary Robert A. Lovett to join ExComm, for Lovett was a leader of New York's Republican establishment. Or Kennedy may have turned to Dillon and Lovett just because he valued their judgment. Whatever the case, he got as a bonus the benefit of long and wide-ranging experience. He had around him men whose memories of dealing with the Soviet Union reached all the way back to World War II. He also called in Charles Bohlen and Llewellyn Thompson, two of the most senior serving members of the State Department's Russian service, and Edwin Martin from the State Department's Latin American bureau. Those three had memories, the first two of Russia and the third of Cuba, which also went far back.[9]

We suspect that this result was not accidental. Looking at the whole record of ExComm, one sees Kennedy himself repeatedly raising questions about the actual history of the issue. "I don't know enough about the Soviet Union," he said on the very first day, "but if anybody can tell me any other time since the Berlin blockade where the Russians have given us so clear a provocation, I don't know when it's been because they've been awfully cautious really." He went on to wonder aloud whether the crisis might have been averted if he had said something more clearly, earlier (in retrospect, a telling criticism). He kept trying to find out when the Russians had decided to install the missiles, seeking in the timing some clue to their possible motives. On his orders the CIA produced a detailed review of the history of Soviet military aid to Cuba. During the terrifying six days between his public speech and Khrushchev's backdown, Kennedy also asked an ExComm planning subcommittee to give high priority to a paper on "the Cuban base problem in perspective."[10]

Third, in unusual degree Kennedy and his ExComm looked hard at key presumptions. During the initial meetings, the President said "it doesn't make any difference if you get blown up by an ICBM flying from the Soviet Union or one that was ninety miles away."[11] When Sorensen summarized for Kennedy the first two days' ExComm deliberations, he wrote: "It is generally agreed that these missiles, even when fully operational, do not significantly alter the balance of power. . . . Nevertheless it is generally agreed that the United States cannot tolerate the known presence of offensive nuclear weapons in a country ninety miles from our shore, if our courage and commitments are ever to be believed by either allies or adversaries." Though no one paused over it at the time, an early exchange between Kennedy and Bundy exposed a weakness in that particular pair of presumptions:

> KENNEDY: It's just as if we suddenly began to put a major number of MRBMs [medium range missiles] in Turkey. Now that'd be goddamn dangerous, I would think.
>
> BUNDY: Well we did, Mr. President.

In fact, since 1957 the United States had had in Turkey Jupiter missiles of greater range than most of the Soviet missiles going into Cuba. Fifteen were still there.[12] The Soviets had "tolerated" them throughout.

In later ExComm sessions the President included one of McNamara's subordinates, Assistant Secretary of Defense Paul Nitze. In doing so, Kennedy dropped another tap into the past, for Nitze had been Acheson's chief planner back in Truman's time. Nitze challenged the proposition that the Cuban missiles did not affect the balance of power. The existing missile gap, he said, gave the United States an unquestionable "second-strike" capacity. The Russians knew the United States could devastate their country even if they successfully staged an all-out surprise attack. That knowledge presumably made them cautious about running any risk of war. With missiles in place in Cuba, Nitze argued, the Russians might reason differently. They might suppose that an all-out surprise attack could destroy enough American missiles and bombers so that Soviet territory would not suffer terrible damage. In any case, they might suppose that their home-based and Cuban-based missiles together posed such danger to the United States that the American government would not risk war over, for example, Berlin. Nitze argued that the missiles in Cuba thus made a real difference.

Given the President's puzzlement as to why the Soviet Union had suddenly ceased to behave conservatively, Nitze's argument had some force with Kennedy. He at least altered his previous presumption, taking thereafter the position that the missiles were more than symbolic. As one result he became clear in his own mind that the missiles mattered much more than did the Soviet bombers also going into Cuba. He pressed for removal of all "offensive" weapons, including the bombers, and the Russians in fact withdrew both; but Kennedy told ExComm that "we should not get 'hung up' on the . . . bombers."[13]

Another presumption tested and changed concerned U.S. capacity for a "surgical" air strike, one that would take out only the missile sites. Since military planners wanted to protect U.S. bombers by suppressing Cuban and Soviet air defenses, they exaggerated somewhat the difficulty of effectively bombing only the missile sites. Because McNamara had misgivings akin to Robert Kennedy's about any air strikes, he may have encouraged that exaggeration. Nevertheless, at least through the first few days, several members of ExComm believed that Kennedy should order a "surgical" strike and would end up doing so.

Like the presumption that missiles were missiles, wherever placed, the presumption that a "surgical" strike could be effected gave way less because scrutinized or explicitly tested against the historical record than because it was questioned by men who had lived relevant history. No one tallied up the precision of past air operations, but some of those present had seen a lot of them. Lovett, himself a one-time Navy flier, had been in World War II the civilian in charge of U.S. land-based air forces. That fact counted when he spoke for a naval blockade in preference to an air strike. Robert Kennedy was ever afterward to treasure Lovett's use of the quotation, "Good judgment is usually the result of experience. And experience is frequently the result of bad judgment."[14]

The thirteen days of the missile crisis saw many other presumptions challenged. McNamara and the Chief of Naval Operations exchanged furious words because McNamara questioned the presumption that the Navy knew how to put in effect the quarantine the President had ordered. Secretary Rusk provoked a lot of paper-writing in his own department and in the CIA by voicing doubt as to whether Castro was truly in the Russians' pocket. In fact, the Navy knew exactly what to do, and, though Castro was sometimes angry with the Russians, he never showed for a moment an inclination to strike a deal at their expense.[15] Nevertheless, Kennedy and his ExComm seem to us exemplary for the extent to which they asked: How well-founded are the presumptions on which we plan to act?

Fourth, Kennedy and ExComm showed uncommon interest in the history in the heads of their adversaries. Kennedy's questions at the first ExComm meeting were about the Soviet Union, conceived as a single rational actor. He asked, in effect, Why is *he* doing this to *me?* Most high-ranking officials involved in international disputes ask that type of question. Early speculation is anthropomorphic. "This is a left hook designed to make him tougher when he comes at us in November, presumably on Berlin," hazarded one ExComm participant endorsing the "Suez" thesis.[16] All that distinguished Kennedy's initial formulation was his retrospection—his interest in when the rational actor had decided to depart from a previous line of conduct. As the crisis continued, however, Kennedy and others began to conceive of the Soviet government more as a collection of individuals.

Coached chiefly by Thompson, members of ExComm began to consider the possibility that certain U.S. actions might provoke Khrushchev to act impulsively rather than out of cool reasoning. ExComm members also took into some account the possibility that pride might affect the Soviet military in case of an attack on *their* missile sites. So far as we can tell, neither Kennedy nor any member of ExComm wondered aloud about the Russian history that Khrushchev and other Soviet leaders had experienced—the Revolution, the civil war, the Great Purge, World War II, de-Stalinization, the split with China, and other great events. On the other hand, Thompson surely had some of that history in his own mind. Probably remembering the Soviet struggle for full diplomatic recognition and the Soviet role in designing the UN, Thompson talked to ExComm of how the Russians might be influenced by a vote of the Organization of American States. They set high store on legal formalities, he said. Also, Thompson predicted that they would press for removal of the U.S. missiles in Turkey: "they like parallels."[17]

According to Robert Kennedy, the President tried constantly to put himself in Khrushchev's position. Once during the crisis he even described to Ben Bradlee of the *Washington Post* how he thought he would feel if in the Kremlin, but he cautioned Bradlee that his words were off the record. "It isn't wise politically to understand Khrushchev's problem in quite this way."[18]

In the climactic hours of the crisis Kennedy received two messages from Khrushchev, the first a rambling four-part cable seeming to offer withdrawal of the missiles in return for a U.S. pledge not to invade Cuba, the second, more curt and formal, seeming to retract that offer. Instead of returning to "left hook" imagery, the President and members of ExComm speculated about factionalism in the Kremlin. They visualized Khrushchev, stamping around his giant office in the Kremlin, possibly not altogether sober, dictating to a secretary, and sending off the text without showing it to anyone. They imagined other members of the Politburo bending over the second cable and tightening its wording. All that made easier their decision to ignore the second cable and simply say yes to the first. Some of them thought later that this tactic was the source of their success, the means to bring the crisis to a close, yet they probably would not have settled on it had they not by then begun to think of Khrushchev as a person, with a history of his own.

Fifth, Kennedy and his ExComm paid attention to organizational histories. They did not do so in quite the way we shall advocate later. They thought of how organizations behaved without asking explicitly how they had behaved over time, and why. But the fact that they took organizational behavior into account at all distinguishes them from ninety-odd percent of the decision-making groups of which we have personal knowledge.

Again, Kennedy himself gave ExComm its cue. He seemed to understand in his bones the tendency of large organizations to act today as they acted yesterday. He pursued his own hunches about American performance. Among other things, he sent the CIA to photograph Air Force planes at Florida bases. The pictures showed that, contrary to his orders, the planes were lined up in the highly vulnerable standard position—wing tip to wing tip—just as at Manila twenty-one years before. Schooled in the inertia of military procedures as a junior officer in World War II, Kennedy was annoyed but not surprised.

Kennedy and ExComm were encouraged toward the quarantine option by Thompson's reminder that Russian military organizations practiced extreme secretiveness. Built into organizational routines, that secretiveness would make the Russians hesitant, they hoped, to risk having their ships boarded and searched.[19] In fact the Russians halted all missile-carrying ships well outside the quarantine line.

Thompson and other Sovietologists also helped Kennedy and the members of ExComm appreciate the possibility that events on the Soviet side could be products of organizational routine or momentum rather than deliberate purpose. Just when Kennedy and his advisers were trying to puzzle out the differences between the two Khrushchev cables, a U.S. U-2 plane was shot down over Cuba. It would have been easy, even natural, to see that as a signal confirming a hardened Soviet line. Kennedy, however, accepted Thompson's counsel not to read political significance into what could well have been just a Soviet air defense unit acting according to the book. Others urged at least tit-for-tat retaliation, but Kennedy chose to wait. As a result, no U.S. strike on a Soviet air defense site complicated Khrushchev's decision to accept Kennedy's terms. (He meanwhile must have had to show equal good sense, for another American U-2 blundered coincidentally into Soviet air space, moving Kennedy to explain, "There's always some son-of-a-bitch who doesn't get the word.")[20]

After the crisis ended, Kennedy said he thought the odds on war had been "between one out of three and even." At the same time, according to Robert Kennedy, the President believed Khrushchev to be "a rational, intelligent man who, if given sufficient time and shown our determination, would alter his position." The historian Arthur M. Schlesinger, who knew the Kennedy brothers well and has written movingly of both, offers an explanation for the seeming contradiction in terms that seem plausible to us, namely:

"Kennedy's grim odds were based on fear, not of Khrushchev's intentions, but of human error, of something going terribly wrong down the line."[21] If that is accurate, then the taking into account of historical patterns in organizational conduct may have been exceptionally important among the unusual practices exemplified by Kennedy and ExComm.

But a final peculiarity in their practice strikes us as perhaps most important of all. In unusual degree, Kennedy and his ExComm saw the issues before them as part of a time sequence beginning long before the onset of crisis and continuing into an increasingly indistinct future. The more Kennedy and ExComm deliberated, the more they weighed consequences and the more they shifted from the simple question of what to do *now* to the harder question: How will today's choices appear when they are history—when people look back a decade or a century hence?

The initial debate in ExComm involved no evident thought beyond the next week or so. As early as the evening of the first day, however, a few participants had lifted their sights. "I don't know what kind of a world we live in after we've struck Cuba," McNamara said. And Bundy: "Our principal problem is to try and imaginatively to think what the world would be like if we do this and what it will be like if we don't."[22]

The President's own way of looking ahead appeared most clearly in his eventual handling of the parallel problem—those U.S. missiles in Turkey. In early sessions the notion of a swap had been dismissed as unthinkable. By the tenth and eleventh days of the crisis, on the other hand, Kennedy and his advisers talked about the possibility in terms of how it might fit a long sequence of events. Most of Kennedy's advisers still argued against removal, predicting that the Turks would protest and that other NATO governments would then make endless trouble. While those advisers were looking back and looking ahead, they did so with the eyes of men whose worlds were made of foreign offices and defense ministries. Kennedy saw the question more broadly. As the minutes of one ExComm meeting record:

> The President recalled that over a year ago we wanted to get the Jupiter missiles out of Turkey because they had become obsolete and of little military value. If the missiles in Cuba added 50 percent to the Soviet nuclear capability, then to trade these missiles for others in Turkey would be of great military value. But we are now in the position of risking war in Cuba and in Berlin over missiles in Turkey

> which are of little military value. From the political point of view, it would be hard to get support on an airstrike against Cuba because many would think we could make a good trade if we offered to take the missiles out of Turkey in the event the Russians would agree to remove the missiles from Cuba. We are in a bad position if we appear to be attacking Cuba for the purpose of keeping useless missiles in Turkey. We . . . have to face up to the possibility of some kind of a trade over missiles.

Robert Kennedy found a way around the dilemma. In very private conversations with Dobrynin, he promised that the U.S. missiles would be out of Turkey in four to five months. He also said not only that he would deny ever making such a promise but that, if any Russian revealed it, all deals would be off. The bargain was struck. No word was said of any trade other than Soviet withdrawal of missiles from Cuba in return for assurances that the United States would not invade Cuba. Five months later the U.S. missiles came out of Turkey.[23]

That the President came to see such issues in a stream of time is still more sharply illustrated by remarks he made to his brother about World War I. He had recently read a book on the outbreak of that war. It had reminded him of having heard in college of a former German Chancellor who, asked about the reasons for World War I, had replied, "Ah, if we only knew." Kennedy was not invoking an analogy, not even in the vein of his brother's reference to Pearl Harbor. Instead, we think, 1914 came to his mind because he saw himself as part of a long procession of political leaders on whose decisions many lives might depend. The book had been Barbara Tuchman's *Guns of August,* and Kennedy said to his brother, "I am not going to follow a course which will allow anyone to write a comparable book about this time, *The Missiles of October.* If anybody is around to write after this, they are going to understand that we made every effort to find peace and every effort to give our adversary room to move."[24]

The missile crisis may have been only accidentally a success story. We do not know—may never know—why the Russians decided as they did, and different decisions by them could have led toward a horrible ending. To the extent that American decisions shaped the outcome, uncharacteristic ways of using—and avoiding—history do not suffice as explanations of their clarity and cogency. Those choices were products of extraordinary conditions: intense concentration; effective secrecy sustained by media cooperation (after Watergate that would be thought treasonous to the First Amendment); a high average of mind—these people were not tagged "the best and the brightest" for nothing—along with breadth of experience. While some staff work could have been better, the run of the mill seldom is as good as the poorest was then. Similar conditions are not often likely to obtain at any level. Few issues can carry on their faces the blazing show of novelty and gravity combined—arresting the attention needed for frontal exploration of concerns and options—as did the first directly military confrontation between Washington and Moscow in the missile age.

Even so, the uses made of history appear to have contributed, demonstrably, to the high quality of analysis and management apparent during the missile crisis. Right or wrong, Kennedy had the wherewithal for reasoned and prudent choice, and resort to history helped produce it. One cannot expect that lesser choices on more mundane matters, either at the top level or down below, will often, if ever, benefit from the special factors present in 1962. One cannot even count on those factors in the next crisis. But why not hope that in choice-making, low-level or high, the preparatory work takes heed of history in ways to emulate—or, better still, improve upon—this Cuban instance?

2 A Second Success

The hope that usual practice might be improved is reinforced for us by an apparent correspondence of unusual endeavors in the Cuban missile crisis to the social security reform of 1983. Although far less is known as yet of the details, the public record makes it plain that there, too, history was used in unusual ways. Those who sponsored and then orchestrated the report of the National Commission on Social Security Reform steered clear of temptations to analogize (except once), studied the substantive, procedural, organizational—and personal—histories involved, and observed with care the cautions those various histories suggested. Who deserves most credit is somewhat in doubt. The legislative strategy group in Reagan's White House, the relevant assistant to the Speaker of the House, the chairman of the National Commission, the executive director, and at least four other commissioners vie for the lion's share. But there is enough to go around. As a group, they accomplished something quite as notable in its way as the work of Kennedy's ExComm.

The story starts in the time of Gerald Ford, when social security financing first began to be a problem. For thirty years before then, the government-run system of old age and survivor's insurance (OASI) had been readily financed from current payroll taxes charged employers and employees: Those who would draw benefits tomorrow, at retirement age, helped pay for the benefits of those who drew them now. This system of pay-as-you-go, understood as distinct from a fully vested system, had sufficed in decades when coverage was limited and benefits low. After 1949 coverage was widened and benefits gradually increased. Since the ratio of employed to aged held up rather well as products of the post-1945 baby boom joined the labor force, the system functioned as before. During the Vietnam War, with employment at peak levels, reserves piled high in the OASI trust fund (the accounting record of tax receipts as reduced by benefit payments).[1]

In 1972 those conditions combined with election year politics to produce substantial changes in the old age insurance system. The proportion of retirees in the electorate was rising, and large numbers lived in sun belt states, thought likely to be pivotal in a presidential race predicted to be as close as 1960 or 1968. The Republican president, Richard M. Nixon, aspiring to be reelected, accepted from a Democratic Congress, albeit with some reluctance, the biggest OASI benefit increases ever.

At the same time, Nixon approved indexing the benefits as a counter to inflation. That was cheek by jowl with his temporarily effective anti-inflation program. Since past decades had seen wages, on average, rise faster than prices, the Administration opted for a relatively conservative approach, tying the benefits to retail prices through the consumer price index.

Taken together, those changes went far to turn OASI from minimal safeguard to adequate pension. For years this had been an objective of the Social Security Administration (SSA) career staff, led by Commissioner Robert Ball. It had also been an objective of liberals in Congress and important unions, particularly the United Automobile Workers (UAW), then riding high. What made it a reality in 1972 was unexpected support from Wilbur Mills, the longtime chairman of the Ways and Means Committee in the House, a living icon for lawyers and businessmen whose lives revolved around the internal revenue code, and not so incidentally a prospective contestant for the Democratic presidential nomination. The usual opposition from Republican conservatives or from traditional opponents in the business world such as the National Association of Manufacturers (NAM), was tempered by fear of offending Mills and of capsizing Nixon, who, though deploring certain increases, dared not go all out against them. After his reelection he contented himself with dismissing Ball.[2]

Then, almost at once, three unanticipated trends were observed. For one, the baby boom was seen to have collapsed, while life-spans lengthened. For another, the 1974 economic indices showed prices going up faster than in any year since 1946 and, for the first time, outpacing wages. For a third, those same indices showed a recession pushing employment down to levels lower than for any of the past fifteen years. Suddenly the long-run future of social security's finances looked terrible, the immediate future bleak. The ratio between workers and the aged was already falling; when the baby-boomers retired, who would be working to pay for them? Meanwhile, in the short run, trust fund reserves already seemed low, worsened by a faulty statute, later fixed. As benefits rose with prices while resources fell with employment, where else was the cash to come from? By 1977 talk of bankruptcy was common.

Jimmy Carter came to office with this problem on his agenda. He called, among other things, for infusions of general revenue. Bipartisan majorities in Congress would have none of that; it jarred the presumption that social security was "insurance," not "welfare." Instead, Congress resorted mainly to a gradual increase in the payroll tax, cumulatively the largest federal tax hike ever.[3] That was supposed to cure everything. And so it might have, except for renewed inflation which appeared in 1978, outpaced all previous rises during 1979, and lasted through the rest of Carter's term. Wages lagged behind; so did employment. When Carter gave way to Reagan in 1981, social security financing seemed to be as much at risk as four years earlier.

Those years had sobered all but the most ardent proponents of expanded pensions. Congress under Carter had rejected almost every move to modify existing benefits but in the process had considered many, several of them stemming from the then Department of Health, Education, and Welfare (HEW, now HHS), one level above the Social Security Administration. Departmental pressure, motivated by financing prospects, had produced in SSA more disposition to endure some curbs on benefits in lieu of further taxes. And repeated airing of the problem had produced on Capitol Hill more interest than before in finding acceptable formulas. At both ends of Pennsylvania Avenue and out among the interest groups, gradualism—allowing ample notice to prospective beneficiaries—was conceived to be the key.

The search for formulas was certainly not discouraged by Ronald Reagan's victory or by surprise Republican control of the Senate. The new President had promised to keep social security—the center of his "social safety net"—intact, but that was not deemed inconsistent with some moves to balance cash flows. The problem was to find a basis for agreement not only among those traditionally concerned: the experts, the committees, the unions, and the business groups, but also the newly organized aged, whose tribune was Florida Congressman Claude Pepper, soon to head the House Rules Committee.

The House Ways and Means Committee had been the usual locus for bargaining out changes in old age insurance. When Reagan took office in 1981, the Democratic chairman of its social security subcommittee, J. J. Pickle from Texas, pledged to seek the needed formulas on a bipartisan basis.

Four months later Reagan inadvertently upset the applecart. A tax cut was the centerpiece of Reagan's economic policy. His Budget Director, David Stockman, frantic for means to hold down the foreseeable Federal deficits, seized on an immediate reduction of some old age benefits, notably for people about to retire early.[4] A former congressman himself, Stockman judged that those reductions could get through Congress. He found allies in three Californians now assigned important roles in welfare policy. They persuaded the new HHS Secretary, a former Senator, to agree to put them to Pickle if Reagan gave assent. Pickle had been pressing for long-run proposals; the short-run reductions could be couched as part of a response. Stockman and colleagues then sought the President's approval in a hasty consultation; until just before the issue went to Reagan they neglected to inform the White House chief of staff, James Baker, and the legislative strategy group chaired by his deputy, Richard Darman. Concerned, those latecomers insisted that the move be HHS's, not Reagan's, and that Pickle embrace it in bipartisan terms. With assurances on both scores, Reagan agreed. But announcement from the White House, a maladroit move, got the cuts billed as Reagan's own two days before the Secretary's presentation.[5]

The political significance of this transcended the immediate issue. One chronicler reports:

> Reagan, going back to the early Sixties, had been skeptical about more than the actuarial soundness of social security. He had reservations about one premise: compulsory participation [preferring annuities, or IRAs, or nothing, for whoever could afford them]. These doubts gave him trouble in both the 1976 and 1980 Campaigns, so he muted them.[6]

But OASI supporters had seized on them as an act of enmity, intended to convert an almost universal system of "insurance" (which Americans traditionally considered a good thing, embodying the notion of earned right) into residual assistance for the relatively poor, akin to "welfare," a bestowal (which Americans increasingly disliked).

During 1980, as in 1976, Reagan had been charged with trying to destroy the insurance system. In reaction, throughout his campaign and since, he had pledged himself to it wholeheartedly. Now sponsorship of immediate cuts threatened his credibility.

Sensing a Reagan gaffe of large proportions, Speaker Thomas P. O'Neill, the Democratic stalwart, urged Pickle to hold back from any favorable response. Democrats pounced; Republicans soon joined them. Within a week the Republican Senate had passed by overwhelming vote a resolution dissociating itself from Reagan's early-retirement cuts. The fact that those were to take effect at once, upsetting the long-made plans of retirees, caused far more indignation than their substance and received far more publicity. The issue of "unfairness" was implanted then and there.

All that occurred in May 1981. If not an early fiasco on the scale of Kennedy's at the Bay of Pigs twenty years before, it was assuredly a "piglet," Reagan's first and worst, exemplifying hazards of transition into office for new Presidents.[7]

Reagan retreated, shrugged off hopes for short-run savings, and repeatedly announced that the Administration was and would be loyal to social security. It did no good. The Speaker and others pursued the opening he had given them; just then, it was almost the only one they had. The issue remained politicized. Pickle was stalled in his tracks. So were friendly Senators. Yet few disputed that OASI seemed on the way to running out of cash, as month by month of renewed recession, starting in the summer, cut employment and hence revenue. Inflation came down too, but not enough to right the balance. Actual insolvency in cash terms was now forecast for July 1983.[8]

In the fall of 1981 the President called for a bipartisan commission to study the issue and report after the 1982 congressional elections. He would appoint five members, including a chairman. The Speaker of the House and the Majority Leader of the Senate, consulting with their counterparts for the minority, would each appoint five more. Precedents cited included the two Hoover Commissions, appointed in similar fashion, and the press drew analogies freely with other advisory bodies created to hold hot potatoes through election years.

Events, however, proved this one to be something special. The commission reported at the start of the new Congress in 1983. To deal with near-term cash flow it offered agreed proposals for many, if gradual, changes both in benefits and in the timing of tax increases. Republicans had sought the one, Democrats the other, and both conceded. They also conceded some disguised, one-shot infusions of general revenue (not acknowledged as such). For the long-term problem posed by baby-boomers, the commissioners split and offered alternate proposals. The President, the Senate Leader and the Speaker all hailed the report and called for bipartisan action. The NAM, the UAW, and other such did not demur. Neither did Pepper. Congress responded quickly. It enacted most of the agreed proposals without major change, as well as one of the alternative proposals for the longer run.[9] The bill reached Reagan's desk in April 1983. He signed it with a flourish, amid mutual congratulations. As far ahead as the political establishment could see, the financing crisis was over.

For advisory commissions of all sorts, at all times, that is an exceptional result. At least four things contributed to its success: First is commission membership, second is a White House reassessment in the nick of time, third is adroit White House involvement thereafter, behind the scenes, and fourth is somebody's persuasiveness with Reagan. We offer a comment on each.

The commission's fifteen members constituted most of the key players in the only game that could produce results: a bipartisan, interbranch, interstaff, intergroup bargain, as in 1972. The Senate Majority Leader, Howard Baker of Tennessee, is credited with having wanted a commission more than most—understandable considering the heat on him. His fellow Republicans downtown and Democratic House members, not least the Speaker, had between them managed to shut off the bargaining arena used before, House Ways and Means; Baker evidently sought a temporary new one somewhere safer for him than the Senate, and he hoped that a commission could be it. He therefore was meticulous in naming to it, as his members, four persons bound to be essential in a deal, and a fifth whose presence added credibility in useful quarters. The four were Robert Dole of Kansas, Gerald Ford's vice presidential candidate in 1976, now chairman of the Senate Finance Committee (the committee with jurisdiction); William Armstrong, a Republican from Colorado, chairman of its social security subcommittee; Daniel Patrick Moynihan of New York, a ranking Democrat on both bodies, once Nixon's assistant in domestic welfare spheres, still earlier one of Kennedy's; and Lane Kirkland, the new president of the AFL-CIO (the union federation which the UAW had recently rejoined), previously its social security specialist. Baker's fifth appointee was Senator John Heinz, the Pennsylvania Republican, less senior than others but chairman of a special committee on aging.

The Speaker of the House, perhaps less committed to the commission's fate, appointed fewer members necessary to a deal but two who were essential. One was former commissioner Ball, now in private life, still very much "the" expert both to Democrats in general and to O'Neill in particular. The other was Barber Conable of New York, ranking Republican on the Ways and Means Committee, widely respected across party lines and in both Houses. The Speaker's other appointees were the redoubtable Pepper; Martha Keyes, a former member of the House and HHS Assistant Secretary under Carter; and the Pickle subcommittee's ranking Republican, William Archer of Texas. But where were Pickle himself and the full committee chairman, Conable's counterpart, the Democrat Daniel Rostenkowski of Illinois? In reserve. Rostenkowski, heir to the once formidable Mills, apparently had no use for a bargaining arena other than the Ways and Means Committee; reportedly he meant to wait until the commission failed, then reassert his own.

Failure was initially predicted also at the White House, a prediction born of snap analogies to many earlier bipartisan commissions and committees. Aside from the first Hoover Commission, in a widely different context and time frame, such bodies seemed to Reagan's aides to have been successes only in the sense of shelving controversies for the length of time it took them to report, after which the issues went their usual way, or nowhere as the case might be, with reports adding fuel to the fire, or vanishing from sight, or both. Presidents Nixon and Ford, among others, had named numerous commissions with such results. Reagan's legislative strategy group, dominated by veterans of those administrations, reasoning from analogy—for the one and only time in this affair—saw Howard Baker's hoped-for bargaining arena as nothing but a closet where the issue could be shut up through the fall of 1982, helping the Republicans and Reagan in particular to avoid it during the congressional elections. The White House therefore took less care in naming its five members than had Baker or O'Neill in naming theirs. Two could be of use in serious bargaining, but three could not. The two were Alexander Trowbridge, a Democrat who had been Lyndon Johnson's Secretary of Commerce, long acquainted with the issues, now by happy chance the President of NAM, and Alan Greenspan, a moderate Republican, once chairman of Ford's Council of Economic Advisers, well regarded both on Wall Street and in Congress, relatively nonpolitical, willing to heed old associates from Ford's time serving now with Reagan—and on good terms with Kirkland too. Reagan named Greenspan chairman. The other three Reagan appointees, who lacked such special virtues, were two Republicans from business, Robert Beck, the President of Prudential Life, and Mary Falvey Fuller, a management consultant, along with Democrat Joe Waggonner, who had been a conservative Louisiana congressman for sixteen years.

Rounding out the group was its Executive Director, Robert Myers, who played for some Republicans a role the Democrats reserved to Robert Ball: in-house expert. Myers too was formerly a longtime career civil servant. He had been generally respected as the Social Security Administration's chief actuary, for many years the voice of caution on Ball's staff and for almost as many years a source of counsel to moderate Republicans. Who first suggested Myers as Executive Director is not clear, but, once suggested, his appointment was taken as a matter of course.

Thus, of a circle that could make or break reform, commission membership included all but three: the Speaker; his chairman, Rostenkowski; and the President. To that result the White House had contributed less than others, but after the congressional elections Reagan's strategists awakened to an opportunity not covered by analogies, the very chance desired by the Senate Majority Leader. For up to the election the commissioners had concentrated on and actually arrived at an agreed definition of the social security problem. Given their composition this agreement might be parlayed into an agreed solution, if the three absent members of the circle could be represented satisfactorily or neutralized. Struck by this (to them) unexpected prospect, James Baker and associates decided to achieve it, if they could, as a matter of high moment for the President and country. They were reportedly spurred on by polls suggesting that the issue hurt Republicans. Abandoning the analogues of failures from the past, Baker and the others set to work to reconstruct the commission and upgrade it without changing it. This they accomplished by creating a backroom body, an informal "Negotiating Group" composed so as to get the necessary representation right.

The White House strategists who took the lead in the endeavor were not strangers to the issue or unknown to key commissioners. James Baker had been Deputy Secretary of Commerce (second to Elliot Richardson) in the Ford Administration. Baker and the then Assistant Secretary for Policy, Richard Darman, had dealt with the first manifestations of the financing crisis in Ford's Economic Policy Board. Darman, moreover, had been with Richardson as far back as 1971–72, when the latter was Secretary of Health, Education, and Welfare while Ball still was Social Security Commissioner and Moynihan just leaving the White House. Now Darman was Baker's deputy. In 1982 another member of their legislative strategy group was Kenneth Duberstein, chief of congressional liaison, who had done comparable work for the General Services Administration in Ford's time and had the confidence of all concerned, not least the Speaker. Still another Reagan strategist, the budget director, Stockman, now somewhat chastened, had not only been a congressman himself but in his graduate school days had been a protégé of then Professor Moynihan. The connections ramify still further; we lack space to trace them. it is enough to say that these four put themselves on their Negotiating Group, along with six commissioners. The six included Ball and Moynihan, along with Dole, Conable, and Greenspan, while Armstrong was in and out. Kirkland and Trowbridge were kept closely informed.

On and off for six weeks, in face-to-face discussions, sometimes among them all, sometimes in subgroups, these twelve cut the deal that eventuated as the commission's successful report. To do so they were frequently in contact with the President through Baker and Darman and with the Speaker through Ball and Duberstein. Agreement from O'Neill as well as Reagan had to be not only gained but also orchestrated so that both would "sign on" publicly to the report at the same time. On that the President, burned once, insisted. As for Rostenkowski, he was first confronted by the prospect of a squeeze between the Speaker and the Republicans, then gratified by the report's deliberate posing of alternatives to meet the long-run problem. Thereby he acquired a piece of the action: His committee could initiate the choice, and later opted for a two-year hike in the retirement age by 2027.

Considering the fact that the Negotiating Group was long on brains and egos, it reached common ground with remarkable dispatch. (One would not have sensed this at the time, reading the newspapers, which were full of doom and gloom—offshoots, apparently, of everybody's tactics.)[11] That testifies in part to the weight of the problem as defined before the Negotiating Group started. The commission had agreed upon the need for new resources over the next seven years in the range of $150–200 billion. Where and how to get them was the problem for the Negotiating Group. The total was too high to be achieved by practicable tax increases only or by benefit cuts alone. Thus would-be Democratic taxers and Republican trimmers both were bound to yield somewhat and knew it from the start. Further, there was no way to achieve so large a sum without tapping general revenues to a degree, and the conservatives opposing this in principle were forced into connivance with the liberals who liked it to find means of doing it in practice without saying so. Sundry "compensations" were devised to funnel money from the Treasury into a trust fund nominally supported only by payroll taxes. And a temporary income tax credit was set to compensate for speeded-up increases in the payroll tax. Item by item, every change of benefits and taxes urged by others in the previous decade was canvassed as a source of funding. Ball and Stockman between them, masters of detail, went down the list, offered ingenious, often contrasting proposals. The others listened, argued, counseled, caucused, compromised. Having put $200 billion as a burden on their own backs, the commissioners among them had no recourse but to chip it away—and they did.

As for the long-run problem of financing baby boomers on retirement en masse in the next century, the group agreed to disagree on whether to raise the retirement age a bit or taxes slightly in the coming century. Seven Republican commissioners opted for the one, five Democrats for the other. Either would serve, under present estimates. The commissioners could well afford to forward two alternatives to Congress, provided that they made them clear, permitting a straightforward choice (and giving Rostenkowski his desired role, at the same time confining it). So they would see.[12] In fashioning a compromise, the Baker group's performance was exemplary.

But there remained the full commission. The Negotiating Group, although more relevantly representative than the commission, could not act without it or despite it since the intended product took the form of its report. Near unanimity on major matters was essential to a maximum bipartisan effect. The product was to be called a "consensus report." Among commissioners left out of the Negotiating Group, Senator Heinz rallied to his colleagues. The Speaker's people, Pepper included, rallied to Ball and Conable. But Reagan's other appointees kicked up a fuss, and since they were important to business support, Beck especially, they had to be persuaded in long sessions at the White House, with the President himself as ultimate persuader—a price paid for the earlier analogizing by his staff.

The commission thus became one with the Negotiating Group, which now dispersed. In the process Reagan and O'Neill (and Howard Baker) had been brought in to play their parts: When the commission publicly reported, they simultaneously applauded. Rostenkowski scheduled hearings, Dole followed suit, and three months later all essential things were on the statute books.

What is striking in this story from our standpoint is that, once Reagan had blundered, the elaborate and successful effort at recovery—for him and trust fund both—involved reversing the usual uses and nonuses of history, just as in the missile crisis. In May 1981, appalled by the Senate's adverse vote and the Speaker's continual needling, members of the Administration went through a first reactive stage of flying to the question, "What do we *do?*" They tried reassurances; as those failed, analogies sprang to mind. Among them were past commissions that had cooled off hot issues. As is so often the case, analogy then became answer. But after that standard first stage, the practice changed. At some point—as in 1962—the people involved seemed to recognize that the issues were too serious to be defined by analogies. So far as we can find, neither White House aides nor the commission and its staff referred again to the experience of other advisory groups. That was wise, since no close counterparts existed for what Howard Baker wanted and James Baker ultimately set out to achieve.

On the other hand—as in 1962—the people who brought off

the success gave attention to the kinds of history usually slighted. Those who did the planning and the choosing displayed sensitivity to the history of the issue, both economic and political. Even more than in Kennedy's ExComm, history walked into every meeting. The Negotiating Group included no one who did not have at his fingertips the whole or a substantial portion of the fifty-year development since social security's start: They all had been participants, at least in the past decade when the trouble had begun. As a result they never let themselves forget that the notion of OASI as "insurance," not "welfare," had long and tenacious roots (to which we return later). Awareness of issue history led them to look at the undersides of presumptions. Earlier negotiators, including even Mills in 1972, had counted on the predictability of controlling factors such as age distribution, ratios of employed to retired, rates of inflation, and relationships between prices and wages. The Negotiating Group decided: better not. Throughout, it acknowledged and defined uncertainties. On cost-of-living adjustments for the longer term it built in sliding scales and automatic shifts by light of economic change.[13]

The make-up of the commission, still more of the Negotiating Group, ensured sensitivity also to the varieties of history in the heads of people concerned with the issue. These were not just advisory bodies with some representation from each organized interest. Together, Negotiating Group members and commission staff remembered almost every approach to OASI benefits and funding ever taken. Greenspan did not let deputies sit for commissioners, so none of those perspectives was ever misrepresented at commission meetings by a surrogate who knew the brief but not the history behind it. And the history then brought into play included that of organizations, for one the Social Security Administration itself, for others the congressional committees.

How far back or how far ahead Negotiating Group members or commission staff looked, we cannot say with certainty. We have not pressed them; others will do that. They are proud people and proud of their product. Memoirs will be written and compared. We are confident, however, that in 1983 as in 1962, success owed something to the fact that the decisive actors saw their choices as part of a series starting long ago and continuing for years to come. If any one feature of their work had to be singled out, it would be the way in which account was taken of time. The formula was not a quick fix, even for the interval until the next election.

But neither did it pretend to be "the" solution for all time. The commission's report acknowledged that hard issues could arise again in the near term and might require still further adjustments. It also made plain that alternative long-term proposals were premised on present projections: many estimates, few certitudes. Yet the longer term was faced and within limits of forecasting was addressed in forthright fashion. Both alternatives for Congress envisaged that younger workers, together with their employers, would henceforth contribute at least the full cost of their benefits after retirement. Behind the forms of pay-as-you-go would emerge reserves so strong as to constitute a step toward vesting—a reversion, in effect, to the original Social Security Act of 1935, before pay-as-you-go was put through in 1939 (another matter to which we return later). Coming full circle was well understood by historically minded negotiators.

One anecdote we cannot vouch for indicates that some of them looked back and looked ahead at least as far as JFK did when invoking World War I and then imagining a future book, "The Missiles of October." While they framed an effective compromise, Baker's negotiators could not nail it down without the Speaker and the President. Both had to be convinced. O'Neill, the Roosevelt Democrat, committed to social security from his cradle, readily let Ball persuade him that the compromise could save the system in the short run and defend it in the long. But Reagan evidently was not wedded to the system, other than rhetorically—not in his private mind. What then persuaded him? The answer is the subject of the anecdote.

Reagan, we are told, liked making advantageous deals at timely moments—which this surely was—but as he showed the world with tax reduction (let alone "star wars") he also liked advancing his own deeply held ideas. Members of his staff are said to have believed the way to move him toward a compromise on such things was to show him how what might appear a U-turn was in fact an S-curve which could take him farther forward than before. So in the spring of 1982 "revenue-enhancement" had been linked to his original tax-cutting goal of 1981, before he outbid Democrats with further cuts to push his tax bill and not theirs through Congress. So now in December 1982, the story goes, reforming social security—nominally strengthening it to Ball's and O'Neill's satisfaction—was linked with something they abhorred.

Stockman and others are said to have argued that the agreed

reforms, taken together, would make social security a system costing baby-boomers in their working lifetimes everything they could get out of it after retirement and more, indeed returning less than they might get had they invested on their own—and once they came to see that they'd revolt: extolling IRAs, demanding voluntarism. "In time these reforms will sink this thing of its own weight," someone is said to have told Reagan: an S-curve!

Only weeks before the President reportedly had said to one of his commissioners in a White House receiving line, "I hope you're going to get me a voluntary system." His auditor, wide-eyed, had told associates all over town. Supposedly, Reagan smiled as he said it. Still . . . .

Moreover, he had another fixed idea, which one of those reforms served quite directly, making it appealing on its own: partial taxation of benefits for the well-off. Reagan reportedly had never seen why his "rich friends" should get benefits at all. Here, aides are said to have told him, was a way to take some back—and once the principle was in the law, more might be made to follow! Reagan, in this respect, apparently saw eye to eye with O'Neill, Irish both and for the purpose populists together.

We cannot vouch for this version of how Reagan was convinced. The closest we can come is to quote a White House source, usually informed although *not* present at key meetings, who commented:

> I don't know; it could have been that way; it's true to life. If that story didn't exist I'd have had to invent one like it to explain his *enthusiasm.* Of course he almost had to go along, given his stakes politically and the trust fund's money trouble. He surely didn't want the thing to go bankrupt on his watch, in the middle of "his" recession. But that doesn't explain his vim and vigor. He even worked over his own dissident commissioners; told them they had to go along for him! The story would account for that. It also would explain why, in the spring of 1984, Don Regan [the then Secretary of the Treasury] remarked publicly that social security was still in trouble for the long run; at the time this seemed at once gratuitous and anomalous to say the least (unless he was guessing that Congress would bleed OASI for Medicare when *that* nears bankruptcy, which Congress might)—but maybe Don was just trying to send a signal to the Yuppies on the President's behalf.[14]

We grant it may not have been quite like this. Rather, whatever his personal preferences, Reagan may have heeded the advice said to have swayed him in his Sacramento years. In effect: When the tank's coming at you and it's too late to escape, don't fall under the treads, jump aboard! This too could account for his enthusiasm.

But whichever way it went (perhaps a bit of both?) the inference for us is plain: Baker's negotiators, some of them, enough of them, apparently knew not alone the issues and organizations but the President as well—and effectively applied the histories of all to advocacy no less than analysis.

We thus have here, both in the missile crisis and in social security reform, two sets of decisions based on preparatory work making better use of history than what we see as usual practice. In both instances analogies were little used; the history of the issue was understood; presumptions were questioned; the histories of persons most concerned as well as organizations most affected were brought into play. This enhances hope that usual practice can be improved.

The two success stories, taken together, help to explain *our* presumptions, as stated in the Preface:

- In employment of government power, particulars matter. Regardless of all else, had Kennedy responded with an airstrike at the outset, it would have killed Cubans and Russians, many of whom are still living. That may be historically insignificant except to them, but it matters at least to them. Possibly it matters to a great many million others.
- Marginal improvement is worth seeking. Putting off the killing of those people for at least a week probably reduced the risk of nuclear exchange by mutual miscalculation. This conclusion is speculative, as any based on a hypothetical replay of events must be, and not every analyst of the episode would agree with it. Kennedy himself felt he should have addressed the Soviets sooner or warned them off deploying any missiles in Cuba instead of drawing distinctions between defensive ones (okay) and offensive ones (bad). And Reagan, obviously, would have done better to send Stockman back to the drawing board in May 1981. But marginal improvement, as we mean it, could consist of even less and still be worth the effort. For marginally better thinking about an issue can lead to much more than marginally better results—as, for example, in a case where the choice is nuclear war: yes or no.
- A little thought can help. When JFK learned of the missiles in Cuba, his first impulse was to do something. Only second

did he think of whether to do anything, in what sequence, keeping open what options. Reagan's case is comparable. Second-thoughts were helpful. Much of the thought was historical. Let others emulate.

Better decision-making involves drawing on history to frame sharper questions and doing so systematically, routinely. That, and not any determinate result, is what we aim at; also, it is what we hope for. Without insistent questioning Reagan let Stockman *et al.* go forward in May 1981. After such questioning, some of it prompted by history, the Kennedy brothers postponed an early, massive airstrike in October 1962. As a matter of judgment, we are sorry for the one and glad of the other. Our judgment puts a high value on prudence and a lower value on capacities of government, American *or* Soviet, to keep control of what it tries to do. Such things as these are arguable. Still, they explain our interest in the laymen's stock of questions.

Lest this suggest that governmental use of history is *only* analytical, we hasten to deny it. As we have already noted, advocacy stands with or ahead of sheer analysis as an objective for the users we have studied. When summarized by JFK for public consumption, the history of the issue of "offensive" Soviet weapons overseas was meant to move his auditors and rally their support—to smother questions, not to raise them. It was slanted accordingly. Other instances abound, not least in social security, as for example the "social safety net." Of course, the line between such advocacy and analysis is thin, the membrane porous. Advocacy smothers questions for the analyst too. Yet it draws on a base of analysis. Kennedy made his side of the case sound better than it was (by leaving out the lateness and ambiguity of his warning); still, there can be little doubt that he believed the Soviets tried to deceive him. Nothing threatens analytic questions more than the beliefs that fuel convincing advocacy. And few things threaten advocacy more than obvious flaws in analysis. From where we stand, considering the choice-maker, concerned for laymen's questions and the insights they can offer, concerned above all for decisions that are enlightened in a literal sense, this becomes a distinction without a difference.

As we said earlier, our purpose is prescriptive; we seek better practice and take aim at marginal improvements. "Usual" practice, we fear, has six ingredients: a plunge toward action; overdependence on fuzzy analogies, whether for advocacy, analysis, or both; inattention to an issue's own past; failure to think a second time—sometimes even a first—about key presumptions; stereotyped suppositions about persons or organizations (stereotypes which could be refined but aren't); and little or no effort to see choices as part of any historical sequence. While we cannot claim to have exhaustively (or scientifically) sampled Washington decision-making in this generation, we see and read enough to know that what we call "usual" is at least not exceptional. And our fear gets regularly quickened by practitioner-students, some qualifying as "crisis managers," who tell us: "That's about the way it is." If "usual" is better than we think, we do no harm. If it is as we fear, we hope to do some good. We seek to turn around what we have encountered in most cases, and to make practice conform more closely to that in the two tales just told. Even these two cases are not for us ideal. After the fact, some participants saw particulars that might have been improved. In later chapters we suggest procedures that we think might have made success more sure, perhaps more swift. Nevertheless, our two success stories point the way toward better things to do with history than was done, on average, in other instances of which we are aware. The two cases suggest the usefulness of *un*usual practice.

3 Unreasoning from Analogies

At 9:20 P.M. on June 24, 1950, a phone rang in the white clapboard, gingerbread Wallace house on North Delaware Street in Independence, Missouri, where Bess and Harry Truman were spending a summer weekend. Dean Acheson, the Secretary of State, was calling from Washington to alert the President that the North Koreans had just invaded South Korea.

The next day President Truman flew back to the capital, his mind already made up. "[W]e are going to fight," his daughter, Margaret, wrote in her diary. Met at National Airport by Acheson, Under Secretary of State James Webb, and Secretary of Defense Louis Johnson, Truman said on the drive into Washington, "By God, I am going to hit them hard."[1]

That night at Blair House, across Pennsylvania Avenue from the White House, Truman held the first of several meetings with Acheson, Webb, Johnson, the Joint Chiefs of Staff, and other advisers. The American delegation to the UN had obtained a cease-fire resolution. Using it as a legal substitute for a declaration of war, Truman within the week had ordered American warships, planes, and foot soldiers to rescue South Korea.

What makes the decisions of that June week lastingly instructive is the fact that the very same men, looking coolly into the future, had previously concluded that South Korea, to paraphrase Prince Bismarck, was not worth the bones of a Missouri National Guardsman. In a top secret paper the chiefs of staff had so advised Truman and his National Security Council back in 1948. With Truman in the chair, the council endorsed the chiefs' opinion. In 1949 the NSC reexamined the subject. The circle now included all those who would be his key advisers in June 1950. They reaffirmed the basic policy, with the military reiterating that Korea "is of little strategic value to the United States and that commitment to United States use of military force in Korea would be ill-advised." The President was again in the chair.[2]

Having appraised South Korea as militarily valueless, why did Truman decide to fight for it in 1950? Partly, no doubt, because of the worsening Cold War: the Russians had recently produced their first atomic bomb; Truman had announced he would go for a hydrogen bomb; and Europeans had begun asking more nervously whether the United States would really risk its own destruction to protect them. Even if Korea was not worth much, failure to defend it could give both Russians and Europeans further cause to doubt American willingness to fight.

Domestic politics must also have played a part. Many Republicans, some Democrats, and a number of newspapers and magazines, including *Time,* the most widely read national newsweekly, had denounced the Administration for "losing" mainland China to the Communists. With a deep recession just ending, public approval of Truman as measured by Gallup polls was 37 percent in April 1950 (the last poll before North Korea's attack), down from 69 percent at his surprise election eighteen months before.[3] The then created Democratic leads in the Senate and House were now at risk in the approaching November elections, the more so since Truman's espousal of health insurance had brought the American Medical Association, bitterly opposed, into congressional campaigning on a national scale for the first time. Political strategists had as much reason as foreign policy advisers for cringing at the prospect of charges that the Administration had "lost" still more of Asia to Communists.

Behind the decision of June 1950 stood also certain powerful beliefs about recent history. They accounted in part for the anxieties prevalent in Europe and among Americans at home. They were firmly fixed in the heads of the President and those meeting with him at the Blair House. In his memoirs, Truman was to write of his thoughts during his Sunday flight from Kansas City to Washington:

> I recalled some earlier instances: Manchuria, Ethiopia, Austria. I remembered how each time that the democracies failed to act it had encouraged the aggressors to keep going ahead. Communism was acting in Korea just as Hitler, Mussolini, and the Japanese had acted ten, fifteen, and twenty years earlier. I felt certain that if South Korea was allowed to fall, Communist leaders would be emboldened to override nations closer to our own shores. If the Communists were permitted to force their way into the Republic of Korea without opposition from the free world, no small nation would have the courage to resist threats and aggression by stronger Communist neighbors. If this was allowed to go unchallenged, it would mean a third world war, just as similar incidents had brought on the second world war.[4]

How much of this recaptured his actual thinking we do not pretend to know. Contemporaneous notes show Truman talking that first evening of how the League of Nations had failed and others referring to events of the 1930s. Given his habit of reaching for historical specifics, we suspect that he did call to mind the episodes he itemized later. When explaining to Congress why he had decided to send in American troops, Truman spoke of the "fateful events of the nineteen-thirties, when aggression unopposed bred more aggression and eventually war." And this was—then—not such ritual phraseology as by the time of Kennedy's speech on the missile crisis. Truman was stating an analogy with irresistible force for almost all Americans of that time.

We do not contend that this analogy led Truman to a wrong decision. Americans have regretted most of their wars. Witness the reputations of wars from those of 1812 to that in Vietnam. Along with the American Revolution and World War II, Korea is an exception. Few historians write it off as a blunder or an avoidable tragedy. Nor do we. Indeed, we shall argue later that Truman's way of using history in June 1950 had much to commend it. We do feel, however, that the President and his aides failed to pause over one important question. They did not ask *why* the analogues of the 1930s came so irresistibly to mind.

For while the initial decision may seem wise, some that followed it do not. The troops sent by Truman helped the South Korean army keep a toehold around the port of Pusan. After more troops reached Japan, General Douglas MacArthur effected a successful landing at Inchon, well behind the North Koreans' advance positions. In danger of being trapped, the North Koreans raced back to their home country. As they retreated they were badly mauled but not altogether destroyed. Truman permitted MacArthur to march north with the aim of extinguishing the North Korean army altogether and then unifying Korea as a non-Communist nation. Paying no attention to muffled warnings from Peking, MacArthur talked of getting his soldiers home for Christmas. But November saw China enter the war with a rush. MacArthur's armies were driven back almost to Pusan again. Gallup polls of October had shown 64 percent of the public in favor of taking all Korea, rather than stopping at the prewar line. By January 1951 they showed 66 percent for getting out of Korea altogether.[5] The battle line finally stabilized just north of the 38th parallel. There it remained for well over two years until, with almost 34,000 American soldiers dead, the Democrats reduced to the minority in both houses of Congress, and a Republican in the presidency, the Chinese and North Koreans agreed to a truce.

Looking back we see some possibility—not overwhelming, but some—that if the Blair House sessions had seen more explicit analysis of the history in use, the intent of Truman's first decision might have been better defined. He himself might have defined more clearly the objective or outcome he had in view, and subsequent events might have been different, perhaps happier.

From reflection on this Korean case—one of success derailed—we extract the moral that for any decision, the first step in analysis should be to take apart and thus define the situation that seems to call for action. We claim no patent for this piece of advice. Put another way, it is nothing but an injunction to get the facts straight before acting. Our version has novelty only in that we suggest a mini-method the habitual use of which can, we think, cut down the number of times when the step is forgotten or bypassed.

Even to seasoned practitioners we propose an elementary procedure, amounting to analysis in the most literal sense (from *anas,* meaning things, and *lysein,* to dissolve). That is to disassemble "now," the situation at the moment, separating the *Known* from the *Unclear* and both from the *Presumed* (presumed, that is, by those who think they have a problem).

The purpose is simple, the procedure more so. Nevertheless, observation teaches us that this mini-method is easier to describe than to apply. So much is *Known* or *Presumed*—or *Unclear.* How do we choose the few items that really matter? How do so in the bustle from crisis to crisis?

The key is to keep in mind the precise aims of the exercise. They are, first, to specify exactly why some kind of decision seems to be called for. The second is to identify the decision's objectives. As a rule, high-level managers pay attention to situations because they have to. What constrains their attention may be a deadline—for a budget, an annual report, or legislative hearing or advisory committee *a la* Reagan in 1981–83. Or the prompter may be, as with Kennedy in 1962 and Truman in 1950, a sudden, unexpected happening. In either case the situation *now* requires attention. It did not yesterday or last week or whenever. Then, it may not have been ideal or even satisfactory, but it could be ignored or left for later. Now it can't. The significant items *Known, Unclear,* and *Presumed* are those which make the situation different now from what it was before, when it did not require attention.

Focusing on matters of evidence provides momentary protection against the natural tendency to react to trouble by saying, "Damn! What do we do?" instead of "What's our problem?" It isolates the decision-maker's concerns. (We prefer "concerns" to "problems" because "problems" imply solutions while "concerns" need not.) It thus provides the person at the top some protection also against being sold a solution designed for a different problem.

To figure out *why* action is called for helps in defining the objectives of action. If the situation was tolerable earlier, then one possible objective is to put it back the way it was. In any case the objectives probably ought to have something to do with the factors that force action; if they don't, the decision-maker should be aware that they don't. In ordinary practice, as we have observed or read about it, that often is not the case. Debating what to do without much thought about why, decision-makers and their aides can easily settle on objectives not clearly related to the matter in hand. In 1950 Truman responded to the North Korean attack on South Korea not only by sending troops there but also by starting the rearmament of Germany, stationing four U.S. divisions in Europe, and tripling his overall defense budget, mostly in order to buy long-range, nuclear-armed bombers. Sorting out particulars can help to preserve some relationship between problems and solutions (or nonsolutions).

If the first caveat is that *Known, Unclear,* and *Presumed* must have to do with the action-issue at hand, the second is that they must be so identified *from the standpoint of the person or persons who have to act.* If you are the decision-maker, the list is yours. If you are an aide or analyst, the items are your inferences about some other person or persons. You need not agree with the presumptions. You may want to combat them. But the point of separating the *Known* from the *Unclear* and both from the *Presumed* is to establish as quickly and economically as possible the particular circumstances that cause a particular decision-maker to feel at a particular time that he must do what he is hired to do.

One last point: We recommend that things *Known, Unclear,* and *Presumed* be written down—even if only on the back of an envelope. As Lee Iacocca comments, from experience as a manager in industry, "In conversation you can get away with all kinds of vagueness and nonsense, often without even realizing it. But there's something about putting your thoughts on paper that forces you to get down to specifics. That way, it's harder to deceive yourself—or anybody else."[6] We agree.

To illustrate, return to the Blair House meetings of June 1950 and imagine what someone might have jotted down as what, for President Truman, was then *Known, Unclear,* and *Presumed.* The results might have run as follows:

Known

- In Korea: North Korean attack across 38° N., South Koreans in retreat
- In the world: Cold War tensions, especially over emergence of two Germanys but also in Mediterranean, Middle East, and Asia; Taiwan and French Indochina potentially vulnerable to Chinese Communists who have just consolidated control over the mainland; at the UN, Soviet delegates temporarily absent, protesting the decision against seating Communist China
- At home: Congressional elections four months away; economic recovery from 1949 recession just achieved; Truman and Democrats still down in polls; "loss of China" issue hot; Senator Joe McCarthy getting headlines with accusations that the Administration harbors Communists; defense spending headed down toward 1930s levels, leaving the United States with meager tactical forces, but occupation units in Japan plus ships and planes from Okinawa and the Philippines suffice for limited operations in Korea.

Unclear

- In Korea: staying power of South Korea if unaided
- In the world: what the Russians intend elsewhere; what the local response would be if they opened a front in Indochina or Iran or Germany; how they or the Chinese would react to forceful American/UN action in Korea
- At home: political conditions by election time; the staying power of the "loss of China" and "Communists in government" issues; the prospective appeal of Fair Deal issues like health insurance

Presumed

- In Korea: The Russians deliberately instigated the North Korean attack. The South Koreans want to stay non-Communist. The North Koreans are militarily stronger than the South Koreans. Though South Korea has a quasi-dictatorship, most Koreans, north and south, would prefer it to a Communist dictatorship if they were free to choose.
- In the world: Given the American lead in nuclear weapons and bombers, the Russians will not deliberately start a new world war. If the United States defends South Korea, that will strengthen the credibility of its specific and general pledges to other countries. If not, the reverse will be true. Most or all non-Communist countries in the UN will favor defending Korea. If asked, some will contribute token forces.
- At home: At least for the time being, a decision to defend Korea will be popular. Only the far left will be critical, and they don't amount to much. On the other hand, if the Administration does not act and South Korea falls, there will be an uproar. Everyone on the right will be up in arms, and there are lots of them.
- Elsewhere: A defense of South Korea will be scrutinized to see if it presages "World War III." Allied and popular support, as well as Soviet prudence, require visible American restraint.

In June 1950 the President's immediate concern arose from the change in the military situation south of the 38th parallel. From the presumption that the Russians started the war and did so for a reason, it followed that other changes might be in prospect elsewhere. From presumptions concerning American credibility, it also followed that there were possibilities of change in the international standing of both the United States and the UN. And so forth.

In this case as in many others, the sorting of things *Known, Unclear,* and *Presumed* would have been only a first step toward clarifying concerns and objectives. In cases that count as success stories, the decision process benefited—and in less successful cases it would have benefited—from two follow-on steps. One, which we shall illustrate here, is quick inspection of analogies that figure or may figure in the decision-maker's mind. The second, to be illustrated later, is review of the history of the issue, tracing how the specific concerns arose.

In the Korean decision of 1950 a pause to look at analogues could have honed understanding of concerns and therefore of objectives.

Truman said in his memoirs that three events of the 1930s had come to his mind: the Manchurian incident of 1931–32, when Japan seized Manchuria from China; Italy's aggression against Ethiopia in 1935; and Hitler's forcible annexation of Austria (the Anschluss) in 1938. He could equally well have called to mind the Rhineland crisis of 1936, when Hitler suddenly marched troops into that presumably demilitarized area, or the Czech crisis of 1938, when Britain, France, and Italy bought temporary peace at the Munich Conference by giving Hitler crucial portions of Czechoslovakia. Others in his circle made reference to those events. No one mentioned—possibly an error—the Spanish Civil War of 1936–39, when the great powers pretended to leave Spain alone while in actuality the Germans and Italians helped the Nationalists, the Russians aided the Republicans, and all were disappointed by the ultimate outcome.

We contend that in June 1950 Truman's aides could usefully have spent a few minutes on the question: Comparing all those seemingly analogous situations with the present one, what are *Likenesses* and *Differences?* Compare "now" with "then" *before* turning to what should be done now.

To do the case full justice, we ought to reconstruct the international history of the 1930s as Truman and other Americans understood it in 1950. But, fascinating as that history is, and much as we may wish that it were better known, such storytelling would take us too far from our main themes.[7] At the risk of mystifying readers for whom "Manchuria," "the Rhineland," and the like are not evocative, we reproduce below what we think someone might have jotted down that June at Blair House.

Likenesses

- In the locale: armed aggression as in Manchuria and Ethiopia; a victim asking outside aid as did Ethiopia, Austria, and Czechoslovakia; treaty violation—the UN Charter in Korea as the League Covenant in Manchuria, Ethiopia, and Spain, the treaties of Versailles and Locarno in the case of the Rhineland, and treaties of Versailles and the Trianon in that of Austria
- In the world: expansionist dictatorships; pacifically inclined democracies
- At home: none to speak of

Differences

- In the locale: The two Koreas are not clearly separate nations; this makes the situation unlike all others except Spain. No major power's troops have crossed a border. (In Manchuria, Ethiopia, the Rhineland, Austria, and Czechoslovakia, the aggressor was a great power).
- In the world: Since 1945 collective security or something of the sort has been successfully maintained. (During June 1950 Truman did draw comfort from experience since then, saying to one White House aide: "Korea is the Greece of the Far East. If we are tough enough now, if we stand up to them as we did in Greece three years ago, they won't take any next steps." At other times he or others mentioned the 1946 demand that the Soviets withdraw from Iranian Azerbaidjan, the 1948 Berlin airlift, and the 1949 signing of the North Atlantic Treaty.)
- At home: There is little evident support for a policy of isolation, less still for one of appeasement.
- Militarily: nuclear weapons exist; the upholders of collective security have the power to threaten condign punishment; and close to the locality they have the conventional power (in occupied Japan) to repel or slow the specific aggression (supposedly true of the Rhineland; not clearly the case in any other instance).

Looking at the analogies, comparing *Likenesses* and *Differences*, even in so cursory a fashion, should have underscored one point: The President's chief concern was not Korea. That place had not gained new strategic importance since the policy papers of 1948 and 1949 wrote it off as militarily valueless. Truman and the others were concerned about the system of collective security that protected entities such as South Korea and, by doing so effectively, could deter a dictatorship like Stalin's from pursuing piecemeal its expansionist goals. Explaining informally to reporters why he did not seek a declaration of war, Truman said, "We are not at war; the members of the United Nations are going to the relief of the Korean Republic to suppress a bandit raid on the Republic of Korea." He accepted—and later had to live with—a reporter's characterization that the United States was engaged in a "police action."[8] But Truman did not put his point as precisely as he might have if his aides, acting routinely, had sorted out the *Known, Unclear,* and *Presumed* and noted of powerful analogies the *Likenesses* and *Differences*, and if his advisers had benefited from such staff work.

The comparisons could have sharpened Truman's definition of objectives and even suggested how to attain them. The point of each analogy from the 1930s was that something had not been done which, if done, might have staved off World War II. What was it that Truman thought those earlier decision-makers should have done? As of 1950, based on what was then known of the past, his answers would have been clear. In Manchuria and Ethiopia the League powers should have threatened or used force to compel Japan, then Italy, to cease aggression and restore preexisting conditions. In the Rhineland and Austrian crises the signatories to the Versailles Treaty should have done likewise, compelling Hitler to withdraw his troops from the Rhineland and Austria. In the Czech crisis the Western powers should have declared their willingness to fight instead of pressing the Czechs to concede.

All those occasions argued for the option Truman actually chose: a use of force to repel the aggression. Thinking in detail about the analogues, however—as comparison requires—would have emphasized that the purpose was "to repel." It was not "to punish," "to seek retribution for," or "to take advantage of." For it was not then a common assumption—and surely not Truman's—that the League powers should have gone beyond restoring the *status quo ante* in Manchuria and tried, for example, to liberate Korea or Formosa, then under Japanese rule. Nor was it supposed that the Western powers should have solved the Rhineland crisis by themselves occupying some portions of Germany. In each instance, Truman and his advisers surely thought the "right" course of action would have been forcible restoration of conditions existing earlier. To have voiced that conclusion—or better still to have written it down—might have helped Truman and the others to define a little more sharply the decisions actually being faced at Blair House.

Had "options papers" been in fashion in 1950, one drawn up for the Blair House sessions might have read:

- Option A. Denounce the North Korean attack but take no other action
- Option B. Add economic sanctions, their lifting to be contingent on restoration of the *status quo ante*
- Option C. Add blockade, with the same condition
- Option D. Employ force to restore the *status quo ante*
- Option E. Employ force and, if opportunity offers, defeat and conquer North Korea and create a unified, non-Communist Korea
- Option F. Act against the Soviet Union itself, either (1) threatening war unless the North Koreans are pulled back, (2) demanding Soviet withdrawal from some part of the world more interesting to the United States, or (3) making a direct attack

As of June 1950 options A and B—using just words or just economic sanctions—were excluded by the presumption of needs to preserve collective security and American credibility. If option C (blockade) were ever in the running, it dropped out once the South Korean army's lines had broken and MacArthur said it would take U.S. troops to check a complete North Korean conquest. Directly threatening the Russians seemed out, because they had declared at once that they had no control over the North Koreans. Besides, it would add to the risk of World War III. If Truman and his advisers had reviewed broad choices at Blair House, they would have regarded option D (restoring the *status quo ante*) and option E (punishing the North Koreans) as the only genuine candidates.

As of June 1950 Truman had no doubt that he preferred D to E. He directed that American forces help South Korea repel the attack. On advice from MacArthur and other military men, he authorized American warplanes to fly missions north of the 38th parallel, the dividing line between South and North Korea, but he explained to his National Security Council, "We want to take any steps we have to to push the North Koreans behind the line." While lower-level officials in the State Department and the Pentagon talked of seizing the opportunity to reunify Korea as a non-Communist state, the President and Secretary of State Acheson spoke only of restoring the dividing line at the parallel.[9] Restoring violated boundaries, after all—or rather, the failure to do so—was not only at the heart of those analogues, Manchuria, Ethiopia, Austria, and so forth, but was what Truman and the others had themselves achieved in Iran, Greece, and Berlin just within the past few years.

Truman and Acheson did not, however, fix that goal in the minds of the public or even in their own. When Warren Austin, the U.S. Ambassador to the UN, made a speech implying that the war aim was reunification of Korea, neither Truman nor Acheson corrected him. Nor did they object publicly when Congressmen, Democrats as well as Republicans, proclaimed that communism would be rolled back. Then in September, after MacArthur had started to pursue the North Koreans into their homeland, Truman and Acheson, like almost everyone else, let themselves slip into a supposition that, since reunification seemed feasible, it was as good a goal as restoring the *status quo ante,* maybe better.

A serious look at the apparent analogues, it seems to us, could have helped Truman, Acheson, and others see more distinctly why their initial preference had gone so strongly just to restoring the *status quo ante.* Truman had a separate reason, and in the first days it sufficed of itself: He sought to demonstrate to everyone he could—in Moscow, London, Congress, and Peoria alike—that his appeal to force was not the start of anything like World War III, at least not at his option. But as the weeks wore on that became obvious. Had he had a second reason, one of principle, already thought through and articulated, it might powerfully have reinforced the restoration option as a war aim, making it much easier for Truman to resist enlarging his aim when the war went well. Had he nailed that down as his sole purpose early on, squelching Austin and others who championed reunification, Truman might more easily have stopped MacArthur's northward march at the first good defense line past the border, hailing UN success where the old League had failed, relishing a victory of principle. Thereby Truman could have spared himself Chinese attack, American retreat, inflationary pressure, allied fears, and two more years of fighting to achieve no further purpose. He could have stood in a Fifth Avenue reviewing stand, taking in the march-past with confetti and cheers—perhaps even before the November elections.

That would have called for Truman to make a speech in the first days of July—two weeks before he actually appeared on Capitol Hill—spelling out the continuity of twenty years, from the Manchurian incident forward, and urging the United States, along with the UN, to stick to principle in its resort to force: Restore a border rather than impose political change. We recognize how fanciful it is to imagine historical might-have-beens. At the outset Truman had at least one reason for not making such a speech: He did not know what it would take to keep a toehold in Korea, let alone restore the border. As the summer advanced, negative reasons multiplied. Since many members of Congress and editorial writers exulted at the chance to deal Stalin a blow, to set him back, such a speech risked breaching the short-run appearance of national unity. A former Republican national chairman early declared that the "Hiss Survivors Association" in the State Department would try "to subvert our military victory by calling a halt at the 38th parallel."[10] In addition, the imagined speech could have been seen as giving Russians and North Koreans unnecessary assurances or as closing off a course of action the President might later want to follow.

Yet nothing short of a public commitment, strongly argued at the very start—while our friends were retreating an increasing distance south with water at their backs—could have nailed down restoration as Truman's only war aim. Squelching, to be effective, would have had to come fast and hard, which means before Truman could know that the UN troops would not be pushed off the peninsula. What could have seemed pusillanimous the following September might have seemed foolhardy in July.

Even such a speech might not have sufficed. We appreciate all too well how easy it was in September—once MacArthur had cleared the south and seemed able to take all of Korea by parading north—for Truman and Acheson to forget the reasoning that had run through their minds in June. Appetites grew with eating. A strong early statement might have made no difference at all to the actual outcome.

With this caveat, we still think it a good exercise to ponder the speech Truman might have made at the war's start, extolling principle and limiting his aims, and when he should have made it, to what audience, mindful of what media, considering what follow-up, and using just what arguments. For doing so helps one recall the obvious truth that analogies are used at least as much for advocacy as for analysis. And when it comes to advocacy, attention to particular *Likenesses* and *Differences* is no less helpful.

The "lessons of the thirties" have provided, among other things, the underlying theme for every argument supporting stern approaches toward Communist regimes abroad from Truman's time forward. As a form of advocacy, nothing is more familiar to Americans of almost any age. Conceiving how one might have used those lessons at the height of the Cold War to argue for confining sternness within limits of a strict, unyielding sort thus calls for ingenuity.

The exercise, however, strengthens the case for regularly distinguishing the *Known* from the *Presumed,* the *Likeness* from the *Difference,* and jotting down phrases that capture the distinctions. For the advocate is judged by the responses of those whose minds he seeks to change, and nothing is more likely to spoil his persuasive effect than to be caught out in a factual mistake, especially if the fact relates to a precedent of which the hearer has independent knowledge. "It wasn't that way" easily transforms itself into "The whole case must be wrong." Nothing defends better against that danger than testing out analogies before putting them on the table. Moreover, the process is bound to turn up points of fact or arguments that make advocacy more effective.

Had Truman's staff done the homework we suggest, and had the hypothetical speech been given, the President could have quoted supporting rhetoric from at least two men whom many of his potential critics would have hesitated to gainsay. Henry L. Stimson, a virtual saint for the Republican foreign policy establishment, had been Secretary of State during the Manchurian crisis, and his memoirs spoke forcefully for the proposition that the League powers should have put things back the way they were, with no retribution against Japan. Winston Churchill, widely regarded as the one man who had been right about the dangers of appeasement in the 1930s, had spoken just as forcefully on how peace could then have been preserved if the League or the World Court had merely insisted that Germany march its troops back out of the Rhineland, restoring conditions as before.[11] Particulars from the key analogues could thus have made more persuasive the proposition that foreswearing aggression was essential to resisting aggression.

Korea by no means exhausts the subject of analogies. We have used Truman's case to illustrate some simple ways of clarifying situations by pulling them apart and by comparing "now" with "then" before addressing options. We think this helps to clarify the options too. We recommend as "mini-methods" with wide application regular sorting of the *Known, Unclear,* and *Presumed* and, when analogies intrude, identification of *Likenesses* and *Differences.* The types of decisions that might thereby be improved come in more varieties than this case shows. We turn now to another.

We classify analogies according to allure. In the Korean case, as the North Koreans stormed across the parallel at the outset of the war, the analogy was irresistible. Everyone saw events of the 1930s being replayed, and everyone agreed about the central lesson of those events: that aggression had to be resisted. Other analogies can be classified rather as captivating, not necessarily irresistible. Some are merely seductive. Still others are like the girl (or boy) next door: so familiar that attachment develops unnoticed.

For the captivating—not irresistible—analogy, a good example is the great influenza epidemic of 1918 as it figured in the swine flu scare of 1976.[12] The earlier of those events remains the most severe flu pandemic (worldwide epidemic) in recorded history, killing half a million Americans and forty times that number around the world. It was a bigger killer than World War I. The later episode, in contrast, was triggered by the brief appearance of a new flu strain at one place only: a crowded army camp where thirteen cases were clinically identified and one recuit died after going on an all-night march against doctor's orders. Two things linked that single death with the half-million. The first connection was technical, a matter for specialists; the second was a matter of folk memory. The latter captured politicians, civil servants, journalists, and not a few doctors besides.

Technically, the new flu of 1976 was chemically akin (the term is "antigenically related") to an influenza virus common among pigs—hence "swine flu"—but not found in humans since the early 1930s and believed to have been then a weakened version of the virus that in 1918 decimated pigs as well as people. With humans suddenly susceptible again—witness those thirteen recruits—questions naturally arose among the specialists: Assuming this is a stronger form of the once-virulent virus, how strong is it? Again a killer? Most immunologists and virologists guessed not, but no one could be sure. That gave an added fillip to their interest as technicians in improved preventive measures against flu pandemics generally. The two most recent ones, in 1957 and in 1968 (neither involving swine flu), had come upon an unprepared United States. Preventive efforts had proved too little and too late. Federal health authorities had been rehearsing ever since how to do better next time. Now next time might be here and might be *worse*.

The link with 1918, running through pigs to people, spurred specialists to try what was already on their minds: "Beat '68." But it came as a bolt from the blue to their superiors, both medical and lay, appointive and elective, career and short-term alike, capturing imaginations and dominating impressions. Though the 1918 influenza holds but a small place in most histories, biographies, and memoirs, it seems that almost everyone at higher levels of the Federal government in 1976 had a parent, uncle, aunt, cousin, or at least a family friend who had told lurid tales of personal experience with the 1918 flu. The killer had been known then as "Spanish flu"; the term "swine flu" meant nothing much to laymen off the farm. But the year 1918—more precisely 1918–19—cited in conjunction with the flu called up vivid images in Washington almost sixty years later. Those images were rooted in folk history and were more powerful because of it.

The 1918 epidemic hit this country in three waves. The first, a spring affair that started here and spread overseas, was relatively mild. The second erupted suddenly in late August—not a flu month, normally, for northern climates—showing itself simultaneously at three seaports around the world, one of them Boston. This one was the killer. It spread rapidly and violently, peaking in October, leaving some 350,000 dead across the country and on ships at sea. (Those also were peak weeks for troop concentration and transport to France in World War I.) At the end of the year, when the second wave had petered out, a third wave followed, lasting until spring. It killed 150,000 more Americans.[13]

The second and third waves were dire. Children sickened by the thousands; so did persons over sixty-five. Youngsters are usually prime carriers of flu, but almost all recover, whereas the elderly, although less susceptible, are likeliest to die of complications contracted or worsened as they weaken with the flu. Bacterial pneumonia stalks in influenza's footsteps, which helps to make those over sixty-five a traditional high-risk group. Those factors held in August 1918 too and there was then no penicillin for pneumonia. But something else, unknown (or anyway unnoticed) in traditional terms, had also happened then: Young adults in their prime, men and women in their thirties, even twenties, were victims of *this* flu, and not alone because of secondary infections. Thousands died within a day or so of getting sick, apparently attributable to flu itself. That is what made for tales told around dinner tables and heard by youngsters who would grow up to be Gerald Ford's advisers. Vigorous young adults, healthy one day, dead the next. Hospitals jammed. Corpses stacked. Mortuaries working overtime.

Given the state of medical knowledge in 1918, there was little to be done. Not for another fifteen years would the virus even be isolated, to say nothing of vaccines produced. Unsure of the causal agent, unclear about proper prevention, lacking a vaccine, local health authorities tried to keep people apart. In some places they issued masks to wear on crowded streets; photographs of those were to be seen in 1976 on TV news shows, adding to the images. For Federal health authorities in the Public Health Service, the only good thing to be said about it all was that no one held them responsible. What they could do they did: offer referral services to medical volunteers, keep watch, and compile statistics.

In 1976, by contrast, the Public Health Service, following the lead of its own specialists and others, overreached itself. The Center (now Centers) for Disease Control and sister agencies, the National Institute for Allergic and Infectious Diseases and the Food and Drug Administration's Bureau of Biologics, arranged worldwide surveillance. For a month after the episode in the one army camp they found no new outbreaks but concluded it was better to be safe than sorry. They also hoped to demonstrate the virtues of preventive medicine. The Center for Disease Control's Director, David Sencer, urged on the Assistant Secretary for Health and on the Secretary of Health, Education, and Welfare an unprecedented effort at nationwide prevention. Sencer aimed to double the numbers in half the time of the largest previous experiment with mass immunization (against polio), a great leap forward.[14] "Beat '68" was very much in Sencer's mind; 1918 figured in his references. While he did not exaggerate, his advocacy played upon those images with effect.

The new flu had appeared in January 1976; Sencer's proposals were made in March, near the end of the flu season. He recommended that a new vaccine for the new virus be developed, produced, tested, and distributed in the next three months, and that inoculation efforts begin after Independence Day, reaching everyone willing and able by Thanksgiving, well before the next flu season peaked. If the new virus reemerged, prevention would exceed all previous endeavors by a long shot, beating 1968 indeed. If not, no harm would have been done except for out-of-pocket costs, comparatively trifling.

The Assistant Secretary for Health, Theodore Cooper, a cardiologist, embraced the recommendations. So did the Secretary of Health, Education, and Welfare, David Mathews, who bucked them to President Ford. The Budget Director gulped but agreed. And President Ford approved the moment he received endorsement from a hastily assembled, expert *ad hoc* panel. Congress followed suit. Production of the vaccine began.

Then trouble started. Contrary to expectations, field trials of the new vaccine showed one dose hard on children, whose immunization therefore was postponed. Shortly afterward, so was everybody else's when, again against expectations, the vaccine manufacturers refused to bottle it because their casualty insurance firms withheld the usual insurance against losses from lawsuits. The President had to go to Congress seeking legislation that would transfer risks of costly litigation from insurers to the government. For a Democratic Congress in a presidential year, that proved an unattractive prospect. Besides, no swine flu had appeared anywhere in the world, not even at the height of winter in the Southern Hemisphere. And this had caused a falling out among President Ford's expert panelists, some of whom now called for stockpiling, which Sencer thought impracticable. With fortuitous help from a publicized burst of (unrelated) Legionnaire's disease, Ford finally shook some legislation loose, but on such terms that his inoculations could not start until October 1, just seven weeks before they were to close, according to the Center for Disease Control's initial scheme.

Actual immunizations had been delegated to the states and on down to local public health authorities or private doctors, with variable results in terms of reach and readiness. Nevertheless, most states had begun by mid-October. Then coincidental heart attacks in Pittsburgh killed two men from the same nursing home just after inoculation. That led local authorities, and several states besides, to suspend immunizations lest the vaccine be at fault. It wasn't, and they soon started up again, but not before TV had publicized the incident. Public confidence, especially among the urban poor, may never have recovered. But that mattered only a short while: Eight weeks later the inoculations were suspended nationwide, not to be resumed. This came about because a severe neurological side effect, not previously linked to influenza shots (indeed not seen with other vaccines either before or since), was established by statistical association through the Center for Disease Control's surveillance system. Legally, each person vaccinated had to be warned of risks; until those were statistically determined, vaccinations had to stop. By January 1977 the determination had been made: one death in two million, a small risk. But by then no one cared or dared to restart mass immunization, for in the entire year since the initial episode there had been, worldwide, not a single case of human swine flu that could not be traced to close contact with pigs.

In ten weeks more than 40 million persons had received flu shots, twice the number in any previous year. Everything considered, that may well be viewed historically as an administrative wonder. In the absence of the flu, however, it seemed to most contemporaries but a waste, or worse. Had a pandemic come, it could have seemed a breach of promise to Americans and callous beyond words to everybody else: President Ford in March, and Assistant Secretary Cooper in April, had loudly voiced the aim of giving all Americans their shots before winter. That would have been delayed; worse, supplies could not have covered anything like "all" and there would have been no help to spare for anyone in any other country. Once CDC Director Sencer's program was launched, the credibility of public health authorities had nowhere to go but down.

The actual outcome, although traceable to incidents and accidents, owes much to luck, much of it bad, yet Ford and his associates had put themselves in a position to be victimized that way. Behind bad luck stood unexamined presumptions. Those stemmed from the original decision process in March 1976. The process was essentially a two-stage affair. First came the turn of specialists assembled by and around Sencer. He made his recommendation after consultation with his staff—along with the National Institute for Allergic and Infectious Diseases and the Food and Drug Administration's Bureau of Biologics—and with support from his Advisory Committee on Immunization Practices, which happened to include the elder statesmen of virology as well as faculty members from schools of public health. While one of them made a mild effort to slow down the rest, asking a hard question (to which we return later), Sencer did not press for answers and, all in all, was encouraged to proceed. Then came the turn of laymen, relatively speaking, at the Assistant Secretary level and above on up to Ford, responding to Sencer's proposal. Not surprisingly they came to his conclusions and decided as he had proposed. The experts Ford assembled at the end included proponents from Sencer's Advisory Committee.

Might our mini-methods have been useful at those stages? It goes almost without saying that in Health, Education, and Welfare and at the White House no one was in the habit of reviewing a current situation quite as we suggest, separating the *Known, Unclear,* and *Presumed* while setting forth *Likenesses* and *Differences* for analogies. However, as a scientific matter, something partial was done naturally, habitually, for Sencer by scientists at his Center and by members of his Advisory Committee. Many points *Unclear,* especially in epidemiology, *were* pulled apart from *Knowns,* while *Likenesses* with and *Differences* from 1918 (among others) were reviewed explicitly in terms much like the summaries above. Little was missing except explicitness about presumptions. Yet in making for bad luck that lack bulked large.

In the "action memorandum" Sencer sent to his superiors, certain presumptions were explicitly identified.[15] Some amounted to scientific hypotheses, for instance:

- Major shifts in viruses occur on eleven-year cycles (1957, 1968).
- The January episode may be just three years early.
- Past shifts were followed by pandemics.
- The absence of new outbreaks proves nothing.
- "Widespread" swine flu is a "strong possibility" in 1976–77.
- This flu might hit young adults as hard as old (as in 1918).

Others were more administrative in character, among them:

- With effort, there is "barely enough" time to produce vaccine for "all."
- And get it into them before next winter.

- By methods short of direct Federal administration.
- With no legislation needed except money.
- And in lieu of stockpiling which "jet spread" could invalidate (the vaccine taking some two weeks to work, with preparations taking two to four weeks more).

One presumption was political; in Sencer's words:

- "The Administration can tolerate unnecessary health expenditures better than unnecessary death and illness, particularly if a flu pandemic should occur."

Time would show that Sencer and his aides and his Advisory Committee colleagues also shared some inexplicit presumptions, not labeled as such. Because they were not acknowledged at his level, they were taken for *Knowns* at the next. Among them:

- Flu vaccine is safe: no serious side effects.
- One dose will do for children as for adults.
- With Federal leadership the country's health authorities can cope through usual channels.
- The litigation problems of vaccine producers won't stand in the way.
- The medical and scientific communities will follow the Center for Disease Control, buttressed as it is by the prestige of the Advisory Committee on Immunization Practices.
- Ditto the mass media.
- While presidential sponsorship facilitates public support.

Every one of these inexplicit, presumptive *Knowns* would turn out wrong in practice, even the last. Ford's role aroused the casualty insurers, fearing claims and suits from angry Democrats or followers of Ford's competitor for the Republican nomination, Ronald Reagan. Many of the things explicitly presumed were wrong in the event as well, among them those scientific hypotheses. Since 1976 flu has behaved in ways that disconfirm the then prevailing theories, not least eleven-year cycles, thus underlining what nonspecialists did not then grasp: How little the specialists understood, how much a mystery the flu remains. Laymen, not excluding doctors with different specialties, grasped this the less because their memories ran to sixty-year-old happenings, and they knew modern medicine had been created since.

With scientific presumptions wrong, administrative ones unduly optimistic, and a fistful of key others unexamined, the specialists gave place in the decision process to superiors who found themselves wedged between Sencer's proposal and their images of 1918. At Ford's level, understandably, and HEW Secretary Mathews's and even HEW Assistant Secretary Cooper's, there was less effort than at Sencer's center to distinguish the *Unclear* from the *Known*, still less to sort out *Likenesses* and *Differences* in that analogy. For with less understanding there was less incentive. It is perhaps significant that several Disease Center virologists and Advisory Committee members later recalled their guesses (not then voiced to one another) putting chances of pandemic at from one in fifty to one in five, while departmental and White House aides were quoted at the time as thinking chances were from one in five to even. The higher the level the fewer the doubts. Below, doubts stemmed from puzzlement: No such single episode had previously been recorded—did the lack of further cases mean this strain of virus could not gain a hold on humans any more? Or might it spread subclinically, carried about by people who did not necessarily themselves fall victim? Virologists were divided. Paradoxically, the chief proponent of subclinical spread expected the pandemic to be mild. The distinction was lost on laymen.

For politically responsible and vulnerable officials, comparable doubts were likelier to follow from unstated presumptions that they tended to perceive as facts (or not perceive at all). Had those been stated and debated as explicit presumptions, then the laymen might have noticed that the expertise involved was mostly managerial, media-related, or political, *not* medical. That might have tempted them to probe. Had they done so they might soon have had as many doubts as the more dubious specialists. This scarcely could have led them to do nothing. But faced with such uncertainties they might have separated the decision to prepare vaccine from the commitment to inoculate and, as to that, might well have publicized more modest goals.

Putting all presumptions on the table and then testing them is one defense of laymen against experts. As the swine flu case suggests, analysis is served thereby. So also is advocacy, for laymen and experts alike. Sencer got his way, as far as the decision goes; but stored up trouble for himself in execution, setting the stage for bad luck. Had he started with tighter presumptions, he might have concluded with more credibility. In the event, he lost his audience, a poor end for an advocate.

To this matter of probing presumptions we shall return, but not before saying more about analogies and then about issue history. This chapter illustrates two kinds of analogies that officials cannot escape. In 1950 no mature officeholder could have shrugged off recollections of the 1930s. The words that had to be used—"aggression" and "collective security," for example—necessarily brought those years to mind. And the lessons appeared indisputable. It was this last point that made the analogies irresistible, for those lessons spoke with such seeming clarity to the question the decision-makers wanted to get to: What should they *do?*

In 1976, faced with cases of swine flu, specialists thought at once of 1918 as well as of the recent and to them more relevant pandemics of 1957 and 1968. Antigenic characteristics compelled them to recall the "Spanish flu," which experts had attributed to the swine strain. And once they mentioned Spanish flu to the nonspecialists, the latter were captured by folk memories. Literally, the analogy was not "irresistible." Its relevance was limited, its application arguable, and its guidance dubious on what to do. It served better as a warning light than as a beacon. Yet it precipitated action on the basis, solely, of "worst-case" analysis without preparing to accommodate the likely case. Captivated, the decision-makers failed to hedge by light of the uncertainty. This caused no tears among the specialists intent on doing better than in 1968. Analysis aside, the analogy was excellent for advocates (in the short run).

In the Korean case Truman and his aides would have served themselves better, we argue, if they had paused just a few minutes to separate the *Known* from the *Presumed* and then to pull apart the irresistible analogies, explicitly identifying *Likenesses* and *Differences.* The exercise would have given them a slightly sharper understanding of why there seemed so little doubt about what to do. Just conceivably, it might have saved Truman from making a heedless choice of follow-up action when MacArthur neared the prewar border. In the swine flu case the lower-level actors had (in other terms) disaggregated the *Known, Unclear,* and *Presumed* and analyzed *Likenesses* and *Differences*—not alone on 1918 but on the two more interesting (to them) analogies of 1957 and 1968. The officials higher up skipped most of that themselves, nor did they probe what had been done below. They took *Presumeds* for *Knowns, Likenesses* for *likelihoods.* Here too, we think, a little more analysis of our kind could have led to hedging of bets, to decisions taken one at a time, with pauses between for scheduled reviews to determine whether conditions were developing as foreseen. But further analysis of the analogy with 1918, captivating as it was to laymen, would have called for more than just pulling apart its elements. Presumptions would have to have been tested, including *Presumeds* at both levels, specialized and lay. The "how" of such testing we shall come to later. First we need to illustrate still other types of analogies and then to touch on cases where the shortcoming is not faulty use of analogues but rather resistance to ones calling into question some presumption the decision-makers cherish.

4 The Seducer and the Kid Next Door

In mid-May 1975, nine months into his presidency and ten months before promising to immunize all Americans against swine flu, Gerald Ford faced the *Mayaguez* affair.[1] He looks back on it as one of the successes of his short presidency. So do most members of his Administration, and we do not take issue with their verdict. It could easily, however, have ended up embarrassing Ford more than did the swine flu scare. As Wellington said of Waterloo, it was "a damn close-run thing." The seductive influence of an analogy—with the *Pueblo* affair of 1968—enhanced the risk of its ending badly. The story thus not only underlines our point that influential analogies ought to be inspected; it also suggests that once is not enough. If an analogy has figured in thinking about objectives and options, then *Likenesses* and *Differences* may need to be re-reviewed periodically as new *Knowns* accumulate.

The *Mayaguez,* a rusty forty-year-old freighter recently replated as a container ship, had been on her regular run from Hong Kong via Sattahip, Thailand, to Singapore and back. On the first leg of that run, her hold and decks heavy with crates of food, clothing, chemicals, paint, hospital stores, and mail, she was wallowing past Poulo Wai island, 60 miles off the mainland of Southeast Asia, when a Cambodian gunboat hailed and halted her, and Cambodian seamen came aboard and seized control. The captain managed to get out one "Mayday" message.

The seizure occurred in the early afternoon of May 12, Southeast Asian time. Washington time being eleven hours earlier, it was 5 A.M. when the captain's message showed up on a ticker in the Pentagon's National Military Command Center. A copy went almost immediately to Air Force General David Jones, the acting Chairman of the Joint Chiefs of Staff. Ford's Deputy Assistant for National Security Affairs Brent Scowcroft (coincidentally an Air Force lieutenant general) informed the President at a regular 7 A.M. briefing. Secretary of Defense James Schlesinger received the news about a half-hour later, and Henry Kissinger, National Security Assistant *cum* Secretary of State, a half-hour after that.

In May 1975 the seizure of the *Mayaguez* seemed a large event. Just a few weeks earlier Americans had played out the final scene of their war in Vietnam. The North Vietnamese, breaking a truce arranged two years earlier, had marched back into South Vietnam. The Ford Administration threatened renewed bombing, but Congress had earlier forbidden bombing, and Congressional leaders refused to suspend the ban. South Vietnam's armies began to dissolve. As the North Vietnamese approached Saigon, the remaining Americans fled by helicopter. Every network news program carried scenes of Americans stepping on South Vietnamese and knocking them away from helicopter doors. All South Vietnam had since fallen. Communists had also taken over Cambodia. The capture of the American-flag *Mayaguez* by one of their gunboats thus pricked a raw wound.

In differing ways, Ford and his chief advisers saw the seizure as a challenge but also a possible opportunity. Ford was a fill-in Vice President become fill-in President because of Watergate and Richard Nixon's abdication. Everyone who read about politics knew LBJ's characterization of Ford as a man who "could not walk and chew gum at the same time." (Johnson's actual verb had been earthier; "walk" was one family newspapers could print.) The *Mayaguez* incident offered Ford a chance to erase some of the memories of those helicopters departing Saigon. At the same time he could demonstrate decisiveness, resoluteness, and fitness to be President. Schlesinger and General Jones saw a challenge to American power and to the principle of freedom of the seas. They also saw a chance to demonstrate the military establishment's competence and thereby to lift morale. Kissinger had felt the fall of Saigon more keenly than others because it had been *his* threat to the North Vietnamese, *his* promise to South Vietnam, that Congress had refused to honor. Having seen intelligence reports suggesting that North Korea might move against South Korea, Kissinger feared worse challenges in the offing. To him the *Mayaguez* incident seemed almost a last chance for regaining lost credibility. At a hastily called meeting of the National Security Council, as Ford recalls it,

> Kissinger leaned forward over the table and with emotion stressed the broad ramifications of the incident. The issues at stake went far beyond the seizure of the ship, he said; they extended to international perceptions of U.S. resolve and will. If we failed to respond to the challenge, it would be a serious blow to our prestige around the world. "At some point," he continued, "the United States must draw the line. This is not our idea of the best such situation. It is not our choice. But we must act upon it now, and act firmly." [2]

No one present disputed Kissinger's basic argument. "There wasn't a dove in the place," one insider said afterward.[3]

Ford and all his advisers agreed that their objectives were to free the *Mayaguez* and its crew and to show firmness. For the moment everyone also agreed about what to do. First, Kissinger was to send a strong diplomatic protest via Peking. Second, reconnaissance planes were to track the *Mayaguez*. Third, available aircraft, ships, and troops were to assemble as rapidly as possible. Fourth, the White House was to appear in control—handle all publicity, be the apparent locus of all decisions, but be seen also as, in the words of Ford's press secretary, preserving "an atmosphere of calm deliberation." To reinforce that appearance, the White House announced that Kissinger would, as scheduled, fly off to keep a speaking engagement in Missouri.

Inside the White House bulletins kept breaking the calm (and Ford's sleep). An early one reported the *Mayaguez* under escort toward Kompong Som, formerly Sihanoukville, Cambodia's port. At 10 P.M. a new report said it was still dead in the water where originally stopped. At 1:30 A.M. another report said no, after all, the ship was on its way to Kompong Som. An hour later yet another put it at Koh Tang, an island about halfway to the Cambodian mainland. The eleven-hour time difference accounted for some of the confusion. Initial snarls in command and communication lines both in the area and in Washington made matters worse. Afterward, Ford said that the succession of contradictory reports gave him doubts about everything the intelligence services said. If they couldn't find a ship, what could they find?[4]

During all that early period, Ford had the earlier *Pueblo* incident much in his mind. He was to write afterward:

> Back in 1968, I remembered, the North Koreans had captured the intelligence ship U.S.S. *Pueblo* in international waters and forced her and her crew into the port of Wonsan. The U.S. had not been able to respond fast enough to prevent the transfer, and as a result, *Pueblo's* crew had languished in a North Korean prison camp for nearly a year. I was determined not to allow a repetition of that incident.[5]

Before writing that passage (or approving it, if the language was actually a ghostwriter's), Ford said something similar to interviewers preparing an official "crisis management" history for the National Defense University. "The similarity of the two situations was obvious to the President," they wrote. "There was no time for a slow 'bubbling up' of analysis through many layers of the bureaucracy." And some of those present at the initial NSC meeting told a journalist not long afterward that Ford there "talked about the *Pueblo* affair: 'How it was similar in some respects,' he said, 'and different in others.' 'It was a benchmark,' he believed, 'from which they could proceed.' "[6]

Talking on the telephone with Schlesinger during the early morning of the second day, Ford again referred frequently to the *Pueblo* precedent. Or so he says in his memoirs.[7] Schlesinger himself does not recall Ford's talking much about the *Pueblo,* nor does he remember it figuring in his own thoughts. Possibly Ford misremembered. Possibly, on the other hand, *Pueblo* references did not register sharply in Schlesinger's ear. At the time of the earlier incident he had been a RAND Corporation analyst concentrating on nuclear strategy. His recollections were those of an interested newspaper reader. Since Ford had been House minority leader responsible for denouncing the Democrats then in office, the *Pueblo* affair figured in his personal history. To the utility of noticing such differences, we shall return in a later chapter. Here, the only point is that the *Pueblo* analogy had a grip on the President's mind, and this probably influenced both his definition of the primary objective and his preferences for action. White House reporters were told right away that the President was considering "the use of air or sea power to prevent the ship being taken into a Cambodian harbor."[8]

After the phone conversation with Schlesinger, Ford convened another NSC meeting. That night, at 10:40 P.M., he did so yet again. By that time Kissinger was back from Kansas City.

To the irritation of both Ford and Kissinger, options for military action remained cloudy. Prolonged uncertainty about the location of the ship, together with the fact that U.S. forces were widely dispersed around the Pacific while the Thai government objected to having any of them stage through the U.S. base at U Tapao, had delayed work by General Jones and other military planners. Also, the absence of a local unified command made their task harder. While the Commander in Chief, Pacific, Admiral Noel Gayler, had overall authority, local control rested with an Air Force officer at U Tapao. He could request but not order action by naval, naval air, and Marine units. Even at the evening NSC meeting Jones was asking for more time in order to obtain better intelligence and get more forces into the area.

For Jones and the military, the prime objective was neat, clean success. Schlesinger shared that wish but was willing to accept somewhat greater risks for the sake of demonstrating that the United States could not be pushed around. Kissinger wanted a maximum display of military might for presumed effect in other Communist capitals. The President remained unshaken in his belief that what mattered was to get the ship and its crew before it ended up as a *Pueblo.* Acting very much the man in charge, Ford overrode Jones's caution. Among the options Jones mentioned, Ford picked out those most likely to effect *his* objective—a helicopter landing plus naval boarding operation to seize the ship and a Marine landing on the island where it was tied up—and he insisted on action at the earliest practicable moment. In fact, he demanded it for the next afternoon and backed off only after Jones said that minimally necessary forces could not get there by then. But Ford at the same time rejected Kissinger's recommendation of massive B-52 raids on the Cambodian mainland. He agreed only to naval air attacks on mainland targets for the purpose of preventing Cambodian reinforcement of the garrison on the island. Ford's eye remained fixed on the aim of recovering ship and crew.

If the *Pueblo* analogy helped Ford keep this clear sense of purpose, it served him well—to a point. We do not know what particulars led him to term the *Pueblo* only a "benchmark." Certainly many points would have appeared in a list of *Differences.* The *Pueblo* had been a Navy vessel, not a merchantman. She had carried sensitive intelligence-gathering gear. Her captain and crew knew secrets that North Korean interrogators might discover. And there had been little doubt of the North Korean government's deliberately planning the provocation. In the case of the *Mayaguez,* Pnomh Penh's part was unclear. In his memoirs Ford reports a chance intervention by White House photographer David Kennerly, who happened once to have visited Cambodia. At one point Kennerly surprised everyone by piping up to ask, "Has anyone considered that this might be the act of a local Cambodian commander who has just taken it into his own hands to halt any ship that comes by? Has anyone stopped to think that he might not have gotten his orders from Pnomh Penh?"[9] But the *Likenesses* were important: an American ship, with American crewmen who could be used as hostages. Ford's sense of what to do was surely influenced by what he believed should have been done before: effect a rescue while there was time.

During the third, late-night meeting of the NSC, however, the President received news that probably should have given him second thoughts about the course of action he had chosen. Earlier reconnaissance reports had said crewmen were being taken off the ship. Now a pilot reported sighting a boatload of "possible Caucasians" en route from the island to the mainland. U.S. planes used gunfire and even dropped riot control chemicals in hope of turning the boat back, but those efforts failed. The boat docked at Kompong Som.

When Ford next met with his NSC in the afternoon of May 14 (early morning in Cambodia), the chief question was whether or not to proceed with the operations ordered the night before. Disregarding Thai objections, aircraft and Marines had been moved through U Tapao. Two U.S. destroyers were in the area, and an aircraft carrier was near. But one helicopter had crashed on takeoff in Thailand, killing all twenty-three men aboard; the two destroyers had been slow in reaching their stations; intelligence was skimpy regarding the ship and the island's topography and defenses; and concern about the possibility that some crewmen were on the island precluded preliminary bombardment. For all those reasons the Joint Chiefs wanted a twenty-four-hour delay. Ford, however, would not hear of it. He ordered that the operation proceed at once.

On a "go" signal from Washington, a U.S. destroyer steamed alongside the *Mayaguez* to carry out the first Navy boarding operation since 1826. About five hundred Marines meanwhile landed on Koh Tang, and carrier aircraft bombed Kompong Som and other mainland targets.

The ship, easily retaken, turned out to have only Cambodian

guards on board. At Koh Tang, the Marines had expected to meet fewer than two dozen Cambodian irregulars. Instead, they found a defending force of nearly two hundred regulars armed with automatic rifles and machine guns. Before the island was secure, eighteen more Americans were dead and fifty were wounded. And not a single *Mayaguez* crewman had been found.

The "possible Caucasians" had been the ship's whole complement. Ford had had one piece of good luck in that the gunfire, bombs, and gas which failed to turn their boat back had not by mischance killed them. He had even greater good luck in that the Cambodians decided to release the *Mayaguez* crew without demanding a ransom. They made the announcement by radio about the time the landings began. Not long afterward a U.S. pilot started a pass at what he thought was a boat bringing reinforcements to Koh Tang. At the last moment he saw white flags and Caucasian faces. Ford's luck held: The pilot did not fire his rockets. The boat turned out to carry all the crew of the *Mayaguez.* They were welcomed aboard one of the U.S. destroyers. Less than three days after their capture, they were headed home.

Ford and his aides were at first exultant. Eight out of nine phone calls to the White House praised the President's actions. In Gallup's index Ford's favorable rating went from 39 to 51 percent. The *New York Times,* not then given to praising the administration or approving presidential use of military force, said editorially that it had to endorse what Ford had done—provided the *Mayaguez* did not turn out to have had some illicit mission.[10]

Those effects did not last long. Soon the press and members of Congress were pointing out that, if one counted the twenty-three men killed in the helicopter accident, the Administration had spent forty-two lives to save forty. Critics charged that bombing of shore installations had been unnecessary—and continued after the Cambodian government announced that the crewmen would be released. Moreover, reporters' rundowns and Congressional inquiries uncovered the extent to which the actual recovery of the crew had been, in the phrase Acheson used for Kennedy's success in the missile crisis, "plain dumb luck." Neither Ford nor Schlesinger and the military nor Kissinger harvested from the *Mayaguez* incident much of what they had hoped for.

We do not hold the outcome to have been a result of faulty decisions or decision processes. Given the general climate in the United States and the world in 1975, Ford and the others did their work reasonably well. As with the missile crisis, we are prepared also to concede that good luck may not be wholly random: Some people make themselves luckier than others.

Still, we do feel that the Administration's decision processes could have worked marginally better. Post mortems by the military, the intelligence community, and Congress would all conclude that the rescue mission was too hastily planned and set in motion. The delay suggested by the Joint Chiefs might have saved a few lives or, in any case, made the operation a better example of what the military services could do. As it was, General Jones looked back on the *Mayaguez* as a model of how not to plan a rescue mission. When he next faced such a task, in 1980, as Chairman, not just acting Chairman, of the Joint Chiefs, he would insist on controlling the timetable and on centralizing both planning and command in his own Joint Staff. In doing so, we are told, he would sometimes refer explicitly to the *Mayaguez* analogy. Yet those helicopters failed to reach the hostages in Teheran. Even if a twenty-four hour delay in 1975 had done no more than make for a less messed-up operation, the nation might have had reason five years later to be grateful, for the *Mayaguez* might then have served as a helpful, not an unhelpful, analogy.

Had Ford made another inspection of the *Pueblo* analogy after the "possible Caucasians" report, he might—just might—have seen more merit in the Joint Chiefs' plea for delay. Up to then the analogy had given him a clear decision rule. He might instinctively have taken a second look at that rule had he trusted the intelligence he was getting. By the final day both CIA and the Defense Intelligence Agency said they couldn't tell where the crew might be. If they had not had trouble earlier pinpointing where the ship was, Ford might have listened harder. As it was, he stayed where previous reasoning had brought him.

Once crew and ship had been separated, that reasoning no longer had the same coherence as in the beginning, when the *Pueblo* analogy had seemed a fitting benchmark. The *Pueblo* had been a prize in its own right. The *Mayaguez* was not: Only the crew mattered. And if the crew had been transferred to the mainland, the President's previous choice among options no longer made as much sense. Where would Ford have been on the day after the attack if, with forty-two men dead, ten helicopters out of action, and the Thai government protesting trespass on its sovereignty, he had had nothing to show but the empty hulk of an old freighter?

The *Mayaguez* case seems to us to reinforce the argument for making it routine to look at *Likenesses* and *Differences* whenever an analogy pops up. The instance argues further for periodically rechecking points of congruence and noncongruence if the analogy seems actually to help in defining objectives or options. For conditions often resemble those of May 1975. A choice has to be made in a hurry. An obvious analogy surfaces. It is seductive, because it helps supply a decision rule when there seems to be no time for analysis to "bubble up." Because it has that attraction, it does not get close inspection. The decision rule then holds even though initial *Likenesses* fade or even disappear.

Irresistible analogies, like those from the 1930s as they came to the minds of Truman and others in June 1950, need a close look to illuminate concerns and options. Captivating analogies need review for the same reason and also, as with swine flu, to uncover questionable presumptions masquerading as facts, especially when laymen confront specialists. Seductive analogies should be examined and reexamined for those reasons and one more: to gain some protection against supposing that a problem is what it used to be when, in reality, conditions have changed.

Last among types comes the girl (or boy) next door—the analogy you don't notice but fall for nonetheless.

Jimmy Carter's early presidency is illustrative. Taking office on January 20, 1977, having already promised to "hit the ground running," he immediately pardoned Vietnam War draft evaders and asked Congress to vote each taxpayer a fifty-dollar rebate. During the next several weeks he proposed, among other things, a batch of election-law reforms, including public financing for congressional campaigns. He tried to kill pork barrel water projects, announced far-reaching plans for reorganizing the executive branch, introduced "zero-based budgeting," and proclaimed his intention to set ceilings on hospital charges. Pledging conservation as the keynote of energy policy, he asked Americans to turn their thermostats down to 65 degrees Fahrenheit.

To set a distinctive style, Carter spurned the traditional limousine at his Inaugural and walked back from the Capitol. During subsequent weeks he gave a televised "fireside chat" garbed in sweater and slacks, was photographed carrying his own suit bag on and off planes, attended a town meeting in Massachusetts, and invited any and all citizens to call him on the phone. (Almost half-a-million did.)[11]

In foreign affairs, he promptly entertained eight heads of state or government, proclaimed his dedication to "human rights," called for a complete ban on nuclear weapons tests, expressed disapproval of West Germany for selling nuclear fuel to Brazil, suggested possible willingness to normalize relations with Cuba, approved Vietnam's admission to the UN, spoke in favor of a "Palestinian homeland," and dispatched Secretary of State Cyrus Vance to Moscow with a "comprehensive" plan for limiting strategic arms.

On April 20, his ninetieth day in office, Carter sent to Congress and presented to the country a "comprehensive" energy program, calling it "the moral equivalent of war." (The issue had not figured in his campaign, nor had the comprehensiveness been tested in Congress, and the characterization was a general surprise—indeed, it was a speechwriter's add-on.) Carter also parceled out, with deadlines to department heads, assignments for comparably comprehensive packages in welfare, tax reform and social security; these were to be presented within weeks or months to the same session of Congress—mostly to the same committees, a monstrous jam up.

Most of Carter's initiatives came to nought. He himself repudiated the tax rebate scheme. Congressional campaign financing died in committee. Most of the pork barrel projects were restored. Reorganization and zero-based budgeting produced disappointing results. Hospital cost containment met unconquerable resistance. Social security reform would be rewritten on the Hill; tax and welfare reform would die aborning. From early on, both congressmen and citizens became irked because *no one* could get phone calls to the White House returned. Nuclear strictures irritated both West Germans and Brazilians. Gestures to Communist states and to the Palestinians further complicated relations with Congress. "Human rights" offended Russians just as Vance arrived, while Vance's mission yielded worse than nothing: It probably set SALT back. (More on that later.) The Senate savaged Carter's comprehensive energy program and did not settle on a policy until three years and two versions later. Carter's original version was to be best remembered by Russell Baker's abridgement of the call for a Moral Equivalent of War: "MEOW."[12]

Viewed in their own terms, however, Carter's first months as President could easily have been scored successful. Until summer, when his Budget director, Bert Lance, was forced to resign for conflict-of-interest reasons, Carter faced no untoward happenings either at home or abroad. He had a rising economy without sharp inflation; slowly increasing employment; no riots at home; no wars abroad; no novel, hostile Soviet initiatives; no serious squabbles in NATO; no shocks to or from Japan; no revolutionary collapses as in Iran the next year; no embassy takeovers as in Teheran the year after. Compared to FDR's first months or to Truman's, Nixon's, or Ford's, Carter's were quiet. Even Eisenhower had his first weeks interrupted by the death of Stalin and unsettled by jostling from Wisconsin's junior Senator, Joseph McCarthy. Not so Carter. Events gave him scant competition in his reach for media, public, and congressional attention.[13]

Some of Carter's early proposals passed the Congress. He got emergency energy legislation, which, in freeing the flow of natural gas, went beyond anything any predecessor had wrestled out of Texan-dominated committees in the House. He also obtained a substantial new public works employment program. He could readily have claimed a winning start on the Hill.

Why then did Carter create—and leave behind—an impression of having rushed in one half-baked proposal after another, scattering his shots, most falling short, so that he looked a loser, not a winner, even in those months of calm before events closed in on him?

The answer doubtless has many elements. Carter had spent most of four years running for the presidency. Some people concluded that he just couldn't stop campaigning, especially since most of his intimate staff had had little experience of or found little excitement in any other line of work. Others saw inexperience itself as the key factor. "They're very smart," one old capital hand said to the *Washington Post* columnist David Broder, "but it's almost impossible to exaggerate their ignorance of what's been going on in government the last 20 years."[14] Still others put the blame on Carter's mind and style: a capacity for intense concentration on detail combined with a curious flightiness, which could carry him from subject to subject or, on a given subject, to one conviction one day and an opposite one the next. Broder himself wrote as early as February 1977 that Carter acted less like the captain of a ship of state than like a "frantic . . . white-water canoeist."[15] Still closer observers have suggested to us that he combined a penchant for "comprehensive solutions" with an absolute misreading of the limits on the uses of initial popularity.

One factor, we venture, was the unremarked, perhaps only half-conscious, influence of an analogy. Carter's own behavior, the language used by his aides at the time, and his own language afterward, suggest a set of beliefs about the startup period of a presidency. They assumed that it involved a "honeymoon period." They also assumed that it came to a first accounting at the end of one hundred days. Carter bitterly (and unfairly) entitles one chapter of his autobiography, "My One-Week Honeymoon with Congress." Not long after the "MEOW" speech, Hamilton Jordan, a key White House aide, described Carter as disappointed only in having been unable to do more. "Carter," he wrote, "would have liked to have done everything in the first 100 days."[16]

Those catch phrases, "honeymoon" and "hundred days," were rooted in specific historical events: the "hundred days" of March–June 1933 (Inauguration Day was then March 4), when Congress passed the first New Deal, and its loud echo during 1965, when LBJ put through the first installment of his Great Society. Carter, Jordan, and the others were probably generally aware of such roots, but there is little indication of their noticing the fact. Had the President explicitly framed the analogy, as Truman framed that of the 1930s or Ford that of the *Pueblo,* we might not single out this case as different from the others. But here one sees the operation of an analogy or analogies left inexplicit, buried in words presumed to describe reality in general but actually derived from a sample of one or at most two.

Our procedures for dealing with other analogies cannot apply to such as these without further thought and adaptation, for these usually arise in a distinctly different context from the others. Rather than a sharp, fresh, frequently surprising situation calling for particular decisions, the context is more likely to be a general set of circumstances, as in Carter's case, at once unfamiliar and anticipated, in which, lacking anything better, a wanderer trusts folk wisdom. In the public sector every arena has its own supply of such "kid-next-door" analogies. General rules based on samples of one or two can be found in every operating agency, every legislative body, and every issue area. In electoral politics such rules of thumb are rife. In presidential campaigns, for example:

- Don't peak too early (i.e., don't be Dewey).
- In a TV debate, be a fountain of facts (be JFK, not Nixon).
- Don't be belligerently ideological (Goldwater in 1964).
- Don't be too specific (McGovern promising every taxpayer $1,000).
- Don't get emotional (Muskie crying in New Hampshire).

Never mind that FDR always peaked early (James Farley, Roosevelt's manager, held that voters rarely changed their minds after Labor Day); or that Ronald Reagan won two gubernatorial and one presidential election being vague or wrong on facts, highly ideological, and very specific in promises; or that John Glenn became a Senator and briefly a presidential prospect because an opponent said he had never held a job and he replied by recounting in a choked voice what it was to be a career military officer. Yet the "don'ts" remain in force.

How are such analogies to be identified in time? Having identified them, what does one do? The best defense, we think, is to begin by asking about any catch phrase: Where did it come from? In short, revert to history again—its history. Often, as with the "hundred days," the particular experiences reflected in the phrase—the analogy or analogies from which it draws its seeming current relevance—come readily to mind. Then, borrowing from previous procedures, think for a moment about *Likenesses* and *Differences.* The question is whether the folk wisdom really applies "now."

Consider what Carter or Jordan or one of their aides might have jotted down after noting where the "hundred days" notion had come from:

CARTER and FDR

Likenesses

Carter in January–March 1977 resembles FDR in March–June 1933 in that he is a former governor and a Democrat, and he faces a number of complex and urgent issues.

Differences

Personally, FDR had behind him twenty years of national political experience. He had held high appointive office in the Wilson Administration and had been a vice presidential nominee in 1920. He knew reasonably well just about everybody who would matter to his initial success as President. He had won by a landslide and carried with him large majorities in both houses of Congress—most of them newcomers susceptible to being led. Besides, Congress convened when he called it, not earlier. Carter, by contrast, has barely squeaked past Ford, exhibits no coattails, lacks much of a majority in either House, and faces a Congress independently led. Thanks to the Twentieth Amendment it is already in session, doing business before his inauguration. When FDR took office, the nation felt itself to be in a grave crisis. Farmers were taking to the roads with shotguns; banks were shutting down; the corpses of starved citizens were turning up in public parks! The country was ready to try anything, and various claimed remedies had already had partial trials either at the local or state level or in other countries. Nothing like those conditions exist in 1977.

Carter and LBJ

Likenesses

Carter resembles LBJ in coming from the former Confederacy, being a Democrat, and facing a lot of hard problems.

Differences

Otherwise, on every count, the two, as newly inaugurated Presidents, are dissimilar. LBJ had spent nearly forty years in Washington, much of the time as a mover and shaker. Like FDR, he had won by a landslide, and enough new Northern Democrats won House seats at the same time to break the power of the twenty-eight-year-old conservative coalition. Having already been President for fifteen months, Johnson had had ample time to prepare. Since his Great Society program opened with unfinished business from Roosevelt's last campaign and Truman's subsequent Fair Deal, Washington lawyers had been working over draft bills for years. Since most of Carter's issues—tax rebates, campaign financing, hospital cost containment, and above all energy—are comparatively new, many of the relevant legal, procedural, bureaucratic, and political problems have not even been detected, let alone surmounted.

To recognize that, as a tag for something Washingtonian, the "hundred days" traced back to FDR and LBJ, and to reflect at all on how much Carter's situation was unlike theirs should have shaken any hope or expectation that Carter's accomplishments in that short period were going to bear comparison. This might have prompted the question: What *can* we do during the "honeymoon"? Which should have led to the question: What *is* the "honeymoon"? Where does that notion come from? And so on.

Here, a bridge would have been crossed. Not conceptually, for "honeymoon" is just another case of a catchword concealing an analogy, but practically, because the question is hard to think about unless one knows some history or has time to look it up. Behind the word there is not one analogue or two but rather ten or twenty. Few Presidents or aides will know them all off hand. The experiences of the 1930s were fresh in the minds of Truman and his advisers. All epidemiologists knew about the 1918 pandemic; so in some fashion did relevant laymen. Ford and those around him remembered the *Pueblo* incident. Carter and Jordan were not much given to reading history, but they probably could have pulled from their heads most of the points about Roosevelt and Johnson. Concerning the "honeymoon," however, they would have had to put questions to someone else. Thinking would have called for reference work.

A little research, a few phone calls to president-watchers in the media and academia, could have made Carter and his aides aware that new men like themselves had usually been given a grace period by citizens more than by congressmen. Gallup Poll public approval ratings first appeared when FDR was already in office. Since then, each new President—Truman in 1945, Eisenhower in 1953, Kennedy in 1961, Johnson in 1963–64, Nixon in 1969, and Ford in 1974—had comparatively high scores during his first three to six months. Thereafter those scores sagged, seldom returning to the same heights. Aside from FDR and LBJ, however, only Woodrow Wilson had a genuinely cooperative Congress at the beginning of his Administration, and he had the advantage that both houses were Democratic for the first time in thirty years, full of newcomers. The other possible exception was George Washington.[17] For the rest, even popular Presidents with long coattails such as Jackson, McKinley, and Harding, even such national heroes as Grant and Eisenhower, got little but grief from Congress during their first year, to say nothing of after. Of course, except for Eisenhower, they had the advantage that under the old constitutional procedure Congress did not meet (unless they chose to call it) until the December following their March inauguration.

Once noticed, the discrepancy between citizens and congressmen should have seemed logical. If presidential popularity can be expected to fade, leaders in Congress have every incentive to wait for that to happen. Except when green, as under Wilson, or in panic, as in 1933, or mesmerized, as by Johnson in 1965, their natural tendency should be to delay, obfuscate, or resist. A look at the history underpinning the tag "honeymoon" could thus have made Carter and Jordan *expect,* not be aggrieved by, an early relationship with Congress less like a honeymoon than like the opening round of a prize fight.

The operational moral might have been the one Zbigniew Brzezinski says he urged unsuccessfully in terms of his own sphere, defense and diplomacy: "to emphasize more the things that we can accomplish . . . and less the things in which we are likely to have fewer successes."[18] On the domestic side the prospects for accomplishment could have been measured by congressional and public preparation and the likelihood that public pressure could be brought to bear in Congress. Concentration on a few developed and familiar themes could then have been the key for turning short-run public favor into congressional acquiescence. So Carter's successor was to see it—and do it—in 1981. Four years earlier, Carter did not. Granting that he and his chief aides might still have proceeded in scattershot fashion, we—as scholars and president-watchers—would feel better if we knew that in doing so they had not been led astray by a well-rouged analogy or two. The memoirs out thus far make us feel worse.[19] Private recollections of participants who urged him at the time to keep his focus tight discourage us still more.

We think Carter made a mistake in not being alert to and therefore trying to counteract overblown press expectations, themselves evidence of public and journalistic susceptibility to this particular "kid-next-door" analogy. Insofar as Carter's advisers shared or encouraged those expectations, they made an even more serious mistake. His staff was packed at second and third levels with bright, young former congressional aides or consultants, bills in hand, who had been waiting on the Hill for 1965 to come again, and thought it had! Of course, Carter could have been lucky, as Ford was with the *Mayaguez* in 1975. Not Carter! The Bert Lance affair started Carter on a run of bad luck unequaled since the presidency of Herbert Hoover, perhaps since that of James Buchanan. The overreaching initiatives of Carter's early months, combined with normal transition hazards and abnormally clubfooted congressional relations, made him more vulnerable than he might otherwise have been. Whatever the cause, bad luck later dogged him. We do not say that somebody in Carter's shoes should have sought nothing but the obviously attainable. Successful leadership probably requires blind faith at least as much as open-eyed analysis. We argue, rather, that the faith should not be reinforced—or guided—by historical analogies that won't stand up to even small amounts of such analysis.

Analogies deemed irresistible or captivating are bound to influence thought and action. People cannot escape them. In 1950 Truman and his advisers could not help thinking of events of the 1930s and the lesson they supposedly taught. Equally, in 1976 public health authorities and their superiors could not ignore the 1918 epidemic and the possibility that it might be about to repeat itself. Prohibition, the 1929 crash, "court-packing," Pearl Harbor, the Manhattan Project, the Marshall Plan, the "loss" of China, McCarthyism, the Bay of Pigs, the Cuban missile crisis, Vietnam, Watergate, Iran, the oil shocks, and the Teheran hostages are among past experiences that can similarly shape reactions if circumstances call them to mind.

In this chapter we have discussed resistible analogies. The *Mayaguez* incident inevitably called to mind the *Pueblo,* but *Differences* were as obvious as *Likenesses* and should have become more so as time went on. Carter and his staff could easily have freed themselves from unthinking expectation of a "honeymoon" or any great record of accomplishment in the first hundred days. While they could not have made the media ignore the milestone, they probably could have minimized attention to it.

We hope our illustrations show sufficiently how one can buy insurance against obvious mistakes—obvious at least in hindsight—by spending small amounts of time and thought to separate the *Known* from the *Unclear* and the *Presumed* in any situation, and to compare *Likenesses* and *Differences,* present with past, when considering claimed analogies or catch phrases that conceal them. We believe such procedures, if applied routinely so as to be readily familiar, can improve the management of public business—perhaps of any business—on the order of other, equally simple practices such as checking for bias in questions on opinion surveys, noting confidence levels in statistical tables, or adding columns of figures twice. We do not promise or predict successes. We do hope for fewer near misses like Ford's and fewer misreadings like Carter's.

5 Dodging Bothersome Analogues

The "lessons of the thirties," Spanish flu, the *Pueblo,* even the Hundred Days were analogies put to use. They enabled members of the Truman, Ford, and Carter administrations to make decisions they wanted to make with a minimum of fresh analysis. Those analogies also helped to create and preserve consensus. In this chapter we turn to an analogy which decision-makers could not ignore but did not want to use. The decision-makers were Lyndon Johnson and his advisers debating in 1965 whether to Americanize the war in Vietnam. The analogue was the previous war in Vietnam waged more than a decade earlier by the French with American aid. The uncomforting element in the analogy was the outcome: France's humiliating defeat.

In the LBJ Library in Austin, Texas, many file drawers full of documents on the Vietnam War have recently been declassified. They open a view of White House decision-making complementary to that of Defense Department decision-making opened by the famous *Pentagon Papers* illicitly published in 1970. Among the Austin documents is a nine-page, single-spaced memorandum for the President dated June 30, 1965, and entitled "France in Vietnam, 1954, and the US in Vietnam, 1965—A Useful Analogy?"[1] The signature on it is that of McGeorge Bundy, the White House

National Security Assistant for Johnson (as earlier for Kennedy).

To appreciate what that memorandum said and what it did not say but might have, one needs a sense of the Johnson Administration's predicament in 1965. For the benefit chiefly of readers for whom the 1960s are a blur—or a blank—we begin with a sketch of the context. We shall then return to Bundy's treatment of the French analogy.

Johnson had inherited the war. When Kennedy's murder made him President on November 22, 1963, the United States had in Vietnam about 16,000 servicemen providing supplies, training, and advice to help the South Vietnamese defeat Communist-led Vietcong guerrillas. The Vietcong, in turn, received supplies, training, and advice from North Vietnam.

The war caused debate in the United States long before it became Johnson's war. After 1954, when the French quit the country, leaving separate South and North Vietnamese regimes as their heirs, the South Vietnamese government was headed by Ngo Dinh Diem. As Vietcong terrorism worsened and the American presence grew, Diem became increasingly despotic and corrupt. He and his family belonged to South Vietnam's Roman Catholic minority. The Buddhist majority suffered discrimination. In 1963 some Buddhist monks went into public places and burned themselves alive. For American media representatives already thronging South Vietnam, human bonfires provided leads for page one stories, cover pictures for newsmagazines, and unforgettable television footage. In the press and in Congress, criticism of Diem mounted.

Kennedy may have begun to think of backing out of Vietnam after 1964. Two close associates later claimed—although without proof—that he had talked of doing so.[2] However that may be, three weeks before JFK died some Vietnamese military officers unseated Diem. They acted with the knowledge and consent of Americans in Saigon and Washington. To Kennedy's horror, they killed Diem too, which was not in the script as most American officials had understood it.[3] Thus, whatever his plans for the future, Kennedy's actual legacy to LBJ included not only a policy of aiding South Vietnam but also responsibility for its having the leaders it did.

Johnson at once faced evidence that South Vietnam's situation was worsening. He was slow, however, to yield to advice that he increase American aid and involve Americans directly in the war against the Vietcong. Many matters more important to him took priority: making the transition to a true Johnson presidency, getting nominated and elected in his own right, readying the legislation that would complete the New Deal and the Fair Deal, bringing on the Great Society. Continuing to reduce Cold War tensions also stood high on his agenda. Doing anything in Southeast Asia did not.

So, from November 1963 to the end of 1964 Johnson temporized while, with his encouragement, the bureaucracy developed contingency plans. As early as March 1964 Johnson gave signs that he might eventually approve bombing North Vietnam in hope of inducing its leaders to stop aiding and encouraging the Vietcong. In August, when North Vietnamese gunboats seemed to challenge American warships cruising the Tonkin Gulf, just off North Vietnam's coast, Johnson used the incident to obtain a congressional resolution—passed unanimously in the House and with only two dissenting votes in the Senate—authorizing "all necessary measures" to repel attack on U.S. forces or "to prevent further aggression." But, running for the presidency against Barry Goldwater, an outspokenly hawkish Republican, Johnson stood before the public as opposing the use of American military power. "What I have been trying to do, with the situation I found," he said in Manchester, New Hampshire, in September, "was to get the boys in Vietnam to do their own fighting with our advice and our equipment." In October, in Akron, Ohio, he added, "We are not about to send American boys nine or ten thousand miles away from home to do what Asian boys ought to be doing for themselves."[4] Until well after the election, Johnson gave no clear indication of his bent. He may indeed have kept his mind open.

During the first six months of 1965 Johnson gradually, perhaps reluctantly, Americanized the war. He decided first to bomb North Vietnam and then to send American ground forces into combat in South Vietnam. In February, during Bundy's first visit to Vietnam, the Vietcong attacked an American army barracks at Pleiku. Reporting army estimates that North Vietnam was sending some of its soldiers into South Vietnam, Bundy recommended using the Pleiku attack as occasion to commence bombing. Johnson had already decided to do so. He ordered "sustained reprisals": continued bombing, gradually increased, to "inflict pain" and thus—he hoped—to raise morale in South Vietnam while giving North Vietnam some reason to want peace.

Johnson was never optimistic that bombing North Vietnam

would, by itself, achieve the desired result. To General Maxwell Taylor, the former Joint Chiefs Chairman and now Ambassador in Saigon, Johnson had written early in 1965 that he thought American soldiers would have to fight the Vietcong on the ground. Taylor did not agree. Neither did Secretary of State Dean Rusk, who, according to Bundy, held "that the consequences of both escalation and withdrawal are so bad that we simply must find a way of making our present policy work."[5] After the Pleiku incident Taylor and Rusk endorsed a limited bombing campaign. Both were probably influenced—and Johnson too—by loose analogizing with 1962, when, it was believed, "graduated escalation" had been one key to success in the missile crisis.[6] Taylor and Rusk also dropped their opposition to the request of General William Westmoreland, the chief of the U.S. Military Assistance Command in Vietnam, for a large contingent of troops to guard the air base at Danang.

The dispatch of three brigades of Marines doubled the number of American servicemen in South Vietnam. Those Marines were soon shooting at Vietcong. Westmoreland then asked for army forces and authority to take the offensive. Taylor objected, arguing that American units should at most make hit-and-run raids from coastal "enclaves."

On advice from Secretary of Defense Robert McNamara and the Joint Chiefs, Johnson agreed to send Westmoreland up to 90,000 men but with orders that they be deployed as Taylor recommended, in enclaves. By May, however, Westmoreland was telling Washington that South Vietnam was on the verge of losing. He asked for forty-four battalions, or 150,000 men, to be committed to finding and defeating the Vietcong. The chiefs backed the commander in the field. "You must take the fight to the enemy," argued their Chairman, General Earle Wheeler. "No one ever won a battle sitting on his ass."[7]

For the most part, debate went on behind tightly closed doors. Pleiku and the bombing made headlines. Reporters and cameramen patrolling South Vietnam detected that the Marines were doing more than guard duty. Some American campuses saw all-night "teach-ins" in protest. The White House, State Department, and Pentagon nevertheless had some success in making Vietnam "not news" and transferring attention elsewhere. At the Johns Hopkins University in April Johnson declared himself willing to talk with the North Vietnamese "without posing any preconditions." He spoke also of putting a billion dollars into Mekong Valley projects modeled on the U.S. Tennessee Valley Authority to benefit both South and North Vietnam. As he very much wanted, Johnson kept the nation's eyes mostly on his domestic programs.

In late April and May of 1965 not Vietnam but the Dominican Republic dominated foreign news. With coup following coup there, many people saw "another Cuba" in the making. Johnson blanketed the place with 22,000 troops. He also sent Bundy to negotiate a settlement (thus keeping him off campuses). A reliably non-Communist government was elected. American forces withdrew. Since senators, columnists, teachers, and students who had started to protest the Vietnam bombing had become even louder concerning the Dominican intervention, critics of the Administration's foreign policy were made to look like hand-wringers. That outcome doubtless fed Johnson's hope that he could do as Westmoreland wanted without slowing the Great Society.

Behind those closed doors, LBJ still appeared open to alternatives. In October 1964 Under Secretary of State George Ball had written a long memorandum arguing, in effect, that South Vietnam was a lost cause. Reading it in early 1965, when it ultimately reached him out of channels, Johnson called Ball in, along with Rusk and McNamara, to debate it. As Ball remembered a decade and a half later, McNamara produced "a pyrotechnic display of facts and statistics to show that I had overstated the difficulties . . . suggesting, at least by nuance, that I was not only prejudiced but ill-informed."[8] Time and again, Johnson nevertheless pressed Ball to argue his thesis. That went on for months, culminating in July, when LBJ spent much of three days with a spectrum of advisers, including Ball and other skeptics. To Ball the President declared himself still open to conviction. To the Joint Chiefs, he said, "remember they are going to write stories about this like they did in the Bay of Pigs. Stories about me and my advisers. That is why I want you to think carefully, very, very carefully about alternatives and plans."[9]

Johnson by then had almost surely made up his mind. Just when he had done so remains a puzzle. As one of his former aides said to us, Johnson believed that what other people didn't know couldn't hurt *him.* He guarded his thoughts from everyone except possibly his wife, Lady Bird. It was his custom, the same aide says, to reach a decision inwardly and *then* organize the process for making that decision appear the result of consultation and debate.

Documents in the LBJ Library suggest that Bundy and other close advisers believed the President's decision on Westmoreland's troop request to be still in doubt as late as the end of June, the time of the memorandum on the French analogy. On June 30 and July 1 Bundy signed two other documents dealing with Vietnam. The first commented on recommendations that Secretary of Defense McNamara was about to send the President. The second, a day later, summarized for LBJ the state of debate in Washington concerning Westmoreland's proposals.[10]

Given the later little-contested denunciation of Bundy as foremost among the "best and brightest" who blundered into an immoral and unwinnable war, the comment to McNamara is an astonishing document. In it Bundy challenged the Westmoreland proposals more sharply and more tellingly than had Ball. Characterizing them as "rash to the point of folly," Bundy ticked off key questions: (1) Could American troops fight a counter-guerrilla war? (2) Would the Vietcong accommodate Westmoreland by accepting toe-to-toe engagements? (3) What, if anything, would keep the Administration off a "slippery slope toward total US responsibility and corresponding fecklessness on the Vietnamese side?" (4) What was "the upper limit of US liability?" Bundy added, "If we send 200 thousand men now for these quite limited missions, may we not need 400 thousand later? Is this a rational course of action?" (5) Was there any threat that could move Hanoi to seek peace, as Eisenhower's threat to use nuclear weapons allegedly had moved the North Koreans to agree to a truce in 1953? (6) Why did a decision have to be made in July on the basis of "fragmentary evidence?"

Bundy does not remember writing that memorandum, although it bears his hallmark: lean, bold prose. He does feel sure that in doing so, he was not just voicing to McNamara misgivings he was hesitant to expose to Johnson. Instead, he thinks it probable that someone in the Pentagon—perhaps Assistant Secretary of Defense John McNaughton, a friend from days when Bundy was Harvard's Dean of Arts and Sciences and McNaughton a Harvard Law professor—had asked him to help McNamara pose hard questions for Westmoreland and the Joint Chiefs.

The memorandum had little apparent effect. McNamara sent his recommendations, backing Westmoreland, to Johnson virtually unchanged.

Bundy's other memorandum, dated July 1, summarized McNamara's recommendations as well as those made by Rusk, Ball, and Bundy's brother, William, then Assistant Secretary of State for East Asian Affairs. William Bundy argued for holding off further deployments while testing U.S. forces, exploring ways of stiffening Saigon, and working on Congress as well as the media. Labeling this "a middle course for the next two months," McGeorge Bundy wrote to LBJ: "My hunch is that you will want to listen hard to George Ball and then reject his proposal. Discussion could then move to the narrower choice between my brother's course and McNamara's." Putting much less sharply some of the points in the earlier communication to McNamara, Bundy listed some "disputed questions" on which, he said, the President might "want to have pretty tight and hard analyses":

1. What are the chances of our getting into a white man's war with all the brown men against us or apathetic?
2. How much of the McNamara planning could be on a contingency basis with no decision until August or September [near the start of the rainy season]?
3. What would a really full political and public relations campaign look like in both the [William] Bundy and the McNamara option?
4. What is the upper limit of our liability if we now go to 44 battalions?
5. Can we frame this program in such a way as to keep very clear our own determination to keep the war limited?"

Bundy knew that Johnson would be inclined to go along with McNamara. As Bundy read his boss, Johnson counted on McNamara to identify the minimum force requirements necessary to prevent the generals from claiming that they were being denied what they needed to do the job. He was very unlikely to cut back on any numbers McNamara genuinely requested. The open question was whether, face to face with the President, McNamara might indicate that the Joint Chiefs and Westmoreland could be persuaded to accept the delay William Bundy urged. That did not occur. The outcome was a fateful decision to make the war against the Vietcong and North Vietnam one to be fought primarily by American military forces.

Bundy's paper on the French, with which this chapter started, was sandwiched between the sharp memorandum to McNamara and the less sharp one to LBJ. Obviously not in our format, which had not yet been invented, it did not distinguish the *Known* from the *Unclear* and the *Presumed.* It did, however, tick off *Likenesses* and *Differences,* using two headings: "Vietnam, 1954 and 1965," and "United States and France, 1954 and 1965." The *Likenesses* were described as almost nonexistent, the *Differences* as numerous, to wit:

- France had fought to preserve a colonial regime. The United States was backing an independent Vietnamese nation.
- France had opposed reform as well as nationalism. The American-supported South Vietnamese regime represented "non-Communist social and political revolution."
- The French in 1954 were fighting Communist regular armies totaling 350,000 men. They had committed nearly half a million French troops, were spending 8 percent of their annual national budget on the war, and were suffering casualties at a rate of about five hundred a month. In 1965 the war was one against about 200,000 guerrillas. It was being waged primarily by a South Vietnamese army, roughly 250,000 strong. For the United States, troop commitments, dollar costs, and casualties were all comparatively low.
- In metropolitan France in 1954 the war was acutely unpopular. The French government was unstable and had lost the will to fight. In the United States in 1965, said the memorandum, there was "considerable concern over U.S. casualties . . . Saigon's political instability . . . the use of air strikes and napalm, etc. but *general support for* the Administration." The memorandum cited in evidence a Harris poll showing 62 percent approval of the President's Vietnam policies. Regarding criticism from Congress, the memorandum passed it off as issuing mostly from "*'reluctant realists'* whose viscera say get out but whose heads tell them the present policy is unavoidable" (emphasis in original).[11]

Despite its length, this memorandum was not on a par with the other two from Bundy described earlier. Its length and wordiness testified to its nonseriousness. So did its security classification, which was merely "Confidential"—two long notches below the "Top Secret" stamped on most Vietnam documents. This memorandum almost surely responded to a request from LBJ for something to wave at Ball or at some senator or newsman needling him with what William Bundy called the "like the French" argument. It was for advocacy, not analysis, and probably more for protection than persuasion. McGeorge Bundy himself has no recollection whatever of signing it, suspects that it was hastily drafted by some not very senior member of his staff, and tells us that, in giving it so much attention, we are "using a hammer on a gnat."

Suppose, however, that it had been routine in the Johnson White House to use history for analysis (or for meticulous advocacy), with procedures along our lines. Bundy's staff would regularly have distinguished among things *Known, Unclear,* and *Presumed.* The concerns animating debate were readily apparent: (1) South Vietnam was losing; (2) its fall might have effects elsewhere: hence "dominoes"; (3) to arrest its fall, the United States might become deeply involved militarily—how deeply and for how long, no one could say—and (4) every possible policy would lead toward pitfalls at home.

Had Bundy's exercise been for analysis, not just for advocacy, the itemization could not have confined itself so narrowly to France in 1954 and the United States in 1965. The memorandum could not have ducked the question: How about France in 1950 or 1951, *before* the French committed half a million men and began suffering high casualties? In 1950, looking forward, the French had embarked on a stepped-up campaign with U.S. support and strong hopes of success—stronger indeed than LBJ's in 1965! And for about a year those seemed to be borne out. A table taking 1950 or 1951 as its base year would have had much more in the *Likeness* column, with many entries adding bite to the questions Bundy posed in his memorandum to McNamara.

As a serious endeavor, examination of the analogy would also have had to look ahead. As of 1965 the Vietnam-related memoranda that were serious, whether written by Bundy or by others, envisioned as a worst-case outcome the Saigon government's collapsing as the Communists took over South Vietnam, while both friends and adversaries overseas said the United States had not done all it could and should have done. In the ideal outcome Saigon became stable and strong, Vietcong fortunes declined, North Vietnam decided the Vietcong could not win, and the two Vietnams continued for the long term, side by side, *à la* Korea. As every memorandum-writer noted, if the ideal outcome were attained, it would appear that the United States had saved South Vietnam, helped defeat the Vietcong, and stripped the North Vietnamese, in the words of one CIA memo, of "grounds for hope that they can outlast the US." McGeorge Bundy had warned in February 1965: "At its very best, the struggle in Vietnam will be long." Rusk wrote in July of "a long and tortuous prospect." McNamara said, "the war is one of attrition and will be a long one." The chiefs told the President victory would require yet another 200,000 men and two to three years.[12] Granting that the United States in 1965 was not like France in 1954, those projections posed the obvious question for analysis: As the war stretches out, costs rise, and more and more coffins come home, what are the chances that American conditions in, say, 1968 will more resemble those of France in 1954?

Several survivors from the Johnson Administration have told us that their great mistake was to underestimate the North Vietnamese. In view of those documents in the LBJ Library, their comment may seem surprising. We have already quoted Bundy, Rusk, and others predicting in general terms a long, hard war. Planning papers sent to the President were more specific, and in hindsight they seem remarkably prescient. By early autumn of 1965, Westmoreland was forecasting need for about half a million men over the next two to three years. With such forces, he said, he could begin to turn the tide in South Vietnam. And with half a million men he did just that, and on just about the timetable he set forth. The North Vietnamese "Tet offensive" of early 1968 was, we now know, an act of near desperation resulting from their recognition that they had begun to lose ground in South Vietnam. Americans at the time interpreted the offensive quite differently, but that is a story for another book.[13] What is germane here is that those survivors from the Johnson Administration, when asked about these prescient documents, say simply that they didn't believe them. They assumed that military planners were putting the worst face on the picture. Some of them remembered how, back in 1961, the Joint Chiefs had told Kennedy to expect that any successful operation in Laos would require 250,000 men *and* nuclear weapons. Johnson's advisers just could not conceive that the North Vietnamese would not come to terms once they saw the opposition they were likely to face and the punishment they might suffer.

How could that misconception have been corrected? How better than by looking back at the punishment the Vietnamese Communists had sustained and survived in their nine-year war with the French? From Ho Chi Minh down, the leaders were the same. One might suppose that they would recognize the United States as far more powerful than France. On the other hand, they could also recognize that the French people had had a great deal at stake in Vietnam—kinspeople, property, wealth, national prestige, possibly the rest of their colonial empire—while the American people did not. Ho had outlasted and worn down the French. Why not the Americans?

Those questions frame themselves—and answer themselves—much more clearly after the fact than before. But how else would they have come to notice in 1965 except as part of an exercise such as the one Bundy passed off on a junior staffer? The President, presumably, had asked for a memorandum on the analogy. Almost certainly his only interest was in using it for advocacy. We think his staff did him—and themselves—disservice by not taking the assignment more seriously. The President needed the memorandum, after all, because he had to deal with men like Ball and Mansfield, who thought the analogy conveyed a warning. The actual memorandum focused narrowly on two dissimilar situations (and included rhetoric about South Vietnam's "non-Communist revolution"), because it might be necessary otherwise to concede that Ball and Mansfield could make a case. General George Marshall (to whose habits of mind we shall return later) used to say to staff officers, "Gentlemen, don't fight the problem. Solve it." Bundy might say that in not wasting time on the analogies exercise, he was obeying such a rule. We feel, on the other hand, that in his place the proper translation for Marshall's precept would have been: "Don't fight the question. Answer it."

By the late 1960s the United States was, in fact, to look a great deal like France in 1954. Some of the lines in Bundy's French analogy memorandum read like prophecies. It said, for example, that Paris "had to contend with *concerted and organized domestic opposition*. . . . Leak and counter leak was an accepted domestic political tactic, and, as a result, even highly classified reports or orders pertaining to the war were often published verbatim in the pages of political journals" (emphasis in original). Identical words could have been written about the United States five years later when the streets of American cities were periodically full of antiwar protesters, and the *New York Times* and *Washington Post* construed it as their patriotic duty to publish the purloined *Pentagon Papers.*

We do not and would not argue that the actual future should have been self-evident three years ahead of time, to say nothing of five. On the contrary, we can see why in 1965 such a future should not even have seemed likely. The American political system differed from the French. LBJ had demonstrated an ability to lead Congress and the public. The United States had no powerful Communist party like France's, and Washington had no large concentration of alienated students and clerks comparable to that in Paris. The issue was different: The United States was not a colonial power (not, at least, in its own eyes). Above all, the might of the United States seemed incomparably greater than that of the Fourth Republic. As a representative of the Joint Chiefs had commented earlier, "The French also tried to build the Panama Canal."[14]

Moreover, any thoroughgoing analysis of risks-by-analogy in American escalation on graduated terms would have had to take account of the pitfalls surrounding *all* options in 1965. Contrast the range of those pitfalls with the few hinted at in the actual memorandum on the French analogy. While the memorandum mentioned congressional expressions of doubt, emphasizing those of left and left-center Democrats, it said almost nothing about the regiments of conservatives, Democrats as well as Republicans, just waiting for a chance to say that the country had to fight a *War,* "no substitute for victory," and therefore could not now afford to fund the Great Society. Nor did it speak of the voices that might charge Johnson—if he followed Ball's counsel—with "losing" Vietnam, as Truman had been charged with "losing" China. And not just by Republicans: Robert F. Kennedy, the late President's brother, had recently warned that withdrawal from Vietnam would be "a repudiation of commitments undertaken and confirmed by three administrations."[15] Bobby's antiwar phase was yet to come. LBJ could easily imagine the Kennedy clan mobilizing American Catholics against the President who had abandoned their coreligionists in Vietnam.

In an explicit list of presumptions, all these could have been implied by some tactfully worded phrases. LBJ would have understood. Later, he said to a confidante:

> I knew that Harry Truman and Dean Acheson had lost their effectiveness from the day that the Communists took over China. I believed that the loss of China had played a large role in the rise of Joe McCarthy. And I knew that all these problems, taken together, were chickenshit compared with what might happen if we lost Vietnam.[16]

A searching look at the French analogy might have stimulated those "tight and hard analyses" which Bundy recommended to LBJ but, so far as we can discover, never conducted. *Might* developments in the United States parallel those in France? Bundy raised that question only generally and glancingly, and more to McNamara than to Johnson. The only person to come near putting it directly to LBJ, so far as the record shows, was Vice President Hubert Humphrey, who wrote him in February 1965:

> American wars have to be politically understandable by the American public. There has to be a cogent, convincing case if we are to enjoy sustained public support. In World Wars I and II we had this. In Korea we were moving under United Nations auspices to defend South Korea against dramatic, across-the-border, conventional aggression. Yet even with those advantages, we could not sustain American political support for fighting Chinese in Korea in 1952. . . .
>
> If . . . we find ourselves leading from frustration to escalation and end up short of a war with China but embroiled deeper in fighting in Vietnam . . . political opposition will steadily mount. It will underwrite all the negativism and disillusionment which we already have about foreign involvement generally—with serious and dire effects for all the Democratic internationalist programs to which the Johnson Administration remains committed: AID, United Nations, arms control, and socially humane and constructive policies generally.[17]

As Humphrey indicated, serious use of history would have required looking not only at French analogies but at others. In relation to Vietnam, the Korean conflict served as what we have called a captivating analogy. Everyone thought of it, but, as with 1918 in the swine flu scare, different people came to it with different stances and drew from it different nuances, depending on their expertise and personal experience. Moreover, since Korea was but twelve years in the past, the experience was firsthand, not vicarious. To LBJ and others, Korea said: Be firm; hold the line; don't shrink at using force in a good cause. Ball argued on the contrary that differences between the two cases showed why we shouldn't be in Vietnam: no march across the border, no solid government; no resilient army; no ward-of-UN status; no UN resolution, and so forth. To many, Korea counseled "beware China." To some it argued: Do not try to fight protracted, limited war; go up (or down).

Of those who put their views in writing, only Humphrey stressed the point that, whatever the merits of the 1950 decision, the long war of 1950–53 had cost Truman and the Democrats their public support—along with the next election. And unlike others who advised Johnson, with the exception of Clark Clifford (who warned that Vietnam could be a "quagmire"[18]), Humphrey had felt the cost himself and sorrowed in Truman's fate. The others were mostly liberal Republicans, Stevensonians, politically unattached, or, like Johnson himself, detached about Truman. We explore those differences in Chapter Nine.

Had regular staff practice required looking closely at all claimed analogies, no matter where they came from, it should have led to thought not only about whether Washington might come in time to feel like Paris *circa* 1954 but also about whether LBJ might be by 1968 where Truman had been by 1952: fighting the good fight but down to about 25 percent approval in the polls while the electorate flocked to the party promising peace. That prospect would have been much harder for Johnson to push aside, for Truman's loss of following occurred on American terms, without any significant Communist party, without, indeed, any antiwar forces like those in France of the 1950s. Explicitness about all versions of the French analogy, and the Korean one too, might have pushed thought farther and farther back—to questions about how public consensus had been preserved in the two world wars, as well as in 1898 to a degree, and why it had been *lost* in all other American wars, even in the Revolution, to say nothing of both sides in the Civil War.

A generation after 1965 most Americans appear to feel that LBJ made the wrong choices.[19] Many think he should have listened to Ball. Others think he got his best advice from former CIA Director John McCone, who said that if he could not abandon South Vietnam, he should move against North Vietnam "promptly and with minimum restraint."[20] We make no claim that if LBJ had only inspected historical analogies, he would have chosen either Ball's formula or McCone's. In fact, the more often we review the case the harder we find it to outline what LBJ could have said in 1965 to explain to the American people why he was dropping JFK's South Vietnamese allies or, alternatively, why he was beginning all-out war against *Hanoi* because of what impended in *Saigon.* Students, young and old, who try to outline the speech Johnson could have given over television, find the exercise distressing. They gravitate, as we do, toward a conclusion that LBJ's one real alternative was one scarcely hinted at even by Ball, namely another dose of the 1963 medicine: engineering a change of regime in Saigon, but this time to bring in a clique that would call for neutralization and American withdrawal. That is said to have been the advice of Senate Majority Leader Mike Mansfield of Montana. It was not far from what the Kennedys might have obtained, despite themselves, had Diem stayed on, under the spell of an enigmatic brother who died with him. But when journalists picked up the scent, as they undoubtedly would, what then?

Even so, if careful review of every claimed or otherwise apposite analogy had been part of standard staff practice, Johnson would have found it harder than he apparently did to brush aside the question of how public consensus could be sustained when costs and casualties went up. If the President's staff had had to look harder at history, they might already have made some headway toward "tight and hard" analysis of what "a really full political and public relations campaign" would have to look like, and LBJ might have had more difficulty putting off the subject. The President might also have paused longer over the question Bundy had posed to McNamara the day before about the "upper limit of our liability." Johnson might have begun to ponder in 1965 the speech he ought to make in 1966 if certain conditions were not fulfilled by then—and what those conditions might be. He might, in short, have planned a test for his presumptions, as, we suggest later, all decision-makers should routinely do.

A last word on analogies. In 1950, at the very start of the Korean War, although not always afterward, Truman and Acheson did their analogizing in a way that seems to us in some respects a model. A distinguishing feature of their effort then is that they drew comparisons with more than single cases. Truman and his colleagues took into account at least Manchuria, Ethiopia, Austria, and Munich (though apparently not Spain). They also thought somewhat of Greece, Berlin, and other recent situations. In short, they generalized from a whole body of potentially relevant experience. So LBJ and his staff would have done had they looked at France not just in 1954 but also in 1951, as well as at a much wider array of other instances. So Carter would have done had he and his staff thought about their "honeymoon" in terms of the whole history of the presidency.

We put in three words what this chapter and the two preceding have endeavored to convey about analogies: *Stop! Look! Listen!* Invoking them often substitutes for thinking hard about things as they are. A first line of defense is to separate out what is *Known, Unclear,* and *Presumed.* That focuses thought on the situation at hand. A second defense is to reach for possibly relevant analogues, the more the better, spelling out *Likenesses* and *Differences.* That helps guard against illusions. We recommend alertness to the various disguises worn by analogies as they occur to people, whether irresistible or captivating, seductive, scarcely seen, or hidden behind catch phrases. As regards the last of these, the best defense is asking where it came from.

Helpful as we hope these "mini-methods" and distinctions are, they offer but a start toward using history effectively.

6 Inspecting Issue History

Our last three chapters have suggested ways to stop, slow, or broaden out analogizing, the most usual use of history. Separating the *Known* from the *Unclear* and the *Presumed,* and specifying *Likenesses* and *Differences* in claimed analogies are techniques for sharpening the picture of the *present* situation and for clarifying what is of concern about it—for seeing swine flu 1976 instead of Spanish flu 1918 or Jimmy Carter 1977 instead of LBJ 1965.

In this and later chapters, we offer positive suggestions on how to make usual the *un*usual uses of history, those illustrated in our introductory examples: the missile crisis of 1962 and the social security reform of 1983. They emphasize the histories of issues, individuals, and institutions.

Our first suggestions have to do with issue history. Even with situation and concerns clearly defined, one set of questions needs to be answered before debate turns to options for action: What is the objective? What is action supposed to accomplish? What conditions do we want to bring into being in place of those existing now? Knowing how the concerns emerged, how the situation evolved, can help. That knowledge by itself will not answer the questions. The future can never look exactly like the past. Usually it should not. But past conditions can offer clues to future possibilities. If a hoped-for situation never existed before, why not? If something like it did exist, why? Besides the concerns of the moment, what else may stand in the way? Answers to such supplementary questions can correct for both too much and too little exercise of imagination. Asking them in 1976 at HEW Secretary Mathews's level or at the White House could have raised doubts early about the wisdom of Ford's promising vaccination for every man, woman, and child. In 1981 a quick look back at social security financing since the 1930s might have enabled Stockman and others to see more clearly in 1981 what could and could not be done, thus sparing the Reagan Administration its early "piglet."

We propose later in this chapter some simple mini-methods for quickly getting up the histories of issues. First, however, two tales. One is of the Carter Administration and the Soviet brigade in Cuba. It illustrates the point that understanding of what used to be is essential for any realistic definition of what needs doing. The second is of FDR and the original old age insurance program. It illustrates what can be accomplished by someone who looks back in order to look ahead.

The story of the Carter Administration and the Soviet brigade in Cuba begins in late July 1979, when Senator Richard Stone of Florida wrote the President of rumors that the Russians had combat troops in Cuba. If so, he said, their presence violated agreements made after the missile crisis of 1962. Zbigniew Brzezinski, the National Security Assistant, told Carter that Stone might be right. Indignant at the numbers of Cuban soldiers showing up at various places in Africa and Central America, Brzezinski had demanded more intelligence on the Cuban military. Communications intercepts and satellite photographs, he was told, showed the presence in Cuba of actual Soviet military units. Learning this, he relates in his memoirs, he "alerted the President."[1]

In the generally unhappy annals of the Carter Administration, the summer of 1979 was one of the sadder seasons. With approval of his performance down to 28 percent in the polls, the President had summoned scores of legislators, governors, and private citizens to Camp David to help him diagnose the state of the nation. From that ecumenical retreat he emerged to proclaim that the nation suffered "a crisis of the American spirit." The media dubbed the speech "malaise." Mildly condemning his own preoccupation with managerial detail, Carter promised better leadership in the future. Thereupon he slightly reorganized his staff and fired three members of his Cabinet while accepting the resignation of a fourth. It is indicative of Carter's public standing at the time that Senator Robert Byrd, the majority leader, did not bother to tune in the speech; he was throwing a party for other Democratic congressional leaders. One of them, Senator Henry M. Jackson, though professing support for the President, predicted coolly that Carter would be defeated in the 1980 primaries.[2]

Carter had just signed SALT II, a long-delayed treaty with the Soviet Union setting limits on strategic nuclear weapons. (More later on why the delay.) Counting on the treaty to help allay the nation's supposed spiritual trouble but fearful that it might be rejected by the Senate with exactly the reverse effect, the President wanted less than almost anything else a public dispute about whether the Russians kept their word. Despite Brzezinski's report, Carter instructed Secretary of State Cyrus Vance to send Stone a soothing letter saying there was "no evidence of any substantial increase of the Soviet military presence in Cuba."

During August Brzezinski and Vance both asked the intelligence agencies to tell them more. Brzezinski quotes from his diary for August 14:

> I briefed the President in the morning on the fact that according to intelligence reports there is now an actual Soviet brigade in Cuba, with headquarters and regular organization and that in fact it is scheduled to hold firing exercises within a week. I told him that this is an extremely serious development which could most adversely affect SALT. The President looked quite concerned.[3]

For the time being, calm nevertheless prevailed. Carter, Brzezinski, and Defense Secretary Harold Brown all went off on vacation. Getting word that a magazine was about to print a story on the Soviet brigade, Vance and some of his aides phoned key members of Congress just so that they wouldn't be taken by surprise. All but one took the news unemotionally.

The exception was Frank Church of Idaho, chairman of the Senate Foreign Relations Committee. Leader a few years earlier of a grand inquest into intelligence agencies, Church had once hoped to become President. Now it was doubtful that he could keep his Senate seat. Idaho voters apparently doubted his commitment to national security. He drew criticism for supporting the

SALT treaty and for having gone to Cuba to meet Fidel Castro. Polls placed him far behind his opponent. Church reacted to word of the Soviet brigade by saying that SALT should be scrapped, the public should be told the facts, and a *demand* should be made for the brigade's removal. He gave that advice to Vance. A few hours later Church decided it was good advice for *him.* Calling in reporters, he told them the news and declared, "The President must make it clear, we draw the line on Russian penetration of this hemisphere." Next day almost every daily newspaper and network news broadcast featured the story.

Now a sense of crisis did build. Congressmen and columnists alike made comparisons with October 1962. In words he later regretted, Vance said, "I will not be satisfied with maintenance of the status quo." The press interpreted him as insisting on withdrawal and, since he was thought to be the Administration's "dove," read ominous portent into his words. It did not calm matters for Brzezinski, supposedly the "hawk," to tell reporters that he thought Vance's language too strong, adding that he himself regarded the situation as less like the missile crisis of 1962 than like the Berlin Wall crisis of 1961.[4]

The President meanwhile had more trouble. UN ambassador Andrew Young broke openly with the Administration's line on Israeli–Palestinian Arab relations. Though Young was a close friend, Carter felt he had no choice but to fire him. On his vacation the President went fishing on a rural pond. In twilight he saw something swimming toward his boat. Thinking it was an attacking beaver, he fought it off with an oar. A photographer caught the scene. When the negative was developed, it showed clearly that the creature had been a rabbit. Across the country, columnists and cartoonists made Carter the butt of jibes about "killer rabbits."[5]

Behind the scenes, meanwhile, Vance argued for playing down the Soviet brigade issue. He hoped to get the Russians to say the troops weren't "combat" troops and thereby to get SALT back on track. Brzezinski, on the other hand, believed the best tactic was to confront the Russians about their "adventurism" all over the world. If the unplanned publicity on the brigade in Cuba made them stubborn to keep it there, the crisis might be defused, he thought, by some Soviet gesture elsewhere. SALT could wait.

The mini-crisis persisted through most of September. As it did, the President and his aides began to learn more of the relevant history. Stone had been right about the Soviet troops, but he had been wrong in saying their presence violated past agreements. Research uncovered the fact that Kennedy had asked for removal of Russian troops, not gotten such a promise, and dropped the subject. A subsequent dispute in 1970 had produced an exchange about submarines and submarine bases. It, too, said nothing about soldiers. Furthermore, examination of old files at the CIA, review of previously unstudied reconnaissance photos, and phone calls to recently purged CIA veterans produced more data about the brigade itself. Vance writes:

> The more resources the intelligence community devoted to the brigade matter, the farther back in time information about it went—eventually all the way to 1962. Appallingly, awareness of the Soviet ground force units had faded from the institutional memories of the intelligence agencies. . . . By late September it was evident that the unit in question had almost certainly been in Cuba continuously since 1962.[6]

On October 1 a television address by Carter brought the preposterous episode to an end. Citing a letter from Soviet chieftain Brezhnev which said that the unit served as a "military training center" and that the Soviet government had no intention of changing its mission, Carter announced various measures for increasing the American political and military presence in the Caribbean. He then called for getting on with ratification of SALT.

In December the Soviet invasion of Afghanistan would finish Carter's SALT treaty. If it had had a chance of getting through the Senate, that chance had dissolved in September's delay, the victim of alarm about the "new brigade" in Cuba. As Vance says in his memoirs, "It was a very costly lapse in memory."[7]

Because of similarities to the 1962 missile crisis, the affair brings irresistibly to mind the observation with which Karl Marx opens his *Eighteenth Brumaire of Louis Napoleon*—that history repeats itself but "the first time as tragedy, the second time as farce."

Could this farce have been avoided? Brzezinski and Vance both say yes—if the intelligence agencies had given them the facts earlier. Brzezinski adds that it could have played itself out wholly in private if Vance and his aides had not blabbed to Church. Their answer seems to us plausible but incomplete. The question of why Soviet "adventurism" should take that particular form at that particular time ought to have provoked more puzzlement. One given inside the government was that the Russians wanted to protect some new installation in Cuba. If so, there should have been signs of some such installation. There were none. Another guess was that

Russian troops were replacing Cuban troops sent elsewhere. That could hold water only on a further supposition that the Soviet Politburo hadn't stopped to think about possible reactions in Washington. The favorite theory around the White House, according to reporters who covered that beat, was that the Russians had sent in the brigade back in 1976 simply to test Carter.[8] But if it was intended as a test for the new Administration, why was it kept secret until the Administration was old? The question of Soviet motivation alone should, it seems to us, have led to earlier asking of the question: Just when did this begin?

We think this episode of the Soviet brigade underscores the uses of an issue's history and the consequences of habitually slighting it. The brigade became an issue only because Carter and his aides did not know the brigade had been there all along, hence supposed it indicative of some new move by the Russians, hence reacted with their own form of the sovereign's complaint, *He can't do that to me.* Since problems or concerns often arise because of some real or apparent change in a situation previously ignored or tolerated, a brief scan backward ought to be standard practice. In this case it would have discovered that there had been no change, therefore that there was no problem, unless the Administration wanted to invent one. (Afterward, Soviet Ambassador Anatoly Dobrynin asked one of Vance's aides, "Do you expect me to get people in the Kremlin to *believe* this story?" In Moscow, apparently, no one did. There was much speculation about what Carter's motives had been.)[9] U.S. intelligence agencies did not have the historical data at hand, because they were not accustomed to answering historical questions. Carter did not ask them. So his aides did not ask them either. Nor were they accustomed to pursuing them with persons out of government, but formerly in it, who might have known the answers, as some surely did. In fact, the style set by the President seems even to have discouraged his advisers from searching their own memories. Vance had been in the Pentagon during the missile crisis, and he must have known *then* that Kennedy decided not to press for removal of Soviet troops. Yet it seems not to have occurred to him to ask, "When did they *leave?*" A little later we speculate on how, at an early stage, the Carter Administration might have adopted different habits. But first a happier example.

To exemplify effective awareness of an issue's history, we return to old age insurance, but this time to the original legislation—

titles II and VIII of the Social Security Act of 1935. This precedes by almost fifty years the success story told earlier of the Commission Report in 1983 on social security financing. That success had had in its background Reagan's misadventure of 1981, his mini–Bay of Pigs, a gaffe at least on a par with Carter's concerning the Soviet brigade. Not long in office and still popular (more so because of aplomb when wounded by a would-be assassin), Reagan seemed likely to become one of the rare examples of a President having a genuine "honeymoon" with Congress. Then, as the reader may remember, he proposed shoring up the social security system's shaky trust fund by, among other things, cutting back at once on payments to beneficiaries retiring before sixty-five, and that proposal brought the skies down: The Republican-controlled Senate condemned it (in effect) 96 to 0. The critical outburst taught the Administration lessons exemplified in the later Commission Report. That the outburst occurred was, however, as the Russians would say, "no accident." Franklin Roosevelt had planned it that way half a century before.

First as Governor of New York and then as President, Roosevelt had been concerned about the aged poor. His concern antedated the Great Depression. He had called for old-age pensions when running for governor in 1928. Taking office in the still prosperous winter of 1928–29, he had said to his Republican-controlled legislature: "No greater tragedy exists in our civilization than the plight of citizens who find themselves, after a long life of activity and usefulness, unable to maintain themselves decently." He had returned to the theme in each year of his governorship and had stressed it when addressing a conference of other governors in 1931.[10] As he often did, he portrayed the problem in terms of actual people whom he knew in Dutchess County, New York. For example:

> I had been away during the winter time and when I came back I found that a tragedy had occurred. I had had an old farm neighbor, who had been a splendid old fellow—supervisor of his town, highway commissioner of his town, one of the best of our citizens. Before I left, around Christmastime, I had seen the old man, who was eighty-nine, his old brother, who was eighty-seven, his other brother, who was eighty-five, and his kid sister, who was eighty-three. . . .
>
> When I came back in the spring, I found that in the severe winter that followed there had been a heavy fall of snow and one of the old brothers had fallen down on his way out to the barn to milk the cow, and had perished in the snow drift.

> The town authorities had come along and had taken the two old men and had put them in the county poorhouse, and they had taken the old lady and had sent her down, for want of a better place, to the insane asylum, although she was not insane but just old.[11]

In Albany Roosevelt had gotten little from his legislature. Few other governors had done better. Fifteen states had no pensions whatever. Those that did paid, on the average, about sixteen dollars a month. Even with bread at six cents a loaf and potatoes at twenty-five cents a pound, that was not enough to buy one square meal a day, let alone provide for rent or heat or pay doctors' bills. Well before becoming President, Roosevelt had defined "economic security" for the aged poor as an objective for governments at all levels. The question was, how?

In view of the Depression, he could not, as President, address that objective or that question in isolation. The aged were not the only ones in need. Dependent children, some of the handicapped, victims of accidents, and the involuntarily unemployed were among others in comparable straits. So, during his first year in the White House Roosevelt concentrated on providing emergency relief to all people in need, meanwhile experimenting with various schemes for restoring the economy. Only during the second year did he turn to longer-term problems.

In June 1934 he created a Cabinet Committee on Economic Security. He made Secretary of Labor Frances Perkins chairman, and he put on it his secretaries of Agriculture and the Treasury, the Attorney General, and, from outside the Cabinet proper, his chief relief administrator, Harry Hopkins. As Perkins comments in her autobiography, that brought to the table the officials concerned with financing and legality and, in Hopkins, someone who could remind them of the "compelling, immediate needs of the people."[12]

Perkins argued that someone else should be chairman. Roosevelt rejected the argument: "No, no. You care about this thing. You believe in it. Therefore I know you will put your back into it more than anyone else, and you will drive it through. You will see that something comes out, and we must not delay. We must have a program by next winter." To her observation that many economists feared taking money away from capital investment and current consumption, Roosevelt responded, "We can't help that. We have to get it started or it never will start."[13]

The President gave the committee generous guidelines. Perkins writes:

> At cabinet meetings and when he talked privately with a group of us, he would say, "You want to make it simple—very simple. So simple that everybody will understand it. And what's more, there is no reason why everybody in the United States should not be covered. I see no reason why every child, from the day he is born, shouldn't be a member of the social security system. When he begins to grow up, he should know he will have old-age benefits direct from the insurance system to which he will belong all his life. . . .
>
> "I don't see why not," he would say, as, across the table, I began to shake my head. "I don't see why not. Cradle to the grave—from the cradle to the grave they ought to be in a social insurance system."

Roosevelt made Perkins the committee's chairman in part because of her relative expertise. As one of the early college-educated social workers, she had dealt with poverty and distress. As a member of New York's Industrial Commission and then in Roosevelt's Cabinet in Albany, she had collected data on the aged poor and studied proposals to help them. She had acted on behalf of Roosevelt in organizing a seminar on the subject for other governors. Having a well-annotated mental index of those whose knowledge went beyond her own, she was able quickly to assemble an expert staff and to enlist advice from, among others, Europeans familiar with foreign social insurance systems. Instructed by Roosevelt to steer clear of "people who were too theoretical and who would take months of research before they could make a brief report" and knowing what advice she did *not* want, Perkins also knew whom among the experts to consult only casually or not at all.

Her committee sifted for the President several sets of issues. One had to do with administration: The system could be state-based, with Washington's funds, or it could be managed by a Federal agency. A second concerned sources of funds: Would money come only from prospective beneficiaries? Would some come from their employers? Would some come from general tax revenues? Another set of issues related to reserves. Would there be a fully endowed pension fund, or would current contributions be used to pay current obligations, with reserves sufficient only for emergencies? Members of Perkins's committee differed on all those issues. So did experts, including several hundred who gathered in Washington in November 1934.

Meanwhile, public pressure intensified. Out in Long Beach, California, two years earlier, a mild-mannered doctor named Francis Everett Townsend had looked out a window. He saw three elderly women scrabbling for food in garbage cans. When he began shouting profanely, his wife protested that the neighbors would hear. He responded, "I want all the neighbors to hear me! I want God Almighty to hear me! I'm going to shout till the whole country hears me!"[14] Aided by a Southern California real estate promoter, Townsend created a movement, with hundreds of thousands joining Townsend Plan clubs to second his demand that all needy citizens over sixty-five get federally funded pensions of $200 a month (Others had urged "thirty dollars every Thursday") provided only that they spent all the money each month. This, the doctor and his disciples argued, would revive the economy. To the complaint that it might simply transfer half the national income to 10 percent of the population, Townsend disdained response. "I myself am not a statistician," he said. "I am not even an economist, for which fact millions of people have expressed thanks."[15]

With "Onward, Townsend soldiers . . ." a rising chorus, a new year approaching, and White House speechwriters already drafting the 1935 State of the Union message, Perkins summoned her committee and its key aides to meet at her house. They arrived at 8 P.M. With phone disconnected, study door locked, and a bottle of whisky on the table, the group argued all night. Morning finally brought something like consensus.

Though the committee recommended that the states administer unemployment insurance (at Washington's expense), the members came down in favor of Federal management for old-age insurance. The probability that many workers would in their lifetime migrate from state to state served as the conclusive argument. On other issues the committee came up with mixed formulas. Immediate suffering would be dealt with as part of Hopkins's relief program. For the longer term, the government would establish a system of old age insurance. Workers would pay a fixed percentage of earnings into a fund and, after sixty-five, would receive benefits graduated according to average wages. Employers would have made matching contributions. In order not to lock up too much of the nation's money, the administrators would keep only emergency reserves. They would use current contributions to pay benefits. At some point, experts reckoned, the reserves would run dry, and the system would have to draw on tax revenues, but that situation was not expected for several decades.

Perkins records Roosevelt's reaction:

"Ah," he said, "but this is the same old dole under another name. It is almost dishonest to build up an accumulated deficit for the Congress of the United States to meet in 1980. We can't do that. We can't sell the United States short in 1980 any more than in 1935."

On the other hand, Roosevelt also told Perkins that he could not delay proposing legislation: "We have to have it," he said. "The Congress can't stand the pressure of the Townsend Plan unless we have a real old-age insurance system, nor can I face the country without . . . a solid plan which will give some assurance to old people of systematic assistance upon retirement."[16]

To satisfy Roosevelt's concern, the final Administration bill provided for a larger reserve fund, and it covered fewer workers. In particular, it excluded farmers and farmhands. A newly elected California Congressman (also the state's poet laureate) introduced a bill incorporating the Townsend Plan. It died on a voice vote, but with two hundred members absent. Townsendites then attacked the Administration proposal as too little. Conservatives attacked it as too much. A newspaper in Jackson, Mississippi, declared, for example: "The average Mississippian can't imagine himself chipping in to pay pensions for able-bodied Negroes to sit around in idleness on front galleries, supporting all their kinfolks on pensions, while cotton and corn crops are crying for workers to get them out of the grass."[17] In an atmosphere heated by Dr. Townsend and others like him (including Huey Long, the new Senator from Mississippi's neighbor state, Louisiana), few members of either house could actually vote "nay." The Administration bill passed the House 371 to 33 and the Senate 76 to 6.

Four years later, with a Social Security Board by then a fixture and Gallup polls reporting 90 percent public approval of old age pensions, the law was amended to bring their financing closer to Perkins's original proposals. Congressional conservatives now favored this to avoid government control of huge reserves. This time FDR did not demur. He evidently judged the system safe, regardless, so the farther future could take care of itself.

Soon after, the President was visited by Luther Gulick, a management adviser. The board's Bureau of Old Age Insurance in Baltimore, Gulick said, was a waste of money. So were clerks in district offices who gave out Social Security cards assigning each individual a lifetime number. The Baltimoreans spent their time filing individual reports by number, entering and totaling each year what the cardholder's covered earnings had been. Any contributor could write in for his total and an estimate of eventual benefits. Thousands did so and were courteously answered. But that was not, in fact, a vested system. Contributors would actually be paid upon retirement from pooled contributions, not personal earnings. It cost at least a million dollars every year in clerical salaries, let alone space, equipment, and supervision,to maintain those accounts just for answering letters.Better save the money. An account had no practical use. So Gulick argued.

Paternally, Roosevelt explained:

> Luther, your logic is correct, your facts are correct, but your conclusion's wrong. Now, I'll tell you why. That account is not useless. That account is not to determine how much should be paid out and to control what should be paid out. That account is there so those sons of bitches up on the Hill can't ever abandon this system when I'm gone.[18]

In creating old-age insurance, Roosevelt studiously made use of the history of the issue, as we define the term. Not that he read up on past experiments or even thought of them, for the history relevant to *his* concerns was not a set of discrete precedents. Particular precedents fell in Perkins's domain. Roosevelt trusted her not to overlook or ignore some relevant wrinkle from Germany's experience or some experiment once tried in Wisconsin or some arcane past dispute among economists. He did not crowd his own mind with such matters. For Roosevelt what mattered most was history in flow—running trends that made the aged poor a concern *now,* not earlier, and in future years would determine whether or not the concern persisted.

Roosevelt did not have to do research on those trends. He had been watching them all his life. One was apparent in demographic and economic statistics. Partly because of better medicine and better nutrition, the number of Americans living to old age was on the rise. In the mid-nineteenth century, only one in forty had survived to sixty-five. By the mid-1930s the ratio was approaching one in fifteen. Meanwhile the country had gone from being largely rural and agricultural to being largely urban and industrial. That meant more old people had to seek jobs calling for young muscles, quick fingers, and sharp eyes. It meant more of them without even a county poorhouse or asylum to provide shelter. A mistaken belief that the American economy was "mature" and unlikely to become more productive made Roosevelt's concern all the greater, but the key fact is that he saw the problem of the aged poor as one that had been developing for decades and was sure to become worse if ignored. He had made that point to his legislature in Albany, citing statistics that showed the increase in population over sixty-five in New York State and especially the increase of those in New York City unable to survive from their own earnings or savings.[19]

A second trend was political. In his own lifetime Roosevelt had seen the country go from the conservatism of Grover Cleveland and William McKinley to the progressivism of Theodore Roosevelt and Woodrow Wilson and, in the 1920s, back to conservatism again. He had seen similar swings in New York and other states and in counties and cities. It had been a common pattern for public enthusiasm to force some reform and then, in the ensuing quiet, for adversely affected special interests to eviscerate the reform. An alert sense of that trend shaped Roosevelt's strategy, explained what he said to Gulick, and accounted, decades later, for the 96 to 0 vote that ended all prospects for Reagan's proposals in the form they took then. FDR had sought to anchor social security in something immune from swings of sentiment. He thought he had found it in "insurance," another shrewd reading of history. But actually, by 1939 it turned out that the symbols of the thing sufficed—the term, the trappings, the account numbers—never mind the vesting. So they still did in Reagan's time, albeit with signs of change. Roosevelt's insurance symbolism might not suffice into the next century, but lasting out this one seems triumph enough.

When we cite old age insurance as effective use of history, we invite the challenge: "Wasn't it just smart politics?" To which the answer is no. It was *wise* politics; that is different. And sensitivity to history accounts for some of the difference.

Consider contrasts between FDR and LBJ. In getting legislation through Congress without significant change, Johnson did better than Roosevelt. On paper the Great Society not only completed the New Deal but promised to leave it in the shadows. Yet Johnson had the lesser sense of history. Witness his approach to Vietnam. In 1965 he did not seem to see either the past or the future of the struggle. He judged it by the light of the (to him) irresistible analogy with "loss" of China. Micawberlike, he hoped for something to turn up. And the same myopia led him to create domestic programs without built-in staying power. Evidently he lacked FDR's awareness of how hard it is in America to build something that endures the way you want it. In consequence, many of his social programs fell far short of their marks; some have not survived through the mid-1980s. Others became expensive out of all proportion to his own priorities, let alone those of his successors.

What now appears invulnerable seems to support our point. The tallest, strongest legislative monument to LBJ is built of civil rights and voting rights laws, aimed in the main at the South. There—in race relations—Johnson, the Southerner, exhibited a sense of history keener than any predecessor, Lincoln not excepted. Consider the extemporized additions to a speech he made during the 1964 campaign before a throng of 2,500, largely white, at the Jung Hotel in New Orleans. Johnson recounts in his memoirs:

> I told the New Orleans assembly a story about Senator Joe Bailey, who was reared and educated in Mississippi and elected to the House and Senate from Texas. Bailey had been talking to Congressman Sam Rayburn about the economic problems of the South and had mentioned the great future the South could enjoy if it could develop its resources.
>
> "I wish I felt a little better, Sammy," Joe Bailey said to Mr. Rayburn. "I would like to go back to old Mississippi and make them one more Democratic speech. I feel like I have at least one more left in me."
>
> I looked over the members of the audience, then gave them the old Senator's final words to Mr. Rayburn on that occasion: "Poor old Mississippi, they haven't heard a Democratic speech in thirty years. All they ever hear at election time is 'Nigger, Nigger, Nigger.' "[20]

That the race issue was hollow and was seen so by congressional colleagues, that it stood in the way of progress for the South, that it was a millstone around the necks of politicians, that release from its worst manifestations would be felt by many segments of the regional community as a decided boon Johnson knew from personal experience. He could remember when the Ku Klux Klan had been a powerful force in his own state's politics. He could imagine a future in which whites and blacks in the South were not possessed by fear of one another but concerned themselves with their common good. And, as FDR with social security, Johnson saw how to effect the change and make it last: Send in federal registrars, get honest voter lists and honest voting (as honest for blacks as for whites, at least: "Landslide Lyndon" was no utopian), and the future would take care of itself. In this domain Johnson's vision reached far back and far ahead.

The hard question for us is not how to distinguish historical judgment from political judgment. It is whether either can be taught. LBJ had taken FDR, in Doris Kearns's words, as "his patron, his exemplar, and finally the yardstick by which he would measure his achievement."[21] Yet Johnson failed to think as FDR had. Does that imply that the crucial variables are inherent and can't be studied or imitated?

In some degree, we fear, the answer to that question is yes. No manual or course of study will make an ordinary politician an LBJ or transform an LBJ into an FDR. But, as we explained at the start of this book, we work at margins. If our students were baseball players, we would not expect to turn out Ted Williamses or Sandy Koufaxes; we would be happy to see a batting average go up from .250 to .265 or an earned run average go down from 6.0 to 5.0. And we do believe that almost any continuous effort to use history routinely will improve the averages of players in the public arena.

How to do so is not easy to prescribe. It is one thing to offer the example of FDR and old age insurance, another to say how the example might be turned to use by other people in another era dealing with quite different situations and concerns. Moreover, the example itself is at best only partially useful, for Roosevelt applied history he himself already knew. In foreign affairs he showed no equally sure sense of trends. Witness his fumbling and ultimately futile efforts in 1933 to make the United States a *de facto* partner in the League of Nations.[22] Yet we write for practitioners usually confronting issues whose pasts they do not know. That is ensured by the American political system and the specialized career systems inside it, which are run at higher levels by semicareer and noncareer officials. Our "government of strangers," in Hugh Heclo's phrase, has a poor to spotty institutional memory, and that holds true at levels well below the whirling dervishes of whom he writes, the political executives.[23] The Soviet brigade with which this chapter started is a cautionary tale with wide application. That being so, what "mini-methods" have a chance of working?

For issue history, the nearest counterpart to separating the *Known* from the *Unclear* and the *Presumed* or *Likenesses* from *Differences* is application of the "Goldberg rule," with simultaneous notation of a "time-line," both to be fleshed out in iterative fashion by judicious use of "journalists' questions." Does this seem complicated? It is not. These are simple notions. They fit well together. Let us now explain.

The Goldberg of the "Goldberg rule" is neither the former Supreme Court Justice nor the inspirer of Bach's "Goldberg Variations." Least of all is he Rube the cartoonist. Rather he is Avram Goldberg, a scholar and gentleman who happens also to be chief executive officer of Stop and Shop, a New England chain of grocery and discount department stores. Hearing once from one of us a brief sermon on the usefulness of issue histories, he exclaimed, "Exactly right! When a manager comes to me, I don't ask him, 'What's the problem?' I say, 'Tell me the story.' That way, I find out what the problem *really* is."

We recommend the "Goldberg rule" to all and sundry. After identifying concerns, or while doing so, ask, "What's the story?" That question might have saved Carter embarrassment in the case of the Soviet brigade. It could have been of use to Ford in the swine flu and *Mayaguez* affairs. It might even have altered the 1965 debate over the number of combat troops to be committed in Vietnam. While applying the "Goldberg rule" may not always help, it can never hurt.

The "time-line" is simply a string of sequential dates. To see the story behind the issue, it can help merely to mark on a piece of paper the dates one first associates with its history. Because busy people often balk at looking very far into the past, we stress the importance of beginning with the earliest date that seems at all significant. Consider what can happen if that is not done with a run of statistics. In a debate on inflation, figures from the Consumer Price Index for the decade after 1973 could be cited to prove that the normal rate of inflation is between 10 and 12 percent. The 4 percent or thereabouts after 1982 seems abnormal. A series starting in 1953 would seem to prove the exact opposite—that the high numbers were the sports. If the run covered prices over two centuries, they would show any inflation at all to be exceptional, for prices in the United States remained more or less constant from the 1780s down to the 1930s. Only with that longer series would one see all the interpretations the data permit. So it is with issues.

After asking "What's the story?"—following the "Goldberg rule"—the next step is to check the story's actual beginning date:

When did it start? If the answer is not known, endeavor to find out! "When" is the traditional first question for a journalist. Think how useful it would have been to Carter, Brzezinski, and Vance if CIA analysts had *expected* that question to be asked and been prepared accordingly. They didn't, so they weren't. Experience, alas, is on their side.

Then come the other journalists' questions, everyone knows the traditional list: "When?" "Where?" "What?" "Who?" "How?" "Why?" The "whens" fill in the "time-line." We include the others not because they need be answered fully for all issues but because—considered as a checklist—they too can help fill in the time-line. They help with the substance of the story as well. Together, they and dates deriving from them offer some insurance that the storytellers will not omit, or the listeners fail to notice, pieces of the story that do not jibe with their preconceptions or policy preferences. By the same token, that checklist helps construct a time-line forward as well as back, into planning as well as into background.

There is of course a limit, frequently severe, to the detail the listeners have time to hear or storytellers to produce. Applying that whole check list to all aspects equally becomes counterproductive. Selectivity is called for, and so are short cuts. But, as we are sometimes asked reproachfully, "On what criteria?" We have no better answers than experience combined with common sense—and buttressed by two rules of thumb well illustrated in the case of Roosevelt on social security.

Our rules of thumb for selectivity are these: For one, get the trends first, forest before trees. For another, try to focus on the trees at points in the story, past or prospective, where politics (whether legislative, bureaucratic, electoral, or international) appears decisive to the outcome. Why politics as against information or technology or physical resources and the like? Because politics has accountability wrapped up in it, affecting not alone substance but office, invoking duty and tenure—both concerns indeed! FDR risked more in 1935 than legislative victories for Townsendism: He risked losing crucial parts of his new voter coalition, drifting "right" toward Father Coughlin, "left" toward Huey Long. He risked, in short, not doing his job, being seen not to do it, and ultimately losing it, in circumstances that brought bad people (as he saw them) to power. As one of us once argued in another connection, "What matters more to a man than his head if he identifies it with the public good?" So we suggest: When seeking specifics to focus on, select those marked by such compelling motivations. Politics affords a clue.

Small specifics sometimes make for large distortions, which can render selectivity as troublesome as it is necessary. For instance, in a famous case at the end of 1962 (about which more later), Anglo-American relations reached a low point because Robert McNamara, Kennedy's Defense Secretary, did not know that two years earlier, when Eisenhower had pledged Britain a crude air-to-surface missile in development (the Skybolt) to extend the Royal Air Force's nuclear capability, the President had not required British bombers to be under NATO.[24] There, however, is where McNamara found them when he entered office, the British having chosen so. When he decided later on performance grounds to cancel Skybolt, leaving no missile for London, and hinted that the British could procure instead a sea-launched missile to be used in NATO-assigned submarines, he thought he was suggesting a straight swap. He therefore was astounded when he was attacked in London for trying to strike down the British nuclear deterrent. For the British Government, then, the very fact of choice was key, politically, as symbolizing sovereign independence. Conditioning the new weapons on NATO assignment was symbolically no swap but rather subordination. It made no difference that the targeting was joint, had been and would be; to the British that was mere operations. Theoretically they could take out of NATO what they voluntarily put in. The same could be said of joint targeting. The voluntarism was the point. McNamara seemed to challenge it. A public row resulted. Until he belatedly requested and examined the fine print of Ike's agreement, McNamara could not fathom why a swap should cause an outcry from those Londoners. Even when he saw the shade of difference, he could scarcely credit it as cause of so much trouble: mere symbolism. Still, the instance does suggest refinement of a sort for one of our rules of thumb: Not only your own politics but your neighbor's is a field in which specifics should be sought, the "trees" inspected, at least if your concerns include keeping him calm. Alas, this merely adds more trees to complicate selection. It puts a higher premium than ever on experience and common sense.

The political specifics that count most in such a case are likely to be clustered around changes of importance in the programmatic content of the issue, that is to say in alterations of its statutory, structural, procedural, or budgetary form. Those occur in relatively fixed and limited periods along an issue's time-line. The points in time at which such alterations happen will be flooded with informative details, worth sifting for their signs about the issue's politics. Historians of social security have often treated Roosevelt's acquiescence in the shift of 1939 to "pay as you go"—which three years earlier he had specifically rejected—as a matter of inattention in the face of the impending European war. By contrast, Luther Gulick's memoir suggests very strongly that FDR, far from being inattentive, was well aware in both years of the programmatic terms of social security financing. He allowed the change precisely because he now accepted what he had earlier rejected, namely that the symbols of insurance, those account numbers, could do as well as dollars piling up in trust funds to keep congressmen from cutting back "his" program after he was gone. What changed his mind, apparently, was overwhelming national acceptance of the program in its first four years. That helps illuminate the social security story, and so does the unchanging character of FDR's intent, a matter of high politics.

Change points, then, in programmatic content, the moments marking substantial alterations of this kind, can be no less significant than trends in helping to define the "problem"—or as we prefer, "concerns"—emergent from the telling of such stories. In the Skybolt instance, on the time-line marking Britain's nuclear deterrent after 1945, the Eisenhower agreement to provide that weapon was a major change point. Precisely for that reason the intended author of the next great change, the man who sought to disrupt that agreement, McNamara, would have done well to study its details, including the political specifics that had led London to ask for Skybolt in the first place and had persuaded Washington to offer it. Not only had the offer left the British free in principle to use the weapon as they chose, but also McNamara's predecessor, Defense Secretary Thomas Gates, no friend to Skybolt, had preferred to see the British shift to submarines in 1960 and had only gone along with the original agreement as a bow to higher interests. Those had been, first, a base in Scotland for American submarines, an implicit *quid pro quo,* and second, Anglo-American comity, a show of friendship, mattering to Eisenhower personally and politically, and mattering in London still more. McNamara until late knew few of the details on either score. What he saw instead was an increasingly expensive, inaccurate airborne weapon compared with increasingly available, reliable, and cheaper land

and seaborne missiles coming on ahead of schedule—a persuasive set of trends. In consequence he framed American concerns as technical and budgetary on an issue that the British, knowing the whole history in full detail, were bound to see as quintessentially political. Hence the crisis of December 1962 in Anglo-American relations.

To gather all the wherewithal needed for effective storytelling, we sometimes suggest drawing the time-line and asking journalists' questions in two rounds: The first round focuses upon the "when" and "where" of trends in economics, demography, legislation, management, production, popular psychology, culture, or whatever may seem relevant. The second round devotes particular attention to the "how" and "why," especially the higher politics, of substantial programmatic changes, point by point. "Journalists' questions twice" is our advice—or, anyway, be mindful of the reasoning behind this advice (acknowledging that time may be too short to take it). The distinctions introduce some rough priorities. We think rough better than random.

These "mini-methods"—Goldberg's rule (asking "What's the story?"), tracing the time-line from the story's start, and asking journalists' questions about trends or change points in the issue's history—can profitably play upon each other to illuminate current concerns. How they do so calls for more than suggestive discussion. We need an illustration in some detail to which readers can apply *their* common sense! That is what we offer next. By way of illustration we return to the Carter regime, not to its later, sadder time but to its hopeful start. For we identify one episode in Carter's first three months as having offered the Administration an opportunity to recognize how history could catch it up—a learning experience potentially as useful as Kennedy is said to have found his Bay of Pigs in retrospect: a spur to reflection, an occasion to begin asking the kinds of questions Carter and his aides still failed to ask in 1980, let alone 1977. The early episode is his Administration's first approach to Soviet–American negotiations over arms control. What was done is reviewed in our next chapter, as is what they might have gained had they applied the "Goldberg rule"—asked what the story was—and then fleshed the story out.

7 Finding History That Fits

In late March 1977, about two-thirds through the Administration's first hundred days, Jimmy Carter sent Secretary of State Cyrus Vance to Moscow. To Soviet leader Leonid Brezhnev, Vance presented a plan for deep cuts in both countries' strategic nuclear forces, that is, in their arsenals of intercontinental, nuclear-armed missiles and bombers. He said that if the Russians were not yet ready to go so far, he would sign terms provisionally agreed to by Brezhnev in a meeting with President Ford in 1974 at Vladivostok. The only condition would be a promise to pursue negotiations soon for a more comprehensive treaty.[1]

Brezhnev did not even stay to listen. In a short, chilly speech, Soviet Foreign Minister Andrei Gromyko called the American proposals utterly unacceptable. On the flight over, Leslie Gelb, one of Vance's aides, had predicted that outcome. He had offered to bet his boss a dollar that the Russians would turn him down and not even make a counterproposal. Gelb won. While Vance was disappointedly flying home, Gromyko called in foreign reporters. In the first such press conference of his twenty years as Foreign Minister, he accused the American government of "a cheap and shady maneuver." At the White House Carter's National Security Assistant, Zbigniew Brzezinski, called his own press conference to protest Gromyko's language and to defend the fairness of the American proposals.

American newspapers and television networks at first characterized this sequence as the opening of a new Cold War. By the time they handed out report cards on the hundred days, they were interpreting it merely as a setback in progress toward arms control. *Newsweek* quoted an unnamed senior official as saying: "We have not gone back to 'go,' but we are back maybe to Vermont Avenue."[2]

In retrospect, both participants and historians judge Vance's mission to Moscow to have been at least a misfortune, perhaps a calamity. Carter, Vance, and Brzezinski all express some regret. Strobe Talbott, the historian of Carter's arms control endeavors, lays on the "ill-conceived" Vance mission much of the blame for Carter's never getting a new strategic arms limitation treaty. In Talbott's opinion, the mission not only delayed practical negotiations but, worse yet, set an unrealistic measurement for judging the negotiations that eventually did occur.

Could different standard operating procedures have produced a happier outcome? We think so. We have argued that it should be routine for staff to invoke something like our "Goldberg rule," to ask, "What's the story?" and after that to draw a time-line tracing the story from its beginning; then, about key moments in the story, to ask "journalists' questions," including "who?" and "how?" and "why?" We believe that, if practiced in the Carter White House, such a routine might have deterred the President from sending Vance on a mission doomed to failure.

We have to present the argument in some detail, because many of the actors *did* know large parts of a closely related story. From his high posts in the Pentagon in the 1960s, Vance had seen the early negotiations between LBJ and the Russians which led, under Nixon, to the 1972 agreement known as SALT I. Paul Warnke, the head of Carter's Arms Control and Disarmament Agency, had also been in the Pentagon in those years. So had Gelb.[3] So had the new Secretary of Defense, Harold Brown, who additionally, as an eminent and not very partisan physicist/administrator, had been in on SALT negotiations under Nixon and Ford. Brown's principal aide for SALT matters, Walter Slocombe, a brilliant young Washington tax lawyer, had earlier been on the NSC staff, analyzing the same issues for Henry Kissinger. While Brzezinski lacked comparable experience, he had served a stint in the 1960s on the State Department Policy Planning Staff, and he had been writing and teaching about the Soviet Union for a quarter of a century.

Also Brzezinski had on his staff, among others, William Hyland, a professional intelligence officer who had been one of Kissinger's experts on the Soviet Union, and Roger Molander, a nuclear engineer who had been following SALT from the Pentagon. Scores of other experts were scattered among the various departments and around the intelligence community.

There was no shortage of either brains or knowledge in the circle of men responsible for the Vance mission, and, at least at the staff level, newcomers had the good sense to ask questions of old-timers. "A lot of us were pretty wet behind the ears," one of the newcomers said to Talbott, "and Hyland and Molander had to spend a lot of time walking us back to reality." In addition, on Brzezinski's orders, Molander prepared for Carter's senior advisers a history of past SALT negotiations. Though the document is still classified, we have every reason to believe it was a good history—of those negotiations—comprehensive, well-informed, and fair. The Carter Administration thus did not lack information about that part of the potentially relevant past. Nor did it lack capacity to analyze that information. What it did lack, in our view, was an inclination to see issues in a longer, still more relevant historical perspective or, as a surrogate, staff procedures designed to stimulate doing so. The missing perspective was the arms race at which negotiations were directed. Shortly we shall turn to this. But first a word on how the new regime came to adopt its ineffectual negotiating stance.

In this as in most areas of policy, Carter's own awareness of history was limited. In his earlier career as a professional naval officer he had been one of the bright young men chosen by Admiral Hyman Rickover for the new nuclear submarine service. He therefore knew more about nuclear technology than most advisers other than Brown. About the central diplomatic and political issues, however, Carter knew little. They had not had much to do with working a submarine, still less with peanut warehousing, which is what occupied Carter after leaving the Navy in 1953, or with Georgia politics, which became his focus until 1974 when, after completing a term as Governor, he began singlemindedly to seek the White House. During most of those years, nuclear weapons interested few voters. Robert McNamara was thought to have fixed the "missile gap," and Nixon and Kissinger, with SALT I and "detente," were thought to have begun to close out the Cold War. So what was there to worry about?

While Carter was beating the backwoods for convention votes, uneasiness about things nuclear began to rise. One of the SALT I agreements of 1972 had frozen for five years Soviet and American long-range missiles, both land-based and submarine-based. Nixon and Kissinger had agreed to that even though Russia was left with a numerical advantage of better than 40 percent—2,400 to 1,700. They believed that advantage to be offset by the U.S. lead in intercontinental bombers, not touched by SALT I; by shorter-range missiles and bombers stationed in Europe and elsewhere abroad, also not touched; and by superior technology. American missiles were soon to be outfitted with MIRVs (multiple independently targeted reentry vehicles). Each missile thus equipped would be able to carry several nuclear warheads and then, over enemy country, to fire them at widely separated targets. (Owing to MIRVs, Carter inherited strategic missile forces which, in spite of SALT I, bristled with twice as many warheads as in 1972.)

Some of the growing public uneasiness was due to increases in numbers not just of intercontinental weapons but of shorter-range and "tactical" weapons. Any American could lose sleep reflecting that there were about 50,000 atomic and hydrogen bombs scattered around the world and that half of them were Russian. But uneasiness was also fed by news that the Soviets had developed MIRVs of their own and were, moreover, replacing old missiles with new ones, some of which were gigantic. With few exceptions, U.S. land-based missiles were of the "Minuteman" type, about 60 feet long and 6 feet in diameter. The new Soviet missiles were more than 100 feet long and more than 10 feet across. People who worried about such matters pointed out that, because of those giant missiles, the Russians gained a large edge in "throw-weight" or the total tonnage of nuclear weapons that could be put up in the skies and dropped on an enemy. Echoing Paul Nitze's concern with the missiles in Cuba in 1962, they expressed fear lest the Russians come to believe themselves able to threaten a Pearl Harbor–type first strike credibly enough so that, in a crisis, they could bluff the United States into backing down.

As one counter, the Pentagon proposed a larger and more accurate new American missile, tentatively labeled MX (missile-experimental). In order that the Russians could not count on knocking them out in a surprise attack, MX missiles were to be based in 10-mile-long underground tunnels and periodically moved from place to place. The pre-overrun price tag was $10 billion for missiles and $20 billion more for tunnels. In prospect also was a new Air

Force bomber, the B-1, at about $90 million apiece and, for the Navy, Trident submarines, at close to $1 billion each, to carry new sea-launched missiles with longer range and greater accuracy.[4]

To fend off huge expenditures on new weapons such as these, Nixon and Ford had sought additional arms control agreements following up SALT I. They had been constrained, however, by legislation. Led by Democrat Henry M. Jackson of Washington, Senators uneasy about the 2,400 to 1,700 lead in missiles conceded to the Soviets by Nixon had passed a resolution requiring that, in any new agreement, the United States get at least numerical parity. At Vladivostok Ford had agreed provisionally that each side should limit itself to 2,400 "strategic delivery vehicles," only about half of which would be allowed to carry multiple warheads. This time American long-range bombers were to be counted, but shorter-range bombers and missiles would still be left out. Lingering questions remained, concerning new Soviet Backfire bombers and new U.S. long-range pilotless aircraft (cruise missiles, so called). Some Americans thought that the Backfires had long enough range so that they should be counted in the Soviet total. The Russians argued not. They, on the other hand, said that U.S. cruise missiles ought to count if over a certain range. In January 1976, at Moscow, Kissinger made some concessions to the Soviet view on cruise missiles. Jackson and other Senators protested that he was compromising the principle of parity. Ford, facing a challenge not only from the Democrats but from Reagan and the Republican right, chose to leave any treaty-signing to 1977 and therefore, as it turned out, to Carter.

At the time of Kissinger's abortive deal in 1976, at least one journalist heard Carter voice misgivings similar to Senator Jackson's.[5] Later in the presidential campaign, after Jackson had dropped out of competition for the nomination, Carter settled into a different stance. He called for more ambitious efforts to control nuclear weapons and promised, if elected, to cut defense spending by $5 billion to $8 billion in order to leave more for human needs. After being elected, he kept that stance. Meeting with the Joint Chiefs of Staff during the postelection transition, he not only asked whether the United States really needed 2,400 missiles and bombers but startled them by wondering aloud whether two hundred might not be enough. In his inaugural address he expressed hope that "nuclear weapons would be rid from the face of the earth." Soon afterward, according to Talbott, he told his staff "with tight-lipped intensity" that achieving that goal was his "most cherished hope." Members of his Administration feel no doubt that this had indeed become his conviction.

Carter ordered preparation of proposals for drastic reductions in strategic nuclear forces. Perhaps with the hundred days analogy in mind, he had already set a tight deadline. In early December, seven weeks before actually becoming President, he had told reporters that he expected to send Vance to Moscow in the spring. He explained that Vance would probably not go until then because "it will take at least some weeks to review the complex SALT negotiations, and sort out internal differences in the bureaucracy that helped to stall the talks."[6] Meeting soon after Inauguration Day with Soviet Ambassador Anatoly Dobrynin, Carter spoke of his hopes for large reductions in both Soviet and American arsenals, but he also said that as an initial step he might accept something along the lines of Ford's 2,400/2,400 Vladivostok agreement. He promptly told the press exactly what he had said to Dobrynin. Soon afterward, in a long breakfast meeting, Carter heard Senator Jackson explain his objections to the Vladivostok terms, namely that the numbers were too high, that Soviet Backfire bombers ought to be included, and that there ought to be clear (and low) limits on big missiles. Afterward Jackson's aide, Richard Perle, sent Carter a twenty-three page single-spaced memo detailing that position.

Through February and into March staff aides in the NSC, State, Defense, and elsewhere worked on papers outlining possible negotiating options. In the Pentagon Walter Slocombe produced an elaborate chart showing the ramifications of three choices. The first, labeled "Vladivostok-Plus," would limit both Soviet Backfire bombers and certain U.S. cruise missiles. The second, "Basic Vladivostok," would leave out Backfires but include the concessions on cruise missiles made by Kissinger at Moscow. (Slocombe labeled this the "As if Ford Had Won the Election Proposal.") The third, "Vladivostok-Minus," would simply cap numbers for ballistic missiles and long-range bombers, consigning Backfires and cruise missiles to future negotiation.

Whenever Carter spoke, he emphasized his personal commitment to drastic cutbacks. Partly at Brzezinski's suggestion, he started writing private letters to Brezhnev. The first was vaguely worded. The second was not. Carter noted in his diary that it was "much more substantive. It's important that he understand . . . that I'm very sincere about my desire to reduce nuclear armaments. If he's willing to cooperate, we'll get something done before four years go by." The letter, however, drew an unencouraging response. "Chilling," Carter called it. Brezhnev insisted on the original Vladivostok plus Kissinger's Moscow concessions—and nothing else.[7]

On Capitol Hill, Jackson meanwhile let the world know that he had misgivings about the new Administration. He came out against confirming Warnke as head of the arms control agency, on grounds that Warnke underestimated the Soviet threat. Other Democrats joined in the attack. Though the appointment went through, the crucial test vote was 50 to 48—figures that called into question the prospects for ratification of any treaty Jackson chose to challenge.

In view of Jackson's criticism of the Vladivostok terms, Carter's desire for reductions in nuclear forces, and his own wish for something new and different, Brzezinski developed for Carter a set of options considerably broader than Slocombe's. There were four instead of three. One was to do nothing: Wait and see what the Russians proposed. A second was to seek a first-stage agreement along Vladivostok lines, probably deferring Backfire bombers and cruise missiles until later. A third was to propose modest cuts, perhaps to 2,000/2,000 instead of 2,400/2,400. The fourth involved deeper cuts, with each side to get rid of perhaps a quarter of its strategic forces. At Harold Brown's suggestion, the modest-cuts and deep-cuts options included proposals that both sides forgo construction of any new missiles larger than the U.S. Minuteman and that both agree to limits on flight tests such as to make harder the development of *any* new long-range missiles.[8]

At the end of the second week in March, at an informal Saturday morning meeting, the President, dressed in blue jeans and a flannel shirt, discussed the options with his top advisers. Brzezinski observed that the Russians wanted ratification of the Vladivostok terms because it would show continuity in American policy. His own recollection is that he expressed a preference for such a course. Others thought he was saying that it would be much better to go for force reductions. In any case, Carter said he did not want just to stay "within the Vladivostok framework." Except for Warnke's remark that an overambitious opening proposal might subject the Administration to criticism if the final result fell far short, no one seems to have raised a question about either odds of success or possible consequences of failure.

Vance and Warnke subsequently sent Carter a memorandum intended to encourage him toward a second look at the option of trying initially to nail down a Vladivostok-type agreement, but intended also to assure him that they would loyally carry out his instructions. Vance writes in his memoirs, "I knew that the President's attempt . . . was a long shot. I disagreed with the decision but I was determined to give it my best. . . . We could not know unless we tried." So tactful were the two, however, that Brzezinski read their memorandum—and reads it still—as endorsing a plunge toward deep cuts.[9]

According to Brzezinski, the President did not in fact make a final decision until after receiving the Vance–Warnke memorandum. Carter liked to see options formally stated in writing so that he could study and perhaps annotate the document, which would then serve as his order for action. Brzezinski did not pull together such a document until after the Saturday meeting, and Carter did not record his choice among the options until a week later, after yet another Saturday morning go-round. In the meantime a letter from Brezhnev had arrived; Carter deemed it encouragingly "businesslike." So he not only reaffirmed his preference for deep cuts but set figures even lower than those of which he had spoken earlier. Vance's assumption was that Carter had already made a firm decision. His recollection is that he thought it pointless to try to change the President's mind. He did, however, ask Carter for authority to retreat to a fallback position if the Russians proved unreceptive, and Carter agreed.

Out of that final Saturday meeting came the instructions Vance carried haplessly to Moscow. He was to push hard for deep cuts. He could indicate that, if this were unacceptable, the United States would, as a temporary measure, accept the original Vladivostok terms without any of the Kissinger add-ons: Backfires and cruise missiles would thus be business for later. Deep in his hip pocket, Vance could keep a proposal for modest cuts, perhaps just to 2,200/2,200. But Carter wanted Vance to pull that out only in extremis. He and Brzezinski insisted that not even Warnke, Gelb, or Slocombe should know that such a proposal was authorized.[10]

Although evidence and testimony abound, much remains mystifying about Carter's decision. It is unclear, for example, how much hope Carter had for Vance's success. A passage from Brzezinski's diary suggests that the President expected Brezhnev and Gromyko to react as they did. Just after the final Saturday meeting, Brzezinski wrote:

> We . . . have instructed Vance to put forth the two proposals [deep cuts and Vladivostok-Minus] and to stick to them, and I think that is quite important. We also stressed to him that the Soviets are likely to reject and ridicule our proposals, but that he has to stand fast.[11]

On the other hand, the President began a serious effort to get approval of a deep-cuts agreement from the Joint Chiefs and from Jackson. Though still in the innocence of transition, he cannot have imagined that either the Joint Chiefs or Jackson would agree to large reductions in American missile forces without compensating increases elsewhere in the defense budget. If Vance was expected to come back empty-handed or with modest cuts or with something like Vladivostok, common sense ought to have said, "Wait."

It is even more unclear how Carter and his staff aides envisioned the negotiations that Vance was supposed to conduct. The President seemed to have ordered close-to-the-vest bargaining, with the predictable result that the Russians and the world would be astonished if and when Vance backed away from his original position. Contrary to custom, no one told Dobrynin until the very last moment what the American delegation would propose in Moscow. Gelb went to Europe to brief the NATO allies, saying authoritatively that the United States would seek only a modified version of the Vladivostok accord. The allies—and Gelb—did not learn the truth until Vance stopped in Brussels on the way to Moscow. At the same time, however, the President was talking publicly of what he had instructed Vance to do. In a speech before the UN Carter said that the United States would seek "a deep reduction in the strategic arms of both sides" and, if that could not be obtained immediately, then "a limited agreement based on those elements of the Vladivostok accord on which we can find a complete consensus." Afterward he told the press that "we're not abandoning the agreements made in the Vladivostok agreement," but the numbers were too high, and Vance would be "taking new proposals to the Soviet Union." Saying just what he had forbidden Vance even to hint, he added, "If we're disappointed—which is a possibility—then we'll try to modify our stance."

From start to finish, the story of the Vance mission seems to us one of muddled planning and muddled execution. It does not quite rank with the Bay of Pigs affair in 1961, but that is because at the Bay of Pigs some humans died and many others were made prisoners. The Vance mission killed only hopes. Purely for pathological study, however, the two are on a par.

At almost any moment any one of the mini-methods outlined earlier could have been applied to useful effect. Those designed to fish out issue history seem to us particularly applicable, but we have to note that some sorting of the *Known, Unclear,* and *Presumed* would have been a necessary first step. Otherwise a search for relevant history would have been equivalent to browsing—likely at best to waste time, at worst to reinforce preconceptions. Carter or his staff might, for example, have taken the relevant history as that, broadly, of arms control and disarmament. If so, they could have seen encouragement for a dramatic deep-cuts proposal in the precedent of Secretary of State Charles Evans Hughes's 1921 "bombshell"—an offer to scrap two-thirds of America's battle fleet if other naval powers would do likewise. That had led to the Washington naval treaties and suspension of a costly battleship-building race. On the other hand, had Carter or his staff supposed the issue to be generally one of Soviet–American relations, they might have thought of the 1961 Kennedy–Khrushchev encounter at Vienna as a precedent—warning that overeagerness on the part of an inexperienced President could encourage the Russians not only to talk tough but also to take larger risks.[12] In fact, neither precedent had much to say about the concerns we think the President and his staff would have identified if they had made the effort.

Look at the concerns that surface if one quickly sorts the elements *Known, Unclear,* and *Presumed* actually figuring in the staff papers and debates of which we have knowledge. The principal *Knowns* included SALT I, Vladivostok, Carter's campaign pledges, Pentagon spending proposals for MX missiles and other expensive new weapons, and figures on the two arsenals—missiles, warheads, "throw-weight," and so on. (These numbers count as *Knowns* even though those for the Soviet side were U.S. counts which the Soviets did not deny; the Soviets never supplied figures of their own.) Important *Unclear* points included the possible lineup in the U.S. Senate for and against a new SALT treaty and the plans of the Russians for future strategic forces.

Under *Presumed,* Carter's staff aides surely would have had to list the following:

- If there is no new SALT agreement, the United States will have to proceed with some or all of the proposed new weapons: MX, etc.

- If so, the President will not be able to keep his campaign promise to cut U.S. defense spending.
- Absent SALT, the Soviets will expand their strategic forces, sending the nuclear arms race into another spiral.
- The Russians want SALT and detente. (After Carter's first press conference mention of SALT, *Newsweek* said that rapid progress was expected because "White House aides—including national security adviser Zbigniew Brzezinski—now believe that the Kremlin leaders are so eager to involve the new Administration in detente," and, when Vance left for Moscow, Carter was to say to the press that everything he had heard showed Brezhnev to be "very eager to see substantial progress made in arms limitations.")[13]

Separation of things *Known, Unclear,* and *Presumed* highlights two concerns above all others. The first has to do with actual and prospective increases in Soviet strategic nuclear forces; the second with the prospect of an unwanted increase in American forces. Obvious as those concerns may seem, once stated, they were not thus specified, so far as we can learn, in any of the papers prepared or passed around by Carter's White House staff. Given Carter's duties and campaign commitments both, those were presidential concerns indeed, deserving something better than a quixotic approach. Had they been defined even this sharply, perhaps they might have gotten it.

For each of Carter's chief associates, key concerns might have been a shade different. In Vance's instance, comparable quick review of what was *Known, Unclear,* and *Presumed* would have produced not quite the same breakdown, for the business of Secretaries of State is to negotiate. Vance's chief concern would necessarily have been what to say to the Soviets about the Vladivostok understanding. The history prepared by Molander for Brzezinski dealt essentially, we gather, with that problem—in short, with Vance's problem more than with Carter's. By the same token, Harold Brown's concerns were what to say about the MX and such to the chiefs of staff, then to Carter's budget director, and then to committees on Capitol Hill. Carter's concerns embraced those of his Secretaries of State and Defense but were broader in scope. Had he defined them for himself, he might have recognized that they posed the question of *whether* to negotiate and, if so, how to relate negotiations to decisions concerning his defense budget.

To such differences in concerns, dependent partly on extent and level of responsibility, partly on the history in each individual's head, we shall return later.

With concerns identified, random analogies such as Hughes's "bombshell" and the Vienna summit should have disappeared from view. There might have been utility in briefly listing *Likenesses* and *Differences* with SALT I. Doing so could have opened up the question: If it took five years to work out those comparatively modest terms, what makes us suppose we can achieve something much more radical in a matter of weeks? But it would have been possible to go directly to issue history, starting with the basic questions: What's the story of past force increases on both sides? How far back does the time-line go, and what are the key moments on it? For those moments, what are the answers to the journalists' standard questions? Those things needed to be asked, however, of the issue relevant for Carter, not alone the issue relevant for Vance.

We cannot overstress the point that what could have helped Carter most, by way of issue history, was the story back of *his* concerns, the issue as defined *by* his concerns. We do not suggest that a review of past negotiations held no interest for the President, but relatively speaking we regard it as peripheral. Yet what he got served up to him by aides and his departments were stories such as Molander's and not the budget story—all periphery, no center—and this combination we conceive to be perverse, worse than no history at all. Still, had he been interested, the indicated questions on strategic forces could have yielded him illuminating answers.

With the focus on strategic nuclear forces, the starting point for a time-line could be no earlier than 1945, when the nuclear era began, but ought to have been not much later—almost a generation before Vance, Brown, and Brezezinski first turned up at high levels in Washington. Much of the time-line could consist of a simple graph, showing actual increases in American and Soviet strategic forces as measured by bombers and missiles or by warheads or by "throw-weight" or possibly by estimates of how much each side spent. (Hyland, Molander, or almost any expert in the intelligence community would have warned against trusting the last of these. While cost comparisons can be very useful in showing how the two sides match up at a given moment, they are not equally useful in showing trends, for the Russians keep their budgets secret; our CIA guesses what they spend by determining what they have and then calculating what such forces would cost us. The biggest rises in imputed Soviet spending occur therefore when *we* raise pay in *our* armed forces, for, since they use more manpower, their apparent costs go up spectacularly.)[14]

For practical purposes, any graphs would have shown the trend lines in Figures 7–1 through 7–4. Given that it takes several years for a decision on building a weapon to translate itself into an actual weapon out in the field, the lines on all of them pointed to two moments when American strategic nuclear forces had been dramatically increased and three such moments on the Soviet side. The U.S. government had decided on large-scale American force increases at the beginning of the 1950s and at the turn from that decade to the next. The Soviet government seemed to have made comparable decisions just after World War II, again in the mid-1950s, and yet again in the mid-1960s. The American decisions showed up in surges of spending followed by surges in deployments. The first Soviet decisions revealed themselves in atomic and hydrogen bomb tests between 1949 and 1953 and the appearance in the skies of a huge medium-range bomber force; the second set of Soviet decisions showed themselves in early missile programs, and the third showed up in the new missiles that had gone into place since SALT I.

The hard part of the exercise, of course, would have been the effort to explain those change-points—to answer "Why?" Here, history is easily harnessed to advocacy. Anyone will be tempted by the explanation that best fits one's inclinations on what to do now. If any way exists of buying protection, it is probably to ask not just "Why?" but instead, "What are *all* the plausible explanations?"

For the two surges on the American side, almost anyone telling Carter the story would have identified four explanatory factors, all in play in various degrees on both occasions: technology, public opinion, elite opinion, and some triggering Soviet action.[15] In the early 1950s Americans had begun to believe that nuclear weapons could be produced in quantity and delivered with some degree of accuracy. Neither assumption had seemed valid earlier, when it had taken immense effort to produce one bomb and, despite the direct hits on Hiroshima and Nagasaki, pilots could promise to drop atomic bombs only somewhere within a few miles of a designated target. For the public at large, that was the period of

FIGURE 7-1. Bombs and Missile Warheads

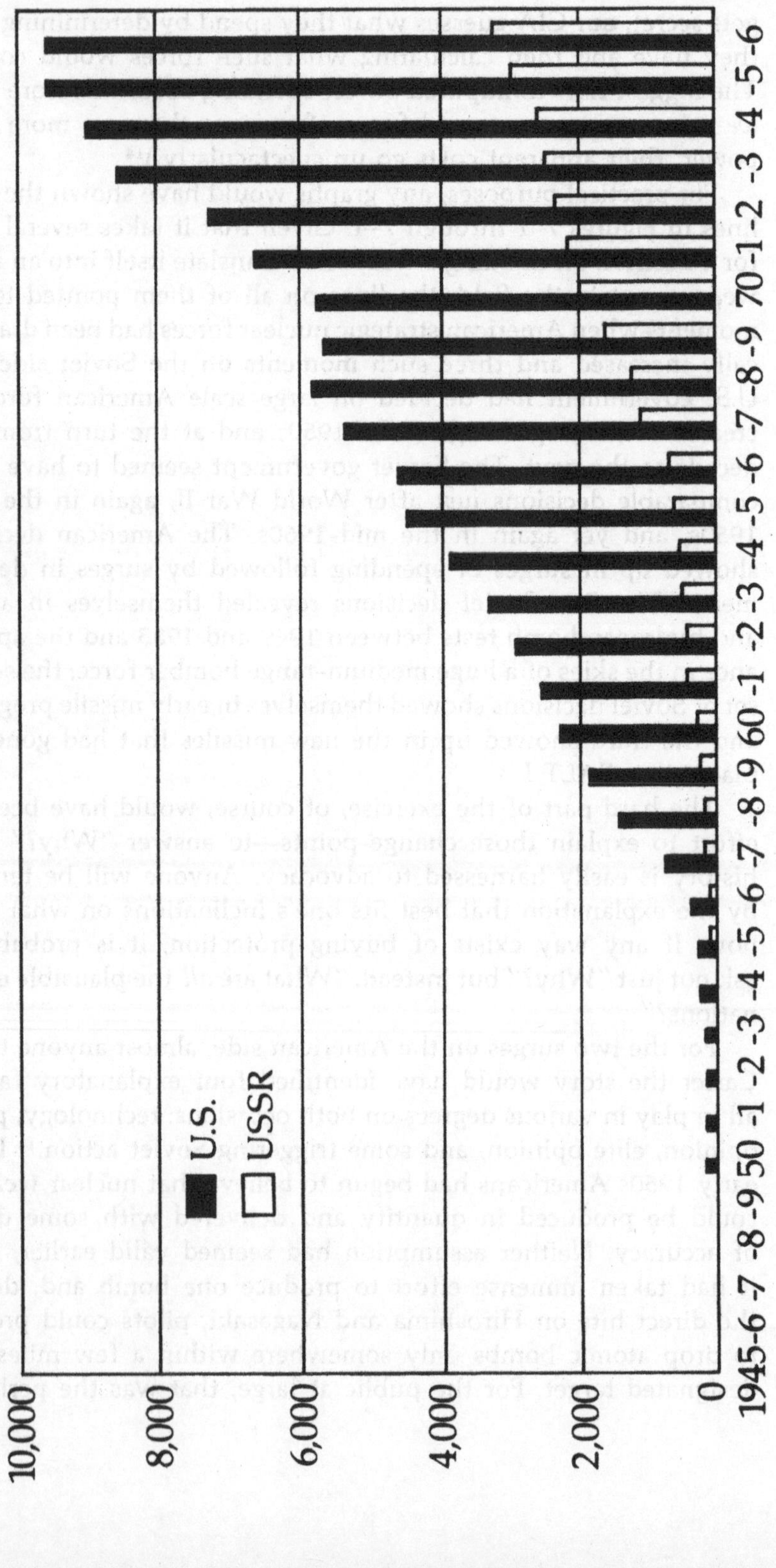

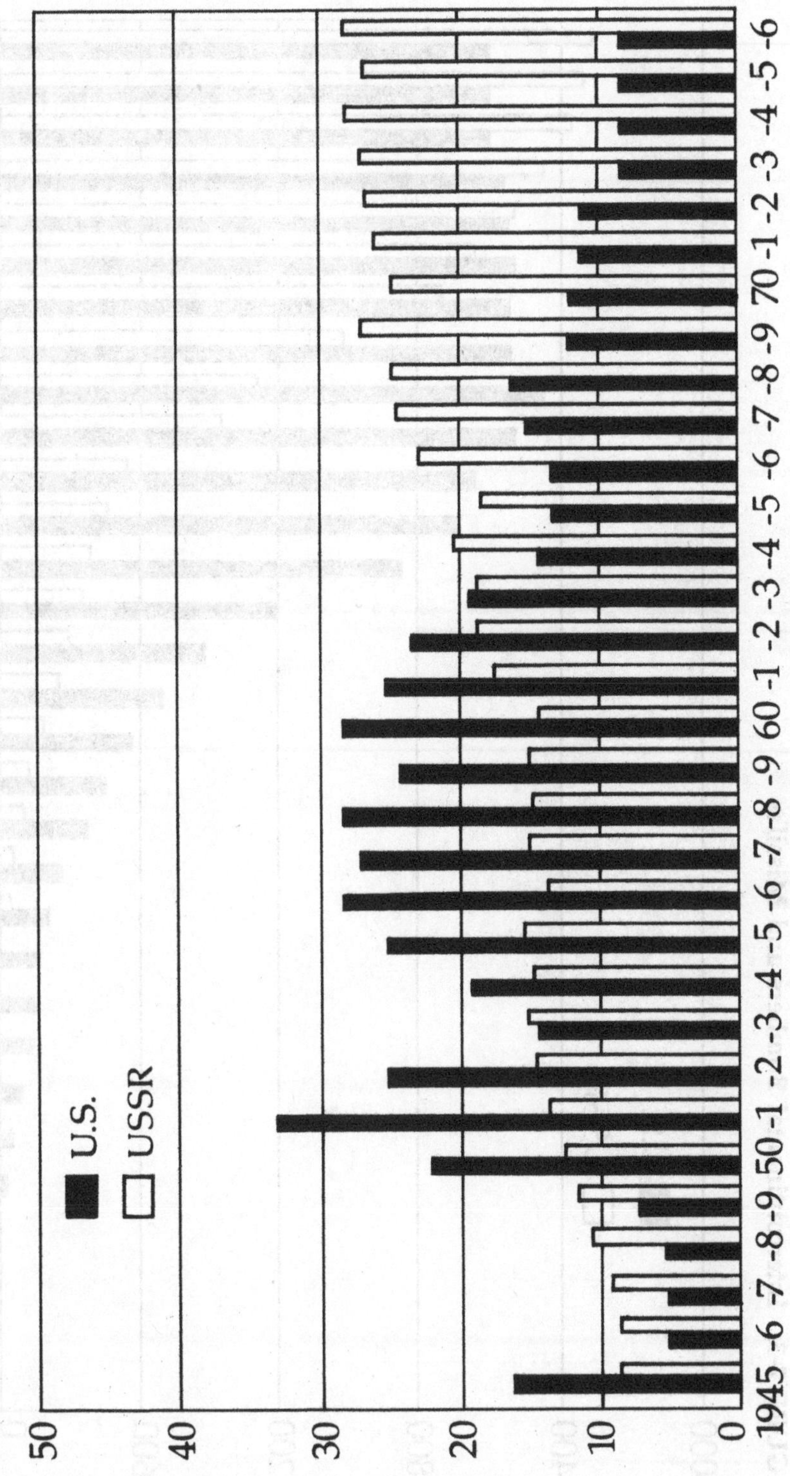

FIGURE 7–2. Spending for Strategic Forces (Bill, FY76 $)

FIGURE 7-3. Intercontinental Bombers and Missiles

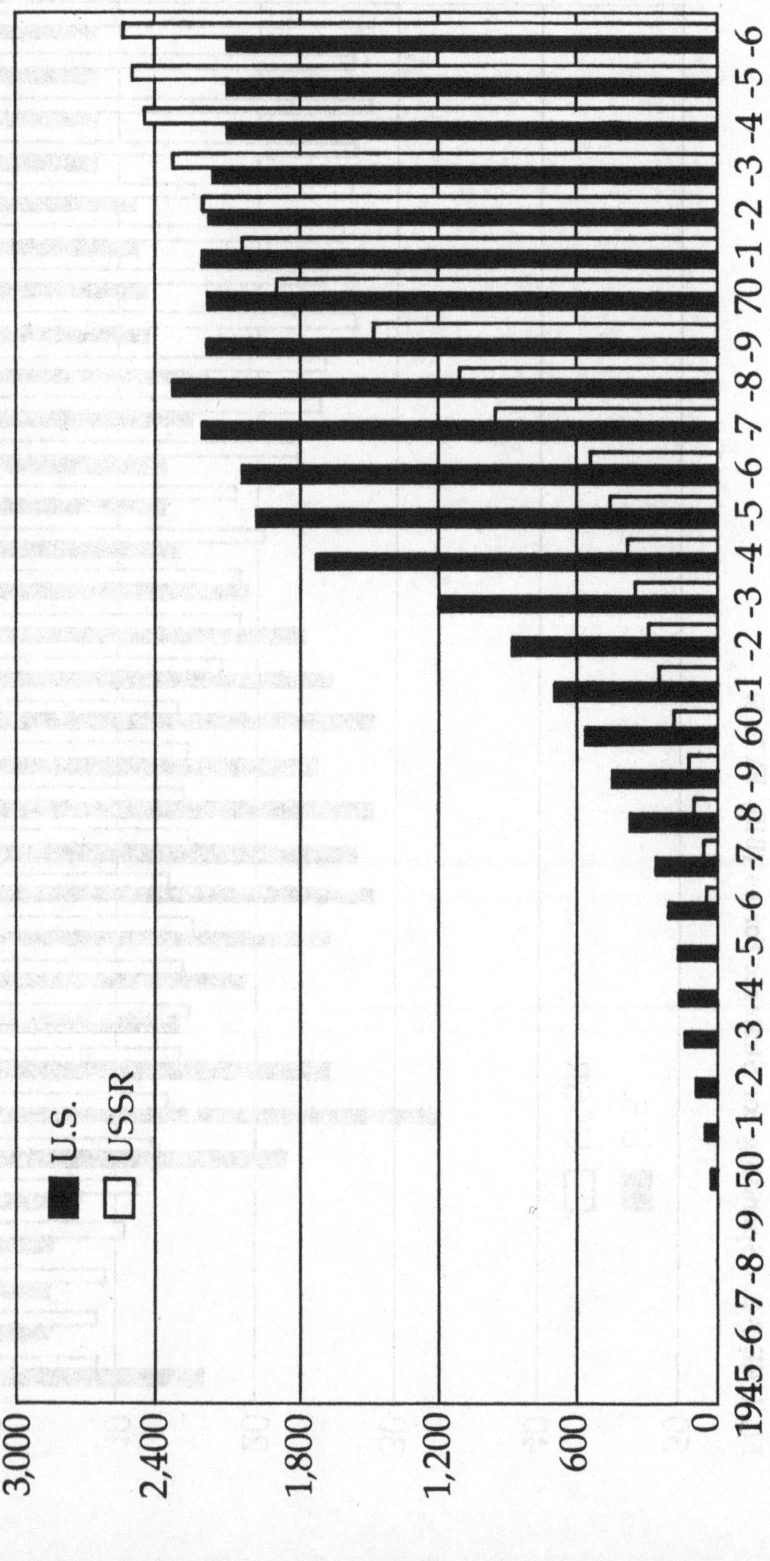

FIGURE 7–4. Megatonnage in Intercontinental Weapons

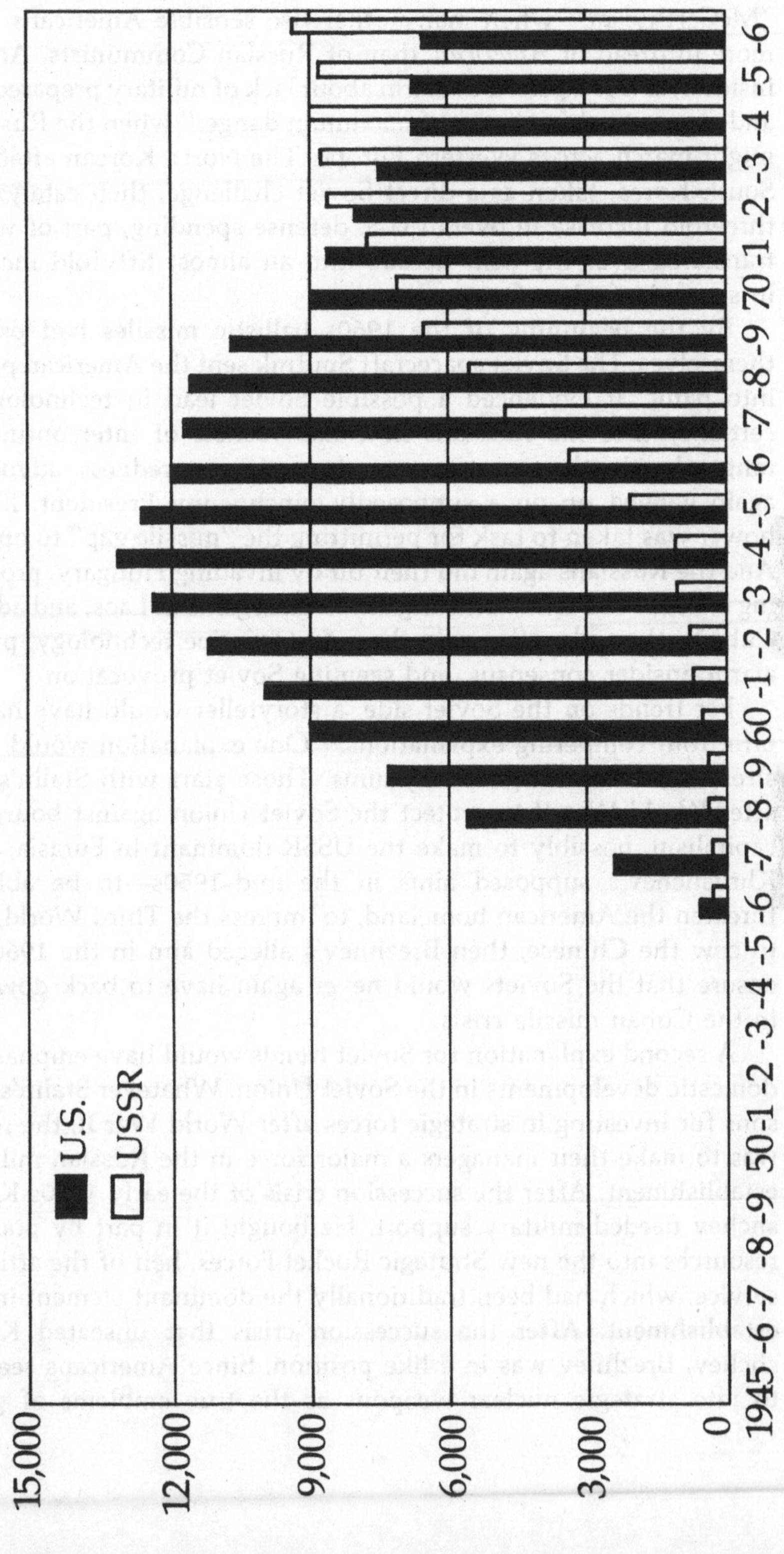

"McCarthyism," when many otherwise sensible Americans lived more in dread of *American* than of Russian Communists. Among insiders, it was a period of alarm about lack of military preparedness and an approaching "year of maximum danger" when the Russians might march across Western Europe. The North Korean attack on South Korea, taken as a direct Soviet challenge, then catalyzed a threefold increase in overall U.S. defense spending, part of which translated over the next decade into an almost fiftyfold increase in strategic nuclear forces.

By the beginning of the 1960s ballistic missiles had proved themselves. The Soviet spacecraft Sputnik sent the American public into panic. It evidenced a possible Soviet lead in technology, a certainty that the Russians now had rockets of intercontinental range. Inside the government, alarmed preparedness advocates again ganged up on a supposedly pinchpenny President. Eisenhower was taken to task for permitting the "missile gap" to open.[16] And the Russians again did their bit by invading Hungary, provoking crises over Berlin, airlifting aid to insurgents in Laos, and adding Cuba to their bloc. So again those factors: ripe technology, public alarm, insider consensus, and seeming Soviet provocation.

For trends on the Soviet side, a storyteller would have had to offer four competing explanations.[17] One explanation would have stressed Soviet foreign policy aims. Those start with Stalin's aim after World War II to protect the Soviet Union against bourgeois capitalism, possibly to make the USSR dominant in Eurasia; then Khrushchev's supposed aims in the mid-1950s—to be able to threaten the American homeland, to impress the Third World, and to cow the Chinese; then Brezhnev's alleged aim in the 1960s to ensure that the Soviets would never again have to back down as in the Cuban missile crisis.

A second explanation for Soviet trends would have emphasized domestic developments in the Soviet Union. Whatever Stalin's reasons for investing in strategic forces after World War II, the result was to make their managers a major force in the Russian military establishment. After the succession crisis of the early 1950s Khrushchev needed military support. He bought it in part by pouring resources into the new Strategic Rocket Forces, heir of the artillery service, which had been traditionally the dominant element in the establishment. After the succession crisis that unseated Khrushchev, Brezhnev was in a like position. Since Americans seemed to rate strategic nuclear weapons as the true emblems of great power, what better for him to give the soldiers? What better to put on display to justify a failure to satisfy consumer needs?

A third explanation would have included relatively little regarding Soviet leaders' purposes, whether foreign or domestic, but stressed the inertia and momentum of the lumbering Soviet state—understandable as a counterpart not of Bismarck's Prussia or FDR's United States or even Exxon or Citibank but rather of the Austro-Hungarian monarchy, the French postal system, a British nationalized industry, or pre-1980s U.S. Steel. This version would have emphasized evidence that the Soviet military establishment gets a fixed allocation of resources with a built-in increase, similar to, and about as untouchable as, that for old age insurance in the United States. The people at the top may supply a course heading, as they did in the mid-1950s when opting for missiles over bombers. But without the missiles there would have been a continuing, ultimately choking flow of bombers. The later surge in missile forces need not have been a product of deliberate decision. It could have been merely a result of the changeover, taking time to achieve a steady state.

A fourth version would have been presented with the caveat that it was popular mostly among people who knew little or nothing about the Soviet Union. It would have described Soviet defense programs as responses to American programs—Stalin's to Hiroshima and Nagasaki; Khrushchev's to the American buildup of the early 1950s; Brezhnev's to that of Kennedy and McNamara.

Laid out before Carter, what would all that history have said? In the first place, the time-line itself should have been eloquent in what it did *not* say. The benchmarks in negotiated arms control, the 1963 Limited Test Ban Treaty and SALT I, did not figure in explanation of trends on either side. They were incidental to the leveling off of U.S. forces, not a cause of it. They seemed to have had little effect on the momentum of Soviet force expansion.

Taking in the fact that the Russians had never, *ever*, done anything but increase their strategic forces, Carter might have felt more doubt about their agreeing to do so now. Experts had already told him that it had probably taken a struggle for them to accept a ceiling of 2,400 for their missile forces. Warnke says one Soviet official told him: "Brezhnev had to spill political blood to get the Vladivostok accords."[18] While Brzezinski's diary testifies that Carter may have suspected Moscow would not accept his terms, the President himself says that he had unrealistic expectations. "In light of what I now know about the Soviet leaders," he wrote five years later, "it is easier for me to understand why the boldness of these first proposals would cause them concern."[19] Had he given some thought to the history of Soviet strategic weapons programs, he might have understood earlier.

Noting the American side of the story, Carter might have been prompted to wonder whether it was true that the Administration would actually have to pour money into MX and those other new weapons if it did not get a sweeping arms control agreement soon. In the past, significant increases in American strategic forces had required ripe technologies *and* public alarm *and* consensus among insiders *and* sudden Soviet behavior that appeared provocative. It had taken all those conditions in combination to move increases in strategic forces into the defense budget, displacing claims for tactical forces, higher military pay, and the like; then to move those increases on through the executive budget process, against competition from other programs and resistance by budgeteers paid to say no; and then to move them finally through authorizing and appropriating committees and into bills enacted by both houses of Congress.

As of 1977 none of those conditions existed. Though cruise missile technology promised soon to pose the kind of "go/no go" questions posed at the beginning of the 1950s by new types of nuclear weapons and at the end of that decade by ballistic missiles, no such situation existed yet. While some members of the public were uneasy about all those big Soviet missiles, others were uneasy about *American* missiles. Polls showed no sense of alarm like that of the early 1950s or after Sputnik. In 1976 Gallup had found less than a quarter of the interested public feeling that military spending was too low and more than a third saying it was too high.[20] Insiders were at odds. Warnke had at least as many fans as critics. And the Soviet Union seemed for the moment on its good behavior: It hadn't invaded another country for almost ten years. Briefing Carter on the history of past increases in American nuclear forces, Brzezinski or someone else from his staff could well have said, "Mr. President, the record suggests that you don't have to worry about being forced to spend money on new strategic forces, not for a while anyway. In fact, you may not be able to spend money if you want to. The conditions that were necessary in the past are just not present now."

By looking at the long history of the ups in Soviet, and the ups and downs in American, nuclear forces, Carter and his staff might also have been more aware that a deep-cuts proposal would not be a cost-free gesture. The review of general trends would not, by itself, have made that clear. Carter's staff would have had to ask the journalists' questions a second time around and then explain to their chief why arms control negotiations and actual arms limitation had not correlated, even on the American side. Kennedy in 1963 and Nixon in 1972 had each had to get support from the Joint Chiefs in order to put an agreement before the Senate with any hope of its being ratified. In the Senate itself they had had to win the votes of men skeptical about any deal with the Russians—Jackson among them. Kind words from the Chiefs and aye votes from marginal Senators had not come cheap. Kennedy and Nixon had had to include in their defense budgets items they would have preferred to leave out. Suitably explored, the history of the issue could have exposed to Carter the danger that if by some miracle he did make progress toward a deep-cuts accord, he might find it *harder,* not easier, to make good on his promise of reduced spending for defense. (The danger would have been even more clear had the President also thought a little about the personal history of "Scoop" Jackson. But more on that later.)

No one, of course, can know what might have resulted had Carter had second thoughts and decided merely to conclude the negotiations begun at Vladivostok. In retrospect, however, almost everyone in the Carter Administration believes that would have been wiser and more fruitful. Just possibly—just possibly—a little attention to the history of the issue might have inspired such second thoughts in good time. But of course it would have had to be the relevant history for the right issue.

When starting to discuss issue history, we noted how the Carter Administration was embarrassed later because no one remembered the specific history of the Soviet brigade in Cuba. As a counter-example, we described FDR's vision of the social, economic, and political trends shaping the past and future of the issue of old age insurance. Here, in our hypothetical reconstruction of how SALT might have been handled in 1977, we have tried to make clear that issue history comprises both trend lines and specifics. It is not a string of analogues or precedents; rather it is a series of connected happenings, which over time take on the form of trends. But an acquaintance with the trends is not the same thing as acquaintance with specifics. No one could possibly learn the details of all in the time available to a decision-maker. The trick is to hit upon a useful combination of key trends and key particulars selected by the light of well-defined concerns.

Concerns guide the choice of trends and of specifics to be emphasized in a review of issue history. Who then has to do what depends a great deal on who the people are and what the issue is. As FDR could rely on Perkins and her committee to get up most of the specifics on the history of social insurance programs, so Carter could have depended on the NSC staff, State, and Defense to bone up on past negotiations with the Russians and on at least the most recent trends in weapons technology. Regarding social security, it fell to Roosevelt to remember the specifics of the relevant political history; it was he who thought explicitly about the Townsend Plan and movement—happening before his eyes—and about the consequences for the coming Congress. The burden on Carter would have been greater. He would have had to get up for himself a sense of general trends in an issue area where he was a comparative newcomer. He also would have had to find someone he trusted who could fill in the political specifics, noting where Jackson and the latter's friends had been in earlier battles over arms control. The combination is not easy to carry. Might someone else have shouldered it better than Carter?

We do not proffer SALT as an example with high confidence, for we recognize how formidable is the ignorance of a new President, Carter perhaps especially but not uniquely. And even if his new Administration had inherited with cheers routine procedure of the sort we recommend, he might well have resisted using and construing what they put before him—this, as James Fallows wrote, because of his ahistorical cast of mind, "his lack of curiosity about how the story turned out before."[21] But less ignorance in certain areas and different operating style are quite conceivable, even in a new President, to say nothing of one with experience. Given moderate changes on those scores, identifying and applying relevant issue history to SALT in 1977 does not strike us as either unduly hard or fanciful. That is why we venture to put this example forward. We hope it suggests what might have been and even what might be.

In this and preceding chapters we have made a consecutive series of points. To sum up our argument thus far, it is that people facing difficult decisions should pause to define their concerns. They should take precautions to avoid being misled by analogies of one stripe or another. Then, to the extent possible, they should try to see their concerns in historical context, asking what major trends are relevant and what specifics in the issue's past—especially, we think, in its past politics—bear on the question of what to do now. Here we offer the "Goldberg rule," the principle that one should always ask, "What's the story?"; "time-lines," the associated principle that the story should always be taken back to its beginning (this reduces the chance of storytelling warped by advocacy); and "journalists' questions," a reminder to ask "where," "who," "how" and "why" of past events, as well as "when" and "what." Those approaches can illuminate both present conditions and future prospects. The three steps build on each other. In the SALT case it is easy to see that.

Is that too much to ask? We hope not. Is it enough? We fear not. For at least three other strands of history ought, in our view, to be drawn in before objectives are finally selected, options sorted, and actions decided. The first is the history underpinning key presumptions. Not obviously analogous and not necessarily connected to immediate concerns, this is the history which induces belief that, if *X* occurs, *Y* will follow. The second is history in the heads of other people—the differing ideas about the past and its lessons that go with differences in age or experience or culture. Awareness of those differences can be useful not only for persuasion but also for deciding what to do. Third is the history of organizations, for options are not abstract, and actions rarely are entrusted to random individuals. Decisions will be executed by organizations with particular routines and operating styles—and it is well to consider how those organizations have learned to work before telling one of them to do something. To those three propositions we devote the next chapters.

8 Probing Presumptions

In March 1976, before finally approving the Center for Disease Control's program of immunization against swine flu, Gerald Ford spent an hour and a half questioning an *ad hoc* group of immunologists and others in the Cabinet Room. They were not an organized panel; some were strangers to each other, and most were strangers to the White House. They were meeting as a group for the first time, at the urgent invitation of a White House aide, because the President had said he wished to hear directly from America's "best scientists."

Earnestly, Ford pressed these strangers for dissent from the opinions of their peers, his official advisers. Hearing only support, he told them he would wait for a few minutes in his office. Anyone who wished to tell him anything in private could enter through a visible doorway. "Just get up, come over and knock and walk in," Ford said as he left the meeting. No one followed. Thereafter, for some months, he thought he had unqualified assent from the "scientific community" to the program he proceeded to announce that afternoon. "When you've got unanimity," he later said, "you'd better go with it."[1]

In the event, of course, Ford's consensus was all surface, lacking depth, without staying power, and the reasons why run back to the presumptions unexamined—or worse, unacknowledged—which were set forth in Chapter Three. The talk around the Cabinet table had left those untouched. Then, month by month, experience intruded to cast doubt upon or disprove them, one after the other. As that happened, doctors all across the country, including some who had been at the cabinet table, fell away. It is no wonder. But not Ford's own officials: They remained loyal to the end to the conclusions with which they began and changed or acknowledged nothing that the facts did not force upon them. Between them and the larger community, a gap progressively widened—a credibility gap. The media seized on it, Ford fell into it, his reputation suffered, so did that of the Center for Disease Control, and the program's reputation was destroyed.

There are obvious parallels with Truman's fate in the Korean War, with Johnson's in Vietnam, or with Carter's in the "hundred days," the SALT debacle, and the Cuban brigade episode. Because of presumptions unexamined or imperfectly acknowledged, concerns were defined in certain ways and not in others (the risk of serious epidemic drew more attention than the risk of serious side effects, for instance). The same can be said of choices: Presumptions gave certain options allure and virtually excluded others. Then came exposure to events—and every fault or failure in those same presumptions was paid for in the coin of credibility. Back of each decline in credibility, of course, were real pains for real people: victims of vaccine side effects, or casualties in war, on down to congressmen who couldn't get a phone call from the Carter entourage and Russians certain that the combat brigade furor had reflected some deep purpose.

The power of presumptions is arresting and bespeaks the need for tests to minimize their shortcomings. We are under no illusion that mere humans can project into the future—which is what presumptions do—unerringly. But we are not content with errors of the sort Ford and those others fell into; some at least, we think, could have been sidestepped with a little thought. This chapter therefore is devoted to the question: How can busy people identify and test their own presumptions (or the ones their aides thrust forward) in a fashion adequate to winnow out the shakiest of them? With the advantage of the intervening illustrations and the widened range of practice they display, we thus return to what we interrupted after writing about swine flu at the end of Chapter Three.

We start with a reminder: Presumptions matter; they are important to decision-makers for three intricately interrelated reasons, all already noted but worth restating. First, presumptions—items *Presumed*—figure in definition of the situation. Second, by the same token they help to establish concerns and, along with a sense of how concerns evolved, shape definitions of aims, of concrete objectives. Third, above all else, presumptions influence options and choices among them. Some they render weighty, others they eliminate. Consider the political presumption that Disease Control Center director Sencer put to his superiors regarding swine flu: better to be seen wasting money than lives. Or consider the evident persistent view of Johnson and his advisers that North Vietnam would make a deal once bombing imposed pain. Or, on the other hand, take LBJ's impression that he couldn't "lose Vietnam" and keep allies or win elections. Or contrast Carter's honeymoon with Reagan's, where reportedly one governing presumption was: "Jimmy did everything wrong." Or reflect on why FDR felt obliged in 1935 to treat social security as really insurance but by 1939 could treat it as only symbolically so.

With regard to situations, concerns, and objectives, we have, we hope, already shown that history can clarify. The same can be said of options. We have urged that those who face decisions identify concerns—the reasons for wanting to do something—before plunging into action. We have also urged that they glance backward as they make up their minds about where to head. But we do not expect them to wait long. Surveying the scene will seldom be more than a warmup for framing options, making choices, trying to follow through—which are what most decision-makers (and the journalists who cover them and the citizens who watch them) take to be the duties they are paid for.

Once choosing among options is the focus, history does not cease to be useful. If anything, it becomes more so. Options are ranked by pros and cons. The pros and cons rest on presumptions, many of which are not specific to the situation at hand, hence may be well below the surface of the choice-maker's mind, out of sight. Those presumptions have to do with cause and effect: If *X,* then *Y.* Many such presumptions are shot through with perceptions of the past—often muddled, sometimes mistaken. Others derive from general beliefs about how people or governments behave. Either way, the presumptions can at least be brought into the light. In some cases they can even be tested: In historical cases of which we have knowledge, did *Y* actually follow *X*? We are not suggesting any complex review of all history, merely a search through data already in memory. Just stop to ask the two questions: (1) What are the presumptions behind the pros and cons for favored options? (2) What experience, if any, validates those presumptions?

For illustration of how options can be colored by presumptions built upon perceptions of the past, Johnson's Vietnam policy in 1965 is a source of compelling examples. His options were not "dos" and "don'ts" drawn from single precedents. Instead, each was thought to have behind it a body of empirical proof. If LBJ bombed North Vietnam, the North Vietnamese government would want him to stop and, in consequence, might cease aiding the Vietcong. He relied on the supposition that a government would respond to pain as a person might. He also assumed that historical experience with strategic bombing validated this supposition. And he accepted the notion of gradualism, of stepping up pain slowly, the so-called slow squeeze, in at least inferential comparison with Kennedy's procedure for the Cuban missile crisis: starting at the bottom of the escalatory ladder while preparing to mount one rung at a time.[2]

Similarly, when LBJ and his associates considered committing their ground forces, they did so with faith buttressed by remembered victories: The United States always won. A French or Italian government might have been open to more doubt. And when Johnson's people thought of peace, they recalled that the North Koreans and Chinese had eventually negotiated an end to the Korean war. They recalled as well that other limited wars, elsewhere and earlier, had also ended in compromise.

Affinities for the remembered past gave certain options added weight and at the same time tended to exclude others. George Ball's preferred policy of heading out, not up, had against it not only the memories of appeasement in the 1930s but also the nation's martial tradition. That helped gain it the label "cut and run." Something similar befell Maxwell Taylor's enclave strategy. It became "hunker down." And JCS proposals for a "fast full squeeze," to say nothing of ideas about invading North Vietnam, were put in a category with previous recommendations commonly judged extreme, particularly General Curtis LeMay's "bomb them into the stone age."

The weight accorded options characterized as "slow squeeze" or "graduated escalation" and the virtual exclusion of "cut and run," or "hunker down," or "bomb them into the stone age" involved much more than debaters' tricks with language. The fact that those labels could win acceptance was evidence of deep-seated shared beliefs about regularities in human affairs—about causes and effects—supposedly validated by experience.

Why tests are needed is obvious. Forced to the surface of consciousness, such beliefs stand a chance of being judged explicitly for what they are, with a not wholly subjective record measuring their realism or lack of it. As a matter of widely known fact, experience had not completely validated the "commonsense" assumption that pain would have the same effects on governments as on individuals. Strategic bombing had *not* always brought the hoped-for results. It did in Italy and Japan during World War II, but only after governments changed. In both Britain and Germany it made governments more stubborn.[3] LBJ knew that. So did everyone around him. Their debates could have been less muddled if one question had been: Why won't Ho Chi Minh react to bombing the way Churchill and Hitler did? As another example, the victorious record of American armed forces stemmed from times when they had the whole nation's resources at their disposal. When put on short rations—as in the Indian wars, the Philippine occupation, various episodes in the Caribbean, and even in Korea, their record had been less glorious. That, too, was common knowledge, at least among Johnson's military advisers.

The beliefs influencing thought about Vietnam options were not necessarily wrong, but they were subject to more qualifications than Johnson or most of his advisers recognized. They seemed so obviously correct as not to be worth stating. If stated with precision, their limited validity might have seemed equally obvious. The point of testing is to give the choice-maker a crack at both perceptions.

This brings us almost to the question of how to test, but not quite. Before we finally tackle it, we pause again over the nature of presumptions. They are not all of a kind.

Some presumptions are mere estimates of what will happen over time. They can range from calculations based on available evidence, to educated guesses, to surmises, to mere hunches. But in any case the central characteristic is that without much delay or pain the presumption can and will be altered as time passes and fresh evidence piles up. American predictions of longevity for the successive governments of South Vietnam fall into that category. So do Center for Disease Control assumptions about starting dates for mass immunization: taken for granted today, refigured tomorrow. Needing shorthand and lacking better terms, we label such things "maybes."

A second type of presumption is at the other extreme. It is so value-laden that it cannot be challenged save in its own terms, by opposed values: Communists are bad, market mechanisms good; life matters more than money; and so forth. All beliefs are tinged by values, some encompass little else. We deal here with beliefs so tightly packed, their value content so solidified, that they are impervious to change unless catastrophe intervenes, if then. Not only anti-Communism but also some naive remnants of the "white man's burden" played a part in Korean decisions, as well as in Vietnam decisions and even *Mayaguez* decisions. A faith in modern medicine, perhaps no less naive, ran through swine flu decisions. In 1983 the symbols of insurance as an earnest of the work ethic remained—perhaps with less force—what they had been for fifty years and were decisive to the social security debate. Basic presumptions about the Soviet Union entered into assessments of data on the "brigade" in Cuba. So, earlier, Carter came to deep cuts in strategic arms partly out of conviction that all humans had to want the world rid of nuclear weapons. He left office never reconciled to the possibility that many Russians, and a number of influential Americans, did not. For shorthand, we call values "truths," since that is how they are considered by those who hold them.

In between "maybes" and "truths" lie presumptions that embody some element of faith but are not impervious to tests of evidence. These are presumptions about what will happen when something else has happened first. If this, then that: two sets of expectations, each a mixture of beliefs and facts, linked by a (usually implicit) causal theory. To those "if/then" presumptions belong LBJ's about the effects of bombing North Vietnam; Ford's about being able to vaccinate everybody; and Carter's that it did no harm to start with a deep cuts proposal. But still more beliefs are packed into such presumptions. If we bomb North Vietnam, South Vietnamese morale will rise. If we cut old age benefits, the voters will retaliate. If we rescue the *Mayaguez*, Americans will feel better. If swine flu should break out again, the country will forgive the aches and pains of immunization. And the reverse twist: If the Chinese meant to rescue North Korea, they would have intervened *before* we crossed the parallel. There are a host of variations on the theme. With hindsight, some of them seem to hold up. Some don't. Distinguishing one from another by foresight is this chapter's chief concern.

The "if/then" form is sometimes used to convey estimates (or "guesstimates"). For instance, if we make vaccine by June, we can complete shots by Thanksgiving. If the Chinese do intervene in Korea, as General MacArthur said six weeks before it happened, "there will be the greatest slaughter." (He proved mistaken only about who would slaughter whom.) But "if/then" estimates are likely, as in these examples, to contain more implicit, unexpressed beliefs than do "maybes" phrased more simply, for instance, that the Chinese have not stood up well against Westerners in the past and won't in the future. So "if/then" is a warning sign, and all presumptions phrased in the contingent form become prime targets for testing.

The first step toward testing presumptions is to sort them, to set aside the "maybes" least weighed down by "truths," and also the free-standing "truths" that cannot well be tested. What remain are likely for the most part to be "if/thens" along with some truth-hiding "maybes." We urge concentration on those remainders.

One more thing we now should do before turning to tests themselves: to illustrate as vividly as possible—in living technicolor, so to speak—the consequences of *not* testing. Although all our examples up to now suggest what they may be, none drives the argument home as hard as we would like. But we do know a case sufficient for the purpose. Having twice postponed discussion of our tests, we do so once again to tell the story of the Bay of Pigs.

The Bay of Pigs affair of 1961 is perhaps *the* classic case of presumptions unexamined. The affair was marked from first to last by absence of explicitness even about "maybes," let alone about "if/thens" and "truths." Participants differed widely at least on the "maybes" and "if/thens," but they explored neither those differences nor discrepancies between what they expected and what was occurring. They skirted doing so in extraordinary fashion. The organizers walled themselves off from colleagues who might have challenged their presumptions. The President did likewise, often inadvertently, for most of those whose comment or advice he asked were too inhibited to plumb his underlying presumptions or to spell out theirs. They were too new to him and he to them. Those things happened at the outset of a new Administration, which was also, in most respects, a change of generation. The details of the story are captured in Peter Wyden's authoritative *Bay of Pigs.*[4] Here we sketch only the outlines.

In 1959 Cuban insurgents led by Fidel Castro capped a long guerrilla campaign by unseating the unsavory Batista government, defeating its police and army, and installing in its place a revolutionary regime. That outcome was hailed initially by liberals in the United States and was accepted tentatively by the Eisenhower Administration. Castro, indeed, came to this country, made a tour of Harlem and of Eastern universities, and sought from Washington development assistance in the form of grants and loans. Washington, suspicious, sought preliminary guarantees that Castro's revolution would not turn too radical, would stop short of suspending property and other rights, and in particular would compensate the private sector—including American investors—for nationalization. Perhaps Castro intended to form a Communist regime from the beginning; some of his closest associates certainly did. In any case, by the spring of 1960 he had proclaimed himself on the side of the Soviet Union against the "imperialistic" United States.

Washington was outraged. The implications for the hemisphere seemed alarming, and a rush of Cuban refugees to Florida made domestic aspects of the problem doubly difficult. Gaining Batista supporters along with mounting numbers from Cuba's entrepreneurial and professional middle class, Miami came to have more Cubans than Paris had ever had White Russians. Other Cubans congregated in New York. The majority settled down, applied their talents, and considered citizenship, with every prospect of soon becoming a force in American politics.

By the spring of 1960 exiled Cubans ranging from ex-Batista goons to onetime Castro stalwarts with no stomach for Moscow-style socialism were plotting counterrevolution. Numbers came in contact with our Central Intelligence Agency; the CIA had Eisenhower's authorization to plan covert infiltrations, which might cumulate into serious opposition, causing Castro trouble and ultimately even bringing him down. The planning fell to Richard Bissell, head of the CIA Directorate that managed spying and covert operations. His audacity and follow-through were thought to have been demonstrated brilliantly when he brought to fruition the new aerial reconnaissance capacity of the United States, the U-2 planes and pilots, "Richard Bissell's air force." CIA Director Allen Dulles, brother of the late Secretary of State, signified his seriousness when he named Bissell to the Cuban planning task. Whether Eisenhower was serious is a question; he is said to have been skeptical. Not so the Vice President, Richard M. Nixon, soon to run for President against Senator John F. Kennedy. Nixon seems to have been serious indeed.

During the fall campaign Nixon, who knew what Bissell was doing, kept his mouth shut. Kennedy, not knowing, lambasted the Administration for passivity. After the election he was told by Allen Dulles, whom he reappointed, and by Bissell, whom he knew. He did not demur, and they proceeded. Already they had Cubans from Miami undergoing covert training in Central America.

During November 1960, apparently on his own motion, Bissell let his planning carry him from small-scale infiltration to a substantial invasion. The CIA's Cubans were to seize a beachhead suitable for installation of a government, formed from exile groups, to rally the country against Castro's regime (in the initial planning he was to be dead by then, assassinated). Risings were to follow the creation of that rebel government. American recognition would come next, helping to sustain a civil war, which Castroites would lose. Recruitment in Miami, training in Guatemala, and planning in Washington were stepped up accordingly, and a coalition revolutionary council was shoved together—all by covert operators from CIA.

In January 1961, soon after his inaugural, President Kennedy received his first full briefing on those plans from Bissell with Dulles's unqualified support. The Secretary of Defense, briefed by his then Assistant for International Security Affairs, William Bundy (a former CIA aide, close to Bissell from Yale days), offered further support. Uncomfortable about it—with his discomfort fueled by sturdy opposition from the held-over Under Secretary of State for Inter-American Affairs—Kennedy sought an advisory opinion from the Joint Chiefs of Staff. In the interest of secrecy he did not let them staff it out. They reviewed only what Bissell put before them. They responded that the operation, which was not to be their doing, stood a "fair chance" of success. The author of that phrase said later that he meant 3 to 1 *against.*[5] The Chiefs offered no such exegesis at the time. The civilians misunderstood. Thereupon, in a series of *ad hoc* meetings with a small but shifting set of top advisers, all adjured to keep the matter quiet, Kennedy toyed with the plan. To reduce its "noise level" internationally, he had the invasion moved 70 miles west from the city of Trinidad to the isolated Bay of Pigs. That shift converted McGeorge Bundy, the National Security Assistant, theretofore a skeptic, who evidently thought deniability the chief issue, now deemed it accomplished, and expressed the view that Kennedy could thus proceed with confidence.[6] Bundy and the President apparently never grasped until after the fact—and no one told them—that the shift had virtually cut off any chance, should the invasion go awry, to fade into the Escambray, the mountains behind Trinidad, and launch guerrilla actions as a "second best," for swamps now intervened. Neither did Kennedy grasp that his revision of the plan was never given—since he never asked—a formal reconsideration by the Joint Chiefs: "Fair chance" rang in his ears as "good chance" until the end.

Nor did Kennedy understand that "fair chance" rested on a presumption of prompt risings throughout Cuba against Castro once the beach was held just long enough to let the rebel government be actually proclaimed on Cuban soil. The military had assumed those risings central to the Bissell plan. Bissell himself had never checked the prospect out with Richard Helms, who, though his nominal deputy, managed the largely separate apparatus for gathering secret intelligence. Nor had Bissell checked with his supposed peer, Robert Amory, the head of the directorate for open intelligence and estimates. Both had been "cut out," walled off. The President was evidently unaware of that. Both would have scoffed at uprisings. Kennedy grasped that least of all. As we shall try to show later, the organizational history of the CIA could have afforded many clues, but Kennedy was shown none of them; he and his aides were ignorant of organization, too.

Through February and March the President fitfully reviewed Bissell's arrangements, while the CIA assembled its materials and anti-Castro Cubans trained at a not-so-secret camp in Guatemala. There were now 1,200 recruits. As Kennedy perceived—lest he didn't, Dulles told him—if they failed to go to Cuba they would end up back in Miami, talkative and angry at the fate of *Eisenhower's* project (which, if untried, was sure to have been successful by their account). Three other factors pushed the President toward a deadline: He was told by the CIA that Guatemala insisted the Cubans depart and that Castro's air force would be much enhanced by May; further, he learned from many sources that security was tight only in Washington. Talk abounded in Guatemala and Miami.

So Kennedy gave Bissell a go-ahead with two provisos: (1) that he could cancel until the last moment and (2) that in no event, including failure, would he sanction engagement of American armed forces. When the time came in mid-April, Kennedy did not cancel the operation. Instead, he let it proceed but stripped it of a protective feature, a second air strike against Castro's military aviation. The first strike, which he had reduced, had partly miscarried. Worse, its "cover" had been blown, and Adlai Stevenson, his UN Ambassador, twice Democratic candidate for President, hotly protested a second strike, saying it was bound to be attributed to Washington. With Secretary of State Rusk arguing the same, Kennedy agreed. Bissell had to acquiesce. Thus the invaders, landing without air cover, were attacked by Castro's few planes flown by pilots more skillful than predicted. The Cuban planes blew up the ship that carried both communications and ammunition, crippling the landing force. They also strafed the troops and pinned them down until the prompt arrival of loyal Castro forces. Most of the invaders were taken prisoner. Castro efficiently jailed many thousands of his fellow citizens lest they be tempted to incite or join any risings. There were none.

Meanwhile, Kennedy for his part stood firm on his second proviso; with very marginal exceptions he allowed no combat use of his armed forces. Naval carriers and destroyers on the scene had to stand by and watch the invasion fail, an experience that equally shocked officers back home and devastated Bissell's men. They had apparently presumed that *in extremis* any President would unleash American forces and that JFK, the war hero, exponent of "vigor," critic of passivity, had not really meant what he said. Not so. On that score he was steadfast. We think it a point in his favor.

In hindsight, one striking feature of the whole affair is that Kennedy did not press many questions on the planners, the JCS, or, for that matter, anyone. All accounts substantially agree on this. Neither did the trio of his close associates, Rusk, McNamara, and McGeorge Bundy. More precisely, Bundy's questioning sank to the level of the others' once the plan was rendered "quiet" by the shift from Trinidad. Partly, the paucity of questions seems to have been a transition phenomenon, a matter of preoccupied new people, all engaged in learning their jobs and learning about one another at the same time, most of them new not only to each other and the job but to executive office in the Federal government. Partly, by all accounts, the lack of questioning traces to the extraordinary personality of Richard Bissell—brilliant, incisive, sometimes charming, analytic, confident, experienced, and cool. Besides,

Bundy, in common with his older brother, McNamara's aide, had admired Bissell since college days; Rusk had known Bissell from the era of the Marshall Plan; and Kennedy, just after the election, characterized Bissell as the only CIA man he knew well enough to trust.[7]

Particulars of other personalities have bearing also. Rusk's reticence was to become proverbial. Here is where it first appeared on something of importance. There is credible testimony that he thought Bissell's plan unworkable, but no other person in the inner circle knew that until twenty years after the fact.[8] In contrast, Chairman William Fulbright of the Senate Foreign Relations Committee, given a gesture of invitation, volunteered total opposition to the whole idea. Fulbright had very nearly been named Secretary of State. Had he sat in Rusk's place, his position probably would have remained opposed and would have been presented without reticence, to say the least. At the outset of the new Administration open opposition from the Secretary of State might have sufficed to win Kennedy. Besides, it would have given cover for the JCS to spell out misgivings that were muffled in the face of a presumably gung-ho young President.

But beyond those partial explanations lies another, on which we focus here, namely that for the President and his associates, particular presumptions reinforced certain expectations and options, excluded others, without anyone pausing to probe even whether those presumptions were testable, let alone the implicit logic about causes and effects. That naturally kept down the stock of questions in their heads.

Had the President or his aides bothered to do so, they would have defined as their concerns Cuba's being (a) a Communist state and (b) a Soviet satellite. Whether (b) was of greater concern than (a) or vice versa is a theoretician's question. Their objective was clear. They wanted a Cuba neither Communist nor allied with the Soviet Union. (But not a Cuba under a new Batista. "Truths" entered in here: if a Batista, then another Castro, then criticism in Latin America, disaffection among Stevensonian Democrats. . . .) Reviewing the history of those concerns could have aided thinking about options. It might have opened up questions as to why the CIA shifted in November 1960 to planning an amphibious landing and thus helped stifle "infiltration" as an option. It would probably not, however, have modified in any way consensus on the objective.

Given that objective—a Cuba without Castro or Batista—the

option of doing nothing seemed a nonstarter. JFK himself, from his reported comments before and after the invasion failed, took it for granted that Castro in Cuba would become more dangerous to American interests and pride and to Latin American neighbors. He and Nixon saw that prospect alike, to some degree. It ruled out doing nothing, if there actually were something doable in sight. The possibilities for doing something included (1) diplomatic and economic pressure only, (2) covert action, and (3) overt military intervention. Reliance only on diplomatic and economic pressure was ruled out by three "cons": First, not much more remained to be done in that line; second, it offered little promise of early results; and third, it would involve calling off an operation well under way, with all the consequences of which Dulles warned. Overt military intervention also seemed out. Berlin and other places were too susceptible to Soviet retaliation. Besides, Kennedy was building his own public image in Europe and Latin America. He liked the results and did not want to spoil them. Throughout the whole affair he was constant in one thing: He blocked overt intervention.

Covert action squared the circle, or seemed to. Dulles and Bissell said it would get Castro out, in the long run if not the short. The Cuban refugees would have nothing of which to complain. Neither would the CIA or the Republicans, for the plan stemmed from Eisenhower's time, as did Dulles's reputation and the CIA's experience. Being covert, not overt, it would invite no countermove by the Red Army. It would have "deniability" both in Latin American capitals and at home. As for the only "con" offsetting all those "pros"—the risk of failure—there was always the fallback of "melting into the Escambray." Besides, Bissell could be canceled until the last moment, and there was always "Kennedy luck," which, after all, within the year had brought him nomination and election.

Covert action seemed clearly the option best suited to the objective. It is hardly surprising that Kennedy and his aides did not pause long over the alternatives. They would have done well, however, to linger over the controlling presumptions that made this choice appear so obviously right. Doing so might have led to more questioning of the particular covert action plan served up by Dulles and Bissell.

Even a little probing would have identified six crucial "if/then" presumptions swaying JFK. Two were organizational: that the CIA had generous capabilities while Castro's still were limited, especially in the air. Two more were substantive: that Bissell's Cubans had to be disposed of, there or here, and that Cubans on the island would be happily rid of Castro. Finally came the justifying twosome: Castro was Moscow's tool, only 90 miles away, and he was taking Cuba away from us.

The effects on thought about options are obvious.

Some of those presumptions were belief-encumbered "maybes." A little thought and inquiry could have turned them into *"Knowns"* or at least put them in the category *"Unclear,"* for instance the "disposal" problem—Dulles put it so—which may have offered Kennedy his most compelling motive. To state it simply, Guatemalans want the trainees out of there, so they must go, and if they go to the United States they must be set at liberty, which they will use to lambaste the Administration in the press. That last presumption almost surely rang a bell in Kennedy's mind. The rest apparently went unexamined. Were the Guatemalans beyond inducement? The training beyond extension? Other places unavailable? Nicaragua? Venezuela? With time, perhaps, the trainees could be retrained back toward the original objective of infiltrating to the mountains in small groups or turned toward other uses and gradually dispersed. At worst, how bad would the press reaction be? Might Eisenhower be induced to temper or absorb it? Before the event, the former President was not in fact maneuvered into any sort of helpfulness, much less consulted. That speaks to Kennedy's own lack of careful reasoning.

Other presumptions were "if/thens." Some rested on cause-effect suppositions that could not have long survived explicit statement. Consider, for example, the presumption that Castro was already felt to be a burden by his people, who were waiting for deliverance (not, of course, back to Batista, but forward to constitutionalism). Kennedy himself may not have put much stock in an immediate uprising, but he evidently took for granted that the government he was about to export from Miami would have more popular appeal than Castro, the supposed burden. Held up to the light, that presumption appears odd indeed: Castro's alleged lack of popular support *in* Cuba was the product of two years when, under a charismatic leader, amid entrancing drama, the masses obtained every sign and symbol of equality while the upper classes left the country. There was austerity, but also there was health insurance, along with education projects, and a vast pride. Western capital had been withdrawn, but the Americans were gone too, tourists and the Mafia as well, and with them the demeaning features of the tourist trade. Everyone was watched and civil liberties were curtailed, but the people who enjoyed them most and cared about them most were living in Miami or trying to get there. Why all that should make Castro feel burdensome *on his island* is a poser. Except for such as Howard Hunt, who then was Bissell's man in Miami (Watergate starts here), the intelligence community acknowledged Castro's current hold upon the island. Kennedy, Rusk, and the others at the top evidently did not. They were not ideologues like Hunt; rather, they seem to have assumed that Cubans were in the same boat as East Europeans, say, and ought to act accordingly, or something of the sort.

If doubts were not awakened simply by making the presumptions explicit, they surely could have been aroused by a few questions about the experience supporting them. Had the Cuban populace in the past risen up for constitutionalism? Put to someone who knew some Cuban history, the question would not have produced a clear yes or no. But that should have been enough in itself. Once Spain's "ever faithful isle," Cuba had been the last Western Hemisphere colony to break with Spain, and the break became final only after years of horrible suffering *and* U.S. military intervention (which allowed the Spaniards to exit gracefully.) Occasional revolutions since had seldom mobilized much support for constitutionalism. New governments came in when old ones collapsed—Machado's in 1933, Batista's in 1959.[9] Five minutes of Cuban history should have sufficed to turn the question on its head: not "Does Castro have opponents?" but "Does he have supporters?" Cuba's past suggested that the odds against his being toppled would be high unless the answer to that second question were "almost none."

The basic presumption escaped scrutiny in part because no one distinguished it from "truths" that gave it force. One such "truth" was that people were and felt oppressed by communism; another was that Cuba should be ours (Teddy Roosevelt had won it at San Juan Hill). Looking back a generation after 1960, young Americans find it hard to grasp how Kennedy, Nixon, and the bulk of their associates could have been so upset by Castro as a Communist and why Kennedy's intelligence agents, in particular, spent time and money during his years in office trying to get the man killed. The vehemence is hard to understand unless one recollects that until 1960 most Americans saw Cuba as a permanent and natural dependency of Washington, almost as much a part of the United

States as the Canal Zone, a cross between contemporary Puerto Rico and Las Vegas with the bonus of Havana cigars (then considered as American as apple pie). Being deprived of all that by a Communist who transfers all to Moscow evidently is what set up perturbations of the sort displayed by JFK and company. It is no wonder. Values were at stake, as well as pride and interest.

The moral is twofold: When you find yourself approving or excluding options on the basis of presumptions (as certainly you will), be sure, first of all, to seize upon the "maybes" that might be turned into *"Knowns"* or at least into *"Unclears"* (thus earmarked for more inquiry) by readily answered questions. If you don't have time for *any* questions-and-answers, you don't. But it wouldn't have cost Kennedy or Bundy many minutes to press such things as: Can they still fade into the Escambray? What would the Guatemalans charge to keep them a while longer? What would Eisenhower say? What do you mean by "fair chance"? And so forth. Secondly, with important "if/thens"—explicit *and* implicit—which depend for verification on the outcomes of decisions not yet made, pause long enough to ask whether the "then" in fact exists: If we go in, are they ready to rise? Who? Where? When? Against what? Illuminating questions are what analysts need most. Decision-makers also need them: Think of JFK, the man who pressed so few. (Think also of his CIA and JCS associates, who evidently never questioned *their* presumption that if all else failed he would sanction American forces.)

The value of such questions can be maximized by making everybody respond, then comparing results. Comparison exposes differences. If differences exist they sharpen every question: They help to set priorities for asking and they help suggest deadlines for answers. "The Castro regime," Fulbright observed to the President, "is a thorn in the flesh, but not a dagger in the heart." Kennedy may not have agreed then. Others surely disagreed. But the causal links implicit in their views were not compared. Had they been, the differences almost surely would have turned on details of Cuban economic and military capabilities, along with levels of prospective Soviet support. A conscious move to that ground would have outflanked Bissell, bringing others into play, because their expertise was now explicitly required, an Amory for instance, or a Helms, perhaps the Soviet specialists at State, even the Cuban specialists, or possibly Secretary of the Treasury Douglas Dillon, who incidentally would have been a tenstrike. Before Kennedy took office,

Dillon had been Eisenhower's Under Secretary of State, and from that vantage point he knew Bissell's plan, about which he was skeptical. He also knew Eisenhower's methods. Kennedy put Dillon at the Treasury but made no use of him on Cuba. Not being asked, Dillon did not offer; his new office bore no relationship to Bissell's further planning. Had Dillon been invited in for any reason, he could have done Kennedy a lot of good. Probing Fulbright's presumption as against those of others on the nature of the Castro threat might have suggested Treasury, where, unbeknownst to Kennedy, that bonus was available.

Or, for another instance, take the matter of Cuban uprisings. The Joint Chiefs of Staff appear to have presumed that those, occurring right away, were the essence of Bissell's invasion plans. He and his associates, by contrast, evidently thought of them as coming a week or more later, *after* the anti-Castro government had been installed on the island. At the State Department and in parts of CIA other than Bissell's, risings of either sort were deemed chimerical. Had Kennedy or some associate but probed the JCS presumption, then insisted on a CIA-wide roundup of opinion, the disparity would have become apparent. Once the causal chain on which the Chiefs relied—even for the "fair chance" assessment—was exposed, Bissell's plans would have gone down the drain with answers to one question, especially had Kennedy pressed it face to face: "What do Amory and Helms think?"

If probing presumptions in two agencies seems too much to expect of a new President, a single question for the JCS alone could have served in this situation as a substitute: "If *you* were doing this instead of CIA, what would you need?" To anyone who can recall supply depots in World War II or the Korean or Vietnam War, it is easy to visualize the answer: Florida might have sunk under the weight of the matériel, to say nothing of air cover. Then how come the CIA proceeded on a relative shoestring? The comparison bristles with insights, which generate deeper questions. A simple question of the right sort—plainly answered, as this could have been—should expose assorted differences that cannot be defended, or even explained, except by surfacing implicit notions of causation. Surfaced, those invite argument, which spurs the search for facts, enlarging *Knowns.*

And an alternative again would have been just to ask: In the past, has "then" actually followed "if"? Dulles and Bissell said so. They cited the easy overthrow in 1954 of a Guatemalan government that flirted with the Russians. In Kennedy's hearing Dulles once said that he felt much more confidence about the operation planned for Cuba than he had ever felt about that for Guatemala.[10] But some pressing of the comparison could have been illuminating, for even a quick check would have uncovered important differences. One was scale: 150 Guatemalans as opposed to 2,000 Cubans and a porous land frontier as opposed to the sea. Second, Guatemala had been partly a U.S. operation, with U.S. pilots flying U.S. planes but using false colors. Third, the President of the United States (then Eisenhower) set less store on avoiding the appearance of overt U.S. involvement. He made it clear to the CIA that no U.S. troops would go in and that, if the rebels lost, he would not rescue them. When the rebels had their bombers shot down, however, he authorized replacing them, even though the State Department warned that "deniability" might thereby be lost.[11] Just a slightly closer look at the historical experience cited by Dulles and Bissell might have armed the laymen with questions to put to the experts. Between "if" and "then," was there hidden a presumption that it was no harder to land a regiment on a beach than to move a company through a forest? Or that Americans in American planes might have to provide the edge for success? Or that, in the worst case, Kennedy's flexibility would be similar to Eisenhower's? The questions deserved asking.

But what helps anyone select and ask the right first question? Of all the questions in the world, how can anyone know and choose a "right" one? To firm up the "maybes" or check out the "if/thens" is valid as an aim, we think, but saying so scarcely offers means. Beliefs can make a "maybe" seem so plainly a near certainty, as faith can make a "then" appear so sure after an "if," that something beyond illustrations framed by hindsight ought to be available for busy men and women to remember and apply. Their time often *is* short, and their distractions are many.

This brings us, finally, to our tests. The need is for tests *prompting* questions, for sharp, straightforward mechanisms the decision-makers and their aides might readily recall and use to dig into their own and each others' presumptions. And they need tests that get at basics somewhat by indirection, not by frontal inquiry: not "What is your inferred causation, General?" Above all not, "What are your values, Mr. Secretary?" Professionally trained Americans are shy about confronting one another, to say nothing of their bosses—or themselves—in such terms on the job. Instead they need associated tests that, like the questions JFK might well have asked but didn't, lead toward arguments or presentations almost bound to bring both causes and values to the surface.

Seeking such tests, we have come up with two. Both are hypothetical. The first amounts to giving odds; the second is an adaptation of "Alexander's question." (Why Alexander? See below.)

First: If someone says "a fair chance" as before the Bay of Pigs (or a "strong possibility" as with swine flu), or more generally, "The Guatemalans won't let us keep our camps there," ask, "If you were a betting man or woman, what odds would you put on that?" If others are present, ask the same of each, and of yourself too. Then probe the *differences:* Why? This is tantamount to seeking and then arguing assumptions underlying different numbers placed on a subjective probability assessment. We know no better way to force clarification of meanings while exposing hidden differences. Judging by our students, millions of Americans are either unfamiliar with numerical notations of probability or are uncomfortable at the idea of stating a subjective judgment in such terms. The doctors of the swine flu case, for instance, recoiled from it, at least outside their own ranks. On odds of a pandemic they refused to give Ford any number beyond "1 to 99 percent."[12] But we have yet to find a fellow citizen unused to placing bets and giving odds on races or at games. So play it as a game and ask for odds on each presumption. If the doctors or their fellow experts hesitate, we offer the suggestion of one academic colleague with extensive government experience: Ask instead, "When I brief the press, with you by my side as an expert, and I tell them the odds are *X,* will I be right? No? Then how about *Y?*" And so forth.

Once differing odds have been quoted, the question "why?" can follow any number of tracks. Argument may pit common sense against common sense or analogy against analogy. What is important is that the expert's basis for linking "if" with "then" gets exposed in the hearing of other experts before the lay official has to say yes or no.

A variant on giving odds is placing bets in the sense of the challenge: "How much of your own money would you wager that the presumed thing actually happens?" Hidden differences are flagged by different sums.

Our second test is "Alexander's question." One of us coined this term for it in another book, and we might as well stick with the label.[13] The Alexander named is not Aristotle's pupil, the great conqueror, but merely the man who asked the question in March 1976 at the Advisory Committee meeting that preceded the decisions to immunize the country against swine flu. Dr. Russell Alexander, a public health professor at the University of Washington, wished to know what fresh data from anywhere, including the Southern Hemisphere, would cause his colleagues to revise or to reverse their judgment that the country should get ready to be immunized *en masse* starting next summer. Mild outbreaks only? None? Time-frames? Locations? He asked but never got an answer. In the circumstances it was the right question, we believe; pursuing it would have flushed out a set of deeper questions, which also did not get asked: questions about tradeoffs between side effects and flu, questions about programming and scheduled review, questions distinguishing severity from spread, questions about stockpiling, and more. In retrospect, they all deserved a thorough airing. This they did not get. Still, the right initial question *was* asked. We draw our term from that.

Adapting but slightly, we put the emphasis on presumptions rather than conclusions, and urge the comparable questions: What new *Knowns* would bring you to change items *Presumed?* When? And why? Passed around the circle, those should sharpen differences, spur debate, and force out inferences, whether of causes or of values. The counterpart question did not do that for Alexander. That is because the director of the Center for Disease Control, chairing the meeting where Alexander asked it, chose not to pursue it. We recommend hot pursuit.

The uses of the second test run as much to future as to present conduct. What "Alexander's question" forces into the light are causal associations thought to be validated by past experience. It is as though someone had said to JFK in 1960, after his election, "list the things which worry you about Bissell's plan and then list all the things which, if they happened in the world or in the planning, would make your worry level rise; then have a watch kept to see if they are occurring. If any do, review."

It is apparent that Kennedy—and Rusk—along with Bundy worried all along about "noise level." Had they asked "Alexander's question" when they first were briefed, they might well have agreed that they associated low "noise level" with (1) minimal press attention and (2) minimal risk that U.S. citizens, especially ones in uniform, would be exposed as directly involved. If asked, they would probably have identified those two as hallmarks of the CIA's past operations. They may or may not have known that the pilots and planes in Guatemala had been American. They did know that there had been no publicity about overt American involvement. Moreover, they knew, as most of the world did not, that the CIA had had a failure in Indonesia in 1958 but had managed a thorough and effective cover-up. But after thinking for just a moment about the experience that allayed their worry, Kennedy and Rusk or the others might have agreed that red lights ought to blink if (1) newspapers got the story or (2) U.S. units began to show up in Bissell's order of battle.

Both happened. In January 1961 *The Nation,* the *New York Times,* the *New York Daily News,* the *Miami Herald,* and *Time* magazine all carried stories on U.S.-backed Cubans training in Guatemala. They even named the site: Retalhuleu airfield. The *Herald* described CIA recruiting among Cubans in Miami, and *Time* for January 27 reported the whole operation to be under a CIA man known as "Mr. B." In January David Kraslow of the *Herald* had known more about it than any member of the new Administration (except perhaps Dillon). A week before the actual invasion Tad Szulc of the *New York Times* was to know almost as much as we know now. Kraslow's full story did not get into print because Bissell got to his editors. Szulc's did not because JFK asked the editors of the *Times* to smother it, and they did. Meanwhile, at least after early March, Bissell called for tactical air support, which meant U.S. planes, no matter how disguised.

Bissell recently has written, wryly:

> With respect to disclaimability it is amazing in hindsight that none of those concerned with planning and decision making ever said "the king has no clothes on" or ever recognized as purely wishful thinking the assumption that official denial of responsibility by Washington would be plausible to anyone, least of all the U.S. press, given the character and scale of the invasion. . . . That this was a major mistake is evident, but it was not a mistake put over on policymakers by operators. Anyone reading the *New York Times* should have known better."[14]

It is our contention that had any of the policy-makers—Rusk, either Bundy, or Kennedy himself—been habituated to asking Alexander's question, they would have been led to set tripwires for themselves against contingencies precisely like the plethora of press accounts.

Had tripwires been set up in advance—which they were not—new, unwanted *Knowns* should have triggered sharp questions. If *Time* knows, doesn't Castro? If air support is needed, has anyone from the Air Staff considered how much, where, and when? In October 1950, during the Korean War, similar advance attention to potentially worrisome *Knowns* might also have produced sharp questions when presumptions of Chinese passivity began not to be borne out by events. The same holds good for Vietnam at any point: We now do such-and-such to make South Vietnamese better off, relative to the Vietcong and North Vietnamese; if they are not—especially if they are worse off—surely some presumptions need review.

So far as we can see, giving odds on presumptions or pushing Alexander's point about what new data might change them are of use not only to prompt questions about options under study but also to test answers obtained. If Bissell acknowledges concern over the "noise level" by offering to cut it with a change of site, the odds of success at the new site become worth soliciting from all concerned, from the JCS no less than the CIA, and the results compared to flush out everybody's fresh presumptions. Those are then worth testing Alexander's way, with "What would change your mind?" One participant in planning for the Bay of Pigs insists to us that questions about consequences of a shift of site were raised at Cabinet level in at least a desultory way. His recollection is the same for prospects of a rising. He cannot claim, however, and the record leaves no hint, that anything but superficial answers were provided—planners' answers, meant to reassure. If so, they were accepted without follow-up or argument. Far from testing answers, that seems the nearest thing to not asking at all.

Regarding questions and answers alike, we urge practitioners never to neglect the tests we here suggest—Alexander's test or giving odds—to use one or the other, preferably both, even if very briefly, before a presumption is let loose among the options.

What of tests for "truths"? They ought to be identified as such, if only because they penetrate the language in which options are described. Once identified, why not question their sources, means, relevance? But calling on American decision-makers to be introspective about ideology would seem like calling for their mass removal and replacement by philosopher kings. We have no such design. Far from it. We relegate that subject, therefore, to the back of the book. There we have a chapter going well beyond proposals for workaday practice. We consider what decision-makers and their analytic aides might do with history in off hours, if they have any, or in off years, of which many have more than they want. Self-conscious and self-critical review of ideology fits nicely.

Meanwhile, returning to the daily grind, we review once again the steps that we recommend become routine. In part we do so to reemphasize how simple they are and how little time they need take. First, sort out the facts: Identify the *Known, Unclear* and *Presumed.* Second, dust away analogies that may cloud vision of exactly what the current situation is and what concerns it gives rise to. Do so by quickly noting *Likenesses* and *Differences* with "now." Third, look back into the issue's history; seeing where concerns came from helps define where to go and also possibly sheds light on options. Fourth, do what you wanted to do first: Identify action options and their pros and cons. Fifth, pause however fleetingly to ask: What are the presumptions behind key pros and cons? How have they held up before? What odds will different people quote, and why? What answers would one get to Alexander's question?

So far so good. Now for two more steps. Sixth, analyze just briefly any relevant stereotypes about people. Seventh, do the same for organizations. To how you take those last two steps—and why—we devote the next four chapters.

9 Placing Strangers

When suggesting how to identify concerns, trace their histories, and test underlying presumptions, we have noted that concerns often differ from person to person. Sometimes the differences seem to be institutional. Even in the urgency and camaraderie of the missile crisis ExComm, Dean Rusk, George Ball, and Robert McNamara all spoke against removing those useless U.S. missiles from Turkey. They were worrying about the reactions of Turks and other NATO colleagues. Theodore Sorensen, Robert Kennedy, and Lyndon Johnson, who spoke in favor of removal, saw the issue more in a domestic context. Rufus Miles's famous law was at work here: "Where you stand depends on where you sit."[1] But sometimes differences seem more personal. Rusk and Ball diverged over Vietnam even though their offices were side by side on the same floor of the same department.

For effective analysis or management, the kind that is not just academically right but gets something done, it is crucial, we think, to anticipate and take into account the different ways in which different actors see the world and their roles in it—not only organizationally but also humanly as individuals. We recognize that such anticipation is mostly a matter of innately sensitive fingertips aided by experience. We recognize also that an effort to make more of it seems, at first glance, to invade the domain of psychologists and psychoanalysts, if not of astrologers and shamans. We have nothing of the sort in mind. But anticipating those differences is too crucial a part of analysis and management to be sidestepped altogether, and we think that some tracking of individuals, some delineation of *their* histories—akin to time-lines for issues—if used very carefully and with awareness of limitations, can yield results useful both for making decisions and for carrying them out.

Just as there is value in taking the history of an issue back to its beginning, so there can be reward from asking about someone else the simplest of all questions: When was he or she born? Where? What happened after that?

Ronald Reagan's admiration for Franklin D. Roosevelt, the President of his young manhood in the Great Depression, became known to the country during Reagan's Presidency and caused surprise. Many commentators suspected him of trickery and only over time came to concede that somehow Reagan meant it. Somehow he believed he was following in Roosevelt's footsteps—not in the letter of policies but in the spirit of innovation. That belief was an important clue to Reagan's behavior. Had it been widely understood before 1981, it might have changed some stereotypes about his probable performance in the White House, where he turned out to be neither sheer reactionary nor mere stage presence.

But before Reagan reached office most of the predicting came, inevitably, from persons who had been too young to see Roosevelt as Reagan evidently saw him or to grasp the difference between FDR seen backward, through the screens of war and of enduring changes from the Second New Deal, and FDR seen forward through the crisis year of 1932, the magic of the "hundred days," and the immense if transient endeavors of the First New Deal, which left their long-term residue in attitudes, not specifics. By 1980 most active journalists and politicians had been children, at the oldest, during the mid-1930s. People under forty, say, in 1980, knew Roosevelt, if at all, only through books, parents, or teachers, in a way that rarely induced consciousness of what a twenty-two-year-old might have *felt* a half century before. For most of them, the "hundred days" enacted social security, cured unemployment, and was followed by Pearl Harbor, whereupon Roosevelt financed the atomic bomb and compromised at Yalta—something like that; we compress only a little.

Yet most prognosticators in our range of observation during

1980 never paused to ask themselves what it might mean to Reagan's outlook on the world and sense of purpose that he had been twenty-two in 1933 and had voted for Roosevelt every time FDR ran. Once asked, the question could not but suggest that—whatever Reagan's substantive objectives, presumed proclivities, areas of ignorance, or operating style—he probably conceived the presidency as a strong, personalized force for change and saw government as capable of bringing about change, even in its own direction (even its own budget!). Those suggestions embody obvious, if superficial, likelihoods.

Such surface likelihoods would have markedly sophisticated the stereotypes of Reagan widely held as election year 1980 started. The obvious suggestions happen to have turned out right; they could, of course, have turned out wrong. In 1980 it was by no means impossible to find men in their seventies whose views about the presidency and government were antithetical to FDR's, despite him or *because* of him. Reagan could have turned out to be one of those, belying surface likelihoods. Still, a stereotype sophisticated in this fashion seems a better guide to observation and prognostication than the frequently held view that Reagan came to the presidency with his mind blank as to what, if anything, Presidents did during working hours.[2]

To take note that someone older or younger may have experienced history differently from you is to begin what we call "placement." A neutral word for a simple concept, "placement" means using historical information to enrich initial stereotypes about another person's outlook—"sophisticating" stereotypes in the sense of adding facets or perspectives or at least shadings to what otherwise are very crude conjectures. Conjecturing about the world view of a stranger with whom one must deal is commonplace in government. Our contention simply is that one improves one's guesses as one "places" her or him against large historical events, the stuff of public history, which *may* mold current views, and also against relatively small details of record in his or her personal history that *might* do much the same. When guessing must be done, we think it ought to be sophisticated in this fashion—another use for history of both sorts, public and personal.

Government officials in this country, not least the in-and-outers lacking long experience, are prone to project upon relative strangers the meanings of things in their own heads, assuming an undifferentiated rationality. Or, at an opposite extreme, officials may take strangers to be what they represent, crudely conceived: "cookie-pushing" diplomat or "military mind" or "narrow specialist" or "mere politician." The American governmental system—in its pluralism both of interests and of institutions, its uncertainty of tenure at the top, and its incentives centered on the private sector—is replete with relative strangers. They tend to view each other in stereotypical ways (and to grow edgy with each other when the expectations founded on such crude conjectures turn out wrong). To effectively convince or oppose one another, which pluralism makes them try repeatedly, they need whatever they can get in terms of more sophistication for their stereotypes. Historical placement helps fill part of the need. Oddly, it seems relatively underutilized, quite unlike analogies.

Taken together, events in the context of details, the public in the context of the personal—Roosevelt's early presidency in the context of Reagan's age—thus offer useful inferences to help refine those inescapable conjectures. That is the promise of placement. Its limitations are twofold, both severe. For one, no inference is a certainty, no guarantees attach. For another, *historical* placement scratches only surfaces compared to psychological assessment, yet we would urge as strongly as we can against either confusing them or practicing the latter without a license. In our view even licensees had best proceed with extreme caution.

Granting those limits, historical placement is worth exploring, and the place to begin is where we are, with the significance of someone else's age. As Reagan's instance indicates, age is the recorded personal detail offering the most straightforward (if not necessarily correct) clue to historical events that may affect the way the other person thinks about the world—provided the observer knows something of the events, as such, or can find out, as with the "hundred days" of 1933. Yet the effects of age are scarcely uniform and sometimes matter less by far than Reagan's case suggests. In June 1950, when Truman flew to Washington with his mind full of the "lessons of the Thirties," as Chapter Three records, some version of those lessons was familiar to all his associates and also to most adult members of the public of whatever age. That helps explain why he encountered little opposition when he changed American policy and threw troops into South Korea. For everybody over twenty-one or thereabouts in 1950, the shocking, great surprise that lent the North Korean challenge its significance had come nine years before, at Pearl Harbor. In

1941 Truman himself had been fifty-seven, not twenty-two, with some isolationist votes in the Senate to embarrass him, but what he then learned shaped his subsequent thinking at least as much as observation of FDR shaped Reagan's—perhaps more—and also that of most of Truman's countrymen. The lesson may not have made literal sense, but its emotional force was enormous: British appeasement of Germans brought Japanese bombs down on *us.*

Such uniformity of sentiment is rarely associated with a public event. Even wars and recessions usually induce divergent lessons. Pearl Harbor was exceptional. More usual is a spread of sentiments, different and sometimes mutually exclusive, as now with the Vietnam War or as twenty years ago with the Korean War, then our most recent conflict.[3] We touched earlier on how LBJ's advisers used the Korean analogy when debating what to do in Vietnam. The policy-makers and observers who cited the precedent agreed, for the most part, on one thing (unfortunately for Lyndon Johnson), namely that in June 1950 Truman had shown admirable courage. But what that signified for 1965—about kinds of American actions, for how long, on what terms, for what reasons—was disputed, with the Korean analogy advanced on every hand.

Which "lessons" of Korea were advanced by whom was partly a factor of age, especially of age when Korea occurred as opposed to twelve years later. Age "then" and job "now" seem tightly linked in that dispute and in most other instances of which we are aware. It is as though Reagan's Roosevelt-mania as a young man was validated, sharpened—also perhaps refurbished—by his incumbency at 1600 Pennsylvania Avenue. Presumably it was. Miles's law about standing and sitting was at work here too, but with the corollary that where LBJ's advisers stood in 1965 depended in part on where they had sat *before.* And some Vietnam disputants who invoked Korea might suggest another corollary: Where they sat depended on where they had *stood* before.

Consider the divergent uses of Korea in relation to their users during 1964 and 1965. General Maxwell Taylor, Chairman of the Joint Chiefs of Staff and later Ambassador to Saigon, was until almost the last a faithful member of the "Never Again Club" (referring to American ground warfare on the Asian mainland). During his late forties he had served in the Korean War as deputy commander of ground forces. General William Westmoreland, by contrast, commander of our forces in Vietnam, roughly the age of Taylor fifteen years before, had fought well as a junior officer through the Korean War, and, taking Vietnam for the counterpart in his career, he willingly prepared to test his mettle as a senior there. Dean Rusk, the Secretary of State in 1965, had been Assistant Secretary for the Far East in 1950 and, like most colleagues, had underestimated the Chinese. That mistake he did not make again. Throughout the 1960s he overestimated them: In counsels on Vietnam he stressed at once their menace as expansionists and the risk that they might do what they had done before, attack.

Rusk's Under Secretary George Ball did not contest the point—which weakened his own argument—but rather focused on the lack of viability for South Vietnam *contrasted* with Korea, including politics, armed forces, climate, terrain, tactics, international support, and the disastrous legacy of French colonialism. Ball had a feel for that: a long relationship with Jean Monnet had brought Ball's Washington law firm as a client the precursor of the European Economic Community, and his work for it made him "European" in his sympathies and an observer of the French political scene. During the Korean War Ball had combined those interests with a role in Adlai Stevenson's first nomination for the Presidency. Keeping his candidate *distinct* from Truman must have been a large part of Ball's concerns in 1951 and 1952. As for the Secretary of Defense, Robert McNamara, his concern then had been with climbing the corporate ladder at the Ford Motor Company. In 1965 he took Rusk's lead on China—knowing nothing about it first-hand—and took upon himself the duty to find military means of sparing LBJ the "loss" of South Vietnam, the more so since he had encouraged John F. Kennedy's involvement there and felt responsible for Johnson's plight.

None of those principal advisers showed much concern for Truman's plight twelve years before as it had manifested itself politically in costs to his domestic program and to his party's hold on office when he put both to the test of a protracted limited war. None of those costs had been paid by those advisers out of their own pockets. The Fair Deal meant little or nothing to them personally. Thus men in Johnson's inner circle seldom cited, perhaps seldom considered, the downside of Korea seen in partisan and programmatic terms. They seem not to have regarded as suggestive for Vietnam the change of aims that protracted the Korean war—the enlargement of objectives from repelling aggression to reunifying the country (which soon had to be scaled back). Judged from the written record of their dealings with each other, they were concerned lest sending troops across the 17th parallel bring in the Chinese but relatively unconcerned lest crossing that boundary by air, meanwhile breaching in South Vietnam the distinction between advice and combat, might have effects on public psychology at home analogous to those produced a decade and a half earlier by crossing the 38th parallel on foot. Or, if they saw that particular analogy, they did not pursue it in writing.

How participants in the debates of 1965 cited Korea—if they did so at all—varied with their own experience of it. For McNamara, seemingly, it might as well not have occurred. For McNamara's closest personal adviser, John McNaughton from the Harvard Law School, it was only distantly relevant; he took a cool, ironic view of Johnson's options quite befitting someone who had been no nearer to Truman's than a young man's stint in Paris with the Economic Cooperation Administration, followed by editorship of his family's Midwestern (Republican) newspaper. Johnson's national security aide, McGeorge Bundy, while occasionally less cool, seems not to have concerned himself with the domestic program and party risks in drawn-out, limited war, although he was unsparing in his concern about the risks of Saigon's fall. But Truman's fall had not affected Bundy. From the distance of Harvard, he had supported Eisenhower.

Along with a few others, Bundy's brother William had a rather different story. Himself a onetime object of attack from Senator Joseph McCarthy, William Bundy as Assistant Secretary for the Far East in the mid-1960s—Rusk's old job—showed continuing, pained awareness of at least one home front consequence in dragging out Korea: the demands to go "all out," to "win," because it was a "war" with casualties—and conscripts. The record suggests William Bundy dragged his feet against the steps that could convert Vietnam into a counterpart.

The two men who recalled firsthand, with interest and regret, the fate of Truman's domestic ventures happened also to be the two who went farthest in warning LBJ that Vietnam could be a quagmire. One was the new Vice President, Hubert Humphrey, fresh to the Senate in the early 1950s and as staunch a supporter then of the Fair Deal as he would be of the evolving Great Society. The other was Clark Clifford, Truman's Special Counsel and in large measure his strategist during the first term, including the election. Clifford had resigned in February 1950 to embark upon a vastly successful law practice and to consult successively with Eisenhower, Kennedy, and Johnson. His consultations were bipartisan, as was his practice, but his sympathies were Democratic, while politics and policy were for him inseparable. Regretting Truman's troubles, he saw Johnson's looming up and tried to warn him off involvement on the scale of "war." Failing that, he counseled winning it (until he replaced McNamara in 1967 and looked firsthand at feasibility; thereafter he became again an advocate of finding a way out).

That LBJ was not himself a source—or not apparently—of recollections quite like those haunting Humphrey or Clifford calls for comment. He had been, like Humphrey, a freshman Democratic Senator in Truman's second term. Johnson had been, even then, a mover and shaker in the party. But he had not been much of a Fair Dealer. "Landslide Lyndon," elected to the Senate in 1948 by eighty-seven votes, was not then the designer of the Great Society. His immediate concern was to hold some margin of support among Texas Democrats, who in 1952 and 1956 were to throw the state to the Republican, Eisenhower. To that end LBJ deliberately distanced himself from Truman. His other main political concern was to gain power within the Senate. (Doing so would increase his electability, and vice versa.) There, Truman's misfortunes worked to Johnson's advantage, for Fair Dealers who lost their seats vacated steps on the stairs to seniority. Without Korea and its ill effects for Harry Truman, LBJ could not have become Minority Leader in 1953 and thus the formidable Majority Leader of the later 1950s. Given that experience, Johnson could look back on the Korean precedent as coolly as the Harvard Bundy.[4]

All this seems clear in retrospect. As of 1964 or 1965, could one have guessed some of it? We think so. It was obvious that some people thought Korea relevant, at least for advocacy, and equally obvious that they saw different lessons in it. It would not have been far-fetched to surmise that those differences might be related to differences in their own experience of that war. In all cases lessons, if any, would have been found to be, if not made predictable by that experience, at least more understandable in light of it. To have been right about LBJ would, however, have required knowledge of him beyond that in his *Congressional Directory* or *Who's Who* sketches. Someone not aware of the Texas background or of the differences between his career in the Senate and Humphrey's could easily have guessed that his lessons, Humphrey's, and Clifford's would be the same. The example warns against putting too much confidence in using "placement" to predict. It also flags the usefulness of putting details in their settings.

Would anyone involved in the 1965 debates have been helped by placing others as to age and previous employment? We think they would, but we hasten to underscore the qualifications. Even someone knowing a great deal about all the participants could have gone wrong if trying to predict present outlook on the basis of past experience. Regarding Vietnam, some Eisenhower Republicans were early "doves"; some Fair Deal Democrats were persistent "hawks." Senators Margaret Chase Smith and Henry M. Jackson, respectively, are examples. In some cases, knowledge of experience might have helped prediction—but only helped; it might have changed odds from 6 to 5 to 7 to 5. Chiefly, placement would have provided hypotheses about how other people *might* view the new set of issues, what they might see as important or unimportant, and therefore what lines of analysis or argument might appeal to them or repel them. Like every other procedure we recommend in this book, placement's uses are diagnostic. It cannot itself work a cure.

So far as we can tell, American officials seldom consciously practice placement. Since the American government is so much a government of, by, and for lawyers, that is a little surprising, for trial lawyers regularly engage in something like "placement" when selecting juries. They start with stereotypes and then sophisticate them by asking questions. (Farmers have it in for insurance companies; is this farmer an exception? And so on.) Trial lawyers then frame arguments with jurors' backgrounds in mind. Why the practice is seldom carried over into government we do not understand, unless perhaps in our allegedly "classless" society the line of questioning seems somehow "un-American." Whatever the case, the comparison with jury selection may help to illuminate both the limitations of placement and its promise. Without guaranteeing a thing, it can contribute to getting a fuller and fairer hearing for a wider range of arguments.

Along with age and work, other details of personal history, perhaps equally well recorded and accessible, affect the ways in which assorted individuals perceive and use big historical events—the "public" history that "everybody knows." Obvious examples include parents, siblings, schooling, geography, and ethnicity. Less obvious, because less well recorded, are mentors, models, and heroes influencing adult life. There are, of course, varieties of other things more personal and private still, shading into psychiatric realms, which, if recorded, are in usual terms not publicly accessible or, even if accessible, fall beyond the bounds of usable, hence useful, history for us. Would it have helped anyone dealing with FDR to have known at the time about his affair with Lucy Mercer and its consequences for his marriage? We doubt it. The "personal history" we have in mind is more that to be found in a reunion handbook than in *True Confessions,* but it still provides plenty of things to use.

In understanding those Vietnam decisions, for example, it helps to know the bits of personal history already noted: William Bundy's brush with Senator McCarthy, McGeorge Bundy's initial Republicanism, Clifford's political activism, Johnson's eighty-seven votes. It helps a little more to know that William's father-in-law was Dean Acheson, and that his father's hero (and his brother's) had been Henry L. Stimson—the Stimson who embodied an ideal of public service and of honor in that service taught at Groton, where both Bundys went to school. Similarly, it helps to understand Ball's Stevenson connection, more importantly his French connection and general European orientation. The one made him useless to Johnson had the latter wished to reverse *Kennedy's* course; the others made him suspect in debates on Asia, not least when he cited French precedents (the French had neither built the Panama Canal nor held off Hitler). With McNamara it appears worth knowing that he made his way at Ford and built his reputation there from a base in statistical control. With Rusk it helps to know that after solid Army service in World War II he was all set to join the regulars when General George C. Marshall summoned him to a civilian job at State, and that Marshall was his ideal and model. And so forth. Each piece of information from the rest of personal history enriches or enlivens guesses drawn from conjunctions of age and job.

Accordingly, if someone wishes to sophisticate his stereotypes of others who can help or hurt whatever he espouses, it makes sense to look for data of two sorts on each. First is the public history, the big events, through which each has lived since gaining bare political consciousness. We suggest drawing a time-line and for safety's sake starting it early, with the lives of parents, plotting events that may have been heard about as well as those presumably read about in the newspapers or viewed on television or actually witnessed firsthand. If the subject is known as a serious student of history, steeped in some period or other, push the line back there as well. Experience can be vicarious. Second is the personal history, the personal matters of record that mount up to location, family, education, career, and the like. To assure that the public history is in the context of the personal and to facilitate comparisons, set those matters forth on the same time-line. For simplicity's sake, the first sort of data can be labeled "events," the second "details"; these are offered as neutral designations, easy to remember and otherwise without significance.

The next step is to mine those events and details for inferences of relevance about the other person, inferences, that is to say, about the other's outlook on the world, the job, the issue, or the like: his or her premises, prejudices, blind spots, commitments, suggested in a strong way by public and personal histories taken together. We urge practitioners never to neglect these three: events, details, and inferences. We also urge all comers to beware of linking up their inferences, one with another, in a causal way. That is all too likely just to build a different stereotype, not a more sophisticated one. Also, it leads in the wrong direction, toward conclusions in place of questions, toward supposing that Lyndon Johnson, *macho* Texan, must behave in such and such a way instead of a working hypothesis, to be discarded if it doesn't test out, that "Alamo" and "San Jacinto" might be words with more significance for him than for the Bundys or for Ball.

Such is placement—as simple as that. Recently we asked a group of temporary students, most of them experienced in government, to consult overnight such reference works as they found readily available, including *Who's Who,* and give us the "details" appropriate to three prominent LBJ advisers: Clifford, Rusk, and McGeorge Bundy. In class the next day we proffered a simple time-line along with historical events for the three, and our students produced their details. Eliminating duplications, the results were as shown in Table 9–1. We then asked for inferences about each man that reasonably could be drawn from stated events and details com-

TABLE 9–1 Three White Professional Men

"Events" Public History (general knowledge)		*"Details" Private History (of record)*		
Date	Event	C	R	B
1908	Taft elected	*Clifford b.* St. Louis	*Rusk b.* Rural Georgia	
1917–18	WWI (US)	well-off	hard-up	*McG. Bundy b.* Boston Brahmin
1919–21	Big Red scare			
1929	Crash	LLB Washington Univ., St. Louis		
1931	Manchuria		Rhodes Scholar Oxford	
1933	New Deal			Groton
1935	Oxford oath Neutrality Acts			
1936–39	Spain	Law practice St. Louis (litigator)	Prof., Mills College	Yale
1938	Munich			
1939	Nazi war			(father joins Stimson, 1940)
1940	Fall of France	Navy	Army Stilwell Burma Pentagon	Harvard Jr. Fellow Army (liaison Navy)
1941–45	WW II (US)	Naval Aide		
1947	Truman Doctrine	HST counsel (1946–50)	State (follows Marshall)	
1948	Marshall Plan			Marshall Plan
	Berlin airlift	Fair Deal proposals	Asst. Sec. UN	Stimson memoir
	Truman election	HST speeches	Asst. Sec. FE	Dewey speeches
1949	NATO			
1950–53	Korean War	law practice Washington		Harvard prof.
	McCarthy			Dean
1953	Eisenhower		Pres., Rockefeller Fnd.	

TABLE 9–1 (cont.)

"Events" Public History (general knowledge)		*"Details"* Private History (of record)		
Date	Event	C	R	B
1960	JFK	Symington 1960 helps JFK	Scarsdale "Everybody's 2d choice"	JFK asst.
1963	LBJ	Helps LBJ	Sec. State 1961–69	LBJ asst. Pres., Ford Fnd.
1965–73	Vietnam War (US)	Sec. Def. (1967–69) Almost State (HHH)		
1969	Nixon		Prof., Univ. Georgia	
1977	Carter	Washington "elder"		Prof., NYU
1981	Reagan			

bined. The answers offered, shorn of a few oddities, amounted to the following:

"Inferences" (within reason)		
Clifford	Rusk	Bundy
confident	conventional	bright
smart	dutiful	confident
savvy	loyal	fast feet
smooth	brainy	golden spoon
daring	nominal Democrat	Groton-honor
actively political	bipartisan estab.	Stimson-honor
Democrat	essentially diplomat	essentially nonpolitical
strategic		
no wrong steps		

For starters, overnight, with only obvious references, this strikes us as a strong result, because for anyone who sought to influence those three at the same time, these lists could have offered some actual guidance as to how (and how not) assistance from each man might best be sought in 1964, say, or in 1965. To be sure, some of those answering had read more references than *Who's Who* or may have had access by telephone to richer sources. But in real life, one or the other or both those conditions would be likely to apply still more than in a classroom. As compared with persons detailed to a university, officials on the ground are better equipped to obtain more information on each other at short notice than that provided by snippets from *Who's Who.* They can ask each other, reporters, or friends or can cultivate the Great Man's secretary, and so forth. Thus we take these products to suggest how useful placement can be and how easily applied.

Consider, as a thought experiment, the advocacy problem facing George Ball when he wrote Rusk, Bundy, and McNamara—not Clifford—in October 1964 urging that they turn their minds to ways of backing out of the American involvement up to then with South Vietnam.[5] Ball addressed his colleagues confidentially, in terms befitting their official duties, not their memories or their styles, appealing more to logic than to world views, offering the outline of a lawyer's brief and asking them to help him fill it in. While the logic was strong, the conclusions were sketchy, and implementation prospects were not weighed, much less set forth. Avowedly, Ball sought to start a conversation, not to offer a plan. Considering his addressees, that may only have weakened his case. At any rate, they gave him no recorded response, although Bundy recalls telling him that Johnson simply would not think about such things until after election.[6] Three months later, through another source, LBJ got hold of that October effort, but by then its tentativeness could have been a crucial flaw, together with its author's personal liabilities in Johnsonian terms. The President thereafter dealt with Ball as his official "devil's advocate," which granted him a hearing at the cost of weight.

Years later Ball's October memorandum would be published and hailed as prescient, and would grow famous as a warning. It certainly was that. But as a piece of advocacy it was almost doomed to fail. The inferences our students draw suggest some of the reasons why.

Ball's problem was a hard one on at least four scores. For one, to question the ability of the United States to succeed militarily was at once to challenge McNamara's capacities, Rusk's confidence, Bundy's honor, and Johnson's pride. For another, to accept the China menace on Rusk's terms was to conjure up domino theories at the Pentagon. For a third, to keep within the bounds of "foreign policy," befitting his subordinate position, as Ball did, ignoring the 1964 election contest with its presidential statements on the stump ("let Asian boys fight Asians" and the like) was at once to downgrade the importance of those pledges—a commonplace within the foreign policy establishment—and refrain from pressing somebody like Clifford, in whose province such things naturally fell. Finally, Ball had to keep his case on this issue distinct from, unimpaired by, workaday hostility he himself might arouse while doing other business with his colleagues and the President.

Those are four hard conditions, and the last may have been hardest of all. From October to December 1964 Ball was engaged with McNamara, Rusk, and Bundy in preparing for negotiations with the British and the Germans on the so-called Multilateral Force (MLF), a naval nuclear arrangement, which that winter Johnson "sank." Ball, its chief advocate, pushed so hard, with so selective a report of European views, that Bundy was aggrieved and the President offended. Besides, they were reminded of Ball's European focus and French sympathies. At almost this same moment LBJ began his postelection study of the issues on Vietnam.[7]

That raises a further aspect of placement. In addition to providing clues about the views of others, it can offer clues about their likely views of you. This, indeed, could well be its most valuable service. In advocacy some awareness of the audience reaction to the advocate himself, his outlook by light of theirs, becomes a boon. Without it disasters can happen.

Long familiarity produces many clues in both directions. Ball and his official colleagues had spent four years in one another's company. He had an opportunity to learn behaviorally, through give-and-take, precisely what associations he evoked inside the heads of others at the table and why, without rummaging into their personal histories or drawing insights from them. He might thus have been as well equipped in this regard as placement could have made him. Fragmentary signs suggest that he was not, but never mind. We do not know. Regardless, for a generation subcabinet officials of his sort have had an average tenure of but twenty months.[8] Disastrous lacks of insight into one's own situation vis-à-vis associates seem all the likelier among such relative strangers. Behavioral acquaintance cannot substitute reliably for placement. Whether or not it did so in Ball's case, his instance seems exceptional in terms of opportunity.

To show the full potential for misunderstanding between

strangers, we must use another case. For the sake of variety, as well as intrinsic interest, we turn from foreign to domestic spheres and also from men to women—to Frances Perkins, arriving in 1933 as FDR's Secretary of Labor (and the nation's first woman cabinet member), confronting a holdover appointee, Mary Anderson, director of the Women's Bureau in the Labor Department. Anderson, thirteen years earlier, had become one of the first women to head a bureau. They were notable people, both of them strong-minded, and their confrontation is a classic.[9]

A protégée of Alfred E. Smith, Roosevelt's predecessor in Albany, Perkins had earlier worked there as what we now would call a "public interest lobbyist," campaigning with the legislature for improved conditions of industrial employment. Occupational health and safety, maximum hours, minimum wages, and the like, achieved through regulation, were her means to make life better in the workplace for both men and women. Child labor she strove to abolish. Her still earlier start in social work had stemmed, as with many in her generation, from religiously based *noblesse oblige.* In that she embodied the Progressive Era: substantial middle class by origin—a Worcester, Massachusetts, WASP—inspired by Florence Kelley and Jane Addams, serious in her Episcopalianism, intent on doing good for those less fortunate, thrilled by Theodore Roosevelt, professionally educated with an MA from Columbia, outraged by the human costs of recent industrialization, determined to use government to ease or reverse its excesses through regulation. Her work with Al Smith had freed her from the usual Progressive prejudices against party politics as an available stepping stone. That was a formidable combination for her time. She made it more so, in her own view, when she deliberately dressed in such a way as to remind men of their mothers, while performing on the job—at least with people she did not know well—as quietly and tersely as men tended to think one should behave.[10] Perkins had been called upon from time to time to mediate labor disputes and knew the labor movement as a sometime ally in her causes. But she was so little of it that William Green, the president of the American Federation of Labor (a confederacy of crafts; there was then no Congress of Industrial Organizations), opposed her appointment as Secretary of Labor.

The contrast with Anderson's career was marked. An immigrant from Sweden to the Midwest in her teens, with neither family support nor education, Anderson had worked as a domestic servant until she gained enough experience (and English) to become a factory worker in Chicago's boot and shoe trade. That was a center for the infant AFL, and she became a dedicated unionist, loyal to the Federation. She was so loyal she even scabbed for it when Massachusetts locals went on wildcat strikes in violation of their contracts, supporting workers from the Knights of Labor, an older rival organization in decline. For the aspiring AFL, upholding contracts was an article of faith. Anderson moved east and helped to break the strikes. She took it as a duty. Returning to Chicago, she put in years of hard work for her union and as organizer for the Women's Trade Union League.

Under pressure to give women workers some representation, AFL President Samuel Gompers gave Anderson various assignments. During World War I he helped make her a women's representative in Woodrow Wilson's agencies for economic management. Working as hard as ever, she eventually became head of the wartime Women-in-Industry Service at the Department of Labor. She also played advisory roles on the American delegations to the Paris Peace Conference and to the International Labor Organization at Geneva. In the immediate aftermath of women's suffrage—which she always had supported and whose leaders were friends—the Women's Bureau was established as a statutory agency, continuing the wartime Service; Anderson was named its first director. Throughout the three Republican regimes that followed Wilson's, she established and stabilized her bureau, husbanding congressional and interest group relations while surviving successive economy drives. She focused on research as against lobbying, limiting her studies to objective questions about women and their work in the contemporary labor force. The Secretaries of Labor under whom she served were relatively indifferent or incompetent or both. Still, the bureau survived, which for her was the main thing, and presently the Democrats returned with FDR, a fellow Washingtonian from wartime. Anderson was thrilled, especially by the appointment of a woman Secretary. "We were all just jubilant," she wrote, "because we thought that at last we would have someone who really understood our problems and would fight for us. . . . I felt I had a friend to whom I could go freely and confidently."[11] She could not have been more wrong.

Perkins, who was new to Washington, had known the Department of Labor only by reputation—unfavorable in her circles—and through sparring publicly with Hoover's Labor Secretary about unemployment figures. (Hers had proved better than his). The Department, then as now, was one of the smallest in the government. It then contained a Solicitor's Office and six principal divisions: the Immigration and Naturalization Service (later moved to Justice), the Employment Service (soon to be expanded), the Conciliation Service, the Bureau of Labor Statistics, the Children's Bureau, and the Women's Bureau. The last three were all engaged primarily in research; from the outset that seemed anomalous to Perkins. The Labor Statistics bureau had great potential; the Children's Bureau was the only Federal presence in a cause left all too pressing by the failure of the states to pass a constitutional amendment outlawing child labor. Also, some of the Children's Bureau's research on working conditions for mothers already overlapped that of the Women's Bureau. Besides, the Secretary evidently had her personal doubts about Anderson as co-worker or colleague. To unfavorable images of perpetual "woman's rep," Republican holdover, AFL careerist, underqualified researchist, Perkins perhaps added another, redolent of class in her era. As one of her then advisers reminisced to us, "Mary Anderson could have been your maid."

At any rate, within weeks of her swearing-in Perkins proposed to Anderson that the Women's Bureau be eliminated and its funds transferred to the Secretary for reallocation elsewhere. That ignored laws on the books, as Perkins's counsel told her, and could not in fact be done administratively; even so, the proposition shocked and infuriated Anderson.

Anderson responded by memorandum. Even after fifty years some of the anger comes through:

Memorandum to the Secretary of Labor

> Following our conversation this morning I have been thinking very seriously of the plans you outlined and I am sending you this memorandum because I am afraid I shall be so occupied with my trip to Geneva that I will not have time to discuss other matters with you.
>
> I am afraid that any action you might take to change the status of the Women's Bureau at this time would subject the Department of Labor to a tremendous amount of criticism from women throughout the country—the times are so critical that I feel we should do everything possible to prevent criticism and consequent loss of confidence in the Department and I am wondering if we can not accomplish

what you desire by some other method while still preserving the identity of the Women's Bureau.

The chief objection to the proposed merging of the Women's Bureau with other activities of the Department seems to me to be that in doing so the law establishing the Women's Bureau will be abolished and while under your administration this fact would not affect the work it might materially alter the situation under future Secretaries of Labor, who may not be interested in the problems of women's employment. If such should be the case and the needs of women should in future years be ignored, the only redress would be to have another law passed, recreating the Women's Bureau and this would involve much time and effort.

It seems to me we should preserve the identity and position of the Women's Bureau at all costs, but to carry out your program we could change its duties, delegate its staff to different divisions of work in the Department and allocate their salaries to this work, in this way meeting the ends of your program and at the same time protecting future policies of the Department.

I am afraid any other course of action would call forth a storm of protest from the organizations that were responsible for the enactment of the legislation creating the Women's Bureau and have given it their ardent support in the 15 years of its existence, and of course we want to avoid this if possible.

Mary Anderson, Director

A case can be made that this was an effective memorandum. In 1933 it could have hurt Perkins to be attacked by women's organizations. Choosing not to run the risk, she left the Women's Bureau intact. It still exists, and Anderson remained its director until her retirement. For purposes of advocacy designed to persuade and to lay a basis for future collaboration, on the other hand, Anderson's approach seems appalling. Her stereotype of Perkins had been sorely disappointed, and she reacted accordingly. There is no suggestion that she tried to grasp and use whatever aspects of the Secretary's past experience might have strengthened her case. Indeed, from that standpoint her threat to use the women's lobby was a sure way to poison their future relationship. Moreover, there is no suggestion that Anderson tried to fathom—and turn to her own account—how she in her career appeared from Perkins's perspective. Had she done so, she might well have invoked mutual friends, of whom they had a few, and mutual interests beyond women's work to try to enrich Perkins's presumable view of her.[12]

So far as we can find, Anderson made no attempt at either of those things. Instead she clung to a stereotype of Perkins as a woman—and one concerned about working conditions to boot—until the latter's unlooked-for threat to her Bureau. Then Anderson reacted in shock with her counterthreat. Though her Bureau survived, she found Perkins not only remote but also unsympathetic—not the experience of others, as for instance Katherine Lenroot, the Children's Bureau chief. And the Women's Bureau was the only part of the Department to receive no budget increase during Perkins's early years as Secretary.

Perhaps that was inevitable. It speaks to the Progressive Era that two prominent women with such overlapping interests could have had such different careers and such fundamentally divergent attitudes, stemming in large part from class position. In that era a Mary Anderson could reach the top of the Federal bureaucracy without being translated by schooling from the working class into the professional middle class. Nowadays such wide gaps in perspective are unlikely, whatever the class origins of the individuals: Higher education is their common lot. Given the divergences between Perkins and Anderson, it could have been predicted that they would have difficulty working with each other (unless some odd personal affinity evolved, which did not happen). Perkins may have foreseen that; at least she came to see it right away. Anderson did not. Our argument is that some exercise of "placement" could have given her warning. If deftly used, it might even have produced a happier result from her standpoint.

We sometimes ask experienced practitioners what they think Anderson might have discovered about Perkins and about the latter's likely view of her had she known and applied placement as we describe it here. On a time-line reaching back into the era of Perkins's parents, our practitioners, standing in for Anderson, plot public events of likely concern to Perkins. On the basis of what Anderson could readily have learned from mutual friends, there then come added personal details of record for Perkins. Our Anderson-substitutes cap the effort with an equivalent time-line for her, tracing events and details of her own life as they might be perceived by Perkins if informed by the same mutual friends. (We offer brief biographies of Anderson and Perkins in lieu of the actual friends). Typically, the response is as indicated in Table 9–2.

TABLE 9–2 Two Women in Public Service

Time-line	*Events*	*Details*	
Years		Anderson	Perkins
1861–65	U.S. Civil War		
1865–77	Reconstruction		
1873–77	Depression Labor unrest	b. Sweden (poverty)	
1878–93	Knights of Labor		b. Boston, to Worcester (upper-mid-class)
1881	Garfield, Arthur Recession Haymarket massacre AFL founded		
		Leaves school Emigrates	
1890	Anti-Trust Act Homestead massacre		
1893–97	Depression Pullman Strike Populists Hull House	Unemployed Schwab's (Chi.)	
1898	Spanish War	Joins BWSU Hull House	Mt. Holyoke College
1901–09	TR, Reformism	Scabs in Lynn	
1905–14	Immigration peaks	Joins WTUC	Hull House, Chi. Commons Episcopal church
1906	Food & Drug Act	Union Label Chi. Fed. Labor	Phil. Research Assn. Socialist Party (brief)
1907	Financial panic	AFL Label League	Univ. Penn., Columbia MA
1910–12	Taft–TR split	Hart, Schaff. strike	Sec. NYC Consumer League Lobbyist, meets Al Smith
1911	Triangle fire 1st AWDC law	Arbitration, WTUC	Witnessed fire!!
1912	Progressives W. Wilson		Sec. Triangle Fire Comiss., meets Robert Wagner
1913–14	Income Tax FTC, Fed.	Organizer WTUC US Citizen Suffrage campaign	Marries P. Wilson one daughter
1914	U.S. in Mexico World War I		

Table 9–2 (cont.)

Time-line	*Events*	*Details*	
Years		Anderson	Perkins
1915	Boom Lusitania		
1916	Child Labor Law (unconst. 1918)		
1917	U.S. in War Women war work Russ. Revolution Prohibition	Nat. Defense Council (women-in-indust.)	Directs Women's City Club
1918–19	Sedition Act Armistice League fight Big Red scare	Women's Div. Army Women's Service, Labor Labor Com. Versailles Int'l Conf Women Head, Women's Serv.	Founds maternity center Husband's breakdown (permanent) Smith Gov. N.Y. Memb. State Indust. Comm. Joins Dem. Party
1920	Women vote	Serv. becomes Bureau	
1921	Recession Open shop drive Immigration curb		
1923	Harding to Coolidge Teapot Dome		
1924–28	Boom (not farm)		FDR Gov. NY
1929	Great Crash		Chair, Indust. Comm. (runs State Labor Dept.)

We then ask our captive practitioners for the inferences they, as Anderson, might draw from these data about Perkins. The usual response includes:

- WASP/upper-middle class/snob?
- Privately religious, upper class church
- Political lobbyist: worldly
- Professional education matters
- Make it as a man
- Help the less fortunate (both sexes, all ages)

- Regulation more than unionization
- Especially safety

Asked to imagine, as Anderson, the stereotypes about herself likely to be in Perkins's head, they produce such terms as:

- Working class
- Immigrant/uneducated
- Union loyalist
- "Token woman"
- "Bureaucrat"
- "Hack"

Armed with these, we ask what they, as Anderson, in prudence, should expect from her new boss and how if at all she could improve her image in Perkins's eyes. Overwhelmingly our practitioner-students argue that the exercise in placement forecasts trouble and that Anderson was woefully naive to stereotype Perkins as a woman. When it comes to what a more sophisticated Anderson might then have done (other than what she did) our students divide sharply. Some argue that she should have moved, well before Inauguration Day, through friends as well as briefings, to stress the Women's Bureau's professionalism—playing down women, playing up research—in relation to working conditions, especially issues of safety. Others argue that she could not realistically have hoped to alter the incoming Secretary's likely view of her and therefore should have coolly planned to take the stand she ultimately did, sparing herself surprise, yielding Perkins neither time nor scope to toy with abolition of the Bureau. Either way, the worth of placement for the person doing it, in terms of useful inferences about how others view her, comes clear in the process of pondering Anderson's plight.

For professional men of more recent time, especially within the foreign policy establishment—a Ball or a Rusk, for instance—placing one another would have been a simpler task than that for Anderson and Perkins in their era. Even with today's widespread professional education, placement of one woman by another may be complicated by questions as to the role of sex in self-identification.

Additional questions arise in placement across sex lines, women of men and vice versa. Which crossing is harder, we do not profess to know. In placing a contemporary professional woman, one has to put among events in "public" history the Supreme Court's 1973 decision on terms for lawful abortion and the losing struggle to enact an Equal Rights Amendment. The person being placed may have paid no more attention to either than did McNamara to the fate of the Fair Deal. Even so, the lack of attention could well seem significant. For a professional man, on the other hand, neither *Roe* v. *Wade* nor the ERA would figure unless it showed up among details of record, as for instance employment, in "personal" history. For most, a nonentry would be clearly indicative of nothing but nonengagement. Our practitioner-students, female and male, argue among themselves as to just how much—even whether—difference of sex is an impediment to placement. Our only sure conclusion is that it is not a factor safely ignored. We say the same of other factors still more complicated, as when placement has to cross lines of race, or race and class combined—a nightmare as compared even with sex and class combined—or lines of nationality or ideology, or those combined, sometimes another nightmare.

10 Placing Across Barriers

Sophisticating one's stereotype by "placing" someone else against historical events and personal experience is uncertain work. Events are all too easily misread. Personal records are prey to gaps, mistakes, and misunderstandings. Inferences are but hypotheses, not even easily substantiated, let alone "proved." Further complications arise when placement is attempted across lines of race, class, or country. Yet the harder placement seems, the more it may be needed. The cruder the stereotype, the higher the returns for sophisticating it. This chapter therefore sketches complicated instances. Forewarned, we hope, is forearmed. We put race first.

The most prominent black American of modern times was Martin Luther King. He was in the public eye at the same time as Ball and Rusk and, roughly speaking, was of a comparable class, the professional middle class, into which he had been born (more so than Rusk). At first glance only color and particular profession—along with commonplace varieties of schooling and geography—distinguish King from such as they. Placement should have been a snap. Yet for white contemporaries in domestic spheres of government it evidently was not easy. In the last years of his life, when his *Who's Who* entry was longer than Rusk's, King's reach for

Northern issues and his opposition to the Vietnam War confounded even Lyndon Johnson. Although LBJ probably practiced his own complex form of placement in his sleep, cared about civil rights, and knew King, he was shocked when King moved past what Johnson thought the proper bounds of civil rights. Angrily, LBJ charged King's change to human weakness, selfish politicking, or deficient patriotism. King's motives may have been mixed, but surely were more complex than LBJ allowed. Despite his special sensitivity to things and people Southern, the President seemed to think of King as essentially white, not black, or "black" in some stereotype that left out the man's sense of race and mission.

A look at King's biography suggests why LBJ judged wrongly. On the surface it is both accessible and conventional in white perspective. Born in 1929, King grew up at the apex of Atlanta's black middle class, the son and grandson of prominent ministers whose congregations rendered them depression-proof and freed them from direct dependence upon whites at least for livelihood. King had gone to college and to Boston University for his Ph.D. He then joined the ministry himself. Returning South to a church in Montgomery, Alabama, he was almost at once thrust into public leadership of the Montgomery bus boycott—the city's blacks refusing *en masse* to ride at all if forced to ride in the back. When the boycott succeeded, King was on his way, his vehicle the Southern Christian Leadership Conference, which he founded, his tactic Ghandian nonviolence, which he studied in India. There followed, among other things, anti–Jim Crow demonstrations in Birmingham, white violence, jail for King, and three thousand Federal troops sent in by the Kennedys. Then came Selma: King leading the marchers, 25,000 strong, more redneck violence, and commitment by Johnson, the civil rights demonstrators' anthem becoming presidential peroration, "We shall overcome." All that culminated in the Civil Rights Act of 1964 and the Voting Rights Act of 1965. In 1963 King had spoken unforgettably to marchers assembled in Washington. In 1964 he won the Nobel Prize for Peace. Then came Northern ghetto riots in 1965 and 1966, accompaniments perhaps of rising expectations. Other leaders called for different tactics. In Vietnam, U.S. casualties were rising too, many of them blacks. King began the efforts that so vexed Johnson. Then assassination cut King off in 1968.[1]

There, in short summary, is King's personal history, an outline of recorded details to provide a context for the general public history affecting him—the big events, according to our formula for placement. In terms befitting any middle-class professional, he was too young for the Depression, not old enough to fight in World War II—although of an age to feel the patriotic surge and see the fruits of full employment—then a witness in his teens to the arrival of the Cold War, in his early twenties to Korea and McCarthyism, and thereafter a participant increasingly in what became known as the "second reconstruction" of the South. Eisenhower, Kennedy, and Johnson take their turns, and the events both foreign and domestic now associated with their White House years.

Suitably fleshed out, those big events combined with King's own history offer wherewithal for inferences. Those in turn provide clues to outlook, to point of view, clues of the sort that LBJ was a master in detecting. But our summary of events here leaves out many things, especially from King's earlier years, that must have seemed to him and to his parents "big" indeed, the essence of recent history—for middle-class professionals *who happened to be black.* And if these are not listed among relevant events, their consequences for the character of personal experience, the quality of "details," as we call them, are all too easily missed. Misleading inferences can follow. Whether that or something more occult created Johnson's problem we do not profess to know. We see it as a danger, though, in anybody's placement across lines of race.

Consider what was missing from our list: the Ku Klux Klan revival which peaked shortly before King's birth; the lynchings which continued in appalling numbers through the 1930s; *de jure* segregation, which remained complete as King grew up; the successive waves of mass migration North, encouraged or impelled by mechanization on the land; the wartime struggle of A. Philip Randolph and others in black labor unions for at least a start on equal employment opportunity; the segregated Army and its slow desegregation, initiated only under Truman; the Civil Rights Commission and its notable report in 1948, followed by years of unsuccessful struggle for congressional implementation. Before the mid-1950s, when King was in his thirties, things like that remained the stuff of specialties, not "history" as generally recalled by whites or widely taught in schools. They were what we now call black history and were then taught mainly in the ancient way, by word of mouth.

Since the 1950s many things of great concern to blacks have seemed to enter general history, among them supreme court decisions, civil rights endeavors, legislative victories, and urban riots.

For a time at least, white history and black converged. But depending on a person's age, however weightily credentialed and however firmly rooted in the upper middle class, if he or she is black the chances are that on his mind or hers lurk certain big events not shared as such by whites, not anyway by most whites. We denote general history by the convenient term "events." So long as the convergence is not total—and alas, it may have stalled—in a disproportionately white society black history becomes "special events." The same applies of course to other races, to sexes other than one's own, to immigrants of every sort, and also to strangers abroad. How do you learn the "other" history? Find somebody to ask!

But suppose the person one would place is both black and by origin a member of the underclass. Here is a harder problem. We caught a glimpse of class differences in Perkins versus Anderson. But they were the same color, and Anderson started in the Swedish working class, suffused with the Protestant ethic, which was Perkins's as well. The complication we would now address runs deeper.

Take the instance of Malcolm X, the Black Muslim nationalist, who was assassinated three years before King, just as they began to jostle each other for the leadership of Northern ghetto blacks. Malcolm X left behind him on the verge of publication an extraordinary autobiography, co-authored with Alex Haley. From it and other sources we have drawn a case study for our practitioner-students.[2] Almost regardless of their age, experience, or race, it stuns them. It should. And those who, having read it, go to the Haley book for more detail are stunned again. They should be. For the net effect is to expose the insufficiency of public history, together with the unavailability of private records, in placing persons with a history of Malcolm X's sort. The big events known to the middle classes do not reach the bottom in their original guise, not as such, not directly, and personal histories, when and if recorded by obscure officials, are locally filed. Whether or not the *Autobiography of Malcolm X* is accurate in all particulars, it seems to put those points beyond dispute.

Malcolm X, four years older than King, was born in 1925. He spent his childhood in Ohio and Michigan, experiencing shades of poverty from poor to poorest. His father, a black nationalist, was murdered by whites; his mother was hounded by welfare officials; a teacher tried to socialize him to inferiority. Rebelling, he ran east to Boston and New York, where he became first a hustler and then an armed robber. At twenty-four he had been caught, convicted, and put away. Jail brought him closer to the mainstream of society. He read voraciously, completed his own education, and became a Black Muslim, a disciplined disciple of Elijah Muhammed. When Malcolm X came out of jail, he went to work for Elijah, became his best organizer and right-hand man, eventually was scandalized by aspects of his leader's life, and broke away to found his own movement in Harlem. He spoke in terms that frightened whites, and he scorned blacks like King. Both tactics brought Malcolm X to national press attention. He also traveled in the Middle East and studied there, encountered his religion closer to its origins, evolved his own position, and returned home to be murdered on Elijah's behalf if not on his orders.

All but the last of this is set forth eloquently in the *Autobiography.* How otherwise could it have become known, especially the earlier part, the hustling in Boston and the misery in Michigan? Police records, welfare files, and school reports tell something. But who finds them and puts them together? Assuredly not *Who's Who.* Moreover, it is plain that until he became politically aware in prison, Malcolm X was conscious of the big events in his time, whether white or black, at one remove, through surrogates, not directly. The Great Depression manifested itself to him through Michigan's welfare system. World War II came to him as employment opportunities, crowded trains, and free-spending enlisted men to serve or fleece in Harlem. We urge practitioners in class to think about those surrogates, contemplating what it means for someone's view and style to take in the impinging world in such a way. Thereby we conceivably induce a certain empathy. We do not—since we cannot—offer better means of getting at the history in such a person's head until well after he begins to read. Then one can ask what books. Books, a different sort of surrogate, are more accessible to the observer.

Sophisticating stereotypes by use of public history and private records runs afoul of the extremes in differences of race or class, especially taken together. Class, as Malcolm X's example shows, seems the more serious obstacle. But we voice this caution without discouragement. Short of the extremes, we think events and details on a time-line are relatively easy to employ. Of course the clues they offer when combined—the things we label inferences—are easily read wrong. Indeed, they rarely can be read wholly right since they exclude the personal psychologies of subject and observer. Here is another caution, but again we are not discouraged.

For it is of the essence to our argument that something is better than nothing. The one thing worse than a sophisticated stereotype is an unsophisticated one. In government and out, the advocate who seeks to be effective with associates, or the analyst who tries to think ahead about the doing, should be wary of all stereotypes yet cannot help but use them. And the ones refined by thought about the interaction of historical events and personal experience hold fewer dangers, we believe, than those not so refined.

This is no less the case when placement has to cross national boundaries, but somewhat special problems then come to the surface. From government to government one usually is dealing with career officials or experienced politicians. Class differences recede. Still, someone from another country ordinarily has little American history in his head, and even that is possibly peculiar to *his* vantage point. Few Americans would include among the principal events of the 1970s Nixon's decision to abandon fixed-price purchases of gold. Few Japanese would leave it out. It was the first great *choku.* Moreover, foreign heads are mostly full of foreign things: events in their "public" histories about which most Americans have weak impressions (or none at all), with echoes in personal experience that few Americans can have heard. To a West German, for instance, price fluctuations are likely to be much bigger public events than citizens of the United States conceive—even after the late 1970s—for the borrowed word *Inflation* brings to a German mind folk memories of the early 1920s, when the mark–dollar ratio plunged in a matter of months from five to 100 million to one.

That Americans who deal with foreigners should "place" them in *their* histories ought to be obvious; one might think therefore that the practice was common. So far as we can tell, it is not. Officials about to negotiate or travel may get canned biographies, some with details like those in doctors' files, and oral briefings that include characterizations. But efforts to match personal records with relevant public events, drawing out hypotheses about how others see the world and why, seem rare. We think the management of international relations might become marginally better if such efforts were part of standard staff routines. Yet even—or especially—in dealings with our close allies that sort of empathetic effort seems remote from usual practice.

For illustration, Jimmy Carter's Administration again offers a made-to-order example. From start to finish, Carter had trouble with his close ally the Federal Republic of Germany. It began with a spat over German nuclear fuel sales to Brazil. Then came the neutron bomb affair. Initially Carter insisted that NATO equip itself with those new and more lethal "tactical" nuclear weapons. *After* German Chancellor Helmut Schmidt spent political capital getting agreement in Bonn, Carter announced out of the blue that he had changed his mind. There followed a speech by Schmidt suggesting that Europeans faced a Soviet nuclear threat they might have to meet on their own. Rushing to knit NATO back together, Washington improvised proposals for new European-based U.S. missiles. That created a whole new set of issues in American–European relations, U.S. defense policy, and SALT (or START, as Reagan would relabel it). Some of the trouble might have been avoided entirely—and all of it ameliorated—if either Carter or Schmidt had bothered to "place" the other and act accordingly.

Schmidt was only half a dozen years older than Carter (and looked younger), but his political experience was incomparably wider. One of the ex-soldiers who made German Social-Democracy pragmatic, nondoctrinaire, and able later to win support outside the working class, Schmidt had been a prominent figure in Germany since the early 1950s. His career had had ups and downs almost as sharp as Richard Nixon's. Schmidt's near oblivion had come in the late 1950s, a result of excessive passion in the losing cause of opposition to NATO nuclear weapons on German soil. He had recanted, had become a pragmatist in that sphere too, had written books which gave him high rank among "defense intellectuals," and had held the Defense and Finance Ministries before becoming Chancellor. Carter and his staff should have been reminded of all that, and of the fact that during the Ford Administration Schmidt had had large influence in Washington (or thought he had: Henry Kissinger was adept at "placing" Germans of Schmidt's sort, more so than at "placing" U.S. Senators). Schmidt told people at home, for example, that his advice had prompted Ford to bail New York City out of bankruptcy in 1975.[3]

The events surrounding those details were the major change points in the history of the German Federal Republic. First came the regime's creation, then the recovery of the 1950s. Spurred by the "economic miracle" of the 1960s, the Christian Democrats gave way to a "grand coalition" followed by an all-Socialist government. The shift was accompanied by a retreat from insistence on reunification, regularization of relations with the Soviet bloc, and (with help from General de Gaulle) the transformation of NATO, at least in German eyes, into an American–West German axis. In 1974 Schmidt replaced Willy Brandt as Chancellor; coincidentally worldwide economic turmoil, produced by OPEC and soaring oil prices, had political effects on Germans. Those were sharpened by fear of *Inflation,* worry that the "miracle" was over, and violence from young leftists all too reminiscent of Brown Shirts. Now, in 1977, there was uncertainty. The last notation on a time-line—both "event" and "detail"—would have been for late 1976, when the Bundestag gave Schmidt another term as Chancellor, but by a margin of seven votes.

From those events, along with the details already noted, it should not have been hard to infer that Schmidt attached value to his reputation for influence in Washington and wanted evidence that, under Carter, it would continue. The appearance of being able to affect U.S. economic policy probably had most utility to him at home, but special sensitivity attached to nuclear matters and to NATO because of Schmidt's past record and expertise. And "appearance" should have seemed the key word. As a veteran politician, Schmidt could be expected to recognize that an American President might follow advice other than his own. Such facts of life would be understood in Bonn. The question there would be: Could some other German do better with Carter? Schmidt would like the answer to be "absolutely not!" He would settle for just "no."

If Carter felt that he might someday want Schmidt to do something for him—or not do something *to* him—those inferences, it seems to us, should have suggested that the President acknowledge the Chancellor's superior experience, listen to him with an air of respect, and, before doing something that might cause Schmidt grief, give him reasons, with a tone of equal speaking to equal, allowing him time to make preparations in Bonn. Good staff work, we think, should have yielded such advice.

The actual tactics of Carter (encouraged, we gather, by his staff) were exactly the opposite. At their first meeting Carter talked to Schmidt about his own hopes and plans. When Schmidt started to offer advice, Carter tried to cut him off. To Brzezinski the President said afterward that he found Schmidt "obnoxious." Though Brzezinski quotes from his diary a passage showing that he advised Carter to remember Schmidt's delicate position at home, the Assistant for National Security Affairs gave no more evidence than the President of noting relevant events and details and inferring anything about Schmidt's *amour-propre.* Brzezinski addressed the Chancellor as "Helmut" and, when the latter protested, rejoined amusedly that, after all, Schmidt called him "Zbig."[4]

But the failure in placement was mutual. Schmidt seems to have taken no notice of events and details offering him possibly useful inferences about Carter. Just a little reflection might have opened Schmidt's mind to the unpleasing truth that the new President probably knew little more about him than that he was a Socialist head of government with a frail majority, and possibly nothing about his country except that it used to be Nazi, now wasn't, but sold Americans too many cars. Schmidt might have expected to meet, as in fact he did, arrogance so innocent as not to recognize that *his* arrogance had some foundation. That Brzezinski was unlikely to orient Carter otherwise, Schmidt might have inferred from the barest glance at details. What was a Catholic Pole, son of a prewar diplomatist—married to the niece of Czech President Beneš, victimized by Munich—likely to think or say about a German socialist born in the lower middle class and once a member of the Hitler Youth?

With a little simple question-asking, Schmidt might have seen Carter's details against the special events of Southern, even Georgian, history—the odd mixture of Old South legend, populism, fundamentalism, New South commercialism, memories of Jim Crow *and* Selma—which made Carter not comparable to Martin Luther King but perhaps more understandable in comparison with King than with Gerald Ford or Henry Kissinger. Schmidt might then have *assumed* that he would be greeted with a sermon and that a great deal of courteous ritual would have to precede any getting down to business. One veteran of the Carter Administration, also long acquainted with Schmidt, feels sure in retrospect that, with only a little imaginative effort, Schmidt could have made Carter a dogged friend and ally. We are inclined to agree. With a good deal less brainpower than Schmidt but, partly for that reason, more experience in the exercise of personal charm, British Prime Minister James Callaghan managed to use Carter occasionally as the equivalent of an extra Labour Party whip.

The Carter–Schmidt example is too stark to stand alone. Few people will believe that they themselves could act like either of them. Moreover, some associates of both men argue that the placement they forebore to do of one another had in fact been done at lower levels and that only their imperviousness to coaching from below kept them insensitive about each other. Precisely this imperviousness, others say, is so characteristic of Carter that he could have heeded our advice no better than that of Vance's underlings, and never would he have practiced placement on his own, least of all in the instance of Schmidt. So the example, seemingly, is not for every day and not, perhaps, for most administrations. We therefore offer another example, this one featuring the characters from one of our success stories, the Cuban missile crisis, acting *after* that success. The occasion was their conflict with the British over Skybolt late in 1962.[5] We touched on that affair in Chapter Six, suggesting that more awareness of issue history might have served as a preventive. More attention to personal history, we think, could have done the same. The relevant history was that of the British Prime Minister. We turn to its utility after a bit of background.

"Skybolt" was the name for a projected early-generation missile designed to be launched from an airplane. Americans had set out to develop the weapon for "defense suppression," a mission requiring high accuracy, whereby some first-wave aircraft could fire at and hit Soviet air defense weapons so that the big bombers could get through to Soviet industrial targets. The British had decided to buy some of the missiles, load them on their aging V-Bombers, and proclaim the combination their strategic nuclear deterrent, capable of hitting somewhere in or near Soviet cities. Accuracy was not a big consideration for the British; economy was. They came to this solution after abandoning on grounds of cost their program for ground-to-ground missiles of their own. Skybolt would be cheap, because it could be bought off the tail of American production.

In 1960 the Prime Minister, Harold Macmillan, had sought assurances from President Eisenhower that the British could buy the needed Skybolt missiles (assuming the Americans found production technically feasible). At the same time—and at some internal political cost—albeit *not* as an explicit *quid pro quo,* Macmillan guaranteed to Eisenhower the Scottish naval base *he* needed for American nuclear submaries, then in development. Scarcely more than two years later Eisenhower's successor, Kennedy, sanctioned the proposal of Defense Secretary Robert McNamara to cancel Skybolt, which was turning out expensive and inaccurate. They agreed that London must be given timely warning, even before they themselves had formally completed budgeting procedures incident to their decision. McNamara undertook to give that warning (which could not yet be entirely definite), expecting that his opposite number, Peter Thorneycroft, the British Defence Minister, would figure out and tell him what the Government in London wanted next from Washington. Thorneycroft understood the warning but assumed that Washington, before finally acting, would have goodwill and sense enough to make London a generous offer, compensating for the trouble, in the spirit of the "deal" that had produced that Scottish base.

Meanwhile, since the *status quo* quite suited the PM and had, indeed, been of his own contriving, he did nothing. Thorneycroft prudently followed suit: His military services were no less wedded to the *status quo* than was Macmillan.

In that lay the misunderstanding: For five weeks the Americans waited to be asked while the British awaited an offer. During the interval McNamara was instructed, at the instance of a State Department faction, not to let the British have the one thing he had heard a hint that Thorneycroft would want, namely a straight swap of submarine-launched missiles (Polaris, then) for Skybolt. McNamara privately thought Polaris the right answer but found it convenient not to quarrel with State's officialdom himself until (and unless) the British forced his hand. Presently he went to London to negotiate with Thorneycroft. A week before he got there, Skybolt cancellation, having cleared budget procedures, leaked into the press. Thorneycroft was tranquil, expecting to be offered Polaris; when the offer did not come, he was angered, smelled betrayal, and went on the attack. Thereupon McNamara hinted at pledging Polaris not to Britain but to NATO. As we previously noted, he mistakenly conceived of this as a straight swap. To Thorneycroft the NATO tie was unacceptable. There had been no strings on Skybolt; to attach them to its substitute was betrayal indeed. He redoubled his attack. Crisis followed.

Two weeks later, to restore relations, Kennedy conceded Polaris to Macmillan in a form and fashion France then used as an excuse to veto British entry into Europe's Common Market, a policy objective dearer to both their hearts, now to be put off for half a generation. And Polaris—to say nothing of Poseidon or Trident, more expensive missiles following on—cost Britain far more money than the Navy or the Treasury or social service ministers, or the PM himself, had ever wished to pay for his deterrent. Kennedy had not wished that for him either.

Had McNamara understood that London would *not* ask and that instead *he* had to *offer* in a show of generosity, he probably could have done so. He and his colleagues, Kennedy included, were disposed toward generosity throughout. Indeed, they could conceivably have done so in a fashion that, while indisputably generous, disposed London toward abandoning its nuclear deterrent, or at least delaying the decision, which is what State's people hankered for. When Kennedy turned his mind to the affair, under the spur of crisis, he produced a politician's proposal: Compensate London with an offer to pay half the remaining development cost of Skybolt exclusively for British use. By the time he put that to Macmillan the latter would have none of it. The day before, the President had spoken to the press of the weapon's shortcomings. "The lady," said Macmillan, "has been violated in public."[6] But the fifty–fifty offer, being eminently "fair," hence generous, might have given the Prime Minister his *status quo,* had it been put to him in private some weeks earlier, before publicity or presidential sneers. It then would have had the added feature, admirable from a State Department view, of adding substantially to British costs. As things then stood, Macmillan's Cabinet colleagues might have balked at that, preferring social services. If so he would have lost both *status quo* and deterrent, but with no blame attached to Washington and no excuse handed to Paris.

Any number of approaches could have freed Kennedy and his associates from the convenient but wrong presumption that a warning would make London bestir itself, decide what else it wanted, and then ask for it. In terms we have used thus far, they might have thought about what was *Known, Unclear,* and *Presumed,* or might have reviewed the history of the issue by light of their concern for British acquiescence, or might have set tests for some of their presumptions. As we suggest later, they might have thought about the history of those British institutions, notably the Cabinet, they supposed they could activate with an indefinite warning. But, failing all else, we think Kennedy and his colleagues could have gotten a better feel for London's likely stance had they but paused to place his opposite number, the Prime Minister.

A bit of thought about the events and details of Macmillan's life could have suggested that McNamara's warning was likely to fail of its intended effect.[7] Upper middle class with some aristocratic connections and comforted through life by revenues from Macmillan publications, Harold Macmillan went the regular route of able men so circumstanced: Eton, Balliol, and, when 1914 came, an officer's commission in the Guards. During World War I he served for four years on the Western Front, survived the decimation of his classmates, friends, and cohort, and returned to civilian life forever conscious of his isolation as remnant of a golden generation, if not age. (Given Macmillan's years and easily caricatured style—grouse shooting in plus-fours, for example—Kennedy had been surprised at how well and quickly the two of them hit it off. But the horror of the war had lent the older man a skepticism about human and political pretensions, about the claims of military planners, and about the uses of armed conflict that the junior officer from World War II, himself by temperament a skeptic, found congenial.)

After the war Macmillan went to Parliament, sitting almost uninterruptedly for more than forty years on the Conservative side of the House of Commons. The Depression of the 1930s reinforced in him two strands of traditional Tory thought: *noblesse oblige* and social consciousness. He became a leader of what was sometimes tagged Tory democracy, an intellectual champion of no-nonsense do-goodism (not unlike Kennedy's own, another bond). In the late 1930s Macmillan's criticism of appeasement put him at odds with his party's then leadership. The second German war changed the fashion and his status. The turning point came in May 1940, as the Nazis marched west, when Neville Chamberlain, the Prime Minister associated with Munich, *won* a vote of confidence from Commons but with forty *abstentions* on his own side. That so compromised Chamberlain's standing in the party, press, and country that he felt he had to step down as Prime Minister. Macmillan never forgot either the event or the lesson: that leaders cannot outlast massive, publicized backbench dissent. Never mind nominal majorities, count the abstentions!

After 1940 Macmillan had risen in his party because colleagues and constituents had four perceptions of him, all of which he fostered. First, he displayed Disraelian readiness to sponsor social welfare programs if but persuaded that they could be made to work. Second, Macmillan stood in foreign affairs for a combination of assertiveness and realism. In 1956 he initially backed Anthony Eden over Suez and then succeeded him, yet afterward Macmillan stressed that Britain must accept a world role different from that of the prewar years. He talked of "winds of change" in the former colonial world and after 1960 hastened British withdrawal from Africa. In 1961 he decided to take Britain into Europe, joining the Common Market, then presumed to be a revolutionary step.

In the third place, Macmillan repaired and championed the "special relationship" with the United States, making much of "interdependence"; this he always coupled with "independence" symbolized by nuclear weapons. (He assiduously clung to membership in the exclusive "club" of nuclear powers.) His restoration of American relations, while simultaneously asserting independence, contributed to a substantial Tory victory at the general election of 1959. Tory budgeting, which held down defense expenditure while boosting social services, also contributed—hence Skybolt.

Fourth and last, Macmillan seemed Prime Minister-in-charge to what was then a notable degree—Margaret Thatcher being unimagined. Though a kindly Edwardian uncle in his television personality and cautious in his chairmanship of the Cabinet (he let Common Market entry drag on for two years), Macmillan sternly used appointive power to police performance and appearances in Tory leadership. Thorneycroft had been one victim, sent into limbo for three years and only let back into the Cabinet in July 1962.

To Kennedy and his associates—a group with many, varied English contacts—there should have popped up from events and details on Macmillan's time-line a whole array of inferences suggesting that he would be wedded personally to the weapon and would be the last in London to bestir himself about replacing it unless he absolutely had to (which no one short of Kennedy could make him feel he must). Besides, by the same logic, he then would feel entitled to receive from the Americans—who still enjoyed their Scottish base—the nearest equivalent *they* could contrive, the initiative (and spare resources) being theirs, not his. An indefinite warning from a second-level source was likelier than not to put him into a defensive crouch, as in fact it did. For Skybolt was his means (literally his, chosen in 1960) to square nuclear status with Tory democracy and to strengthen transatlantic ties while awaiting fruition of "Europe"—all at the lowest cost in sight and long since approved by the Cabinet. From Macmillan's perspective, Skybolt might well square all sorts of circles *better* than any substitute at higher cost, even Polaris. (He could have had the latter for the asking two years earlier, and hadn't asked). Others, like McNamara—or Thorneycroft—who thought it mattered that Polaris was a better *weapon,* were bound to reason differently, of course. But the survivor of World War I, who governed a small island under constant Soviet threat, might not take the particulars of nuclear weapons seriously *except* in symbolic terms, where one served as well as another, the cheapest best.

In the event, of course, Macmillan did switch from supporting Skybolt to insisting on Polaris, which he wrangled as a virtually straight swap at Nassau.[8] But it is worth noting that he never took the issue to his Cabinet and never sought support there from the Treasury or social services for that expensive substitute, until the President's own public deprecation of Skybolt forced his hand—and only did so then, by cable from afar, when he could add that time was of the essence because Kennedy was waiting. The Cabinet got the issue only then, and with a twenty-four hour deadline for reply. That will suggest how loath Macmillan must have been to risk Cabinet support for Britain's nuclear deterrent by discussing it at length when he had nothing but a warning that entailed prospective costs nobody wanted, himself included. If that seems unpresidential, it is well to note that Macmillan was *not* President, and the Cabinet was "the Government."[9]

Having said that any of our mini-methods, applied in time, might have helped avert the Skybolt crisis, we have to acknowledge that the same result could also have come from fingertip-feel for Macmillan's situation, coupled with some empathy for him as a politician. Once the crisis had began, Kennedy en route to Nassau, spurred by the deadline, informed himself on Macmillan's political plight and saw all this and more. As with FDR and social security, we expect some readers to accuse us of calling less for use of history than for exercise of good political judgment. We repeat our earlier pleading. Good political judgment rests, we suspect, on historical understanding, even if that understanding is largely intuitive or unconscious. For those not Roosevelts, not even Reagans, conscious and regular resort to history may whet political judgment. If it does not, probably nothing can. Or so we believe. For more, see our final chapter.

11 Noticing Patterns

Placing people has a use that until now we have not stressed: helping to think through objectives. Most of our illustrations of placement have emphasized its potential usefulness for advocacy: for George Ball to persuade others about Vietnam, for Mary Anderson more effectively to champion the Women's Bureau, for Schmidt to propitiate Carter or vice versa. Concerning Martin Luther King and Malcolm X, we spoke chiefly of improved understanding for the sake of insight and effective interchange, a matter again of persuasion. In connection with Skybolt, however, we suggested that early reflection on events and details for Macmillan might have had some value to JFK *et al.* when they discussed their own desired outcomes. Let us underline the point.

Events, routinely reviewed in context of the details of an individual's life, with sensitivity, as needed, to sex, race, nationality, and indeed to ideology, can offer decision-makers aid in thinking about what to do as well as how to do it. Treating those two subjects—what to do and how to do it—as separable seems to us an almost certain route to going wrong. Analysis and implementation, "policy" and "management," are inextricably interlaced. Thinking about what one can get other people to see as in their interest is part and parcel of thinking through what can be done and what ought to be done.

To illustrate as pointedly as possible, we return to the Carter Administration and to the might-have-been example cited to illustrate possible uses of issue history—the comprehensive SALT proposal carried to Moscow in March 1977 by Secretary of State Cyrus Vance. Timely exercises in placement, we think, might have improved the Administration's judgments not only about how to put its case but about what case to put and where, when, and to whom.

Could placement have made up the lack? We think so. We think Carter and his aides might have improved their judgment about what to do if they had thought intently, even if not long, about events and details for three key actors outside their own circle: Soviet leader Brezhnev, Ambassador Anatoly Dobrynin, and Senator "Scoop" Jackson.

Brzezinski easily, Carter and the others with a little tutoring and a little effort, might have been able to imagine the large events—the public history—possibly entering the heads of Brezhnev and Dobrynin as they thought about strategic nuclear weapons and arms control. Stalin surely dominated that history, long dead though he had been. While Brezhnev and his colleagues had collaborated in Stalin's purges and climbed professionally over the bodies of the victims, they probably remembered best their own terror of being next.[1] Still, they had to look back on Stalin's era as a golden age in which Russia at last became a modern industrial nation, beat the Germans (almost singlehandedly, as they saw it), built its own *cordon sanitaire* in Eastern Europe, and gained recognition as a nuclear superpower. Nothing since had matched that period of accomplishment: certainly not Khrushchev's regime of clumsy domestic amelioration and clumsier foreign adventurism, and not Brezhnev's own time, marked as it had been by whining complaints against the domestic bureaucracy's noncooperativeness. Brezhnev's achievements had been to hold the empire together and to protect Russia's status as a military superpower. Given Russia's history and his, how could anyone suppose that Brezhnev would want his last days or years as General Secretary to be remembered as the moment when the Soviet Union came down from its pinnacle of military might? The Vladivostok accord could be rationalized as evidence of America's crying "uncle!" But cuts? *Deep* cuts?

Dobrynin, the second key actor, was the Soviet Ambassador in Washington. For nearly fifteen years he had been the primary communication link with Moscow and also a figure in capital society ranking practically with Alice Roosevelt Longworth, the surviving daughter of TR. The large events on Dobrynin's time-line would have come from American as well as Russian history. He had been on the Washington end of those early SALT negotiations—closer to them than Vance. During the Nixon–Ford years Dobrynin had cultivated Kissinger and vice versa. SALT I and the rest of detente were as much his as anyone's. Of course, he did what Moscow ordered, and it was reasonable to suppose that he protected himself against a sudden shift in Moscow's climate by never becoming identifiably the sponsor of a particular policy line. But even a glance at events and details in Dobrynin's life should surely have suggested that his career was built on accurate knowledge about the American government and corresponding ability to explain its often odd behavior, sometimes even to predict it.

Thought about Brezhnev should have reinforced—or offered another way of arriving at—a conclusion that the Russians would probably not be receptive to a U.S. proposal involving force reductions, deep or even modest. A little effort at empathy with Dobrynin might have raised a question as to how the Russians would greet *any* U.S. proposal other than one to ratify Vladivostok exactly as amended by Kissinger in 1976. With Dobrynin kept in the dark (or at least told no more than the *New York Times* was told), how could Moscow judge the significance of even minor wording changes?

For Vance and his aides, such thought about the two Russians could have prompted more resistance to the President's deep cuts formula and more argument for early and candid communication through Dobrynin. Deep cuts seemed sure to be a loser at that stage in Brezhnev's career, whenever or however brought forward, but even an inherently workable proposal was likely to run into trouble if sprung on the Russians without ample warning conveyed through familiar channels.

For Carter and his White House aides, independent thought about Brezhnev and Dobrynin, perhaps encouraged by protests from State, should, we think, have suggested questions reaching farther: Why must we seek an agreement as early as March? Why must it be done in Moscow? Why must it be done at all on *our* initiative?

Questions somewhat similar could also have emerged from a

serious effort to place Senator Jackson. In the actual thinking of Carter and probably others, Jackson cut a large figure. He was the first person to whom the President confided the instructions he was giving Vance. Though in their memoirs neither Carter nor Brzezinski even mentions Jackson in connection with the President's decision, Vance writes (accurately, we think) that hope of winning Jackson's support—together with fear engendered by Jackson's roundup of forty votes against confirming Paul Warnke as chief SALT negotiator—was a key factor in the President's mind, second only, perhaps, to his own personal feelings about nuclear weapons.[2]

One likely reason for the reticence of Carter and Brzezinski is the fact that their hope proved to have been misplaced. We think a review of events and details for Scoop would have warned them of that. It would not have required deep research. Any number of people near Carter could have met the request: "Tell me Scoop's history."[3]

A dozen years older than Carter, Jackson had been in college when the Great Depression hit the State of Washington. Maturing in the 1930s, absorbing its "lessons," he had come to the capital in 1941 as a freshman member of the House. The previous spring Hitler had overrun his parents' homeland, Norway. In the 1970s that memory stayed with him. Asked on "Meet the Press" if he was not "obsessed" with national security, Jackson replied:

> Yes, I am concerned about the security of my country. I think it is priority number one. My parents, you know, came from Norway. They were immigrants. There was a country that thought they could be neutral. They had a thousand years of freedom. They had clean air, clean water, clean land. They had a fine system of social justice. What good did it do them when the Nazi hobnail boot took over?[4]

Though hesitantly, given the strong isolationism of his district, he supported Lend-Lease and other interventionist measures. He felt that Pearl Harbor proved him to have been right.

After World War II Jackson made his first trip to Norway. He saw Red Army guards herding released POWs for involuntary and unwanted return to the Soviet Union. The sight helped make him an early, vocal Cold Warrior. After assignment to the Joint Committee on Atomic Energy, he championed the hydrogen bomb and more and better "tactical" nuclear weapons. Time and again he warned that the Russians were probably building strategic forces faster than most people supposed. When Jackson took those positions, they were not plainly popular. Even within the Democratic party he stood against the wind. Truman, after all, swung over to supporting high defense spending only after the Korean War began. Jackson saw himself as having been part of a courageous minority eventually proved right.

In the 1950s, after moving to the Senate, Jackson helped bring down Joe McCarthy. Right again! Then he fought Eisenhower's effort to cut defense spending. Scoop called early for a crash program to develop long-range missiles. Against the Navy establishment as well as against the Republican Administration, he backed Admiral Rickover and the nuclear submarine. Again the same pattern: in the minority but eventually vindicated—by Sputnik and the threatened "missile gap" and by Polaris.

When Kennedy ran for President in 1960, Jackson, a Senate friend, nearly became the vice presidential candidate. He served instead as chairman of the Democratic National Committee and prepared himself to be a close adviser of the new Administration. But JFK ignored him, McNamara snubbed him, and with dignity Jackson turned back into the Senate.

By every sign, Jackson saw his career after 1960 in exactly the same terms as before. On domestic issues he remained an unreconstructed Fair Dealer, supportive of liberal programs as then defined, and consistently so, whether Kennedy zigged or LBJ zagged or Republicans opposed. On foreign policy issues he remained consistently anti-Soviet and was to be the nemesis of Nixon's detente policy, sabotaging its centerpiece, a reciprocal trade agreement. On defense issues Jackson remained with equal consistency committed to the Truman–Acheson philosophy adopted after the Korean outbreak: "Positions of strength" were keys to peace. Jackson had thought Adlai Stevenson wrong to advocate halting nuclear weapons tests. Sudden large-scale resumption of testing by the Soviets occurred just as Scoop had warned it would. When Kennedy in 1963 then negotiated the Limited Test Ban Treaty, Jackson voted for it but made no secret of his skepticism.

In 1969 Jackson fought successfully to get funds for the ABM, the antiballistic-missile weapons system, only to have Kissinger and Nixon, three years later, give away ABM development as part of SALT I. Jackson had no doubt whatever that they had made a big mistake and that future events would again prove him right. Nor had he any doubt that Administrations, Republican and Democratic alike, acted unwisely when they failed to fund new long-range bombers, cruise missiles, or strategic forces of any type. "As I see things," Scoop said in the late 1960s, "international peace and security depend not on a parity of power but on a preponderance of power in the peace-keepers over the peace-upsetters."[5]

Looking back over Scoop's career, it should have been hard for anyone in 1977 not to bet that he would take a critical line toward any SALT proposal, assuming history would eventually show him right. Richard Perle, Jackson's principal staff aide for such issues, had given deep cuts qualified support, probably on a well-grounded assumption that the Russians would never accept them. Had that assumption proved wrong, Perle would probably have found some previously unnoticed reason why deep cuts were not acceptable either. It was Perle's consistent view that *anything* the Russians liked had to be against U.S. interests.[6] People who knew Jackson well say that quick and adroit intervention could sometimes short-circuit Perle, but once persuaded, the Senator was immovable. The details for that inference, and the inference itself, were easily available to Carter and Brzezinski. Placement of Jackson suggested that negotiations with him needed at least as much preparation as negotiations with Brezhnev.

A little more inspection of events and details on Scoop's time-line could have given that inference double force. It would have required recognizing that placement across institutional lines has some similarity to placement across national lines. In the Skybolt affair, Americans needed to remember first of all that prime ministers were not presidents. In 1977 Carterites needed to remember that Jackson's country was Capitol Hill and that he was a Senator, not a Cabinet member or White House adviser.

Carter himself may have been understandably deceived. He perhaps drew false analogies with the Georgia Senate. Moreover, he had given a nominating speech for Jackson in 1972; perhaps he thought the favor had some carryover value. In 1976 Carter had defeated Jackson in the Pennsylvania primary, forcing him out of the presidential race. Members of the White House staff whose job it was to worry about Senators did not worry about Scoop; Carter had "cleaned his clock" the year before. And Scoop in person was so mild-spoken, so seemingly reasonable, so woodenly affable, that it was easy to forget what he was. There is an *a propos* line in James M. Cain's novel *Mildred Pierce,* when Mildred with shock asks Mr. Treviso, the voice teacher for her daughter,

Veda, if he is characterizing Veda as a snake, and Mr. Treviso replies, "No—is a coloratura soprano, is much worse." Jackson was not just a human being, he was a United States Senator. Carter and his aides would have done well to think of him as, for practical purposes, a small but powerful foreign country, with his own independent interests and his own equivalent of government departments (in Perle and other aides). Except for Vice President Mondale, formerly a Senator from Minnesota, and Brzezinski's deputy, David Aaron, formerly a Mondale aide, no prominent figure in the White House had Capitol Hill experience to bring to bear. Since it was "Bay of Pigs time" in the new Administration, the early weeks of office when people still were feeling one another out, neither Mondale nor Aaron could comfortably offer tutoring. So far as we can tell, neither did.

If knowledgeable about both the Senate and Scoop, Carter or his aides could reasonably have added to presumptions bearing on SALT the following: Any words spoken to Jackson to reassure him will be recorded and then, to the extent possible, turned into a binding pledge.[7] This could have given rise in turn to the proposition: If the Administration wants ratification of a SALT treaty, it will have to negotiate with Jackson *while* it negotiates with Moscow, for any advance concessions to either party will doom the treaty.

We hazard that if those presumptions had been voiced and then probed by tests such as we suggested earlier, officials in the Administration who knew Jackson would not have offered less than fifty-to-one against his agreeing to modifications *after* the Administration committed itself. Few would have offered less than ten to one against his supporting any SALT treaty, whatever its terms. The means for keeping track—for following up "Alexander's question"—would have been a watch on Perle.

Unfortunately for those who wanted a treaty (certainly Carter and Vance), understanding of Jackson developed late rather than early. Two years afterward, when they finally got a SALT II treaty, Jackson, it seems clear, would have voted—and campaigned—against its ratification, had Carter not abandoned it. By then, of course, Scoop had abandoned Carter and was backing Edward Kennedy. It has been suggested to us that the Senator's progressive disenchantment with this President reflects a failure of placement in reverse. Like most professional politicians, Jackson evidently started with the stereotype that Carter was one too.

We hope our readers will remember placement and, as part of normal routines on the job, will note time-lines, events, and details for anyone they find important to the work they have to do, whether setting objectives or trying to advance them persuasively. In logic, placement is often but a form of probing presumptions—usually implicit ones—which center on individuals. For Carter in early 1977, two were (1) Brezhnev will make some SALT concessions because he badly wants to keep detente, and (2) Scoop can be won over if we start with *his* proposal and then, if it doesn't fly, back off to something more realistic. Both, we think, might have been recognized as wrong had it been routine practice to identify *all* key actors and quickly run through the events and details on their time-lines.

We would leave a wrong impression, however, if we halted discussion of placement here, since we have so far touched but glancingly on the complicating force of ideology. For LBJ's advisers, placing one another would have been largely a matter of asking, "What would be *my* frame of mind if I had had *his* experiences." For Mary Anderson thinking about Frances Perkins or vice versa, the exercise would have been harder: ". . . and if I were of her social class." So, too, for Schmidt and Carter or Macmillan and Kennedy vis-à-vis one another: ". . . and of his country." For Martin Luther King and Malcolm X, it would have been harder still: with race *and* class in the questioning, perhaps too hard to be doable but worth trying nonetheless. So it is if one adds—as one certainly should for a Brezhnev or a Dobrynin and also if a Carter looking at a Jackson: ". . . and I saw patterns of history as he or she sees them."

The people one may seek to heed, help, influence, or shun in given instances all carry in their heads not only their own memories of direct or of vicarious experience but also beliefs about persistent or recurrent patterns. They amount to models relating effects to causes. Each model is buttressed by impressions from the past so strong as to seem proofs. The model and those firm impressions, taken together, help their holder to explain, predict, and act upon historical events, including the next of the same sort to come along.

Such patterns will not necessarily be in the forefront of a holder's mind (or even fully formulated, much less articulated), and from mind to mind they will not be all the same. Different persons may have very different concepts of recurrent cause–effect relationships in history. Some even opt for randomness, others for forces, divine or human (capitalist-imperialists, Communists, "secular humanists," and so on), acting purposefully. In between lie speculations informed by technical philosophy, along with social science, and a plethora of improvisations. What they all have in common are historical events; the differences relate to claimed causation and results.[8]

Wrapped up in those claims, differentiating them still further, are implicit values. For the models undergirded by historical impressions are built of beliefs, not of demonstrable certainties. Many are beliefs about how fellow human beings behave or ought to behave. All are, in terms we have used earlier, presumptions tinged by "truths."

Effective stereotyping of the persons one must deal with on particulars includes effective guesswork about their beliefs. That surely was a part of Carter's need with respect to Scoop Jackson. The guesswork is facilitated, obviously, by prior knowledge of events as such and also by acquaintance with the intellectual currents running through the years, and the locales, of those one seeks to place. The currents convey patterns, values included. Jackson, no less staunch a Fair Dealer than cold warrior, responded to events in the context of such currents, not by any means the only ones, but strong ones in his time and place—and differing somewhat from those that had tugged at the younger Southerner, Carter.

Among Americans, at least among people who think of themselves as doers, underlying beliefs rarely get pulled to the surface. Here too Scoop is a prototype, perhaps part of Carter's confusion. And differences in opinion rarely get interpreted as perhaps due to differences in value-rich presumptions. Our pragmatic, essentially lawyerly society supposes that if people differ, they have either different facts or different interests. If the one, the solution is research; if the other, arbitration or compromise. Most Americans find it hard to accommodate the alternative possibility that differences may be due to differences in concepts of causation at a level *beyond* tests of evidence or of "getting to yes" conciliation.[9]

To our practitioner-students, most of whom are pragmatic and lawyerly (some in fact practicing lawyers), we introduce this additional dimension with an exercise that many find unsettling. We ask them to imagine themselves economic planners working in the Soviet Union. For the purpose they are given a primer on Marxism-Leninism, some statistics, and some samples of exchanges in Soviet economic journals between defenders of centralized economic planning and advocates of greater decentralization.[10] They are then asked to frame arguments that conscientious Soviet officials ought to make to the Politburo.

The readings offer evidence of the lengths to which actual Russians go to keep their arguments inside orthodoxy. Corresponding Member of the Soviet Academy of Sciences S. Shatalin, to make a case for decentralization, has to say that the aim is to transform the Soviet economy "into a single national economic complex—an ever developing, living, dialectically contradictory system continuously and deliberately improved according to plan." He has to claim, in other words, that he wants only to make central planning more efficient.[11] Participants in our exercise are not forced into such verbal acrobatics. They do, however, have to use language that protects their recommendations against charges of threatening to reintroduce capitalism, foster worker alienation, encourage "commodity fetishism," weaken the leadership role of the Party, or otherwise betray the promise of the Bolshevik Revolution.

Being themselves fans of a relatively free economy and recognizing the current beset condition of the Soviet economy, most Americans who play the game argue for decentralization there. In practice, they find it hard to do so without going on to argue that ideological purity has to be compromised; that the system must not only let some workers be exploited but acknowledge the fact; that the Party must allow the social order to be shaped in part by managers and investors making decisions according to profit criteria; and so forth. They find that the language they have to use—the values they have to pretend thereby to protect—limits the array of options they can present and changes the character of some.

It is natural then to ask: How does value-laden language affect *us,* Americans in America? The answer: much the same. Many imaginable options for dealing with our economic problems are also precluded by rhetorical norms reflective of values, enshrined in impressions of history. Were Russians pretending to be Americans, they would find it difficult to work centralized planning into the menu of options for serious consideration. Comprehensive central planning of a national economy may be stifling to say the least. Soviet experience conveys innumerable warnings. The relevant point, however, is that those words are so nearly taboo as to make the very concept almost undiscussable in the United States. The option can get on the table only if put in different words and, as a result, substantially changed. Nor would Russians playing Americans easily get serious attention for a policy of ending unemployment through massive public works. Chief among the obstacles, more serious even than money, would be fundamentals on the status of employers and trade unions somewhat comparable to those, in the Soviet Union, on the status of the Party. For Americans such fundamentals are conveyed by words like liberties and rights and "sanctity of contracts."

Clever people, thinking hard, can often circumvent the constraints of value-laden language. Look at the Hungarians! Their "market socialism" allows for landed gentry, millionaires, and banking houses comparable to Switzerland's. But such ingenuity requires recognition first that the constraints exist, followed by hard thought on how to get around them. To accept them is to chain the imagination. To ignore them or to run at them headlong is to invite frustration. Witness the fate of New Dealers and Fair Dealers who sought national insurance for comprehensive health care but could not avoid the label "socialized medicine."[12] Their quest has lasted fifty years to date, and they are nowhere near their goal.

This exercise serves as a reminder that, for thinking about Soviet leaders, the context of SALT and START negotiations may be special, even unique. Nuclear weaponry has been for decades the focus of a branch of analytic philosophy not unlike that which produces large books on the various meanings of "between." While Russians and Americans have different approaches, they draw on a common store of concepts and definitions, making their debates in some respects comparable to those of Roman and Byzantine theologians disputing over the Apocalypse. When Americans discuss with Russians other matters, such as European security treaties or pipeline deals or human rights, our exercise suggests, they do well to remind themselves from time to time that they and their Soviet counterparts may see causes and effects in different terms.

But the exercise has limited value if its only lesson concerns dealings with Russians and other Marxist-Leninists. Its greater utility is in calling attention to *American* ideologies. We therefore use for reinforcement a second exercise, involving only Americans, in this case debating the subject of economic growth.

At the outset we offer the text of a famous speech from 1932 given by FDR, then running for his first term, before the Commonwealth Club of San Francisco.[13] It is amazing how few readers understand right away what Roosevelt was saying. They see him denying that the nation's "mood of depression" is justified and going on to declare, "America is new. It is in the process of change and development. It has the great potentialities of youth." So they assume that the speech must embody the optimism associated with the New Deal, must look forward to the boom that will follow the Great Depression. They usually have to read the speech a second or third time before they take in its central message. "Our task now is not discovery or exploitation of natural resources, or necessarily producing more goods," Roosevelt said. "It is the soberer, less dramatic business of administering resources and plants already in hand, of seeking to reestablish foreign markets for our surplus production, of meeting the problem of underconsumption, of adjusting production to consumption, of distributing wealth and products more equitably, of adapting existing economic organizations to the service of the people." The nation had finished its growth, he was arguing. The chief problem for the future was to see that finite resources were fairly distributed. Once they grasp FDR's message, many of those who take part in our exercise are shocked, not only because it is so out of keeping with conventional images of him but also because it sounds so much like what economists are thought to have just recently discovered, namely upper limits.

After analysis of the Commonwealth Club speech, the next step in the exercise is to read excerpts from Walt W. Rostow's *Stages of Growth,* the Club of Rome's *Limits to Growth,* and some works in between.[14] Rostow's book, published in 1960, generalized to all human history and to all the future a model based on the experience of eighteenth- and nineteenth-century Britain, partially repeated by the United States. In the early 1960s his model captivated many European and American imaginations. The usually restrained and ironic London *Economist* hailed Rostow's work as "one of the most stimulating contributions made to economic and political thought since the war." Writing of Rostow's "powerful new framework of ideas," the *New York Times*'s economics writer,

Harry Schwartz, likened him to Marx.[15] Rostow's presumptions became the premises of Kennedy's foreign aid programs, notably the ambitious "Alliance for Progress" in Latin America. Rostow's proclaimed pattern also influenced policies elsewhere.

By 1972, when *Limits to Growth* appeared, the Alliance for Progress had foundered, "population explosion" had become a cliché, and pollution of the environment preoccupied politicians and citizens' groups from California to West Germany and beyond. Meanwhile, Vietnam-driven inflation in the U.S. dollar put industrial products, not to speak of capital goods, farther and farther beyond the reach of people in poorer countries. Rostow had envisioned humankind barrelling toward collective 3 to 5 percent growth annually. That now seemed preposterous; also, to many, it seemed pollutive and hence morally wrong. While the Club of Rome hardly won immediate, universal acceptance for its Malthusian projection of population outstripping resources and producing "a rather sudden and uncontrollable decline in both population and industrial capacity," *Limits to Growth* set the terms of debate, much as Rostow's book had done a decade and a half earlier. A new conventional wisdom subsequently took form around the notion that if growth did continue, it ought to take a slower pace, with more attention paid to social and environmental effects.

Points of resemblance between the new orthodoxy and what FDR said back in 1932 can stick in memory as a reminder that macroeconomic explanations impose patterns on the jumble of data from the past—relatively formalized, articulated, circumscribed, but nevertheless imposed, creating an appearance of order. Underneath each is a model, bolstered by pieces of history, controlled by presumptions about future trends, and reflecting the theorist's values. A few years hence prevalent presumptions may be different, along with predicted trends and implicit values. From that future vantage point, what now seems "right" may well look "wrong." Or vice versa.

Our exercises, taken together, are suggestive of what might be done by other teachers for other types of students or by officials for themselves, off the job or even on it (in the course of a day's travel or some other pause), to sharpen sensitivity toward patterns in the heads of others—and by the way to sharpen recognition of their own. The quicker they can spot and then inquire into the patterns, the likelier they are to make the most of placement, in the process making up (if necessary, as it probably is), for lack of general background on the history of ideas. We wish we could go beyond mere suggestions aimed at sensitizing oneself, and add a definite procedure to our mini-method for placement. We cannot. Patterns are too subjective in their actual hold on people; intellectual currents are too variable in their actual effects. So, lame as it may be, we fall back to a plea for sensitivity.

For whom does placement work, and why? For anyone, we think, who seriously tries it. The formula can vary and the time spent can be slight. What matters is the seriousness of purpose. Some people do it by instinct. Those who do may leap where we have feared to tread, into psychology, mingling inferences from history with probes of personality. Lyndon Johnson did so when he thought it worth his while, probing for the weakness, for the human vulnerability, in his associates and using that to harness them to him. "I never feel really comfortable with a man," he is said to have remarked, "unless I have his pecker in my pocket." Yet the process almost certainly included a meticulous concern for what was in the other's mind by way of those things we label events and details, perhaps even for patterns. Overall LBJ must have spent a good part of his time learning the personal histories of those around him whom he thought he had to master or might someday want to master—or might simply enjoy feeling he could master if he wanted to—and calibrating them against what he knew of the public history they had experienced. It took no book to teach him how or why.

In 1957, when planning his campaign for the 1960 Democratic nomination, Johnson set out to woo the Adlai Stevenson liberals. The historian Arthur M. Schlesinger, Jr., a former Stevenson speechwriter, describes Johnson's approach to him. LBJ, he writes,

> . . . poured out his stream-of-consciousness on the problems of leadership in the Senate. He described the difficulties of keeping the conservative southerners, whom he called the Confederates, and the liberal northerners in the same harness; he analyzed a number of seemingly insoluble parliamentary situations which he had mastered through unlimited perseverance and craft; and he gave a virtuoso's account of the role which timing, persuasion and parliamentary tactics played in getting bills through. Saying "I want you to know the kind of material I have to work with," he ran down the list of forty-eight Democratic Senators, with a brilliant thumbnail sketch of each—strength and weakness, openness to persuasion, capacity for team-

> work, prejudices, vices. In some cases he amplified the sketch by devastating dashes of mimicry. . . .
>
> He talked for an hour and a half without interruption. I had carefully thought out in advance the arguments to make when asked to justify my doubts about his leadership; but in the course of this picturesque and lavish discourse Johnson met in advance almost all the points I had in mind. When he finally paused, I found I had little to say. It was my first exposure to the Johnson treatment, and I found him a good deal more attractive, more subtle and more formidable than I expected. After nearly two hours under hypnosis, I staggered away in a condition of exhaustion.[16]

One of Johnson's biographers reports encountering a freshman congressmen who had just left the leader's presence. "The congressman," he writes, "had a numbed look, 'It was like talking to my campaign manager, he said, 'only I wish he knew that much.' "[17]

Something more restrained, more modest in its purposes, requiring less artistry, although not much less seriousness, is all we have in mind when we suggest that placement become routine practice in government. It can, as we have tried to argue, sophisticate the stereotypes humans must use to deal with one another, especially if the dealings are official, infrequent, or both. A little could have gone a long way if prompting Mary Anderson not to type Frances Perkins as "a woman" or warning centrist Republicans and Democrats during the 1970s (and after) not to dismiss Ronald Reagan as "an actor." But we cannot stress too much that, like everything else we recommend, placement gives no guarantees. Lyndon Johnson, the master of the art, was wrong about Martin Luther King. We suggest why, but we can offer no assurance that looking beyond "big" events to "special" ones will always work a correction.

Among other things, the backward look at events, even special events, and at details as well, even combined, may miss the mark because they don't catch capacity for change—whether in individuals or in conditions that affect patterns of belief. Study of Harry Truman's biography as of April 1945 might have produced only a few right inferences about how he would behave as President. A study of Robert Kennedy as of 1960 would almost certainly not have projected the RFK of 1968. How could it? His whole outlook on life was to be deepened by tragedy, his brother's fate. Who could have foreseen that in 1960? Even correct reading of FDR's suppositions, as of the Commonwealth Club address, would have been a poor guide for prophesying his performance in the White House. So, while urging that placement be standard practice, we add a caution: Remember that its only purpose is to produce a better working guess, a more sophisticated conjecture; the result is still a guess—a hypothesis—and it may be wrong.

12 Placing Organizations

Government agencies are in some respects like people. The organizations have public histories usually composed of "big events" like statutes assigning them powers and money, changes in top personnel, and controversies over programs. They also have equivalents for personal history made up of details not interesting to people other than insiders but recorded and traceable from back-page news stories, published regulations, legislative hearings, or like sources. The details of institutional history include changes in internal organization, resource allocation, or operating procedures, including the procedures that constitute the organization's personnel system (incentives and training included).[1] Useful inferences are often to be drawn from those two sorts of history combined: in short, from "events" and "details," thus defined, arrayed on the same time-line. Not many years ago Secretary of State Cyrus Vance objected to the point of resignation against military plans to rescue Americans being held hostage in Iran. The Secretary's objection he is said to have put pithily: "too many moving parts." He earlier had spent three years as Deputy Secretary of Defense in wartime, and he evidently knew whereof he spoke. He was overruled, whereupon implementation made the same point.

Organizations can be placed as well as people, which is fortunate, because an organization's history can help just as an issue's does to serve up questions useful for a government decision. We do not yet know all the questions asked, suppressed, or left unthought in April 1980 at the time of the abortive hostage rescue mission, but a fully documented instance from a generation earlier will illustrate the point: the Bay of Pigs affair, outlined in Chapter Eight. The organization is the CIA, the Central Intelligence Agency. Had its development been understood, even in capsule form, and had JFK's own stereotype of the Agency been sophisticated even slightly in organizational terms (beyond Allen Dulles, the living legend, and Richard Bissell, the man to trust), the President might have been led to those critical questions: Where's Robert Amory? Where's Richard Helms?

We often give practitioners studying with us a history of that affair to February 1961, when Kennedy began his helter-skelter meetings, and then add a twenty-page account of the CIA's development through 1960, drawn from a published report for the Senate Intelligence Committee and from Thomas Powers's biography of Helms.[2] We ask students: Had you known this much and been advising Kennedy, what questions do you think you might have urged him to ask Allen Dulles? High on the list of responses, almost always, come requests to hear from those two absent men. For even published history, innocent of secrets, emphasizes three things about institutional growth in the CIA. First, it had evolved from separate organizations with separate personnel systems of varying repute, many of their people still in place. Second, the separateness persisted, in fact had been institutionalized. Third, the separateness was reinforced by the nature of CIA business, which required and encouraged compartmentation, tightly contained "need to know" among those organizations and within them, even among Deputy Directors such as Bissell and Amory, and compartmentation had been built into operating procedures. The published history skirts other features of interest and significance, but those three seem sufficient in the classroom to provoke these crucial questions.

Why they were insufficient at the time and on the job is very probably because not even this much about the CIA was known to JFK or his immediate advisers. Unlike Vance in 1980, but rather like his nemesis, Zbigniew Brezezinski, they had never been close to the "moving parts." Their own experience was of settings such as the Senate, Harvard, the Rockefeller Foundation, the Ford Motor Company, theaters of operation in World War II, or the State Department—all places where secrets were traded, not hoarded, and few were kept for long.

To have had useful questions then—to have done as well beforehand as our practitioner-students can do by hindsight—Kennedy and his associates would have had to learn at least the same things about the Agency's development as those in our twenty-page handout. Is that a big requirement? Too big for busy women and men in the real world, outside classrooms, on the job? We think not. To make the point, we summarize the facts behind the threefold emphasis of that handout.

In modern times, in modern governments, "intelligence" has four meanings: (1) analysis, including estimation and prediction, along with research, starting from open sources; (2) collection, chiefly clandestine; (3) dirty tricks (covert action, nowadays "special activities"); and (4) counterintelligence, or finding the spies of others.

Governments organize those activities differently. Consider the contrasting models of Germany, Britain, and France in World War II. In Hitler's Reich every user—the party, the foreign ministry, the army, the air force, the navy—had its own analysts, collectors, and counterspies. Only covert action, the domain of Admiral Canaris's *Abwehr,* was centralized. World War II Britain was the opposite. A Joint Intelligence Committee did analyses for the Cabinet; a government-wide body handled cryptography; the RAF, aerial photography; MI6, espionage; a Special Operations Executive, covert action; and MI5, counterespionage. In Germany the users fought. In Britain the suppliers did. Pre-1940 France by contrast had just one organization. The army's Deuxième Bureau did everything. And France, coincidentally, lost its war in six weeks.[3]

Only during World War II did the United States even begin to organize. Earlier the State Department, the Army, and the Navy each did its own analysis and collection. The services were good at cryptanalysis, as witness "MAGIC."[4] No one had any human agents to speak of. There was no covert action. J. Edgar Hoover hunted spies. When war approached, the FBI extended its reach. Hoover recruited Spanish-speaking lawyers and former policemen to track Nazis and Fascists in Latin America. Then FDR asked the Wall Street lawyer and World War I hero William J. "Wild Bill" Donovan to create a separate intelligence organization. He formed what was eventually called the Office of Strategic Services (OSS), the forerunner of the CIA. It actually comprised four separate organizations, with Donovan as overseer. One did research and analysis, sending papers through him to a Joint Intelligence Committee, which prepared estimates for the Joint Chiefs of Staff. A secret intelligence branch developed agent networks everywhere except Latin America, which remained the FBI's. That branch's information went as a rule to theater commanders. A third set of people conducted covert operations, aiding resistance groups, arranging sabotage, broadcasting "black" propaganda, and so forth. They acted more or less on their own. Finally, the OSS had a counterintelligence branch.

After World War II Truman dissolved the OSS. The Army took over its agent networks and added some new ones, chiefly in Eastern Europe, while State took over the remnants of the research and analysis branch. Otherwise conditions became as they had been before 1941. Then, with the Cold War, Truman decided to reinvent the OSS. In 1947 he re-created it with statutory sanction as the CIA. More precisely he partially re-created it, for the new agency was assigned only research and analysis, secret intelligence, and, in a small way, counterintelligence. It did not have a warrant for covert operations.

The CIA's research and analysis people and its secret intelligence people had little in common, except for being in the information business together. Researchers liked to write for people outside the Agency. Some researchers were scholarly types inclined to produce long papers describing and evaluating sources; others, more like news reporters, served up juicy stories for the President and lesser officials who subscribed to their daily intelligence reports. The secret intelligence gatherers, on the other hand, put a premium on developing informants and protecting them. Spending effort and time—often years—to cultivate trustworthy agents, they were loath to risk losing them, perhaps having them shot, because someone on the research side wanted to prove a point or have a "scoop." Since much of their information in the early years actually came from other intelligence services, they themselves were not always sure what tidbits might compromise sources. So the CIA's secret intelligence people tended to look on the researchers almost as enemy agents. They were, to say the least, sparing of information, and the most they would divulge about a source was a grade based on past reliability. (A "D," say, for someone who might be a drunk and double agent in Teheran.) The researchers in turn tended to hold back what they learned from, for example, listening to open broadcasts or reading communications decoded by the armed services or studying photographs taken by the Air Force. In the CIA the secret intelligence collectors and the analyst-researchers were part of one family only as the Air Force and Navy were part of one Department of Defense.

While the two groups regularized their nonrelations inside the CIA, a new covert action organization took form separately. The Cold War was turning ferocious. The Russians were believed to be up to dirty tricks everywhere. All Truman's advisers thought the United States needed to match them. All but one of those advisers thought the assignment should go to the State Department. The "no" came from General George C. Marshall, then Secretary of State, and the "noes" carried. Instead, the President established an independent Office of Policy Coordination answering to the Secretaries of State and Defense but not belonging to either. Its assignment: to conduct "propaganda, economic warfare, preventive direct action, including sabotage . . . ; subversion against hostile states . . . ; and support of indigenous anti-Communist elements in threatened countries of the free world." Its only formal limitation was that operations be "so planned and conducted that any U.S. government responsibility for them is not evident to unauthorized persons and that if uncovered the U.S. government can plausibly disclaim any responsibility for them."[5]

Headed by Frank Wisner, an OSS veteran legendary for energy, quickness of mind, and personal magnetism, the Office of Policy Coordination flourished. It secretly channeled money to anti-Communist groups all over the world. It organized propaganda campaigns and tried, though without much success, to foster resistance movements in Eastern Europe. To prepare "stay-behind" forces in the anticipated event of a Red Army attack on Western Europe, Wisner's office also developed an organizational capacity for and interest in training and equipping paramilitary units.

With the Korean War, both the CIA and Wisner's organization received new resources and new assignments. General Walter Bedell Smith, who had been Eisenhower's Chief of Staff and in-house s.o.b. during World War II, became Director of Central Intelligence; as such he was both head of the CIA and nominal coordinator of all intelligence activities throughout the government. In the CIA he built up the research side. Its Directorate for Intelligence soon had talent and expertise sufficient to go to the mat with service intelligence agencies over military issues. It also had an office pulling together—and presenting to the National Security Council—National Intelligence Estimates representing collective judgments by the "intelligence community" based on all available evidence. (That office got least evidence from the secret intelligence people under the CIA's own roof.)

As patriotic young college graduates, Ph.D.s, and lawyers signed up to fight the Cold War, the wing of the CIA collecting secret intelligence also acquired an army of new talent. So did Wisner's outfit. Before long they were competing with each other in recruiting all over the country and in foreign capitals as well. By 1952 each employed about 6,000 people, and Wisner had increased his independent field stations from seven to forty-seven.

"Beetle" Smith finally intervened. He claimed a right to oversee Wisner's Office as well as the CIA. Key people in his secret intelligence organization, Richard Helms and Lyman Kirkpatrick, tried to talk him into putting it all under them. Wisner, fans of his, and fans of covert action successfully protested. Smith instead chose a looking-glass version of Solomon's solution. He ordered that the two bodies be sewn together. A new Directorate of Plans in the CIA was to include both, but on an understanding that someone from Wisner's office would head it while someone from secret intelligence would be nominally number two, actually autonomous, as its Chief of Operations. Wisner went into the first slot, Helms into the second.

Competition between the two different approaches continued within the CIA. Recruits into the Agency's clandestine service were pulled during training toward one orientation or the other almost as if in a mixed-denomination theological seminary. In headquarters two sets of offices sent instructions to officers in the field. Wisner himself, along with functional staffs for political warfare, psychological warfare, paramilitary operations, and economic warfare, developed or encouraged development of "projects." Helms and various geographic divisions meanwhile undertook to keep stations at the quiet, slow work of developing sources of information.

Field officers were torn. "Projects" brought in money and gratified the desire to see results. At least as much as telling tales to the Intelligence Directorate, however, they risked killing sources, blowing cover, or otherwise compromising the intelligence mission.

In 1953 Allen Dulles succeeded Smith. The OSS station chief in Bern during World War II, he was famous for organizing covert action in Germany and occupied Europe. Though a lawyer of keen mind, respected for his judgment, and in a position to influence policy because his brother was the Secretary of State, he showed less interest in either analysis or secret intelligence than in covert "projects." Gossip said they occupied three-quarters of his time, while designing the CIA's Virginia headquarters took much of the rest.

When Wisner fell victim to mental illness, Dulles put Bissell in his place. That maintained Smith's two-headed solution. It also testified to Dulles's preference for operations. No one inside the Agency was in any doubt, however, that Helms, Kirkpatrick, and others who shared their view of the intelligence profession were maintaining efforts to prevent the information-gathering mission from being contaminated or compromised. And James Jesus Angleton, as head of a counterintelligence staff, operated independently of either Bissell or Helms, keeping secrets from everyone.

Thus CIA was (and, we suspect, is yet) a confederacy, in some respects similar to the Pentagon. Covert action and secret intelligence both came under the Directorate for Plans, and people in the field worked together, but they were at least as separate as, say, submariners and fliers in the Navy or missileers and fliers in the Air Force. Certainly the Plans and Intelligence directorates were as far apart as the Army and the Navy. There was no Secretary of Defense, nor even a Chairman of the Joint Chiefs. The set-up resembled what the Pentagon would have been if it had no head other than one service chief acting as coordinator. Moreover, the separateness in CIA was sanctified by a doctrine that *no one* should be told *anything* without an established "need to know." Operating procedures reinforced the doctrine.

There are a dozen ways in which those facts about the organization—and their obvious implications—could have been acquired by the man who was about to make himself depend on it for action, namely John F. Kennedy. He could have spent time meeting and questioning old hands. More simply he could have searched out someone knowledgeable to brief him in person or to brief an Arthur Schlesinger, who could write it up in style for him to read. Simpler still, he could have asked a McGeorge Bundy to inform himself on statutory highlights in their substantive settings and on administrative evolution too, align both on a time-line (as with "events" and "details" for people), then devote some minutes jointly to pursuing inferences while framing questions.

But who would so intrude into an esoteric sphere like Dulles's and Bissell's? Only somebody who did it everywhere and all the time as a matter of working style, which Kennedy plainly was not, or someone keen to the full meaning of dependence on strange organizations, which Kennedy had not yet become. Never in his short tenure did he find it easy to consider organizations apart from individuals. Like many politicians and virtually all Senators he tended to see agencies as tantamount to personalities within them—true of course as far as it goes—which downplays the dependence of results on training, traditions, routines, and incentives. Kennedy's perspective may have been enlarging with experience, not least in Cuba. By his fourth year, had he lived, he seems less likely than a Carter to have set aside the organizational issue posed by Vance, likelier indeed to have shared Vance's fear of many "moving parts." But the point is moot, which limits the utility of Kennedy's example. It illuminates what not to do, but only in the classroom can it be done over to display the helpfulness of organizational history, much less the handy use of something like our time-line, events, and details.

Defense and diplomacy are not the only spheres in which an organization's history sheds light upon decisions. Domestic spheres show comparable effects. The Public Health Service is a good source of examples. So is the Social Security Administration. Those agencies already have been introduced as frames for substance in previous chapters. We return to them now for aspects of their organizational histories potentially or actually of use to decision-makers.[6]

During the swine flu scare of 1976, which centered on the Public Health Service and its component, the Center (as it was then) for Disease Control, almost every misadventure had an organizational source contributing to if not itself creating trouble. Many of those were known to the decision-makers in advance and could have been but were not used to pose hard questions or elicit timely warnings. The presumable emergency stood in the way of that. So did the presumptive expertise of specialists. So did a faith that they could "doctor their way through" (their term), improvising around hurdles, organizational and others. The swine flu instance thus is crammed with negative examples, where the public health authorities and their superiors failed to turn organizational history to their account. But it was all around them, ready to hand.

To return to a few instances already introduced in Chapter Three, the swine flu program rapidly outran its assumed base of scientific and medical consensus. In the absence of flu it was plagued by poor public relations. Had a pandemic come, those might well have been worse: Inoculating children would have been a hassle, local competence variable, vaccine limited. And structural features foretold such results, had anyone cared to notice.

Consensus among specialists and medical practitioners that swine flu was an active risk against which the whole country should be immunized had been a *sine qua non* for Gerald Ford when he approved the program. He judged it to be so because the *ad hoc* group arrayed before him was unanimous. In this the group followed the verbal lead of two members, Dr. Jonas Salk and Dr. Albert Sabin, the famous inventors of rival vaccines against polio. Despite their rivalry, which was personal as well as scientific, those two had agreed on the need for swine flu shots. They thus had backed the government's two doctors who were sponsoring the program, CDC Director David Sencer and HEW Assistant Secretary for Health Theodore Cooper. No one in Ford's hearing said them nay. *Ergo* consensus. But the other presumed experts in Ford's *ad hoc* panel had been Sencer's own suggestions, for the most part, drawn from among members of the Advisory Committee on Immunization Practices he had already consulted. The most doubting expert in that body, Dr. Alexander (who rarely spoke up anyway), was not offered a crack at Ford. The others were already committed to Sencer's plan. Their unanimity meant less than Ford assumed. It neither kept Sabin and Salk together (Sabin turned against the program three months later) nor reflected firm views in the medical community, where opposition (and indifference) mounted as the months passed without swine flu.

Ford's advisers did not serve him well in two particulars: in making Salk and Sabin symbolize consensus, for those two were sure to disagree wherever and as soon as they could manage, and in packing the assembled group with acquiescent members of the Advisory Committee, for their concurrence was too readily assured to make them representative. Granting that the first misstep was psychological, the second certainly had organizational roots.

In 1976 the Advisory Committee on Immunization Practices, although nominally attached to the CDC's parent Public Health Service, had long since come to operate as an adjunct of Sencer's office. There had been an accretion during the decade of his directorship. He served as the committee's chairman, presiding at meetings and summing up, controlling agenda, circulating minutes, and deciding on new members. Those he drew in part from the virologists and immunologists specializing in flu, two tiny groups, and in part from other specialized circles, including faculties of public health. He was scrupulous in seeking advice on substance, narrowly defined, and he expected support on implementation, which he took to be everything else. Sencer had been ten years on the job and felt himself its master. Members felt that too. The Advisory Committee was a clubby group and deferential to him, the more so since its members could expect sought-after invitations to assorted panel meetings in the Public Health Service domain.

After 1976 Sencer's successor put a separate chairman between himself and the Advisory Committee. He thus applied a lesson of the swine flu program, namely that argument, not deference, inside the group as well as with the agency, is needed in advice-giving. This more or less acknowledged, after the fact, the Committee's weak performance a year earlier. Anyone familiar with its operating procedures could have foretold that before the fact, discounting its conclusions as a guide to scientific-medical consensus especially when strained through its then chairman. Understandably, Sencer proposed for the presidential meeting only Advisory Committee members who agreed with him. Unfortunately, by the time inoculations started six months later, Alexander's views were probably more representative of medical opinion as it had evolved, in the absence of flu, than were those of more favored members. But the White House aides who improvised Ford's meeting were not cautioned by the fine points of procedure in an obscure group four levels down; they did not know them. The President's Science Adviser could not assist. That post had been abolished and was just then being re-created.

The public relations problems of the swine flu program were in part the product of diminishing consensus but were fed as well by gaps between initial claims and actual performance. In March 1976 the program had been premised on achieving immunization for most Americans before the winter influenza season. In April Cooper had incautiously announced the aim of immunizing almost all, roughly 200 million. Ford had spoken of vaccine for "every man, woman, and child." Then came the wait for unforeseen insurance legislation. No program starting in October could have met goals remotely like those before winter. By then that was both obvious and embarrassing. But it was outweighed by other embarrassments mentioned in Chapter Three: the dosage problem for children, the publicized deaths in Pittsburgh, the lagging acceptance rate, the severe side effects, all in the absence of swine flu. Combined with waning support among doctors, those accumulated into something of a public relations fiasco.

Some of the troubles were unavoidable, others not, but something rather like them could have been predicted from the fact that Sencer's Center for Disease Control had dominated Federal plans while actual operations were in state and local hands. The CDC professionals, for the most part, were unaccustomed to conceiving of the media and public in other than traditional, expert terms: as laymen to be told no more than would be good for them, especially not doubts. Communicating with their fellow doctors was conceived in terms just as traditional, essentially research terms: journals, articles, and public-health advisories. And the CDC was organized to suit. Its information staff was actually a publications group, a virtual publishing house, not a source of expertise in media relations. Sencer himself had previously dealt with the mass media as a research director, running laboratories and pronouncing expert judgments, rather than as point man for a crash attempt to corral the whole country in the name of Gerald Ford.

As planner—then coordinator—for a national crash program, the CDC had an unlikely history. Until the 1970s it had been named "Communicable Disease Center." The older title reflected its original concern with traditional public health functions. First was epidemiological investigation into ancient scourges of sailors, whose care had initially justified the Federal health service: venereal diseases, smallpox, cholera, malaria, typhus, tuberculosis, and plague, among others. Second, as an adjunct, now grown skilled and famous, was laboratory work identifying strange outbreaks of a communicable character. CDC labs had become a combined court of last resort and detective service for state and local public health authorities. Third, and growing since the 1930s, especially under Sencer, was technical assistance to those authorities in terms at once of funds for special programs and of personnel on loan. The latter included both epidemiologists (M.D.s) and public health advisers (nonmedical, administrative staff) on assignment. As the Center evolved, the funding to build up both groups of staff had been scraped off the top of categorical grant programs offered the states by Congress to control national threats such as venereal diseases during World War II.

With medical knowledge and drugs transformed in the 1940s and 1950s, the old diseases came under increased control or were eradicated, malaria even earlier, smallpox still later. Congressional interest in aiding state efforts through the CDC had shifted from control to prevention and so had the prospect for funding those staffs. Smallpox, rubella, measles, and polio had all attracted Federal grant programs for immunizing children. Staff expenses were defrayed in part from these. To stabilize his agency, Sencer naturally sought more of the same; influenza was a prospect both before and after swine flu. And he managed to change his agency's name without changing initials, no small feat. The new name signified the new thrust.[7]

From quarters near the campus of Emory University in Atlanta (testifying to the patronage of Senator Richard Russell of Georgia), Sencer profited somewhat by distance from his chiefs in the Public Health Service and HEW, while handing out on their behalf both money and assistants to the state health commissioners, and through them to local bodies, where control and prevention met the actual population. As a member of his staff asserted for the swine flu program, "They had to do it through us, we're the only ones with state connections."

True to a degree; the connections were often (not always) close. But they were not command relationships, nor comprehensive across state activities, nor uniform among all states. (Nor were states uniform in their relations with localities). Rather, the CDC's connections were a web of funding here, a staffer there, a friend elsewhere. From this one could, and Sencer did, build a confederacy for swine flu shots in summertime. How well it would have held up in a winter epidemic, no one knows.

Instead of shifting weight from sickness toward prevention, CDC might have adapted by a move in one of two other directions, but those were blocked—although not by enemies. One direction was research, but the National Institutes of Health, a burgeoning arm of the Public Health Service, was already there. In influenza, for example, the Institute for Allergic and Infectious Diseases funded work across the country (and still does). The other direction was testing preventives, but the Food and Drug Administration and its Bureau of Biologics did that (and does). To exemplify, again with influenza, vaccines were marketed—and are—only after Bureau of Biologics tests and approval.

Even without trying to compete directly, the CDC could not help overlapping the Institute for Allergic and Infectious Diseases and the Bureau of Biologics. In acknowledgement, the three perfected ways to work together where their interests intersected, as was bound to happen with a dangerous disease remaining as mysterious in its behavior as was influenza. When swine flu was identified in humans, the three consulted constantly at top and middle levels. Those were manned by doctors, most of them careerists in the Public Health Service commissioned corps. The CDC reviewed state plans, dispensed administrative money, and developed a surveillance system using Institute researchers among others. The Institute designed the field trials. The Bureau of Biologics prepared and ran the tests of swine vaccine. All kept in touch with the vaccine producers through their laboratories, a further element in the cooperation. It was informal, continuous, friendly, cohesive, and mutually accommodating, effective in its way and of its kind. Sencer and his collaborators found it satisfactory.

Cooper, their superior as Assistant Secretary for Health, sought to give them personal guidance; in fact he danced to every tune they sang in chorus. He had wished, for example, to carve out central roles for private physicians and voluntary groups, but most state public health plans predictably left them peripheral. Resorting to Sencer's connections, Cooper was stuck with their product.

Inevitably mistakes were made, and those were of a kind (reflecting accommodation). Someone proposed, but no one followed through on, weekly information bulletins for medical practitioners. Someone suggested field trials of two half-strength shots for kids, but that was lost from sight in confidence that there would be no problem (there had been none before with other vaccines, after all), combined with lack of thought about the media. Somebody proposed informing states and cities of statistical expectations for "coincidental deaths"—like those Pittsburgh would publicize—but this was quashed on grounds that it would leak and lessen public confidence in shots. How confidence would fare if local health authorities confronted the condition without warning was not faced. The statisticians foresaw that inoculation of unprecedented numbers might expose some previously unknown side effects, and they expected neurological ones, like that which did appear, but not of much significance statistically. No one asked whether numbers would seem significant to laymen or, more to the point, what it would take to quantify the risk for a consent form, or most pointed of all, how to continue shots while that was going on. Alternatively, how could they be suspended without shutting down the program? The CDC, in particular, had not had to face questions like those before and was not structured to do so, or staffed to do so, and didn't.

Had swine flu erupted in this country or abroad by late 1976, many such questions would have been mooted—but others would have arisen. Those others seem likely to have left the program still less creditable than in fact it was. The likelihood arises from confederal organization for operating purposes, combined with accommodating peer groups at the Public Health Service and limitations on vaccine supply built in before October. For down at the low level where shots actually were given, everything depended on the ingenuity and skill with which state plans had been prepared and local services enlisted, as well as on cooperation in the doing among doctors, clinics, support groups, and employers, both private and public. All those would have intersected with supplies of vaccine insufficient to inoculate adults once and children twice if the demand ran high. Adults were the principal victims of previous flu strains. Yet children had been the prime spreaders. If those relations held this time, if the disease spread fast and if, above all, it turned out to be severe, a national program that entered October with battered credibility could well have emerged the next spring, after flu season, credited with disaster.

In some quarters that was feared, and organizational decisions were briefly contested. The Vice President, to whom few listened, a usual fate in the job, suggested consulting the Army. The HEW Secretary felt around for an emergency organization of temporary character. The permanent units prevailed. They, of course, knew their histories; Sencer, for one, had lived the CDC's, but suffered from a sort of managerial (or medical) hubris. His superiors, who mostly did not know it, mistook the CDC for a command center and let him play the part without the capability. Had they known better they might have called on the Army—improbable—or run a "crash program" from Washington—unworkable (?)—or set about reducing expectations.

Failures are dramatic and we hope illuminating, but successes add to understanding too. In the same time period, only a year later, and the same Federal department, HEW, the incoming Carter Administration broke with the expansionist approach to social security, which for nearly forty years had shaped all legislation on the subject. That was no success initially; in 1977 key elements of HEW's revised approach were roundly rejected by Congress (another comment on Carter's "honeymoon"). But the then proposals marked out ground that has confined all subsequent debate, namely that "the social security program had gone far enough and . . . the time had come to stabilize it."[8] In 1979 a second set of HEW proposals, furthering the same assumption, was again rejected on Capitol Hill; yet its direction, if not all details, was confirmed four years later by the bipartisan commission and ensuing legislation noted in Chapter Two. That occurred despite severe initial opposition from the permanent establishment, the Social Security Administration and traditional, supportive interest groups. Yet the new direction was not brutally imposed by politicians. Rather it was worked out in detailed discussion with the SSA's career officials on a basis according them due process. That contributed to its longevity and ultimate success.

The credit for this contribution (or the blame, depending on substantive preference) goes in part to the then HEW Under Secretary, Hale Champion. Carter had come in determined to take fresh initiatives on many fronts; several involved HEW, and the new Secretary, Joseph Califano, had divided up the field with his Under Secretary. Rising costs and falling revenues had just squeezed social security trust funds. Since Champion had been a state finance director, that problem fell initially to him. He then put together two pieces of institutional history, known to him from previous work in Washington and California. Acting on what he knew, he set the stage for that new direction.

One piece of history concerned the Social Security Administration; a high-quality career group with a proud tradition which included a pervasive ideology about its programs. Training and incentives in the agency were deeply influenced. That was the legacy of a strong-minded founder, Arthur Altmeyer, the first commissioner, and his hand-picked successor, Robert Ball. They had dominated the agency from 1935 to 1973, along with Altmeyer's onetime assistant, Wilbur Cohen, later HEW Secretary, who still was actively advising the congressional committees. Cohen had been active in almost all the legislation since the original Social Security Act; he remained dedicated to the proposition that there should be more of the same: more entitlements, more coverage, more benefits, more of the tasks of welfare handled in this fashion, but no stigma, no means test, and instead the symbols of insurance—while American pensions rose to match the best in Europe.

By no coincidence those ideas warmed most hearts in the Social Security Administration as late as 1977. The exceptions were actuaries, not policy planners.

The other piece of history, a shorter piece by far, concerned the Office of Planning and Evaluation (P-and-E) at the Secretary's level in HEW. It had been established by John Gardner as Secretary in 1966, modeled roughly on Robert McNamara's Pentagon "whiz kids," then still in relatively high repute. Gardner had been both admiring and frustrated by his own lack of analytic staff resources not tied to some operating agency or other. Gardner's successor, Cohen, had made little of the innovation, feeling less need. But during Nixon's term two of his three Secretaries, Elliot Richardson and Caspar Weinberger, had each in his way encouraged P-and-E, bringing on strong directors who built up the staff, forcing entrée for it elsewhere in the Department. Weinberger remained with Ford for a full year, and his successor, Mathews, kept the same director, who grew stronger. Califano had changed directors while adding staff in good analytic repute. That had encouraged the career civil servants, who were raring to go.

What Champion saw was that this gave him not a match for Social Security's career staffs—the operating agency with its own planners had a staying-power P-and-E could scarcely muster—but at least a useful foil if he could set them at each other under the right circumstances. He arranged the circumstances, which included Califano and himself as referees. Carter's proposals were the end product. In Champion's words:

> I found soon enough what I rather expected, that the planning people, the analysts, in SSA were imbued with the same philosophy as everybody else there. Left to their own devices they'd predictably come up with a solution to the Old Age Insurance financing bind that left benefits essentially untouched and hiked payroll taxes way above what Carter would conceivably put forward. . . . Congress later shoved them down his throat but that's another story.
>
> So I decided on a set of meetings. I'd be there and Joe [Califano] as often as he could: the Social Security people on one side of the table, Henry Aaron (the new head of Planning and Evaluation) with his people on the other side; every point of each critiqued by the other, one by one, no generalizations, no skipping, first to establish an agreed base of facts—that came pretty quickly—then to air every programmatic proposal either side wanted us to keep on the table for Carter. . . . What the SSA people saw was another set of experts

> as knowledgeable as they were, often more ingenious, and both sets were going to be heard on everything where it counted, by Joe and by me.[9]

Califano in his memoir of the period has commented:

> For hours, sitting in the green chairs, we listened to [the two] staffs debate different approaches. At first the disagreements were sharp; the memos and tables put forth by one side were criticized severely by the other.
>
> But as the staffs talked, and as Champion and I listened, elements of common ground began to emerge.[10]

So the two political appointees were eventually equipped with proposals premised on the need to reform the existing program without expanding it. Many hard choices about benefits were set aside by virtue of a plan for occasional resort, in recessions, to financing from general taxation. Congress rejected that flatly (shades of FDR!) and instead hiked payroll taxes, the traditional financing source, far higher than expected. When even those taxes proved insufficient to keep trust funds flush, benefits were scrutinized again at HEW in a review of the same sort as Champion's original. By late 1978 he and Califano had persuaded Carter to tax a portion of pensions, gradually step up retirement age, and step down assorted fringe benefits. Then Carter distanced himself, the affected interests fought back, and Congress balked. Three years later, as we note in Chapter Two, the Reagan Administration precipitously grabbed up some of those proposals, stripped of gradualism, then under fire let them drop, opting for bipartisan review. This debated mostly the same questions. The dialogue of SSA with P-and-E had turned up all the issues and prefigured the alternatives. Precise results in 1983 differed somewhat from the details of 1979, but Champion had plainly set downward revisions in motion, reversing forty years of meaning for the term "reform."

For that he deserves credit (or again blame, if preferred), but not too much. He was not the first Under Secretary who, given the assignment, could have used his departmental analysts to balance in an innovative, program-building way the preferences of such an operating agency as the SSA. Yet if not the first he was only the third or fourth. Not before 1972, at the earliest, would the Planning and Evaluation staff have had the strength, standing, and confidence to bring it off. And not before 1974, in the course of sharp inflation followed by recession, was there any serious worry about near-term solvency for social security trust funds. So the possibility and need approximately coincided with a man who happened to have in his head those two pieces of organizational history. He had them there by reason of experience, not study. Still, he fitted them together and made use of the result. Such is the stuff of success in public management.

Putting it another way, Champion in this case came to HEW with relatively sophisticated stereotypes about those organizations. With both he was bound to deal. In doing so he did not have to learn from scratch or change a misconception or climb up above a prejudice; rather, in these instances, he started off approximately right (remembering that everything is relative). Compare him, say, to Secretary Mathews in the swine flu case the year before, whose starting stereotype of HEW's then legal staff was flawed by overconfidence in its proficiency. His lawyers told him he would need no legislation; he took their word for it; they were wrong. The reason they were wrong is that they did not understand procedures and incentives among casualty insurers.

What had contributed to Champion's relative sophistication? A series of exposures, snapshots in the course of time. Unlike Mathews's lawyers, Champion had seen or at least heard about the organizations that would now be crucial to his cause. At the end of the 1940s, when social security coverage was decisively expanded and comprehensive health insurance seriously pressed, he had been legislative assistant to a Fair Deal congressman. Lobbying for the Administration, Altmeyer and Cohen were in touch. During the Kennedy–Johnson years, Champion had been Finance Director—in effect deputy governor—of California until 1967. Thereafter he served on a Johnson task force critically reviewing Federal organization (with an eye to the third Johnson term, which never came). In the one capacity Champion had dealt recurrently with the Social Security Administration from the state side; in the other he was briefed on analytical resources for domestic agencies, emphatically including the Department of HEW.

Lacking such acquired snapshots, it could have been open to Champion, as with anyone else, to seek at least a comparable sophistication from another set of sources, those we have identified with organizational history: on the one hand, successive laws and leaders and the like; on the other hand, the internals that matter so much to managers, the training, the incentives, and the SOPs. That brings us back to time-lines, events, and details, and to the inferences which are the point of it all. Students, even ones with years of experience, are often baffled at being urged to seek insights from such things: Who has the reading lists? Where are the books? But on the job the problem usually is different. Books may be irrelevant or unavailable. The thing to do is ask around.

Why ask about history? Why bother about "big" events and "small" details on time-lines instead of just asking how a place runs? We know three reasons at least. The first is bias. Kennedy probably would not have gotten a useful profile of the CIA by asking Dulles or Bissell how the Agency worked. Had he asked Amory or Helms, he might not have believed what he heard. Even in more collegial organizations, any one person's picture may magnify the part he knows best. Asking several persons is time-consuming. That gives us our second reason: speed. The quickest way for a greenhorn to get an objective picture of an organization is to look at how its current powers, resources, and personnel system compare with those of the past—provided, of course, that the greenhorn will periodically ask "why?" The third reason is that the person getting oriented probably needs to know not just what the organization does now but what it might do or is unlikely to do. Even an unbiased profile of the CDC as of 1976 would probably not have alerted Cooper, Mathews, or Ford to the nature of its relationships with state and local authorities. A briefing on its history—with "Why?" asked now and then—might have done so. Without some sense of how the SSA and P-and-E had evolved, Champion would have been unlikely to hit on the procedures he adopted. With organizations as with issues, looking backward can help one look forward.

The problem is that, in a Champion's shoes, all too many people lack patience for inquiry. Or else pride gets in the way. Or the results are incomplete and imprecise or contradictory and therefore frustrating because ambiguous. Organizational history can be deceptive, especially acquired by word of mouth, catch-as-catch-can. As usual, caution is called for. Yet least cautious of all, we think, is the approach that does not seek because it may not find.

If institutional memory were more structured and better treasured in American government—or if constitutional history and institutional development were seriously studied by Americans in school—there might be less need than we here suggest for newcomers on jobs to use their snapshots or to ask their questions, filling in, *ad hoc,* the history of where they are or what they may encounter, "learning the way to the bathroom" as American bureaucrats say, but also learning where it used to be and why the fixtures were or were not changed, lest finding it prompt inappropriate proposals, untoward or undoable. But in our present state of governmental practice and of higher education, the burden of that learning seems to fall, idiosyncratically, on individuals who may be so ill-trained in thinking about institutions that they scarcely know they bear it, and so don't do it. Placing events and details on time-lines can serve, we hope, as a usefully simple reminder.

13 What to Do and How: A Summary

Thucydides, the exiled Athenian, argued that his history of the Peloponnesian Wars could arm future decision-makers to do better when comparable choices came around again on time's enduring track (he saw it as a circle). He said he wrote for

> . . . those who want to understand clearly the events which happened in the past and which (human nature being what it is) will at some time or other and in much the same ways be repeated in the future.[1]

Implicitly: Vicarious experience acquired from the past, even the remote past, gives such guidance to the present that history becomes more than its own reward. Knowledge conveys wisdom; ignorance courts trouble. Persons of good sense are bound to study history in sheer self-interest, reaching out for reference points of likely future relevance and cramming in vicarious experience from each.

That is the claim traditionally made for history, the use traditionally advanced for it, even by the many who deny its circularity. The course of human affairs sheds light on "now" and "next"; a prudent choice-maker seeks light. Twenty-four centuries after Thucydides, five thousand miles from Greece, attentive to American decision-makers, we wish the claim carried conviction. But in our observation it does not. The people who should heed it don't believe it. Neither work nor schooling gives them much of an incentive to believe.

To be sure, Thucydides' account of the expedition to Syracuse enthralls some of our practitioner-students. American experience in their own lifetimes makes them see Athenian ignorance about Sicilian history, psychology, and capabilities as a strong warning for the likes of Lyndon Johnson when he contemplated warfare at long distance with Vietnamese, of whom he and his aides knew little if anything more. Then why, we are asked in the 1980s, do not the memoranda of Rhodes Scholar Rusk in the mid-1960s invoke Thucydides? Why don't the memoranda of the Bundy brothers? Surely they had read *The Peloponnesian Wars* somewhere, sometime, at least in snippets. But the very notion of their invoking for LBJ the Athenians of the fifth century B.C. boggles our minds. Not because LBJ had his B.A. from Southwest Texas State Teachers College; his mind could grasp anything it could use. As Arthur Schlesinger comments of FDR, "Detail stuck in his mind like sand in honey."[2] But LBJ's advisers did not themselves know what to say if Johnson asked, as he was wont to do, "And therefore?" The concept of progress and the manifestations of technology, to say nothing of American exceptionalism, curtained off the classical past for them no less than for their President. Senator Fulbright did invoke the reference, we are told, but he was by then estranged from Johnson and busy making speeches, many on college campuses. What could the story of those ancients, armed with spears, propelled by oars, maintained by slaves, deprived of electronics, knowing nothing of air power, convey to men managing a modern war?

An answer, we grant, can be offered. All else aside, the blinders self-imposed by senses of superiority, the rash or over-cautious tendencies of generals, the frailties of intelligence, the fickleness of publics, the faithlessness (or anyway, self-interest) of allies, and the uncertainty of luck—these the two expeditions, Athenian and American, do share to a degree, and although not analogous in specifics, the one surely offers reference points for the other. Yet Lyndon Johnson needed no Greeks to teach him things like those. Unfamiliar references could not make such things clearer.

And familiarity would not have guaranteed him against stumbling into war without a grasp of its prospective attributes. Fifty years earlier, across the Atlantic, the decision-makers of July 1914 had the Greeks at their fingertips. Their sons died in the trenches, nevertheless. The premier sources of vicarious experience, on which educated persons in the West—so called, Americans included—had relied since the Renaissance, failed to spare Europe the decisive civil war that cost that continent its world supremacy. Johnson and his advisers must be forgiven for neglecting to identify their country with one episode in another, smaller war twenty-four centuries earlier. The men of 1914, on both sides, had mostly failed to see or heed the parallels between what *they* were launching and the painful struggle, known to every educated European, that had so weakened the Greeks that in the aftermath they all lost independence. Those modern Europeans, much like Johnson in his turn, drew rather on their own than on vicarious experience, seized on the aspect most comforting to them (no continent-wide war for a century), and took it to prove "truths" (that war had become too expensive to last long or reach far). The example of the Europeans in 1914, much more than that of Americans in 1965, mocks the traditional claim for history.

We offer in this book some modest substitutes for that traditional claim, backed up by modest methods, yet we do so with a hope scarcely mentioned until now. We hope that if the mini-methods we suggest were to become routine they might rouse such a hunger for vicarious experience as to renew and justify the larger claim. On this we shall elaborate, but two things intervene. We need first to remind our readers of those methods and second to consider certain practicalities. The question first becomes: In sum, what have we urged practitioners to do? And second, how can they find out enough to do it? Answers for those questions will provide us wherewithal to take up that hope again. We postpone its discussion but briefly.

Our first task is to summarize what we have urged. It is easily done, which testifies, we think, to the simplicity of what we recommend for government routines. For the logic behind our proposals is the essential logic of staff work, or at least of good staff work as we have read about it or observed it. And there is nothing esoteric in that.

Faced with a situation prompting action, the first step in good staff work is to grasp its manifestations: What goes on here? The second step is to identify one's boss's concerns and one's own: If there is a problem to be solved (or lived with), what is it? And whose is it?

Essential if these steps are to be sure-footed is an early effort to clear away impediments embedded in impressions of the past. Whatever the locus of action, from national government down to precinct, whether in an executive body or a legislative committee, some participants are almost sure to start with favorite, long-developed schemes. Their inclination will be to ignore whatever seems not to fit and to define the problem as one calling for solutions they have handy. Their arguments will be supported, more than likely, by analogies. (The new flu could be as severe as Spanish Flu and anyway will spread like previous pandemics. Or "slow squeeze" succeeded in the missile crisis and should do as well for Vietnam.)

We urge that it become standard staff practice to start out by listing in three separate columns key elements of the immediate situation, namely those *Known, Unclear* and *Presumed.* That simple procedure puts attention on the situation itself instead of on the question "what to do" (which thus is kept at bay a little while). The procedure helps establish from the outset what, if anything, is generally agreed. It also points up answerable questions embedded in presumptions or uncertainties, which a little information-gathering might convert to *Knowns.*

An associated procedure is explicit identification of any past situations that appear analogous or someone who matters seems likely to cite as such. Quickly jotting down the *Likenesses* and *Differences* can block use of potentially misleading analogies. Listing *Likenesses* and *Differences* can also help define concerns. If the breakdown of things *Known, Unclear,* and *Presumed* has not by itself established what those concerns are, such *Likenesses* and *Differences* may do so. For the Truman Administration in June 1950, the North Korean attack was the *Known* that caused concern. Inspection of analogies from the 1930s could have sharpened recognition that the basis for concern had less to do with territorial and political arrangements in Asia than with the principle of peaceful change enforced by collective security.

Once situation and concerns have become tolerably clear, the next staff step, in logic, is to define the objective—that is to say, the situation desired in place of the one at hand, the happier "then" to substitute for the bedeviled "now." Here, issue history can help. We recommend routine resort to three devices.

- The first is the *Goldberg Rule.* With some definitions of concerns in hand ask, "What's the story?" How did *these* concerns develop. Take care not to pursue the wrong story. Recall how Carter's staff served up to him the history of SALT negotiations when what he mainly needed was the story of how the two arsenals had expanded. Remember that the "issue" for your boss consists of the concerns appropriate to him, derived from his presumptions (or yours on his behalf) in face of knowns and of uncertainties before him.

- The second device is *time-lines:* Start the story as far back as it properly goes and plot key trends while also entering key events, especially big changes. Don't foreshorten the history in ways that may distort it. Don't neglect changes with high political content.
- The third device is asking *journalists' questions:* As the time-line answers "when" and "what," don't omit to ask also "where," "who," "how," and "why." Answers can illuminate still further the potential incongruities in favorite courses of action. That is part of the point of invoking issue history: to get more thought on where to go and on how to get there before taking off.

Issue history—provided it is the right story, relevant to the appropriate concerns—highlights a range of objectives. In most cases what precipitates concern is a perceived change making current conditions different from those of the past. The earlier conditions may not have been satisfactory, but they weren't crying for attention. Some recent happening—some equivalent to North Korea's attack on South Korea—makes the situation now not what it was before. One possible objective is just to put things back the way they were before. Another is to bring into being for the future a new and more satisfactory state of affairs.

Issue history can help define the desired future. For one thing, looking back at past realities suggests the limitations on some future possibilities. Recognizing that the Russians had never reduced their strategic forces would have made it clearer that Carter's deep cuts proposal asked for radical changes in Moscow's behavior. Recognizing that social security had never been self-financing after 1939—or meant by its sponsors to be, even in 1935—would have helped identify the primary risk incurred in 1972, with cost-of-living adjustments piled on top of benefit increases, namely credibility for the sustaining myth of earned insurance, now rendered much more vulnerable to birthrates, employment, and prices. Issue history enhances recognition of what may be hard to attain, what less hard, and at what cost, and thus aids in *selection* of objectives.

Moreover, issue history sheds light on the next logical step, the selection of options for action once objectives are set. What succeeded in the past might succeed in the future. What failed then might fail now. (But don't neglect the *Likeness/Difference* test. Logically these are analogies, with all attendant hazards.)

Now, at last, we have reached the step where many people yearn to start and often leap for: arraying options. Except as it may be suggestive of the future, history has but a limited role here. For the most part options are defined by current conditions and capabilities. In 1950 Truman had the option of sending ground forces into Korea, because U.S. occupation forces were nearby in Japan. For his immediate decision, it made relatively little difference when or why the troops had been sent to Japan. And that is the usual case, for options are initially arrayed in answer to the question: What can we do *now?* The rush to get to that question explains in part the customary neglect of logically precedent questions, such as whether the situation calls for action at all and, if so, how it got that way.

"What can we do now?" brings forward issues of feasibility. Nowhere else around the Asian rim of Russia did Truman have troops he could bring to bear against agression. In judging feasibility, physical limitations can render history irrelevant. So can technological ones, at least for the near term. Administrative and political limitations, on the other hand, being more subjective, evoke historical considerations of the sort we saw at work in LBJ's Vietnam decisions: For instance, can Americans accomplish what the French could not? Or for another instance, will Truman's fate befall the Democrat who "loses" South Vietnam? Those, in short, are judgments of the future as a product of the past affected by presumptions about the present. This playing off of future, past, and present is important work. We wish we could suggest a mini-method the decision-maker could reliably employ in juggling the relationships. We cannot. This brings us to the absolute frontier of our considerations and experiments up to now. We have no more to offer than a general attitude, a cast of mind, an outlook, not a method—along with our tests for presumptions. To that outlook we return later, proffering examples: Time is viewed as though it were a stream.

Once options have been screened somehow for feasibility and

choice impends among the ones left on the board, then history again can help, we think, by way of tests for presumptions. If not done before, now is the time. The question becomes: What expectations about causes and effects make certain options preferable to others? To attempt an explicit answer is to force review of potentially determinative presumptions. Kennedy and his aides need only have tried on a yellow pad to complete the sentence: "For the objective of bringing Castro down, a landing at the Bay of Pigs is the best option because . . ." (. . . Cubans may rise up in support; . . . if the brigade fails it can fade into the Escambray; . . . in any case, the United States is not overtly involved; and so on) Even had they sidestepped basic beliefs ("truths"), they would have confronted key "if . . . then" presumptions. Those they could have tested—or discarded—on sight.

As simple tests we suggest *bets and odds* and *Alexander's question.* The first involves nothing more than stating odds on an expected outcome (or perhaps saying how much of one's own money one would risk at certain odds). In that way the lay decision-maker can discover differences among experts otherwise masked by terms like "fair chance" or "strong possibility." The second—imitating Dr. Alexander in the swine flu affair—is to ask what new evidence might change a current presumption. Then set a watch to see if the evidence appears. If not, good enough, but if so, perhaps review the roster of options once again.

Finally, both before deciding on an option and afterward, continuously, in the course of implementation, comes the step we label *placement.* It amounts to probing presumptions about relevant people and organizations on whose active aid success depends. The need is for improvement in the starting stereotypes by which persons and institutions at some distance will be categorized, while mindful of the time squeeze that necessitates stereotyping. To this end we suggest *time-lines* arraying *events* and *details* for individuals or organizations, as the case may be, with relevant "public history" appearing as events and personal or internal organizational history as details. Don't stop with the first stereotype: "woman" or "actor" or "bureaucracy" or "interest group." Note the large events to which the person or the organization has been exposed. Add, where useful, *special events,* the public history particular to the set (black history for Martin Luther King). Then put down details, discernible items of individual experience or of internal organizational development. Reviewing both and remembering that different people may see causes and effects in different *patterns,* then draw out *inferences*—working hypotheses one hopes are more sophisticated than those derived from the initial stereotype—and use them to refine it: for instance Frances Perkins as professional in a man's world, regulator, lobbyist, Al Smith Democrat, FDR loyalist, all qualifying "woman."

We identify placement with implementation; the need for it, however, could arise much sooner. If the boss is a stranger or his job unfamiliar, placing both the person and the organization helps define concerns.

Placing an organization and placing a person call for the same kind of reasoning. That is why we use "events" and "details" as terms for both. But we recognize that most people find it harder to think about institutions than to think about individuals. Almost any American with a sense of his country's history (alas, not every American) can be reminded that Ronald Reagan voted four times for FDR and can recognize that fact as one with possible implications for his concept of the presidency. Not every American so equipped will recognize equally readily possible implications in, for example, the fact that the Department of Energy was originally the Atomic Energy Commission, engaged chiefly in producing weapons; that the Department of Housing and Urban Development grew out of the Federal Housing Administration, dating from the late New Deal and engaged mainly in guaranteeing mortgages on private homes; or that the Navy had been a wholly autonomous department and service from 1798 to 1947, engaged almost exclusively in tasks it set itself. Lack of recognition is in part because the history of organizations has so small a space in the history generally taught. In part it is because people are easier to empathize with than institutions.

When we surveyed men and women who had taken our course, asking their experience in applying our mini-methods on the job, only a minority said they regularly looked at organizational histories. Those who did were nearly unanimous, however, in designating placement of organizations as the most helpful notion they had drawn from the course. And some of their uses went beyond what we originally imagined. One, a lawyer in private practice, had refined his stereotype of a law firm, learning thereby—as he saw it—how first to win a partnership and then how gradually to change some of his partners' conventions. Another, a senior civil servant, congratulated himself (and disquieted us) by reporting that study of his agency's past had enhanced his own ability to manipulate the political appointees supposedly directing it. But we accept the general finding of the survey.[3] Placing the organization, partly because it is the least natural of the various steps we suggest, may yield a high return in terms of questions that might otherwise be left unasked or answers left unexamined.

We put our recommended steps in terms of staff work, but our eyes are on the choices. If decision-makers are their own staff, or if staffers make the choices, fine: The steps apply regardless. So do the procedural devices we propose. Our mini-methods are for anyone who needs them, boss included.

The point is to get forward, as soon as possible, the questions that ought to be asked before anyone says, "This is what we should *do*" or "Here's how to do it."

Our list of questions is far from comprehensive. Many others may need to be asked and answered. As examples: What are the measurable costs? How do they relate to measurable benefits? How are costs and benefits to be tracked? What are the comparative utilities of the various objectives? How do they trade off against each other? A comprehensive list may include technical questions. The swine flu risk did call for judgments by epidemiologists and other doctors. Social security financing involved issues best addressed by economists, demographers, statisticians, accountants, and lawyers. Even in taking the first step toward SALT II, Carter needed advice from physicists, engineers, systems analysts, and experts not only on arms control verification technologies but also on budgeting techniques. Theorists of various types have worked for decades to develop capital-M Methodologies—even entire professional codes—which cope with those components of public policy decisions. What we try to do in this book is give slightly more systematic form to the components usually lumped together as "experience" or "common sense" or "judgment." Combined with formal Methodologies and professional expertise—not substituting for them—these mini-methods can, we think, add marginally to the decision-maker's sense of knowing where he is going when he says, "Okay, *this* is what we'll do."

One query always thrown at us when we run through our mini-methods is: "If I don't already know the piece of history and I need it in a hurry, how do I get it?" That puzzle has to be dealt with directly. We shall argue later for using leisure—or even time in school—to learn some history that just might have future use. But the particular problem could arise for anyone. How many Americans, however educated, could have been expected in the 1960s to know the history of Vietnam or in the 1970s that of the petroleum industry or in the 1980s that of Lebanon or El Salvador or the Federal income tax?

To state the puzzle is almost to solve it. Historical information is no different from any other kind. You just have to recognize that you need it. If in a position to do so, you then say to someone else, "Go find out . . .," leaving it to that someone to figure out how and where, possibly even what. Alternatively—or if you are the someone—pick up the telephone.

The numbers to be phoned start with ones in the Rolodex. During the *Mayaguez* affair, it was David Kennerly, the White House photographer, who had the brass to ask whether everyone was sure that the Cambodian government had ordered the seizure. Had Kennerly wanted also to ask questions about the *Pueblo* precedent, he might well have rung up Y. R. Okamoto, who had been LBJ's White House photographer. Okamoto could at least have given him the names of other old hands to call. Similarly, when faced by the Soviet brigade in Cuba, Vance or Brzezinski might have phoned Dean Rusk. He tells us that he could have "straightened them out . . . in five minutes—but no one called." Rusk, a professor at the Law School of the University of Georgia, would have been easy to find.

However found, old hands are likely to be the first, perhaps only, sources with whom to check recent analogies, issue histories, personal biographies, and organizational histories. They may have axes to grind. None will know more than part of any story. Those are good reasons for keeping in mind the "Goldberg rule," timelines, and journalists' questions, whatever the subject of inquiry. If asked to "tell the story," the old hand will find it harder to serve up just a biased, present-day cut of an issue, person, or agency. The injunction to "go back to the beginning" helps give the story order. Supplementing "when" and "what" with "where," "who," "how," and "why" makes it fuller.

Reporters or broadcasters can serve as surrogates for or supplements to old hands from officialdom. If an issue has been around for a long time, people actually in government are likely to have bills of goods to sell; that may be true of journalists, too, but also it may not. Veteran journalists have a lot of the information useful in placement, for part of their business is hoarding gossip. The obvious caution is that newsgatherers seldom give up information except for a price. Members of Carter's staff could not have questioned the newspapermen who had done research on Senator Jackson without at least saying why and running a risk either that something more about the SALT initiative would leak or at least that Scoop himself would learn they were nosing around. Still, the good journalist is a source officials should not ignore.

Last among those to be phoned will be people who make a living out of having history on tap. Sometimes it will be a mistake to put them last. In the Federal government and in a number of state and local governments, various agencies have in-house historians. The Senate has had one now for a decade. The House has just installed one. Sometimes those official historians qualify as particularly objective old hands. They rarely have high status. (In the early 1950s Oliver Clubb, one of the State Department's China specialists, resigned from the Foreign Service rather than serve in the Division of Historical Research. He took it as equivalent to internal exile.)[4] On the other hand, in-house historians have been licensed to look at records from all levels of the organization, and they have lived inside it. Had McGeorge Bundy's staff wanted his memorandum on the "French analogy" to say something about France and Indochina in years prior to 1954, one good source would have been mid-level civil servants in the State Department's Historical Office who were just then pulling together, for volumes of *Foreign Relations of the United States,* documents dealing with Southeast Asia in the early 1950s.

If the professional historians are not in some sense in-house, officials probably do right to put them last (here, as elsewhere, we use "historian" to include also a number of people who happen to call themselves economists, political scientists, or sociologists, and some who also qualify as journalists). The reason is that the government official probably will have trouble specifying just what he wants to know. The scholar will know too much and may well have trouble saying anything without qualification. Conversations can resemble those between Chinese speaking different dialects, with writing the only useful form of communication. (Though we dream of a day when officials and historians will talk to each other more easily, we have seen little earthly evidence to sustain hope. Officials who talk a lot with historians come to imagine that they are historians themselves. Historians who talk even a little with officials come to imagine themselves "advisers." The exceptions are rare.)

If telephone calls aren't enough and someone must himself turn to written texts, where does he go? What does he look for? (Or she, as the case may be.)

Answers could fill a large book. In fact they fill several. Perhaps the most interestingly written is *The Modern Researcher* by Jacques Barzun and Henry Graff.[5] We offer here only the sketchiest of advice, but tailored to the overworked staff aide with an urgent deadline.

Bibliographies can save time. The venerable *Reader's Guide to Periodical Literature* has up-to-date subject indexes of magazine articles. There are special indexes of congressional documents, social science publications, statistics, laws, and so forth. There are also biographical directories by the score. Ask a librarian for help. That's their business.

If an index points you toward periodical articles and the *National Journal* or the London *Economist* or *Science* is cited, go there first. They are apt to provide both current news and background. Among less frequently published journals, others on which to keep an eye, for the same reason, are the *Congressional Quarterly, Foreign Affairs, Foreign Policy,* and *The Wilson Quarterly.*

For information about events farther back in time, it may be necessary to go to books. *The Harvard Guide to American History,* edited by Frank Freidel, is a little out of date but still useful.[6] The Library of Congress publishes on microfiche a subject index of recently published books. Librarians can point you toward other finding aids. If you have access to a data base such as Lockheed's DIALOG, your computer can fetch you titles and abstracts not only from book lists and news and magazine digests but from specialized guides prepared for historians and various types of social scientists.

Once you have articles or books in hand, you may discover that they disagree. How do you decide, in a hurry, which ones to trust? As a starter you should presume that the one most recently published is best because it probably takes account of, and tries to supersede, everything written earlier. But you should check that presumption against the work's bibliography or footnotes or other indications of sources. If it doesn't mention earlier writings you know about or if it seems to be based on skimpy research, turn to something older.

Especially if the article or book has no footnotes, pay heed to the author's credentials. If he (or she) is based in a reputable college or university, you know that he had graduate training in research and that the results have gone through some form of peer review. If he is a journalist, you won't know about his research training unless some headnote mentions it. On the other hand, if he is attached to a good newspaper or magazine, you can be sure that he has been tested on his ability to get facts straight. Note also, if you can, what else he has published. That may give some indication of whether or not he knows his stuff.

A glance through opening and closing paragraphs can sometimes tell you all you need to know about the author's interpretation. If he claims to have discovered some truth never before suspected, especially some dark conspiracy, try another book. If, however, the author seems sensible, then skim the work. We shall say a word later about articles or books you might *read.* Here we speak of ones you leaf through because you have work to do. Remember that you are looking for an answer or answers to questions that arise in the process of defining a situation and what to do about it. The clearer those questions are in your mind, the faster your fingers can flip through even the most massive fine-print tome. It isn't hard, and it gets easier with practice.

Plainly, the more history one carries in one's head about more centuries or countries—or institutions, issues, individuals, whatever—the less one has to scramble in these ways when need arises. In the missile crisis, having just read Barbara Tuchman's *Guns of August,* Kennedy did not depend on staff to raise with him the sobering reference point of 1914. A memory check (accompanied ideally by a check *on* memory) is a relatively fast, efficient way to cut time and curtail dependence—provided one's memory has some things of use stored up in it.

That brings us back to history's traditional claim that study of the past in general helps decision-makers in particular. We hope we can strengthen the claim. We think we can; indeed we think we have. For in at least two tangible respects the mini-methods we propose, tailored as they are to the particular, put premiums on general knowledge already at hand, already stored away.

The premiums attach to inventory and to context. Explaining those takes but a moment.

"Inventory" simply means the stock of historical knowledge, the accumulated points of reference readily available within a given mind from which to pull analogies or time-lines as occasion warrants, or to test those drawn by others. "Context" has a simple meaning too: The more history one knows, the better one understands the options. Anyone compiling events and details for Scoop Jackson, say, would have been hard put to leave out his persistent advocacy of increased defense spending from the very start of the Cold War. But only someone who recalled the period just after World War II, either from living through it or vicariously from reading, would be likely to grasp that up to 1948 at least, if not up to Korea, a Northern Democrat so staked out was about as rare as, then, a Southern Republican. Thinking about actual *use* of *Likenesses* and *Differences* or events and details on a time-line or the "Goldberg rule" (asking what the story is) or even "Alexander's question" (what new *Knowns* would change a *Presumed*?) cannot but suggest the usefulness of general historical knowledge.

Unhappily, as we commented when explaining the origins of our joint endeavor, general knowledge of history is less and less characteristic of American decision-makers and their aides. Our educational system turns out lawyers who may know only the history they learn through the constricting prisms of court opinions; economists who may learn neither economic history nor much if any economic thought except their own; scientists who may know next to nothing of the history of science; engineers who may be innocent of history entirely, even that of their profession; graduates of business schools with but a smattering of theirs; and generalist B.A.s who may, with ingenuity, have managed to escape all history of every sort. Our government and politics are peopled by such as these. To ask them to take seriously Thucydides' claim for history in his terms seems a lot. But that is tempered by the fact that reading histories, his included, can be represented readily as fun for anyone who takes an interest in the human comedy, a point to which we shall return.

Throughout this book we have stressed that our hopes have to do with margins: a little sharper sense of purpose here, a little clearer sense of danger there. Regarding education, formal as well as informal, our hopes are similarly constrained, but no less strong. If Americans who see themselves potentially as decision-makers, or as aides or even choosers of decision-makers, come to think it useful to accumulate inventory and context, as we define the terms, more of them may put part of their time, in school and out, into study of the past.

If so, we see a likely byproduct perhaps even more useful to decision-makers than gap-filling in inventory and context. The byproduct is visualizing issues in time-streams. To link conventional wisdoms of the present with past counterparts and future possibilities; to link interpretations of the past with the experiences of interpreters, and both with their prescriptions; to link proposals for the future with the inhibitions of the present as inheritances from the past—all these mean to think relatively and in terms of time, opening one's mind to possibilities as far back as the story's start and to potentialities as far ahead as relevant (judged, of course, from now, hence subject to revision later). That entails seeing time as a stream. It calls for thinking of the future as emergent from the past and of the present as a channel that perhaps conveys, perhaps deflects, but cannot stop the flow. (Conveys? Deflects? In what degree? A critical concern!) Perception of time-in-flow cannot help but be encouraged by purposeful study of stretches of history, regardless of whose it is or what the focus. Or so *we* think—and hope.

That brings us to our final point, a final use for history. Seeing time as a stream has an enormous value, in our eyes, to government decision-makers. Since they may not have been schooled in any past except their own, perhaps not even that, they should welcome any sort of practice. History can provide it. Every prior illustration in this book has something to contribute on that score, over and above its other purposes, an indication of the riches history holds. Those and the uses of such thought we find a fitting subject for a final chapter.

14 Seeing Time as a Stream

In the spring of 1943 George Marshall called John Hilldring to his office. It was the middle of World War II. The Germans were still deep in Russia; the British and Americans had cleared North Africa but not yet invaded Sicily or Italy. The Japanese controlled most of the Western Pacific. Marshall was Chief of Staff of the U.S. Army. Hilldring, a two-star general, had just been given the job of organizing military governments for countries to be liberated or conquered. Years afterward Hilldring reported what Marshall said to him:

> I'm turning over to you a sacred trust and I want you to bear that in mind every day and every hour you preside over this military government and civil affairs venture. Our people sometimes say that soldiers are stupid. I must admit at times we are. Sometimes our people think we are extravagant with the public money, that we squander it, spend it recklessly. I don't agree that we do. We are in a business where it's difficult always to administer your affairs as a businessman can administer his affairs in a company, and good judgment sometimes requires us to build a tank that turns out not to be what we want, and we scrap that and build another one. . . . But even though people say we are extravagant, that in itself isn't too disastrous. . . .
>
> But we have a great asset and that is that our people, our country-

> men, do not distrust us and do not fear us. Our countrymen, our fellow citizens, are not afraid of us. They don't harbor any ideas that we intend to alter the government of the country or the nature of this government in any way. This is a sacred trust that I turn over to you today. . . . I don't want you to do anything, and I don't want to permit the enormous corps of military governors that you are in the process of training and that you are going to dispatch all over the world, to damage this high regard in which the professional soldiers in the Army are held by our people, and it could happen, it could happen, Hilldring, if you don't understand what you are about.[1]

Marshall's injunction to Hilldring illustrates what we mean by seeing and thinking in "time-streams." Though busy fighting a war, he paused to ponder possible futures. He looked not only to the coming year but well beyond, and with a clear sense of the long past from which those futures would come. At least in some general way, he brought to bear an understanding of how military–civilian relations had evolved in other countries: in Britain before the Mutiny Act; in the France of the Dreyfus Affair; in Imperial and Weimar Germany. He recognized what was genuinely exceptional in America. He thought of what his concerns (or his successors') might be if Hilldring made day-to-day decisions without regard to imaginable long-term consequences. By looking back, Marshall looked ahead, identifying what was worthwhile to preserve from the past and carry into the future. By looking around, at the present, he identified what could stand in the way, what had potential to cause undesired changes of direction. Seeing something he had power to reduce, if not remove, he tried to do so.

Another instance of such thought on Marshall's part comes five years later, during 1948. By then out of uniform, he was Truman's Secretary of State. One of his main concerns was China. In the civil war there, the Communists seemed to be winning. Like just about everyone else in Washington, Marshall wanted the Communists to lose. He asked General Albert Wedemeyer, once his chief planner and at the end of the war commander in the China Theater, to review whether anything could be done. After touring the area, Wedemeyer recommended to Marshall that the United States dispatch a few thousand military advisers. Brigaded with Chinese Nationalist units, Wedemeyer predicted, those advisers could turn the tide, perhaps even enable the Nationalists to win. Though Marshall respected Wedemeyer's professional judgment, he concluded that the United States should not go beyond giving the Nationalists money and supplies. As he explained to the Senate Foreign Relations Committee in executive session, he felt that anything more could involve "obligations and responsibilities . . . which I am convinced the American people would never knowingly accept." In the long run, he added, the Chinese would resent foreign interference. Besides, he doubted whether there were enough qualified Americans. In all events: "It would be impossible to estimate the final costs. . . . It certainly would be a continuing operation for a long time to come. It would involve this Government in a continuing commitment from which it would practically be impossible to withdraw."[2]

Here again, Marshall looked at an issue in the present with a sense both of past and of future. Reading and experience alike had taught him that American public tolerance for war was short. His first assignment had been in the Philippines after the Spanish–American War, when public opinion, once exultant about the new empire, had shifted to sympathy with Filipinos resisting conquest. He had witnessed dire disenchantment on the heels of World War I and a dislike for even small-scale military actions, such as that in Nicaragua in the mid-1920s, once they lasted a little while. Recently he had spent his final weeks as Chief of Staff coping with "bring the boys home" demonstrations. Moreover, he had served in China more than once before World War II and spent a year there afterward trying to mediate between the Communists and the Nationalists. He thus had some sense of the history and character of China as well as of his own country. Though he shared the general yearning for a China not Communist, his judgment on what to do was disciplined by awareness of what had gone before and might arrive again, and also of potentials in the present. He knew firsthand that Chiang was out of steam while Mao was not. Calculating that he could not stop the change without unacceptable cost, if at all, he counseled living with it.

Marshall's habit of thinking in time-streams did not always make him negative. Perhaps the boldest act of his whole career was espousal of what history remembers as the Marshall Plan. After less than six months in the Secretaryship of State, though little acquainted before with either international economic issues or the people allegedly expert about them, Marshall concluded that economic conditions in Europe called for drastic and unprecedented remedies. Others, of course, provided diagnoses and suggested possible treatments. But the particular prescription was his own. He wrote the text of his speech, delivered at the Harvard Commencement in June 1947, which outlined the plan. The State Department had no advance copy. The elements were majestically simple. First, Marshall identified the target as "not . . . any country or doctrine but . . . hunger, poverty, desperation and chaos." Second, he said, the approach "must not be on a piecemeal basis as various crises develop": Action should "provide a cure rather than a mere palliative." Third, the Russians and their satellites were welcome to take part, provided they genuinely cooperated and did not "seek to perpetuate human misery in order to profit therefrom politically or otherwise." Finally, the initiative had to come from the Europeans. They should collectively define what they needed and ask the United States for help.[3]

Not given to explaining himself, Marshall did not say, then or later, why he crafted the plan as he did. But his choices almost surely emerged from his looking toward the future with a long look at the past. Couching the proposal in humanitarian rather than anti-Soviet or anti-Communist terms expressed an awareness that Americans were traditionally eager to help the hungry, but no less traditionally suspicious of anything "politically motivated." Making it a one-piece plan acknowledged that American attention spans traditionally were short. Only so could it hold public and congressional support long enough to be effective. And putting the onus on the Europeans recognized not only the American propensity to respond to appeals for help but also the European propensity to bridle at dictation from upstarts across the Atlantic. What Marshall proposed was unprecedented in both character and scale. It was breathtakingly imaginative. Yet underneath was cautious concern about what might go wrong, and underneath that (we think—we cannot prove it) was deep awareness of long-running currents in both American and European experience.

Marshall made mistakes. In 1941 he was as blind as other Washingtonians to Japanese perceptions of Japan's dilemma. Pearl Harbor astonished him. In 1948, at the same time he was choosing against military involvement in China, Marshall played the starchy diplomat on Palestine, insisting to Truman that neither sympathy for displaced persons nor Britain's one-time pledge to Jews, nor even (least of all) the Jewish vote in that election year should influence American policy. (Clark Clifford heard the Secretary lecture the President in "a righteous, goddamned Baptist tone.") Marshall feared, among other things, that the public would not long support a policy seen as so influenced.[4] His fear was baseless (or seems so thus far), for recognizing and backing Israel proved enduringly popular. After the outbreak of the Korean War, Marshall, then named Secretary of Defense, adhered to the traditional principle of noninterference with the field commander, the more so since the latter had an old suspicion of him, and accordingly did little to restrain MacArthur's feckless march toward the Chinese border.

Nevertheless, overall, Marshall seems to us, as generally he did to FDR and Truman and to almost everyone else, a preeminent example in the governmental sphere of someone with "good judgment." It is our contention that at least in his case—we believe in others as well—his judgment was the better for that habit of thought about time as a stream.

Thinking of time in such a way appears from our examples to have three components. One is recognition that the future has no place to come from but the past, hence the past has predictive value. Another element is recognition that what matters for the future in the present is departures from the past, alterations, changes, which prospectively or actually divert familiar flows from accustomed channels, thus affecting that predictive value and much else besides. A third component is continuous comparison, an almost constant oscillation from present to future to past and back, heedful of prospective change, concerned to expedite, limit, guide, counter, or accept it as the fruits of such comparison suggest. Judging from examples offered here and many others, those components in some fashion, perhaps explained quite differently by Marshall to himself, were present in his habitual thought and so define it for us.

Examples drawn from Marshall will suggest a further point, namely that thought about time as a stream does not necessarily call for great historical learning. John Melby, a Foreign Service Officer who once traveled with Marshall, wrote disappointedly that the general "had little sense of history. . . . His conversation never goes beyond the scope of his experience; he sees a movie every night he is home, and reads cheap fiction endlessly." Melby did not see enough of Marshall to get a full picture. Marshall had lectured on military history at the Infantry School. During World War II he sometimes read history for relaxation. On the return flight from the Casablanca Conference of 1943 he finished off one of Arthur Bryant's three volumes on England in the Napoleonic wars and also J. H. Haskell's *This Was Cicero.* Reading of

Pitt the Younger and of Julius Caesar reassured him, as he wrote a British friend, that "grave problems of leadership were neither new nor insoluble." Still, Marshall was no scholar, and he certainly never paraded knowledge. "Avoid trivia," he told staff officers, and he obeyed the rule himself.[5]

Marshall may have been better off for *not* singling out particular signposts from the past. When working on the Marshall Plan, for instance, he surely thought of Lend-Lease as a precedent, but it was probably just as well that he did not mention it. At best, it could have been a seductive analogy. At worst, it could have distracted his auditors, if not himself.

In that respect Truman is a contrast to Marshall. Truman had read a good deal of world history and had almost encyclopedic knowledge of the political and military history of his own country. (Some of it actually came from having, as a child, pored over encyclopedias.) He enjoyed his knowledge and liked to put it on display. In his memoirs he contended that it had been helpful to him and could equally serve others. He made his case in terms of analogues he said he had consulted during his Senate and White House years: the Committee on the Conduct of the Civil War as a bad precedent for his own Senate committee in World War II; Andrew Johnson in comparison with him as accidental President at war's end; Lincoln and McClellan as counterparts for him and MacArthur; the 1930s with their lessons, and so on.[6] Yet the case seems rather weak. As nearly as we can tell, the truly historic choices of Truman's presidency—with the exception of aid to Greece in 1947 and his move to save Korea in June 1950, a story already told—were made with little or no reference to all those precedents stored in his memory. We do not question that he showed a strong capacity to follow arguments couched in historical terms, concerned with the significance of present or prospective change. If no one else drew an analogy, he often did. No doubt he gained some insights and much comfort from his stock of them. But in decision-making style he was a case-by-case man, each on its own terms, not constantly comparing either across issues or through time.

To contrast Truman with Marshall is not to make a case against the usefulness of knowledge. Far from it. But knowledge as such, we do suggest, the knowledge of historical specifics, cannot substitute for (even though it supplements) the kind of mental quality that readily connects discrete phenomena over time and repeatedly checks connections. That is a special style of approaching choices, more the planner's or the long-term program manager's than the lawyer's or judge's or consultant's or trouble-shooter's—and surely more Marshall's than Truman's. (The question of which approach, if either, is characteristic of a given man or woman lends itself to testing via events and details on a time-line.)

To clarify the distinction further we return to FDR, whose aptitude for thinking of time as a stream was well illustrated by his contributions to the original Social Security Act. Roosevelt referred to historical events more often than Marshall did. Sometimes, especially in foreign affairs, he used them as Truman would do with Korea. Roosevelt's extra-careful approach in creating the UN owed something, for example, to the captivating analogy with Wilson and the League.[7] Usually, however, Roosevelt drew on history in a different way from Truman.

How differently one can see in the Commonwealth Club speech of 1932—the one that so surprises students by its forecast of no economic growth.[8] Most of that speech dealt with the evolution of government since feudal times. Roosevelt talked of the rise of opposition to government and how that had helped lead to the American Revolution. He summarized the differences between Hamilton and Jefferson, saying that the one had focussed more on the need for governmental power, the other on the dangers inherent in it. He described how, since Jefferson's day, factories and financial empires, together with the rise of cities and the closing of the frontier, had created new conditions. All that led to his central proposition:

> Government is a relation of give and take, a contract, perforce, if we would follow the thinking out of which it grew. Under such a contract rulers were accorded power, and the people consented to that power on consideration that they be accorded certain rights. The task of statesmanship has always been the re-definition of these rights in terms of a changing and growing social order. New conditions impose new requirements upon Government and those who conduct Government.

Roosevelt was mistaken in going on to say that one of the new conditions was an end of economic growth. But by looking at "now" in light of a long past and by recognizing processes of change, he saved himself from being permanently a prisoner of that mistake.

For the essence of thinking in time-streams is imagining the future as it may be when it becomes the past—with some intelligible continuity but richly complex and able to surprise. Someone who has acquired the habit is thereby made wary of "problem-solving." (Not despairing, not even distrustful, just wary.) During World War II William S. Knudsen briefly headed the American defense production effort. A genial self-made man, risen from auto mechanic to the presidency of General Motors, he approached his government assignment as if he were organizing assembly lines, getting the kinks out with determinate quick fixes. "You bring it to the shop door, and I'll cut it up," he said repeatedly to the military services and other claimants.[9] Since the need was for no less than transformation of American industry and of its labor force to produce different goods in novel ways, on a scale and schedule outside his experience (or anyone's) for an unknown duration in a most uncertain world, Knudsen did not do well or last long. A quarter-century later, the onetime president of Ford, Robert McNamara, did better and lasted longer, but his country sometimes suffered when he slipped into a similar approach. McGeorge Bundy's critique of McNamara's troop buildup in 1965 addressed the larger, longer implications and potentialities in terms quite close to those that had warned Marshall away from China eighteen years before. Rusk, who idolized Marshall, also saw them; recall his early warning to both Bundy and McNamara that some way had to be found of neither abandoning Vietnam nor stepping up American involvement.[10] But McNamara, in 1965 anyway, seemed to feel sure that if the problem were brought to his shop, he could cut it up. At any rate he thought it his duty to make things appear so. Someone who saw the future as part of a stream running continuously from the past, both America's past *and* Vietnam's, might have been more cautious, especially if he also saw that when it happened it might well be like the present in confounding previous hopes!

Thinking of time as a stream need not induce discouragement about the future. Thinking so helped FDR envision a social security system that could outlast him and his children: It has kept at bay "those sons of bitches on the Hill" (and off) for nearly fifty years now. Thinking so helped Marshall see in the downhearted Europe of 1947 the prosperous community that a large dose of dollar aid could foster. Sensing that the present was alive with change, they knew the past would be outmoded by a future that had never been. But their image of that future could be realistic because informed by understanding of its sources in the past. Equally realistic, because similarly informed, could be their sense of how much care and effort it would take to shape the future as desired, how crucial therefore to survey the obstacles and count the costs beforehand.

Carter provides an object lesson of someone who apparently thought otherwise. His basic approach resembled Knudsen's: one problem at a time; solve it, get on to the next. In addition, he showed confidence amounting to self-delusion in the face of likely difficulties. Recall that after the election he collected and reiterated all the promises he had uttered during the campaign, filed them in his Press Room, and passed them out in Congress, ceremoniously committing himself to fulfill them all without remanding any to a third year or a fourth, or to a second term, or to indefinite study. Rather, all were out there, seemingly labeled "soon."[11] Combined with falling for the analogues of "hundred days" and "honeymoon," that contributed to his undoing.

It may not be fortuitous that our source of examples for thought in a time-stream, George Marshall, was a soldier or that, when Harvard gave him his honorary degree in 1947, the citation compared him with George Washington, also a soldier. For the military profession, probably more than any other, fosters thinking about the future. This is not to say that all soldiers do it. Far from it! But the good planner, the first-rate staff officer, as Marshall surely was, works imaginative foresight to the limit. A successful operation plan provides for essentials to be in place when and as called for, down to the last rifle and ration. In the trade of public management, such plans are sometimes made by "backward mapping," more often by forward probes. Thinking in a time-stream can amount to the same things: visualizing a desired future in realistic terms and figuring out, step by step, detail by detail, what "then" requires all the way back to "now," or conversely how "now" might be turned by stages into something approaching "then." Or the future can be undesired and the plans made to avoid it, as with Marshall and Hilldring—or if need be to accept it, as Marshall might have had us do a generation before we did with Communist China.

In the soldier's case, thought about the future is made specially serious by awareness of the stakes, professional and personal, especially if the soldier is also, as Marshall was, a willing citizen of a democracy. As Chesterton once observed, the military profession has less room than most for illusion: "If you have lost a battle, you cannot believe you have won it." And the reckoning comes in human bodies. Late in life, after having been both Secretary of State and Secretary of Defense, Marshall said he still believed that military men should not, as a rule, be involved in political decisions. "[T]he effects are too wide-reaching," he explained:

> Also it must be remembered the military responsibility in operations is very, very large, and it has with it a terrible measure of casualties. I know I was very careful to send Mr. Roosevelt every few days a statement of our casualties and it was done in a very effective way, graphically and . . . in colors, so it would be quite clear to him when he had only a moment or two to consider. I tried to keep before him all the time the casualty results because you get hardened to these things and you have to be very careful to keep them always in the forefront of your mind.[12]

One does not have to plan campaigns or calculate outcomes in dead and wounded to learn to think in time-streams, but it may help. Surely it does help to bear in mind that futures arrive detail by detail and that decisions lightly taken sometimes carry awful costs.

Suppose we persuade somebody that thought about time as a stream is a good habit to have or acquire. But how to begin? How do it at all? How come to do it regularly? How guard against forgetting? How interpret ambiguities? Apart from citing individual examples, what do we say to such questions?

As with noticing "patterns," we cannot propose useful "mini-methods." Thinking in time-streams is not something we see how to do by following particular routines. We wish we did. We would like to repair the lack, if indeed it can be done, but not this round, not in this book. Analogizing and invoking issue history and testing presumptions and placement have preoccupied us until now. Possibly, with concentration, we might find some simple means to aid in answering those questions. But we do not have them yet. Whether we ever shall is speculative. All we can offer now are a couple of tests (for oneself or others) to show how hard or easy such thought comes, and a couple of experimental exercises similar to those for "patterns"; further, some suggestions for spare-time reading; finally, a few words of personal perspective. We proceed down this list.

As an initial test of anyone's propensity to think in time-streams, we put forward "intervals," a two-level game we invented for the purpose. On the first, simplest level ask, "What does 'decade' mean to you? What does it signify if someone tells you something is a decade hence?" See whether the answer is "ten years" (with a stare and a shrug) or something like: "the time between Harding and FDR" or "the length of the (American) war in Vietnam" or "about as far from now as when the North Sea oil supposedly runs out" or "when I was in Junior High." Alternatively, one could ask about the meaning of "year," "century," "generation." Whatever the question, if the answer comes in terms like those, however personal, not numbers, it is likely that what is in evidence is the appropriate imagination, an imagination sparked by time itself and by its meaning for the march of human generations. To probe that likelihood, move up a level to a question on the order of: "How do you react when someone says the social security trust fund may run out in 2050 or thereabouts?" If the response resembles "I worry hard; there won't be enough workers to support the oldsters from the baby boom," then the talent for thinking in time-streams may be limited. If, rather, the response approximates, "recalling what has happened in the world and the economy and U.S. population—and to successive demographic projections—in the sixty years just past, I cannot worry yet . . . too soon . . . don't know . . . birthrates . . . immigration . . . ask again in 2020," the talent is probably there.

As a second test of talent, check the frequency with which the subject (whether you or someone else) inquires of the day's news, "What's so new about that?" In thinking of time as a stream, the preeminent challenge is to judge whether change has happened or is happening or will. The imperative need is to get that reasonably right. This mode of thought contributes to the chances of doing so by continuously posing comparisons of present with past and future. The affair of the Soviet brigade in Cuba illustrates in caricature what can occur when people perceive change where there is none. The social security amendments of 1972 suggest what can result from failure to see that change is actually in progress. On both occasions activists were guilty of careless comparisons. To challenge the newness of news suggests caring, at least, if not carefulness.

In the United States, to an extraordinary degree, the national political agenda is a product of careless comparisons—a series of Soviet brigades. The media contribute to this. Every night the networks have to produce "news"—evidence of change. Absence of change can become news through the hypothesis that change is supposed to occur. ("This is the hundreth day of the 'hostage crisis.'") The morning papers have to keep up with the networks, and the weeklies have to outdo both. Almost continuous political campaigns also contribute, for "ins" have to allege that things are better now than they used to be, while "outs" have to charge that things are getting worse. And the public at large has little immunity, first because change inheres in "the American way of life" (brands of beer, cars, houses, spouses); second because most people have not had much schooling in history; and third because they have been so deluged with "news" denoted "crisis" that the memory cells are cluttered.

Even people who should know better, who ought to *remember* that the past was not that different from the present, fall into the trap. Consider, for example, one alleged problem widely and solemnly discussed, at the time we write, by columnists and other would-be setters of agenda, namely the need for a "new consensus" on foreign policy. The premise is that back in the period from World War II to the Vietnam War there was general agreement about the world role of the United States and how it should be played. An "establishment" centered in New York at the Council on Foreign Relations provided bipartisan leadership. Now, by contrast, there is absence of agreement, controversy, partisanship, politics beyond the water's edge, and perceived absence of purpose. From that premise it follows that the challenge for would-be American leaders is to identify and take account of ways in which conditions have changed and then, having done so, to rebuild the lost "consensus."

Whatever one may say about the goal, the premise is almost pure fantasy. The reality is that in the early Cold War years a coalition of Democrats and Republicans successfully prevented a revival of isolationism. They obtained wide and lasting public and congressional support for the proposition that the United States had a vital interest in a peaceful and stable Western Europe. Ditto Japan. Agreement also existed that the Soviet Union was bad and represented the principal threat to those vital interests and to peace and stability everywhere. About other matters, however, consensus would have been hard to find. The years from 1945 to 1960 saw bitter, partisan, and utterly consensus-free debate about the "loss" of China, the long-term stationing of troops in Europe, the limiting of warfare in Korea, and whether a new war ought to be risked for Dien Bien Phu or Quemoy and the Matsus. Democrats blamed Eisenhower for what happened in Latin America, whether it was dictatorships replacing democracies or, as in Cuba, Communists replacing dictators. Over recognizing Israel in 1948 and the Suez affair of 1956 there was also little accord.

If ever anything existed like consensus across the board, it developed from efforts by Kennedy and Johnson to gain protection against attacks such as Republicans had made on Truman and they themselves had made on Eisenhower. The period marked by *least* public disagreement over foreign policy extended from the winter of 1962, after the Cuban missile crisis, until the spring of 1965, following the bombing of North Vietnam and the invasion of the Dominican Republic—a period of about twenty-eight months.

On the limited set of issues where consensus had developed between 1945 and 1960, it persisted thereafter. Indeed, it grew stronger. In the earlier period the Taft wing of the Republican party had stood for a "fortress America" alternative. In the 1980s Taft's political heir, Reagan, was as ardently pro-NATO as any Democrat or Eastern establishmentarian. Concerning Latin America, the Middle East, and Asia the spread of opinion in Reagan's time grew wider than in 1963–65 but not nearly so wide as during many of the years from 1945 to 1960. Yet in the 1980s those would-be agenda-setters—some of whom had witnessed the 1950s—talked as if an ideal future could be found by looking back to years when State Department China hands were being purged and Senators talked of impeaching Truman because he had fired General MacArthur!

So much for Golden Ages.

Our second test for a propensity to think in terms of time is thus the frequency with which one reads or hears about some alleged change, pauses to recall the past, and says, "But that is nonsense! It has been that way, more or less, for at least *x* years." If that happens often, you are probably well along toward being able to recognize real changes when they take place. You may even have made headway toward identifying changes that might be *made* to take place.

After tests come exercises. They involve taking a stand in the past and trying to imagine how, or whether, one could have foreseen what was soon to come.

Our first such exercise deals with the likelihood and character of civil war in the United States in 1861. When inviting our practitioner-students to try it, we hand out a small collection of contemporaneous documents: the article on the United States from the 1860 edition of the *Encyclopaedia Britannica,* copies of *London Times* stories filed from various American cities in the winter of 1860–61, and dispatches of the same period from British diplomats stationed in the United States.[13] We ask the readers to pretend that they are British merchant bankers, holding an option on shares of the Baltimore & Ohio Railroad. Acquired during the short-lived stock market panic that followed Lincoln's election in November 1860, the option has favorable terms. Exercising it will make money for the banking house in almost any circumstances, even if the split in the American union becomes permanent and even if shots are exchanged, provided only that there is no prolonged ground fighting in the Virginia-Maryland-Pennsylvania region. The option expires on April 12, 1861. On that day, in historical reality, Confederate artillery would bombard Fort Sumter in Charleston harbor, setting in train the four-year Civil War. Situated in England, our hypothetical bankers cannot know that and will not even know of Sumter for at least twelve days, for there is as yet no trans-Atlantic cable; all communications come by ship. Our students, playing the British bankers, are asked to make their business decision with information of no later date than March 28, 1861. Their senior partner (as indeed was true) is close to the Foreign Secretary, which accounts for access to dispatches; as of that date they are as current as could be.

We ourselves believe that Englishmen so situated would probably have exercised the option and bought the shares. The *Britannica* article called to mind many past crises settled by compromise, including two previous threats of secession. Employed in the usual way, American history thus offered seductive analogies to suggest that the same thing would happen this time. Neither the correspondents for the *Times* nor the diplomats offered much evidence to challenge such a presumption. They saw or heard little sentiment except in favor of peaceful arrangements. Whether reporter or diplomat, nearly all believed that economic calculations controlled human choices. "Peace is dictated as a financial necessity," a *Times* correspondent wrote. The best clues to what would actually happen appeared in incidental and easily ignored reports from the British Consul at New Orleans. He wrote with puzzlement of how traditional, pro-Union conservatism seemed to have dissipated and of how little concern was in evidence about the prospective loss of the rich Mississippi River trade; "even the motives of interest have given place to antipathy and hostility to the Northern and Western states." But bankers in London would not have known to pay more attention to these dispatches than to more soothing ones from Washington, New York, and other centers. Or so we believe.

Knowing what actually happened, our practitioner-students naturally struggle to find in the documents a basis for predicting a long and bloody war. Being ingenious, many succeed. But even those who compose the best such briefs appreciate better, as a result, how very hard it is to foresee at a given moment what later may seem an inevitable future. Even the British diplomats reporting from America who came to think hostilities more likely as the spring advanced gave no hint in dispatches of conceiving "war" in other terms than skirmishing along frontiers accompanied by an attempted blockade and the naval actions needed to enforce or break it. Six hundred thousand dead after four years of bitter fighting on the ground, in a total population of some 31 million—nothing of the sort was hinted at by even the most pessimistic observers. As would be the case in 1914, they looked back to see what war might mean and missed the clues around them. That is obvious *in retrospect.* The exercise thus has the effect of encouraging both caution about forecasts and awareness that the future may surprise. It surprises because something in the present, hard to see, weakens the past as a guide.

In 1982 we had an unusual opportunity to play present against past and future. Our class discussion of the British bankers' dilemma took place on April 12, the anniversary of the firing on Fort Sumter. It happened also to be ten days after Argentinian forces had seized the Falkland Islands (or the Malvinas, as they term them). After discussion of 1860–61, with the class dividing about fifty–fifty on what the bankers should do, we invited guesses as to what was likely in the South Atlantic. All but a handful of those in the room predicted that no angry shots would be exchanged: Surely the British and the Argentinians would find some peaceful exit; they had done so for a century and more. It was left that, as of five weeks later, when the semester ended, we would meet again informally. By then the *Belgrano* and the *Sheffield* had been sunk. Soon there would be a thousand dead and nearly twice as many wounded, and the British would have their possession back. The future, turned to history, had reinforced the lesson of our exercise.

Our other exercise has to do with the onset of the Great Depression. We hand out a brief history of the previous four decades and review statistics from the 1920s.[14] The data cover the stock market crash of October 1929 and stop in early 1930 at the point of near recovery. The question then becomes to estimate economic trends from March 1930 and to frame hypotheses about the party outcomes in that year's congressional elections, as well as in the presidential race two years hence. This is the counterpart for choosing whether to buy B&O stock in April 1861. Given their capacity for retrospect, students are left in a quandary. The financial panics of 1907 and 1921, even the depression of 1893–97, yield them—along with Herbert Hoover—no solid footing to predict what they, unlike him, know is coming: an eventual one-third drop in prices, a near halving of GNP, and a tenfold increase in unemployment. The middle 1890s pale by comparison. But no such things have happened yet or even appear likely in the spring of 1930. As in the spring of 1861, aspects of the present, hard to see or weigh except in retrospect, were altering the relevance of past to future. Accustomed signposts were about to lose their usefulness, while other aspects of the past, previously unregarded, were about to take their place.

In short, change of a massive kind was really taking place. But nothing plain was written in the stars to warn contemporaries that it was not evanescent. Change often is short-lived and often had been in the 1920s and the 1850s. The accustomed past might reassert its sway and serve as guide again, or be revived with relatively small adjustments. *Plus ça change*. . . . Students know it cannot be so for those particular occasions, but they find that shorn of retrospect they might well have assumed the opposite. And while we cannot tell them how to draw reliable distinctions in advance of retrospect—distinctions between changefulness and continuity, between the rumblings of the present and the patterns of the past—those exercises do enhance awareness that, reliable or not, distinctions will be drawn because decision-makers must. They then risk rude surprise. The exercises lodge in players' minds (how long retained, who knows?) that futures can be far worse than, anyway far different from, what reason guided by the past, at least by obvious analogues and surface trends, foresees. In 1930 as in 1861 what came differed dramatically from what had gone before and from what was anticipated by decision-makers. All else aside, the students learn to pity Hoover.

Our tests and exercises reinforce each other. To play with the meanings of "intervals" or to ask "what is *new* in the news?" keeps continuity in mind. Replaying 1860–61 or 1929–30 reminds that continuity is not all. Human experience also includes discontinuity, sudden, sharp, and hard to foresee, if foreseeable at all. The person who learns to watch the present for signs of either, or still better both, may well have learned to think in time-streams. If so, such tests and exercises promise much. Also, as a bonus, the two exercises tighten language. No one who has lived vicariously through secession or depression can use "crisis" as loosely as is now the American way. A twenty-five-cent price hike in gas at the pump or seizure and imprisonment of Embassy employees in Iran becomes a problem or an incident. But a "crisis"?!

Books are our next subject: more precisely, historical writings. Anyone can use our tests, and all who wish can liberate our exercises from the classroom, trying them on anybody anywhere, herself (or him) included. But books may help still more to hook somebody on the habit of thinking in time-streams. Books, after all, contain the wherewithal for innumerable exercises, to say nothing of sophisticated answers for those tests. Besides, books are a storehouse of vicarious experience, the ready source of reference points for inventory and context. Indeed they ought to help.

We wish that we could say this more assuredly, that we could point to individuals and say, "Look, he learned that from what he read (or, for that matter, what he studied in school)." Unfortunately, we cannot. Marshall and Washington read history. Washington cited Roman history much as FDR cited that of America in Washington's time—as a past from which the present had grown. But neither Marshall nor Washington was a bookish man, and others who were, such as John Adams and James Madison, or Douglas MacArthur, for that matter, had less of a knack than they did, as we see it, for thought about the present as transition from past to future, viewing all three comparatively. The bookish men, perhaps coincidentally, had more trouble than those two with their own egos.

We can only say that reading history *may* help. Some people could be born to think historically, as others—a tiny minority—are born to think mathematically. Possibly an instinct for the time dimension is either in the genes or not, and if not, nothing can be done. We disbelieve in that dichotomy. It follows, then, that the majority of humankind, ourselves included, learn to think in streams of time as we learn to think mathematically—if we do either or at all—from teachers and books. It probably also follows that the learning comes through pieced-together stories about real people better than through abstract constructions from philosophy or social sciences, or even through invented characters in fiction (a close question). We are not confident that anyone who reads can gain proficiency, if what he reads is history and what he does is govern, but we cannot think of any better way.

Besides, the reading can be fun. Of that we are sure, even if of nothing else. We grant that history is not necessarily relaxing. It certainly is not the best way to escape the real world. After all, those things happened! History books are not in competition with "M*A*S*H*" reruns or Redskins games or even Elmore Leonard thrillers. But in spare time given over to improving one's ability to do a job, the fun to be had from reading history has it all over that of reading almost anything else about real people.

Which brings us to the question of what to read, for we are prepared to argue that "fun" is a principal criterion in choice. When making points about how to look things up, we suggested giving a premium to recentness of publication, tempered by the author's credentials, the density of footnotes, and seeming reliability. With books to be taken home and read all the way through, the standards are different.

In the first place, one ought to feel doubt about any new history book. In the course of the twentieth century professional historians have come more and more to write like social scientists, that is, with little or no concern about entertaining readers or holding their attention. Of any book written by a professor, the presumption should be that its intended audience is other professors. There are fortunately a number of exceptions, but not enough to warrant a different rule.

For learning history, in any case, newer books are not necessarily more useful than old ones. Fresh discoveries usually add only incrementally to the basic story. While interpretations found in an older book are almost surely out of date, so, soon, will be those in a newer book, for practically every important set of events gets reinterpreted every few years. What is probably of most use is simply experiencing another time. The particular vantage point is important but secondary. Francis Parkman's explanation of why the English won out over the French in the colonial struggle for North America assumes the superiority of white men over red men,

Anglo-Saxons over Latins, and Protestants over Catholics. But a reader repelled by every one of those prejudices can still put down *The Discovery of the Great West* or *Montcalm and Wolfe* having had, unforgettably, the experience of living for a period in the great American wilderness of the seventeenth and eighteenth centuries.[15]

Nominating a few of our own favorites, we begin where we started the chapter before this one, with Thucydides. The effect of his *Peloponnesian Wars* is not like that of one of Parkman's books. No one can come away from it feeling that he has lived in fifth-century Greece, seen how people lived, understood what stirred them about honor, city, or the Gods, or even smelled the battles whose brutal rhythms Thucydides chronicles. Such things he takes as givens, alludes to dryly, or passes over in silence. The impact of *The Peloponnesian Wars* comes, rather, from its seeming contemporaneity. If the translation is up to date, almost any reader sees his own period foreshadowed. So it was with Englishmen who read Thomas Hobbes's translation in the seventeenth century or Richard Crawley's in the nineteenth, and so it is with contemporaries reading the one Rex Warner prepared in the 1950s. The contest between Athens and Sparta is the Cold War; the expedition to Syracuse is Vietnam (or El Salvador). Of course, they aren't. The exact analogies do not hold. But it is not the exact analogies that stay in a reader's mind. It is instead the illustrations of Thucydides' proposition that human nature remains constant—or better, perhaps, that dilemmas of human governance remain so—the indications, in short, that 2,500 years ago bad and good political judgment were to be found in about the same proportions as today. Anyone who reads and remembers Thucydides should have acquired some immunity against imagining that this week's crisis is the worst, or last, in human affairs. Some other ancient historians, also a pleasure to read in translation, can make the immunity stronger. Among them are Livy, Polybius, Plutarch, and Tacitus.[16]

Another category of works we recommend are those by historians who also practiced politics. Not all of them are worth reading. Woodrow Wilson's *History of the American People* is unfailingly tedious. George Bancroft's ten-volume *History of the United States,* written almost a half-century earlier, remains by contrast one of the liveliest narratives of the Revolutionary War and the early republic. Bancroft wrote as an unashamed patriot. He also wrote as a partisan. His history, it was said, "voted for Jackson." But his prior experience as an actual patronage-dispenser for "Old Hickory" and as Secretary of the Navy under Polk gives his story-telling an edge of realism that otherwise might not be there. Albert Beveridge's life of John Marshall is comparable. The author was an Indiana Senator sufficiently master of English so that, as a college student, he won a prize for composing a speech without a single word in it of other than Anglo-Saxon derivation.[17]

Theodore Roosevelt's *Winning of the West,* though written while his political career was just beginning, has some of the qualities of both Bancroft's history and Parkman's. Readers of the four volumes will not easily forget either the sometimes conniving, sometimes idealistic Americans who organized settlements in and across the Appalachians or the physical realities of the "dark and bloody ground." Of practitioner-historians, the greatest, surely, is Churchill. His biography of his ancestor, the Duke of Marlborough, and his multivolume *History of the English-Speaking Peoples* belong on the bookshelves of anyone who even suspects that reading history improves understanding of politics.[18]

Then there are books by writers who were primarily historians but whose experience or observation was enough to give them something of an insider's perceptiveness. Machiavelli is a prime example, particularly in his *Discourses* on Livy's history of Rome. Macaulay's *History of England* owes some of its pungency to his own experience in Parliament. Henry Adams's *History of the United States During the Administrations of Thomas Jefferson and James Madison* reflects not only his feeling that the White House belonged to his family but also intimacy with real politicians of his own time. Although nine volumes long, it is such lively reading that it seems too short. Arthur M. Schlesinger's *The Age of Roosevelt* belongs in this company. The three volumes published thus far, coming up to the election of 1936, total more than 1,700 pages, but readers who once start the work will find themselves hungering for more.[19]

If pressed for additional titles, we tend to emphasize autobiographies, biographies, and memoirs. The biography of Lincoln by John Nicolay and John Hay has the virtue of being by men who worked with Lincoln in the White House, one of whom (Hay) was subsequently both a poet and U.S. Secretary of State. Ulysses S. Grant's autobiography is so well written, in a style so modern because so terse, that one understands at once why contemporaries charged it had been ghost-written by his publisher, Mark Twain. They were wrong which makes it all the more worth reading. Churchill's autobiographical works on World War I and World War II are at least as good as the biography of Marlborough. They include artful dodges to burden scholars, but practitioners in search of vicarious experience will be well served. Harold Nicolson's biographies of British diplomats and his own reminiscence of the Paris Peace Conference, *Peacemaking 1919,* enable one to live through the transformation of Edwardian England. Lord David Cecil's *Melbourne,* alleged to be the favorite biography of JFK and Harold Macmillan both, and surely one of the things that initially brought them together, suggests much about all three and pre-Victorian England too. Robert Sherwood's *Roosevelt and Hopkins* and Schlesinger's fine *Robert F. Kennedy* go on our list because in different styles they provide such vivid vicarious experience. So do the memoirs of Henry Kissinger. We cannot say in good conscience that we wish either of the volumes so far published was longer, nor would we argue that he offers the last word. But he has had the art to fashion a "first word" so compelling in its narrative that readers enter into his experience, thereby gaining insights for themselves no matter what they make of him.[20] And finally among biographies, partisan though they are, we cannot resist listing Shakespeare's plays on the Plantagenet Kings.

Those happen to be books we both have found especially useful in imparting vicarious experience on which to draw for insight. The chief principle of selection is given. The stories should be told well enough so that they become permanently part of the reader's experience. Just what will fill that bill varies enough from person to person so that our final suggestion is simply: Browse. If the browsing strays across the fine line to fiction, so be it, provided one remains aware that nature surprises art.[21]

We write as though we thought vicarious experience could cumulate into a talent for thinking in time-streams. So it might. Certainly it adds to inventory and fills in context. It also builds up definitions: Words acquire content, witness "crisis" once again. Maybe these are steps along the way. Probably vicarious experience heightens sensitivity to patterns in the minds of other persons, thereby aiding placement and abetting tendencies to see the truth as relative, the future as contingent. And possibly it informs judgments of the past as a predictor for the future, given what is happening at present. We write "possibly" because we do not, cannot, know.

If possible, is this worth reaching for? We take the answer to be an emphatic yes. In so doing we of course express our biases, our values. Readers will have noticed that those make us conservative about such consequential and—to us—uncertain things as government decisions. We have employed, approvingly, such words as "contingent" and "relative" to characterize judgments we term "good." We have invoked, approvingly, such examples as those generals, Marshall and Washington, who were famous above all for "character" and also for consistently pursuing moderate courses in excited times. No ideologists they, or more precisely no extremists, settling rather for essentially consensual ideals. Is that, when all is said and done, what we seek from the thing we call thinking in time-streams? Is that what we hope can come of it? Indeed so. For in our view, facing government decisions—and it is a view, not "truth"—the prize in the package is prudence. Thinking of time as a stream seems to us most important for that.

To aim at prudence-in-the-large is to aim high, and yet to hope for general application of a mode of thought we cannot even characterize precisely is to invite disappointment. Prospects in these large terms remain clouded by our inability (by no means ours alone) to specify criteria reliably distinguishing the boulders from the sand, the changeful from the evanescent. Lacking specifications we fall back on exhortations, urging those who make decisions or their aides to learn by doing, to practice doing, to test themselves, or to immerse themselves vicariously in the doings of as many others as they can. Well and good, but the effort is all theirs, and we cannot in conscience press our hopes on those for whom we do so little.

But when it comes to prudence-in-the-small we are prepared to press harder. Here we think we offer the specifics, mini-methods, which entitle us to do so. Prudence-in-the-small, one decision at a time, is what the previous chapters of this book address, aiming at whatever margins of improvement might be had from case to case. Improvement is dependent on personalities and circumstances. Those often are recalcitrant, and the margins slim. We are convinced, however, that in almost every instance margins do exist. We are convinced also that thinking on the lines our mini-methods offer makes for opportunities and reduces risks. We urge them, therefore, on all comers.

Consider our illustrations: they surely counsel modesty, but also they suggest room for improvement and patently imply that even marginal improvements might contribute to happier outcomes. Even the relative successes with which we began, the Cuban missile crisis and the social security reform, reflect propensities to leap without looking where a small amount of looking might do large amounts of good. For both those cases comprise chancy measures of recovery from previous failures to ask simple questions. The missile crisis, or at least the surprise that fueled it, might have been averted had officials pressed upon themselves the questions, six months earlier, why are *we* so confident the Soviets will never export medium-range missiles? What might tempt them to do differently? Are the temptations out there? From such questions as those it would have been but a small step to a timely warning. And in 1981 the collapse of normal channels for bipartisan changes in social security might have been averted with some questions early on to David Stockman: Which Democrats have signed up? What of the others? How do *we* know?

Enlightening questions are the point of every method we propose, questions that shed light almost regardless of the answers. In no sense are historical records, references, or memories the sole sources of such questions. Other sources, more consistently and consciously applied, range from statistical to legal analysis, encompassing decision theory and the social sciences. History is but a source of last resort, or anyway the last refuge of laymen. Yet even as an add-on it has more to offer than is made of it in current American practice (so far as our unscientific sampling shows). For Washingtonians, both now and in at least two previous generations, tend to overuse analogies, especially in argument, and to underutilize all else—the histories of issues, individuals, and institutions—while making wholly idiosyncratic efforts, perhaps none, to open up the treasure house of reference points they mostly were deprived of in their schooling.

Our refrain to practitioners in class and now to readers: Since one way or another, consciously or not, you use history now, why not try doing a bit better with simple methods in a short time? "Simple" because no one will—or should—stand still for complicated ones incapable of yielding determinate results. "Short" because no one commands, or thinks he does, much more than half an hour of discretionary time. Doing a bit better is a modest aim, but it suffices us. Our methods match, from *Known-Unclear-Presumed* to *Likeness-Difference* to the Goldberg rule—"What's the story?"—to bets and odds to Alexander's question—"What new knowledge would change a presumption?"—to events and details on time-lines—for people *and* organizations. Those and the rest are simple to the point (not past it, we hope) of being simple-minded. And none should take more time than busy people can afford before they start to spark enlightening questions.

Seeking to serve prudence-in-the-small, we sympathize with those whose duty it is to seek it, the decision-makers. Our methods are meant for their staffs at least as much as for them, but our hopes run to them directly. Those hopes, at the last, we reduce to one. We hope that with a modicum of care as well as luck, care of the sort suggested by this book, future decision-makers will be spared the Kennedy complaint to Theodore Sorensen at the moment of disaster in the Bay of Pigs: "How could I have been so stupid?"[22] Kennedy was scarcely stupid to think Castro a problem. Most Americans thought so too, not least Eisenhower and Nixon. Nor was Kennedy stupid to hold firm against the overt use of American force. Law and morality were buttressed by military considerations: Cuba is big, and other places were vulnerable to retaliation. So the stupidity for which he blamed himself comes down to a handful of judgments and presumptions on small particulars: moving a landing 70 miles west, cancelling one air strike out of two, failing to notice that he already had lost deniability, or taking it for granted that a Dulles would believe his ban on overt intervention, and so forth. Misjudgments of those sorts are mostly in the realm of feasibility: "Will it work?" "Will it stick?" "Will it help more than it hurts?" "If not, what?" Our hope is for more such questioning.

Acknowledgments

For the course that preceded this book some fifty case-studies were prepared as teaching materials (listed in our Appendixes). These are available for courses and colleges across the country. Their preparation was assisted by the National Endowment for the Humanities, to which we remain very grateful.

We hasten to add the John F. Kennedy School of Government at Harvard, which has supported us in innumerable ways with time, funds, course assistants, interested colleagues and more; we are deeply appreciative. The Woodrow Wilson International Center for Scholars in Washington gave one of us a berth during part of the period when the book was written. It also provided a forum for discussion of an early draft. We are in debt to that Center and its admirable staff.

With respect to draft chapters of the book itself, particular thanks go to readers and commentators, both in the academic community and outside, including many of those mentioned in our illustrations. Among those who hold no blame for what we say but who do not object to our acknowledging that they tried to set us right, we can list: Nancy Altman Lupu, Robert Blackwill, James Blight, John Bross, Harold Brown, Zbigniew Brzezinski, McGeorge Bundy, William Bundy, Brewster Denny, Stuart

Eizenstat, Thomas Eliot, Harvey Fineberg, Anthony King, Don K. Price, Dean Rusk, Thomas Schelling, James Schlesinger, Brent Scowcroft, James Sebenius, Theodore Sorensen, and Charles Wyzanski. For their time, thought, candor, warnings and encouragement we continue to be grateful, more than we can say.

To Melanie Billings-Yun, who served as staff director of the project that produced most of our case-studies and to her crew of case-writers we also owe our gratitude. All performed earnestly, some brilliantly. The writers of each study have been listed on its title page. Editorial supervision was Melanie's and ours.

We owe thanks as well to Erwin Glikes for his sharp eye and judgment, to his editorial associates at the Free Press, and to our literary agent, Maxine Groffsky, for their good work and help.

Finally, to Sally Makacynas, our secretary who put up with us and with our separate scrawls, as well as with May's word processor, for all the years the book has been in preparation, thanks and thanks again—there is no way to say it enough.

Appendixes

A. Methods
B. Courses
C. Cases

A. SUMMARY OF MINI-METHODS

I. *K-U-P/L-D*

- To help *define* the immediate *situation* ("now") and the decision-maker's *concerns* (problems) in it, from which to draw objectives.
- For use with or without analogues from the past ("then")

Step 1. Separate what is *Known* "now" from what is *Unclear* and both from what is *Presumed* (by the person with the problem or his agent).

Step 2. Do the same for all relevant "thens" that come to mind or others urge (fill in each "then" from *present* knowledge).

Step 3. Compare then with now for *likenesses* and *differences* (skip if no analogues).

Step 4. Articulate specifically what now is of concern and, if possible, commensurate objectives.

N.B.: If concerns and objectives don't come clear, add placement (VII below) and try articulating again; if still unclear, review the history of the issue (II–IV below) and try once more.

II. *The Goldberg rule*

"Don't ask 'What's the problem,' ask 'What's the story?' That way you'll find out what the problem really is."

III. *Time-line* (for the issue)

The dates from "now" back to the story's start

IV. *Journalists' questions:*

"When" (time-line) "What" "Where" "Who" "How" "Why"

- Used together to help trace and articulate the history of the issue (the issue is defined by the decision-maker's concerns), for more light on objectives, thence options.

Step 1: With respect to the issue, invoke the Goldberg rule.

Step 2: Plot on the time-line relevant trends, asking journalists' questions as helpful.

Step 3: Plot on the time line any changes in specifics that appear to have especially high political significance.

Step 4: Articulate objectives and options to match concerns as refined by issue history.

V. *Bets and Odds:*

What odds will you give that the presumption proves correct?

and/or

How much of your own money would you wager on it?

- Used to test presumptions uncovered in I above or later.

Step 1: Ask either question (or both) of each adviser, in presence of others.

Step 2: Require each to specify what makes his answer different from the others.

Step 3: Encourage argument, promote articulation of differences.

Step 4: Review presumption accordingly.

VI. *"Alexander's question"*

What fresh facts, if at hand, by when, would cause you to change your presumption? (Your direction? Your decision?)

- Another way to test a presumption. Also a way to set up warning signals in advance and schedule contingent reviews ("If we should find these facts, then . . .)

Step 1: Ask the question.

Step 2: Put agreed answers in a tickler system.

Step 3: Commit to a review of presumptions—or decisions—if tickler shows facts found.

Step 4: (contingent) Review accordingly and amend, as indicated, definitions of situation, concerns, objectives, and options.

VII. *"Placement"*

	Individual	*Institution*
Time-line	Since parents' adolescence	Since start of key components
Events	Public history widely taught or reported	laws, leaders or controversies widely reported
(Special events)	widely known to distinct publics	(same as for individuals)
Details	Personal history of record and available	Internal history: structures, procedures (esp. incentives)

- To help "place" relative strangers, either people or organizations, by inferring personal outlook or institutional proclivity from the history external signs suggest may be in someone else's head or built into incentives in somebody else's bailiwick

Step 1: Articulate initial stereotype about the other person or organization.

Step 2: Lay out the relevant time-line.

Step 3: Plot relevant events (and/or special events) and details appropriately defined, with approximate dates.

Step 4: Draw inferences about the person's likely outlook or the organization's likely approach in order to sophisticate initial stereotype—subject to reality checks as (if) direct evidence comes in.

B. COURSES AND COMMENTS

We refer often to our "Uses of History" course in the Kennedy School of Government at Harvard. Anyone who has read this book knows plenty about it, for the course and the book make the same points and draw on many of the same examples. In this appendix we describe a few other courses with aims similar to ours, and we report what our own practitioner-students say about on-the-job use of our "mini-methods."

Our course began in the early 1970s as an experimental part-semester seminar. By mid-decade we had the courage to offer it as a *full*-semester elective. Toward the end of that decade, the National Endowment for the Humanities gave us a grant to improve our course and, if possible, make it an export product.

Until then we had mainly assigned piles of xerox. This limited the numbers of cases we could put before students. It also opened us to suits for copyright infringement. With the NEH grant, we signed up Dr. Melanie Billings-Yun as project director. Overseeing a number of part-time casewriters, she created half a hundred compact ten- to twenty-five-page cases. We, she, and others tested the cases in classrooms. They were then modified or rewritten, as experience suggested. Appendix C contains a full list with abstracts.

Most of the schools using our cases or otherwise joining in the experiment were, like ours, schools of public policy or public administration training post-B.A. professional students for careers in public affairs. Each, however, had its own clientele, and each its own emphasis and style.

Joel Tarr offered a course, "Historical Perspectives on Urban Problems," in Carnegie-Mellon's School of Urban and Public Affairs. He and his colleague Peter Stearns had started work on such a course about the same time we started on ours. Designing his course particularly for engineers and others planning to work in city power, water, transportation, or sanitation services, Tarr started with a question we postponed. Inviting students to define "the urban crisis," he asked implicitly: How different are conditions now? What has *not* changed? He then emphasized issue history, looking seriatim at the evolution of urban economies, transportation systems, neighborhoods, suburbs, ethnic and religious communities, and political organizations. He wound up by pressing students to assess the future of Pittsburgh's "urban Renaissance"—asking them, in our terms, to set the subject in the stream of time.

At the Harriman School of Urban and Public Affairs in the State University of New York at Stony Brook, David Burner, followed by Michael Barnhart, designed a different course. Although most of their students were also aiming at careers in state or local government, fewer had technical backgrounds. More were looking toward general managerial assignments. The Stony Brook course therefore put its emphasis on organizational history, using not only our Bay of Pigs case but also one on the United Mine Workers union and, from the private sector, the famous Harvard Business School "Dashman" case, each illustrating some different way in which standard operating procedures had evolved and played out.

In some schools the approach to the subject was different from ours. At the RAND Graduate Institute in California, where all the students are Ph.D. candidates already fitted with M.A.s, all working part-time on RAND Corporation projects, and nearly all oriented toward hard quantitative analysis, the initial reaction to a course copying ours was, to say the least, mixed. Some students said it smacked of "history appreciation." RGI's Stephen Schlossman then taught the course as one in which students looked at analogies, issue history, and the like in terms of their own particular research projects—private pension systems, "TVAs" for other countries, airfield attacks in the early phases of wars, and so forth. In that form the course "worked" for even the most mathematical-minded participant.

In the public policy program at the University of Chicago, Barry Karl moved in exactly the opposite direction, putting more stress on "history appreciation," less on workaday utility. His course treats in broad terms the development of the professions, of management, both public and private, of government regulation, and of policy issues relating to education and social welfare. It concludes with a wide-ranging review of American ideologies.

These various experiments suggest the range of possibilities open to schools of public policy and public administration.

In the Graduate School of Business Administration of the University of North Carolina at Chapel Hill, Lester Garner has created a course on uses of history in decision-making suitable for inclusion in M.B.A. programs.

Though case-focused, the course at Chapel Hill differs from ours and the others just described in that it deals with only a few cases during a term, attempting to get students to look at each one from a number of different angles. One such is a decision case in which students choose whether or not to recommend to an electronics firm that it bid on a component for a new tank. Garner writes: "They must make this recommendation without sophisticated financial data, which even at a late stage in the course, generates startled responses. During the module, we discuss factors such as the political web of relationships that direct weapons procurement decisions, American attitudes toward the military and big business, and the problems of manufacturing when dealing with new technologies, all of which in fact should influence the firm's decision on the bid. We look at these factors throughout their relevant pasts, and by the end of the module many students perceive that the financial data may be the least influential factor to consider in such a decision."

Another case used at Chapel Hill simulates U.S.–Mexican negotiation over compensation for Mexico's nationalization of oil properties in the 1930s. Getting to a definition of the issue requires exploring the different historical experiences of Mexican officials, American officials, and oil industry executives. But the issue, once understood, turns out to be solvable only by application of sophisticated accounting techniques.

Measured by enrollment curves, student ratings, and the like, all of these professional school courses can claim early success. But nothing in such data rebuts suspicion that many students may like the courses because they are or seem more comfortably liberal-artsy than other curricular offerings at these schools.

Partly for this reason, partly for our own guidance, we organized in the early 1980s a questionnaire survey of students enrolled in the first six full-semester trials of our Kennedy School "Uses of History" course. We located the addresses of about two hundred alumni and sent out a single mailing. Sixty-eight filled out and returned the questionnaires. Impressively, all but a half-dozen respondents volunteered comments, most writing on the back as well as the front of the form and many adding extra sheets.

Not everyone complimented the course. Answering questions as to which course concepts he remembered and which he applied, one former student now a practicing physician wrote "None" and "None." Two Washington policy analysts said the course needed more rigorous conceptualization. One management consultant and one journalist told us they doubted that many people would find it useful in their work.

On the whole, however, the respondents said emphatically that the course did help them at work. Almost everyone singled out at least one course concept as both memorable and useful. Asked to rate "on-the-job usefulness" on a scale of one to five, those who mentioned one or more of the following gave scores averaging out as follows:

Alumni Ratings of On-the-Job Usefulness of Course Concepts
Scale: 1 (a little) to 5 (a lot)

Concept		Avg. Score
O-H	("Placing" Organizations)	4.53
PL	(Placing Individuals)	4.19
I-H	(Inspecting Issue History)	4.04
A-Q	(Testing Presumptions)	3.93
K-U-P	(Defining Situations)	3.93
L/D	(Comparing Analogues)	3.76
PER	(Broadening General Perspective)	3.14

The numbers of alumni citing "organizational history" were comparatively small—only about 20 percent of the sample; but their ratings were uniformly high and their written comments strong. "I became much more attentive to the history of policy issues and of government institutions. This kind of attention I exercise *all* the time," wrote a Wall Street banker. "The histories of organizations often determine their culture and management style today," commented another banker, this one based in London. A management consultant wrote: "Five years after graduation I still find Uses of History, itself, one of the most useful courses I took at Harvard. Most of my work involves helping corporations make major shifts in their strategic orientation by making changes in their organization. Successful organization change requires a good bit of understanding of the company's past—especially a close analysis of how its *past* strategies are embedded in its *current* organization structure and culture. The Uses of History course, while dealing primarily with public policy issues, provided me with strong tools to use to analyze corporate histories." A lawyer in private practice commented that the course had alerted him to the utility of studying the history of the courts before which he practiced, and another, more junior lawyer wrote that he was profiting from having studied the history of his own firm: he was better able thus to forecast decisions of the senior partners.

Though alumni in the public and private sectors did not differ in statistically significant degree in their ratings for organizational history, most of the additional testimony to its usefulness came from ones in profit-making lines of work. One exception was a middle-level official of a state agency who wrote: "The history of any issue and the history of the bureaucracies that deal with those issues are absolutely essential to policy formulation and agency management." Another was a foundation executive who said, ". . . the background from 'Uses of History' helps me apply a conceptual framework to predicting how effectively grantee organizations are likely to carry out their proposed activities."

The high ranking for "placement," on the other hand, represented a judgment by approximately three-fifths of the alumni. Along with need for prophylaxis against false analogies, the need to think about differences in individual human histories was the moral of the course best remembered. And here the supporting testimony came mostly from people in the public sector. One lawyer did write, after ranking "placement" as the most useful course concept: "The 'Uses of History' course is a great marketing tool. It is one of the few courses I can identify as having improved my practice." But the strongest testimonials came from Washington bureaucrats. "[P]lacement has been an extremely useful concept for facilitating constructive relationships with political appointees (or at least for avoiding destructive ones)," wrote one. "I personally found ["placement"] useful in explaining certain direction changes in policy after reorganizations and new leadership. . . . ," wrote another, adding disquietingly: "The knowledge gained in general placement allows you a framework to manipulate the decision maker." A congressional staffer wrote that he used placement "almost daily," and a city planner asserted that he used it and related concepts "to tailor my explanations of policy and program decisions to communicate more effectively with people unlike myself."

Though the actual occupations of our alumni are too diverse to permit ready statistical discrimination, these comments highlight the obvious fact that organizational history is most likely to seem useful to people such as investment bankers and management consultants, who work chiefly with large organizations, while "placement" is more likely to appear valuable to people whose careers lie inside organizations or who, for other reasons, trade in the coin of persuasion. One alumnus wrote that, when a policy analyst, he had found discrimination among analogies the most useful tool taken from the course. Now, as a lobbyist in a state capital, he ranked "placement" first.

Issue history, probing presumptions, and scrutinizing analogies all tended to be favorites for alumni engaged, one way or another, in analytic work. Despite the fact that they had been exposed to issue history solely through the domestically-focused social security case, three military officers wrote to say how useful the time-line technique had proved to be in briefing more senior officers and civilians, preparing congressional testimony, or drafting Defense-wide guidance papers. An Air Force officer serving in a senior staff position in Europe wrote that he made K/U/P and L/D lists "all the time—the essence of my job." Tying together utilities for analysis and for advocacy, a Washington lawyer wrote: "Stated succinctly, much of argument is intimidation; historical argument is very intimidating."

Worth momentary note is the fact that the least utilitarian element of the course—a segment we labelled "perspective", identified with traditional claims for history—received distinctly the lowest rating from alumni. Moreover, not one of the sixty-odd volunteer commentaries even suggested that enthusiasm for the course stemmed from its having had a liberal arts flavor or effect.

Like those on the negative side, positive general comments from alumni nearly all had to do with applicability on the job. The closest thing to an exception was a statement by the president of an information industry firm. "The *prism* the course offered has been a constantly useful one," he wrote. Rating the course among the most valuable of all he had taken in professional schools, a management consultant explained: "The course makes a significant contribution toward the development of rigorous 'hard' assessment techniques to deal with some of the 'softer' qualitative issues that form the majority of those found in the real world." Putting the same point somewhat differently, a lawyer wrote: ". . . the course is one of the few at the Kennedy School which requires analysis of both 'market failure' and essential nonmarket decision-making."

Describing the course in terms which we suspect inflate its potentialities, another management consultant said that the course was conspicuous in the curricula of Harvard's professional schools because it "ensured that the leadership component, providing direction and not only efficiency, was not overlooked." What we think the course can actually accomplish in that line was best put by the lawyer who wrote also of the power of history to intimidate. The concepts of the course were useful outside government, he remarked, but more useful inside, for "government problems tend to have lengthy histories [and] . . . turn on various enduring themes. . . ."; hence, he wrote, "The best way to manage and to lead is to help people understand the significance and direction of what they are doing and to help them to realize the stream of forces of which they have become a part."

Following our own prescription, we are prepared to offer even odds or better that our course will remain a long-term part of the Kennedy School curriculum. We are equally sure that at least some of the counterpart courses are destined for long lives in their respective institutions. Whether seeds will sprout in large numbers of professional schools is another matter. We are hopeful but less confident. The reasons for uncertainty are embedded in three lessons we have drawn from our own experience and that of others:

First, the evidence *is* strong (a) that professional school students could perceive a course on using history as beneficial in career terms and (b) that people who have had such a course would look back on it as actually helpful at work. But these conclusions do not produce the prediction that such a course will soon become an *expected* part of professional career preparation. "Uses of history" courses will probably have to prove themselves for a generation before they acquire such status.

Second, such courses will stand or fall on their continuing to have perceived value as providers of effective, workaday analytic techniques. Neither pre-career nor mid-career students will, in any large numbers, trade off skill-building courses for courses designed primarily with the worthy, pleasurable, but nonutilitarian purpose of broadening their general level of knowledge and culture. The moral for instructors to keep constantly in mind is that they are equipping students for the work they will do and not, as in college, for the lives they will lead.

Third, each student population is different. Those in the graduate public policy programs at Carnegie Mellon, Stony Brook, and the RAND Graduate Institute were different from those at Harvard, and the business school students at Chapel Hill were unlike any of the others. Even within schools, there were important variations. At Harvard, pre-career, mid-career, and executive program students had quite dissimilar expectations and needs. The less practical experience our students have, the more we have to explain and justify asking them to spend time thinking about particular situations and people of the past. The more experienced the students are, by contrast, the more we have to combat skepticism about the applicability of general rules, whether they be "mini-method" rules of thumb or formulas from fields like decision theory and bargaining theory. The moral is that instructors teaching "uses of history" courses had better spend some of their own effort placing the students whom they confront.

C. CATALOG OF CASES

The following case studies were prepared at Harvard between 1975 and 1983 in conjunction with our efforts to teach uses of history for public policy-making and management. The teaching was done at the Kennedy School and elsewhere. In several of those years we had assistance from the National Endowment for the Humanities, which markedly enhanced alike the quantity and quality of cases and is gratefully acknowledged. The Endowment hoped to see our case material widely distributed for use in many different kinds of courses around the country. We hope so too.

Each case was originally designed to provoke discussion of and practice at, or otherwise to illustrate, a particular use of history in actual decision-making. While each case is in form a closed narrative or a summary of points of view or documents, most can be converted into open decision cases by the simple expedient of asking: "Suppose you were "X" in the case and the "Y" variable were changed as follows. What would you have done?"

In addition, taken as closed narratives, the cases can serve purposes remote from our concern with history's uses in decision-making; we ourselves have introduced a number into undergraduate history and political science courses where they meet a variety of other needs nicely. We invite experimentation.

Below, case studies are grouped by the particular uses for which we initially prepared them. Where feasible we created several examples of a given use. One reason was to give instructors (ourselves included) flexibility in choosing among issues, times, and actors. Another reason was to guarantee ourselves alternative examples we could use in class once we had scooped the heart out of a given case to make an illustration for this book. Thereby we kept an option open in the future teaching of our course: namely, to assign the book and cases too. For we could then ask students to apply our mini-methods and the like to past examples *different* from the ones the book conveys. So, for convenience, we list cases under headings that comport with the book's categories. Many cases fit almost equally well under several of these headings. (To get the flavor, we suggest scanning them, or at least sampling the teaching notes we offer with them.) And they could easily be listed in other ways, as for instance alphabetically. That is the order chosen by the Publications Distribution Office of the Kennedy School, which circulates a listing so arranged for the entire output of school cases, ours among them. Anyone who wishes it should write to:

Publications Distribution Office
JFK School of Government
Harvard University
79 John F. Kennedy Street
Cambridge, MA. 02138

Copies of our cases, either single or in bulk, can be obtained, at cost, from the same address. Teaching notes are available if requested. Case numbers must be indicated. For that reason they are shown below.

1. Drawing Analogies

Americanizing the Vietnam War (C15–80–271) 28 pp. plus notes
Vietnam Documents (C15–80–271S) 80 pp.

The case and the selection of documents (from the Pentagon Papers and others recently declassified) deal with U.S. decision-making during the first year and a half of Lyndon B. Johnson's Administration. This culminated in commitment of large ground forces to South Vietnam for sustained offensive action, in effect taking over the war. The many, varied, sometimes contradictory "lessons of Korea" (America's previous war) cited by participants in this decision-making to and against each other are highlighted. So are analogies with French experience in Vietnam itself. (A memorandum on the French analogy from McGeorge Bundy to LBJ, June 30, 1965, is included in the *Documents.*) Case and documents can be used separately or together, and documents in whole or part, depending on audience and purpose.

The Coming of the Cold War (C14–76–144) 16 pp. plus notes
Supplement (C14–76–144S) 21 pp.

In February 1947 the Democratic Truman Administration received a pair of urgent requests: to replace Britain as the supporter of the Greek government, beleaguered by Soviet-backed leftist guerrillas; and to bolster Turkey against Soviet encroachment. For response with definitive action, Truman would need authorization from the newly elected Republican Congress. One Senate leader, Arthur Vandenberg, was supportive. Another, Robert Taft (believed the likely Republican presidential nominee in 1948), was skeptical. Members of the Administration also ranged in their degrees of warmth to active U.S. involvement in Europe.

Coming of the Cold War takes readers from the end of World War II up to the critical meeting at which the decision was made to go to Congress and present what became known as the Truman Doctrine. The case provides the arguments on both sides of the Greek–Turkish aid question but leaves the resolution open. Analogizing Stalin to Hitler is pressed by some, shrugged off by others.

Cold War Supplement contains brief biographies of the principal actors in the decision, selected U.S. public opinion polls, and chronologies of Soviet and German political/foreign policy (a basis for testing the analogy by way of *Likenesses/Differences*).

Korea and the Thirties A & B (C14–80–298/299) 10 pp./15 pp. plus notes
Supplement (C14–80–299S) 37 pp. plus notes

In June 1950, five years after World War II, a surprise attack by Soviet-supplied North Korean forces against South Korea evoked in the mind of U.S. President Harry S. Truman a powerful analogy, "The Thirties," more specifically, "Manchuria . . . Austria . . . Munich" and the like. His associates felt the pull of this analogy as well. Following his lead they reversed their own established policy toward South Korea and rallied to its support, overwhelming doubts within their ranks. The *A* case traces previous policy and its reversal in successive Blair House meetings during late June 1950. The *B* case summarizes the events in the decade from 1931 to 1941 encompassing the "lessons of the Thirties" commonly cited thereafter. Together the two cases cover a well-documented instance where events trip off in a decision-maker's head an analogue of decisive power. The *Supplement* contains documents pertinent to the policy-making on Korea.

Swine Flu D (C14–81–410) 20 pp. plus notes

To be read in conjunction with Richard E. Neustadt and Harvey Fineberg, *The Epidemic That Never Was* (New York: Vintage Books, 1983). This case provides historical analogues in the earlier flu pandemics of 1918–19 (Spanish flu), 1957 (Asian flu), and 1968 (Hong Kong flu). The case also reviews the successful campaign to eradicate the polio virus in the 1960s, invoked during 1976 as an analogue for swine flu immunization.

Verdun and Versailles (C14–83–494) 14 pp. plus notes

As Truman harkened to the "lessons of the Thirties" when confronted with aggression in Korea, British Prime Minister Neville Chamberlain saw German demands in the 1930s by light of "lessons" drawn from World War I and its aftermath. In hindsight his "appeasement" policy is usually accounted a disastrous mistake; but at that time in Britain, appeasement had massive support, born of the last war and the last peace. This case evokes both as they appeared to participants.

2. Inspecting Issue History

The Mayaguez Incident (C14–81–443) 27 pp.

In his first ten months as President, Gerald Ford faced formidable challenges: to redeem his office after Nixon's disgrace, to wrest back control of foreign policy from Congress, to live down America's humiliating defeat in Indochina, to cope with stagflation, and to overcome his own weak image. Then, in May 1975, the Khmer Rouge captured the U.S. freighter *Mayaguez.* Ford seized this opportunity to win public confidence and to show the world that the United States still intended to guard its interests abroad.

This case treats the decisions made by the President in the three days between the *Mayaguez's* capture and the launching of the U.S. rescue mission. It raises the question: Did the solution precede, indeed define, the problem? It also raises questions about analogies, explored in this book's Chapter Four.

The Pittsburgh Machine

A. Pete Flaherty: Nobody's Boy (C14–82–468) 4 pp. plus notes
B. Rise and Fall (C14–82–469) 15 pp. plus notes
C. Detente (C14–82–470) 3 pp. plus notes

These cases take the history of the Pittsburgh Democratic Organization from its dramatic birth in 1933 to its questionable state of health in 1977. "A. Pete Flaherty: Nobody's Boy" sets the scene at 1973 and poses the question whether the Democratic machine is alive or dead as an electoral force. "B. Rise and Fall" provides historical background material for greater insight. "C. Detente" brings the issue up to date.

Social Security

A. Critiques (C14–77–197) 18 pp. plus notes
B. Issue History (C14–77–198) 26 pp. plus notes

Social Security A examines both the short- and long-term financial difficulties confronting the social security system at the start of the 1980s and summarizes the views of a number of prominent economists as to basic causes and cures.

Social Security B describes the establishment and subsequent expansion of the system from 1935 to 1981. The political and personal factors that influenced the Roosevelt Administration help explain the particular form of the early system; later modifications suggest the enduring importance of early decisions, as well as difficulties faced by most proposals in the A case. For continuation of the story into 1983 and further emphasis on these points, see this book's Chapter Two.

Wage and Price Controls

A. The Debate in 1980 (C15–83–489) 6 pp. plus notes
B. The Nixon Controls (C15–83–490) 25 pp. plus notes
C. From FDR to Eisenhower (C15–83–526) 11 pp. plus notes

Wage and Price Controls explores the applications of the history of an issue to finding its current solution. The A case sets the "problem" in the late 1970s, as the Carter Administration battled to reduce inflation. Although Carter rejected the imposition of mandatory wage and price controls, persistent double-digit inflation spurred renewed consideration of such policies, and both sides turned to the historical record—especially alleged "lessons" of Nixon's controls—to support their positions.

The B case, "The Nixon Controls" describes the implementation, structure, and effects of the previous American experiment with wage-price controls (1971–74) in the context of both political and economic forces. This facilitates either evaluating the "lessons" for current policy analysis or judging the allegations made about them in 1980, or both.

The C case, "From FDR to Eisenhower" goes back still farther in time, to the experiences from which Nixon and his contemporaries drew "lessons." The case very briefly outlines the World War II controls program and the more problematical attempts under Truman.

3. Probing Presumptions

The Intelligence Process

A. U.S. National Intelligence Practices as of 1980 (C14–81–361) 11 pp. plus notes
B. Operation Barbarossa (C14–81–362) 19 pp. plus notes
C. The Structure and Practice of Soviet Intelligence as of the Late 1970s (C14–81–363) 10 pp. plus notes

The Intelligence Process, B: "Operation Barbarossa" concerns Stalin's failure to foresee the German invasion of Russia that occurred in June

1941. The case outlines the strengths and weaknesses of Stalin's intelligence system and details the preconceptions of Soviet military planners regarding Germany's intentions and capabilities. For comparisons see *The Intelligence Process* A and C.

Kennedy and the Bay of Pigs (C14–80–279) 25 pp. plus notes

The formulation and unsuccessful execution of the CIA's plan to invade Cuba using a brigade of U.S.-trained exiles. The case focuses on President Kennedy's first three months in office, during which he first heard of, then revised, and ultimately approved the plan, leaving unexamined manifold presumptions, his and others. (See Chapter Eight of this book). Used in conjunction with the *CIA to 1961* (C14–80–280), an organizational history of the agency, the case provides the basis for considering institutional questions that, had they been addressed, might have helped the President better to assess the information on which he based approval of the invasion attempt. Can also be used to illustrate hazards of presidential transitions. These can be compared with Lincoln's in *Secession* C (C14–82–427), or with Carter's on SALT in Chapter Seven of this book.

Korean War Aims (C14–82–484) 9 pp. plus notes

A short account of America's incremental steps into war in Korea and the eventual establishment, then hasty abandonment, of Korean unification as the U.N. war aim. Poses questions of shifting presumptions and what it would take to test them, or alternatively to hold fast early on. Can also serve to introduce differing explanations in Allison's models or other decision theories. Further, can be used to round off *Korea and the Thirties A*.

4. Placing People

Mary Anderson and the Women's Bureau (C14–81–368) 27 pp. plus notes

A biographical sketch of a prominent woman labor leader and Director of the Women's Bureau of the Department of Labor from 1920 to 1945. Covers her life from birth to the beginning of the Franklin Roosevelt Administration (when she became involved in a damaging controversy with Secretary of Labor Frances Perkins), illuminating events, public and private, that helped mold her perspectives and style in office. Used in conjunction with *Frances Perkins* (C14–81–369), this case frames an exercise in "placement" as a tool of analysis or advocacy.

James William Fulbright (C14–82–488) 8 pp. plus notes

Sketches the life of the Senate Foreign Relations Committee Chairman from his birth to the start of the Kennedy Administration. Used in conjunction with *Vietnam Advisers* (C14–80–272), this case adds an eventual, key dissenter from White House policy on Vietnam. In conjunction with *Kennedy and the Bay of Pigs* (C14–80–279) it adds a mite.

Martin Luther King (C14–81–365) 26 pp. plus notes

Treats the life of civil rights leader Martin Luther King from his birth into the black middle class of Atlanta in 1929 to his receipt of the Nobel Peace Prize in 1964. It shows how his family background, his mentors, and his education in theology and philosophy helped shape King's dream for black equality through nonviolence. Used in conjunction with *Malcolm X* (C15–81–366), which chronicles the life of a contemporary black leader who sought similar ends through dissimilar means, *Martin Luther King* illustrates how placing a person in historical context deepens one's assessment of him/her beyond initial stereotypes.

Malcolm X (C14–81–366) 35 pp. plus notes

Treats the life of Malcolm X, a leader of the Black Muslims and a powerful voice for black pride, from his birth as Malcolm Little in 1925 to his break with the Muslims in 1964. It shows how his philosophy was shaped by his long personal struggle from a childhood of poverty and violence and a youth of crime to his achievement of respectability through the Nation of Islam. Used in conjunction with *Martin Luther King* (C14–81–365), which chronicles the life of a contemporary black leader who sought similar ends through dissimilar means, *Malcolm X* illustrates how placing a person in historical context deepens one's assessment of him/her beyond initial stereotypes.

The Fates of Martin Luther King and Malcolm X (C14–82–426) 4 pp. plus notes

Completes the biographies of the two black leaders, from the start of 1965 to their separate assassinations.

Frances Perkins, Secretary of Labor (C14–81–369) 25 pp. plus notes

A biographical sketch of the first woman U.S. Cabinet member, Frances Perkins, FDR's Secretary of Labor. Covers her life from birth through her first Cabinet meeting, illuminating events, public and private, that helped mold her perspectives and style in office. Used in conjunction with *Mary Anderson* (C14–81–368), this case frames an exercise in "placement" as a tool of analysis or advocacy.

Vietnam Advisers (C14–80–272) 19 pp. plus notes

Dean Rusk, Robert McNamara, George Ball, McGeorge Bundy, and Clark Clifford were prominent figures in the Kennedy and Johnson administrations who had in common race, class, sex, exceptional ability and a keen interest in foreign affairs. They also shared the role of principal advisers to President Johnson on Vietnam. But beyond those similarities—and others such as age-range (ten years) or length of public service—they had many differences in outlook. This frames an exercise in placement. By presenting short biographies of these Vietnam advisers, highlighting significant events and molding experiences, it seeks to provide insight into the origins of each man's particular world view, sophisticating cruder stereotypes of their perspectives. See this book's Chapter Nine.

This case is well utilized in conjunction with *Americanizing the Vietnam War* (C15–80–271) or *Vietnam Documents* (C15–80–271S).

5. Placing Organizations

The CIA to 1961 (C14–80–280) 27 pp. plus notes

The organizational history of the Central Intelligence Agency (CIA) from its establishment as OSS during World War II to its role in the Bay of Pigs invasion. Emphasis is placed on factors which served to shape distinct institutional identities and points of view within the Agency, providing perspective from which to assess "its" analysis and advocacy of the invasion plan. Used in conjunction with *Kennedy and the Bay of Pigs* (C14–80–279), the case suggests a number of organizational questions that, had they been addressed, might have helped the President to assess better the information on which he based his approval of the invasion attempt.

The United Mine Workers of America

A. The 1977 Contract Negotiations (C14–81–357) 11 pp. plus notes
B. John L. Lewis's Union (C14–81–358) 29 pp. plus notes
C. The Church Contract (C14–82–267) 4 pp. plus notes

The most powerful union in America in the 1940s and 1950s—dominated by powerful John L. Lewis—the United Mine Workers has in the past two decades appeared weak, rebellious, and confused. Wildcat strikes have threatened not only the fortunes of the union and coal operators but the reliability of coal as a basic national energy source. What accounts for the change? Can it be reversed?

These three cases review the history of the organization for light on these questions. "A. The 1977 Contract Negotiations" describes the 1977–78 negotiations, showing the difficulties faced by Arnold Miller in trying to lead an increasingly militant union. "B. John L. Lewis's Union" looks back at the early years of the union, through the dark rebellion that ousted the corrupt W. A. "Tony" Boyle and propelled Miller to the presidency. "C. The Church Contract" brings the reader up to the 1981 contract period and poses the question, "What next?"

6. Noticing Patterns

Economic Growth

A. Three Theories (C14–76–186) 18 pp.
B. Four Statements (C14–83–515) 17 pp.

Economic Growth A describes the theories of groups of American economists who argue for or against pursuing economic growth policies as the key to achieving maximum societal good. Examination of the analyses of Walt Rostow, the Club of Rome, and Lester Thurow shows that they are based on different perceptions of the historical patterns of economic development and achievement of social good.

Economic Growth B includes three political speeches (one by FDR, two by Reagan) and an excerpt from a 1939 government report—all dealing with growth from a policy perspective. Can be used either before or after *Economic Growth* A. For one use see this book's Chapter Twelve.

Keynes and Friedman on the Great Depression (C14–82–427) 15 pp. plus notes

Examines and puts into theoretical context two differing interpretations of the Great Depression: that of John Maynard Keynes and of Milton Friedman. The case outlines Keynes's and Friedman's analyses of the Depression's origins and their policy prescriptions for overcoming the economic crisis. Their disputes over economic theory have in many ways established the parameters for current economic discussion and, even more, for political action. To be read in conjunction with *Keynes and Friedman: Two Economists* (C15–82–428).

Keynes and Friedman: Two Economists (C14–82–428) 16 pp. plus notes

Presents biographical information to supplement the theoretical sketches on Keynes and Friedman drawn in *Keynes and Friedman on the Great Depression* (C15–82–427). By outlining their differing historical, national, economic, and educational backgrounds and their varying experience with government, the case illuminates the personal circumstances which helped form the two economists' world views. For a third, less easily "pegged" economist, see *Paul A. Samuelson* (C15–83–532).

Paul A. Samuelson (C14–83–532) 5 pp. plus notes

A third portrait, an American Keynesian, to supplement those of Keynes and Friedman in (C15–82–427/428). Outlining his historical, national, economic, and educational background, and his experience with applied economics, the case illuminates the personal circumstances that helped form Samuelson's world view.

Marxism-Leninism (C14–80–284) 12 pp. plus notes

Introduces concepts central to Communist thought: dialectical materialism, the labor theory of value, commodity fetishism, alienation, Communism, dictatorship of the proletariat, democratic centralism, and imperialism.

U.S. Analyses of the Soviet Economy (C14–81–373) 20 pp. plus notes

Presents three views of the Soviet economy by American experts. Used in conjunction with *Marxism-Leninism* (C14–80–284), this case provides a basis for the question how, in terms not wholly inconsistent with Marxism-Leninism, could Soviet officials concerned with reforms justify them to their leaders?

Soviet Views of America (C14–85–642) 26 pp.

Presents assorted views of American society and economy by members of Soviet elite groups in the late 1970s. It provides a basis for the questions how, if you were in their shoes, might you view contemporary U.S. economic problems? Where would you as an American argue with that view? Why?

7. Judging Change

The Great Crash (C14–81–376) 31 pp. plus notes

Follows the trends of the American economy and stock market from the peak of prosperity attained in the 1920s to the edge of the Great Depression in the spring of 1930, a half-year after the stock market crash. Also indicates what happened afterward. Drawing heavily on contemporary reportage of events surrounding the crash, the case points up the slowness of commercial and political leaders to see or acknowledge the severity of the impending economic downturn. Past experience bulks large in assessing current events and in forecasting future trends, hence: How do you know something *new* when you're in it? And if not the past, what?

Secession

A. Foreign Reports (C14–82–435) 45 pp. plus notes
   Supplement (C14–82–435S) 14 pp. plus notes
B. A Southern View (C14–82–436) 5 pp. plus notes
C. The Near Fiasco (C14–82–427) 20 pp. plus notes

Secession "A. Foreign Reports" chronicles events from Abraham Lincoln's election in 1860 to the brink of the Civil War five months later, as reported by British diplomats. Past events, possibly analogous, are summarized in excerpts from an 1860 English encyclopaedia. Stopping just short of the confederate attack on Fort Sumter, the case poses such questions as: How do you know when a crisis is a *crisis?* How do you know what "war" means if it comes?

Secession "Supplement" contains biographies, chronology and statistics to be used in conjunction with the A case. A map of the Baltimore and Ohio Railroad frames the student exercise described in Chapter Fourteen of this book.

Secession B and C examine the events leading up to the first military engagement of the Civil War from different analytical perspectives, posing questions of their relative utility for explanation and prediction.

Secession B summarizes the argument of a prominent Southern historian, Charles W. Ramsdell, who asserts that the Confederate attack on Fort Sumter was cleverly maneuvered by President Lincoln in order to give the North the moral advantage. *Secession* C challenges Ramsdell's "rational actor" interpretation, by illuminating the confusion and rush of events facing the newly elected Lincoln. His decision to resupply Sumter evolved in his first month of office, at the same time he was trying to launch his government, make appointments, assert his authority, and preserve the Union.

Secession C can be juxtaposed to *Kennedy and the Bay of Pigs* (C14–80–279) or to Chapter Seven of this book on Carter and SALT, or both, to pose further questions about continuities and changes in institutions, personalities and operations over time.

Prohibition

A. Enactment (C14–83–492) 21 pp. plus notes
B. Repeal (C14–83–493/493S) 4 pp. plus notes
Supplement (C14–83–493S) 10 pp.

On January 16, 1920, the Eighteenth Amendment to the Constitution, outlawing the manufacture or sale of alcohol, became law.

Prohibition A chronicles the century-long effort to secure prohibition legislation, culminating in the victory of the Anti-Saloon League; the final section analyzes the forces behind Prohibition's success. *Prohibition* B very briefly recounts the life and death of the Eighteenth Amendment. The *Supplement* contains a number of recent articles on the Moral Majority and Christian Political Action Committees, to provide points of comparison.

George Marshall (C14–82–480) 20 pp. plus notes

The renowned Army General, World War II Chief of Staff, Secretary of State, and Secretary of Defense, as seen through the eyes of his contemporaries. Quoting liberally from their assessments, both good and bad, the case points up qualities perceived during the lifetime of someone judged "great" by history.

George Washington (C14–82–479) 16 pp. plus notes

The Commander-in-Chief of the American Revolutionary Army and the first President of the United States, as seen through the eyes of his contemporaries. Quoting liberally from their assessments, both good and bad, the case serves the same purposes as that on George Marshall and can be used comparatively.

Notes

Preface

1. The Appendixes contain a summary of a survey of course alumini and alumnae, with additional extracts from their comments.
2. James Fallows, "The Passionless Presidency," *Atlantic Monthly,* May 1979, p. 44.
3. 89th Cong., 1st Sess., U.S. Senate, Committee on Government Operations, Subcommittee on National Security and International Operations, *Hearings,* June 29 and July 27, 1965, Part 3, pp. 121 ff.

Chapter 1: Success Story

1. This estimate is based on the President's private calendar, which shows periods during which the key CIA official, Richard Bissell, was with the President either alone or in the presence of others privy to the secret. Bissell's attendance was always noted as "off the record." The calendar may not reflect colloquies held out of hours or off the premises, but none such are reported in various accounts of the affair. Participants with whom we have talked voice surprise at the figure but cannot dispute it on the basis of their own calendars or specific recollections.

2. Dean Rusk to the authors, August 22, 1984.
3. Important works on the missile crisis include Elie Abel, *The Cuban Missile Crisis* (Philadelphia: J. B. Lippincott, 1966); Graham T. Allison, *Essence of Decision: Explaining the Cuban Missile Crisis* (Boston: Little, Brown, 1971); George W. Ball, *The Past Has Another Pattern: Memoirs* (New York: W. W. Norton, 1982), chapter 20; David Detzer, *The Brink: Cuban Missile Crisis, 1962* (New York: Thomas Y. Crowell, 1979); Robert F. Kennedy, *Thirteen Days: A Memoir of the Cuban Missile Crisis* (New York: W. W. Norton, 1969); Arthur M. Schlesinger, Jr., *A Thousand Days: John F. Kennedy in the White House* (Boston: Houghton Mifflin, 1965), pp. 794–841; *idem, Robert Kennedy and His Times* (Boston: Houghton Mifflin, 1978), pp. 499–532; and Theodore C. Sorensen, *Kennedy* (New York: Harper & Row, 1965), chapter 24. Except where otherwise noted, documents to which we refer can be traced through *Declassified Documents Quarterly Catalogue,* issued by the Carrollton Press of Washington, D.C. The key information needed is the source of the document (White House, State Department, and so on) and the date of declassification.
4. Sanitized transcripts of the White House meetings of October 16, 1962 (I: 11:50 A.M.–12:57 P.M.; II: 6:30–7:55 P.M.) were released by the John F. Kennedy Library in October 1982. The story of the note is in Kennedy, *Thirteen Days,* p. 9. The rest is from Sorensen, *Kennedy,* p. 684, and Sorensen's memoranda of October 17 and October 18, 1962, declassified from White House files in 1978.
5. Johnson on the blockade option is in Transcript I, p. 20; McNamara's comment is Transcript II, pp. 46–47. Robert Kennedy completely forgot Johnson's role. In a retrospective memorandum written in November 1962, only a month after the crisis, he commented on "the inability of Johnson to make any contribution of any kind during all the conversations." Schlesinger, *Robert Kennedy,* p. 525.
6. Dean G. Acheson, "Dean Acheson's Version of Robert Kennedy's Version of the Cuban Missile Crisis: Homage to Plain Dumb Luck," *Esquire,* LXXI (February 1969): 76 *et seq.*
7. Schlesinger, *Robert Kennedy,* p. 509; Dillon oral history, Kennedy Library.
8. Sorensen to the authors, October 19, 1984.
9. The comment about Capehart and Keating is from Kenneth P. O'Donnell and David F. Powers, *Johnny, We Hardly Knew Ye* (Boston: Little, Brown, 1970), p. 378. Detzer, *The Brink,* pp. 102 ff., speculates about Kennedy's reasons for composing ExComm as he did. Abel, *The Missile Crisis,* p. 33, says that, on the first day of the crisis Kennedy consulted by phone with John J. McCloy, Lovett's wartime colleague in the

Pentagon and the putative dean of the New York foreign policy establishment, but McCloy himself has no recollection of hearing from Kennedy until later, when called back from Europe to negotiate with the Soviet Ambassador to the UN the exact terms for removal of the missiles.

10. "I don't know . . . ," Transcript II, pp. 35–36. It was in the same brief soliloquy that he said, "Now, maybe our mistake was in not saying sometime *before* this summer that if they do this we're [word unintelligible] to act." Slightly earlier he had said, "Last month I should have said . . . that we don't care" (*ibid.,* p. 15), but the context makes his meaning ambiguous. His requests for historical studies are recorded in NSC ExComm Planning Subcommittee minutes, October 24, 1962, declassified in 1975, and NSC ExComm records of action, October 25, 1962, declassified in 1982.
11. Transcript II, p. 13. The "missile is a missile" argument has usually been ascribed to McNamara. He echoed it, but the recordings indicate that the President was the first to voice it.
12. Transcript II, p. 26.
13. NSC ExComm Meeting No. 10, Summary Record, October 28, 1962, declassified in 1982.
14. The image of a "surgical" strike was introduced by Bundy: Transcript I, p. 17. The best analysis of the debate over a "surgical" strike is in Allison, *Essence of Decision,* pp. 123–26, 204–10. The Lovett quotation is from Schlesinger, *Robert Kennedy,* p. 532.
15. On McNamara and the Navy, Abel, *The Missile Crisis,* pp. 157 ff.; Allison, *Essence of Decision,* pp. 127–32; and Dan Caldwell, "A Research Note on the Quarantine of Cuba, October 1962," *International Studies Quarterly,* XXII (December 1978): 625–33. On Rusk and the Cubans, NSC ExComm meeting No. 5, Summary Record, October 25, 1962, declassified in 1982, and Schlesinger, *Robert Kennedy,* pp. 525 ff.
16. *New York Times,* November 3, 1962, p. 6.
17. Thompson oral history, Kennedy Library.
18. Kennedy, *Thirteen Days,* pp. 102 ff., and Detzer, *The Brink,* p. 158.
19. Kennedy, *Thirteen Days,* pp. 37–38.
20. NSC ExComm Meeting No. 8, Summary Record, October 27, 1962, declassified in 1982; Schlesinger, *A Thousand Days,* p. 828.
21. Schlesinger, *Robert Kennedy,* pp. 528–29.
22. Transcript II, pp. 22, 29. Ambassador to the UN Adlai Stevenson wrote an early note to Kennedy, cautioning him that "the judgments of history seldom coincide with the tempers of the moment." But

Stevenson was a marginal figure in the affair. Most members of the Kennedy circle thought him pompous and preachy. He did not count as a key decision-maker.

23. NSC ExComm Meeting No. 7, October 27, 1962, declassified in 1982. Schlesinger, *Robert Kennedy,* pp. 526 ff., gives the best account of the secret bargain.
24. Kennedy, *Thirteen Days,* p. 109.

Chapter 2: A Second Success

1. Interest is an add-on to receipts. For more detail, see "Social Security: B," Kennedy School of Government Case No. C14–77–198.
2. *New York Times,* Jan. 6, 1973. On the day of Ball's dismissal, Nixon's press secretary, Ron Ziegler, announced a "new direction" in the social security program. In response Wilbur Mills warned that Congress would not allow the program to be politicized.
3. The plan approved by Congress raised payroll taxes $277 billion over ten years. By the mid-1980s employers and employees would each pay 7.15 percent, with an estimated wage ceiling of $44,100.
4. *Congressional Quarterly,* May 16, 1981, p. 842. The Administration's plan also included measures to phase out limitations on outside earnings, tighten up disability requirements, and delay for three months an annual cost-of-living increase.
5. For details see, among others, Laurence I. Barrett, *Gambling with History* (New York: Doubleday, 1983), pp. 154–59. See also William Greider, *The Education of David Stockman and Other Americans* (New York: E. P. Dutton, 1981) pp. 44–48.
6. Barrett, *Gambling,* p. 155.
7. For more on presidential transitions, see Richard E. Neustadt, *Presidential Power,* Revised Edition (New York: John Wiley & Sons, 1980), chapter 11.
8. *Report of the National Commission on Social Security Reform* (Washington, D.C.: U.S. Government Printing Office, 1983), Appendix J, p. 14.
9. *New York Times,* March 22, 1983. To provide for long-term financing, Congress approved a gradual increase in the retirement age from sixty-five to sixty-seven by the year 2027. Among the short-term proposals were measures to (1) extend mandatory social security coverage to new federal employees; (2) increase payroll taxes to 7.65 percent for employers and employees by 1990; (3) postpone for six months the cost-of-living increases for 1983 and after; (4) increase payroll taxes

for the self-employed; and (5) tax half the social security benefits of individuals with incomes over $25,000 ($32,000 for couples).

10. James A. Baker III served as Deputy Secretary of Commerce in 1975 but left the position in 1976 to work on President Ford's election campaign. Richard G. Darman worked at HEW, the Department of Defense, and the Justice Department under Nixon and served as Assistant Secretary of Commerce under Ford. Kenneth Duberstein was Director of Congressional and Intergovernmental Affairs for the General Services Administration from 1972 to 1976.
11. During December 1982 and early January 1983 the *Washington Post* frequently and the *New York Times* on occasion ran circumstantial stories blaming one faction or other for imminent breakdown.
12. The commission alternative for raising the retirement age, which Congress adopted with amendments, would have pushed it up in monthly increments to age sixty-six during 2015. Congress substituted sixty-seven by 2027. Under "intermediate" demographic estimates (neither "optimistic" nor "pessimistic"), the latter was expected to keep the trust fund solvent up to 2050 despite all the retiring baby-boomers, provided the economy avoided long-term depression or sustained, high inflation in the interim.
13. The commission also urged on Congress three alternate v suggestions for a "fail safe" mechanism to assure benefit payments even if a sudden economic change should run the trust fund down faster than foreseen while Congress was out of session or in need of time to think. Nothing precisely like that had occurred in the past or was even considered probable, but the commission was in a mood to take contingencies seriously.
14. Another White House aide, as of then, also close but not himself a witness, has encouraged us to think the link to voluntarism worth noting as a live possibility. But we were not at the meetings where the words "fall of its own weight" might have been spoken, and we lack effective access to the few most likely to have used them with the President. The Reagan papers may eventually decide the point, but also they may not. Little appears verbatim in memoranda of conversations with a President; often enough there are no memoranda.

Chapter 3: Unreasoning from Analogies

1. Margaret Truman, *Harry S. Truman* (New York: William Morrow, 1973), p. 455. Glenn D. Paige, *The Korean Decision* (New York: Free Press, 1968), p. 124.

2. United States, Department of State, *Foreign Relations of the United States, 1949,* VII, pt. 2 (Washington, D.C.: Government Printing Office, 1980): 969–78. Further details are in the official JCS history declassified during the Carter Administration: United States Joint Chiefs of Staff, *The History of the Joint Chiefs of Staff: The Joint Chiefs of Staff and National Policy,* vol. III: James F. Schnabel and Robert J. Watson, *The Korean War* (Wilmington, Del.: Michael Glazier, Inc., 1979), Part One, pp. 1–130.
3. George C. Gallup, ed., *The Gallup Poll: Public Opinion 1935–1971* 3 vols. (New York: Random House, 1972) II, *1949–1958:* 784, 939.
4. Harry S. Truman, *Memoirs,* 2 vols. (Garden City, N.Y.: Doubleday & Co., 1955–56), II, *Years of Trial and Hope:* 332–33. The role of analogies in Truman's decisions regarding Korea is traced in greater detail in Ernest R. May, *"Lessons" of the Past: The Use and Misuse of History in American Foreign Policy* (New York: Oxford University Press, 1973), pp. 52–86. Except where otherwise noted, quotations and other specifics are to be found there, appropriately referenced. That account relies heavily on Paige, *The Korean Decision,* a book based primarily on extensive soon-after-the-fact interviews with key participants. Accounts drawing on more recently available documents include Bruce Cumings, "Korean–American Relations," in Warren I. Cohen, ed., *New Frontiers in American–East Asian Relations* (New York: Columbia University Press, 1983), pp. 237–82; Robert J. Donovan, *Tumultuous Years: The Presidency of Harry S. Truman, 1949–53* (New York: W. W. Norton, 1982), pp. 187–248; and William Whitney Stueck, Jr., *The Road to Confrontation: American Policy Toward China and Korea, 1947–1950* (Chapel Hill: University of North Carolina Press, 1981). By far the best document-based account of the American decision and its aftermath is the Schnabel and Watson work cited in note 2 above.
5. Gallup, *The Gallup Poll,* II: 943, 961.
6. Lee Iacocca, *Iacocca* (New York: Bantam Books, 1984), p. 47.
7. "Then" as understood in 1950 can be recaptured from period pieces such as Winston S. Churchill, *The Gathering Storm* (Boston: Houghton Mifflin, 1948), and William L. Shirer, *The Rise and Fall of the Third Reich* (New York: Simon & Schuster, 1960). The entire range of analogues as viewed in 1950 is presented, one by one, in brief in our case study, "Korea and the Thirties (B)," Kennedy School of Government Case No. C194–80–299 (see Appendixes).
8. Donovan, *Tumultuous Years,* p. 212.
9. Truman, *Memoirs,* II: 339.
10. Donovan, *Tumultuous Years,* p. 277.

11. Truman's speechwriters could have found apt quotations in Henry L. Stimson and McGeorge Bundy, *On Active Service in Peace and War* (New York: Harper & Brothers, 1948), chapter 9, and Churchill, *The Gathering Storm,* chapter 11.
12. Except where otherwise noted, what follows draws on Richard E. Neustadt and Harvey V. Fineberg, *The Epidemic That Never Was* (New York: Vintage Books, 1983). Also see Arthur M. Silverstein, *Pure Politics and Impure Science: The Swine Flu Affair* (Baltimore: Johns Hopkins Press, 1981).
13. Alfred W. Crosby, Jr., *Epidemic and Peace, 1918* (Westport, Conn.: Greenwood Press, 1976), p. 210.
14. The largest previous mass immunization, which took place over a year's time, had been the successful effort against poliomyelitis in 1963 using the Sabin "live virus" vaccine. For a summary, see "Swine Flu (D)," Kennedy School of Government Case No. C14–81–410 (see Appendixes).
15. For text see Neustadt and Fineberg, *Epidemic* pp. 198–206.

Chapter 4: The Seducer and the Kid Next Door

1. Basic sources are Gerald R. Ford, *A Time To Heal* (New York: Harper & Row, 1979), chapter 5, and 94th Cong., 2d sess., House Committee on International Relations, "Hearings: Seizure of the *Mayaguez.*" Richard G. Head *et al.*, *Crisis Resolution: Presidential Decision-Making in the Mayaguez and Korean Confrontations* (Boulder, Colo.: Westview Press, 1978), is a study prepared by the National Defense University. Central Intelligence Agency, "Post-Mortem Report: An Examination of the Intelligence Community's Performance Before and During the *Mayaguez* Incident of May 1975," *Declassified Documents, 1978* (microfiche), no. 5D:7, explains how information reaching Washington was routed to Ford and his advisers. Commander in Chief Pacific, *Command History, 1975,* Appendix VI: "The S.S. *Mayaguez* Incident," *Declassified Documents, 1981,* no. 33B, describes the initially confusing command and control arrangements in the area. "'Mayday' for the *Mayaguez,*" U.S. Naval Institute *Proceedings,* CII (November 1976): 93–111, assembles reminiscences of various U.S. officers who took part in various phases of the rescue operation. Roy Rowan, *The Four Days of MAYAGUEZ* (New York: W. W. Norton, 1975), is a colorful and well-researched account by a journalist. We also drew upon Douglas King, "The Capture of the *Mayaguez,*" a prize-winning undergraduate honors thesis at Harvard College in 1981, on file in the

Harvard College Library. A summary of the episode is in "The Mayaguez Incident," Kennedy School case no. C14–81–443 (see Appendixes).

2. Ford, *A Time to Heal,* p. 276.
3. *Time,* May 26, 1975, p. 21.
4. Head, *et al., Crisis Resolution,* p. 113.
5. Ford, *A Time to Heal,* p. 277.
6. Head, *et al., Crisis Resolution,* p. 108; see also Rowan, *Four Days,* p. 68. "We were all haunted, of course, by the *Pueblo* affair," writes a senior White House staff member, "Ford wasn't sure at the outset what he would do, but he was sure he had to do *something.*" Robert T. Hartmann, *Palace Politics: An Inside Account of the Ford Years* (New York: McGraw-Hill, 1980), p. 326.
7. Ford, *A Time to Heal,* pp. 68–69. Kissinger seems to have referred frequently to the *Pueblo* precedent. That may have been because he perceived its force with the President. It may also have been partly because of his own experience. In 1968 he had been an adviser to Nelson Rockefeller, then seeking the Republican nomination, and had almost surely helped Rockefeller frame a comment on the *Pueblo,* which Rockefeller's rival, Richard Nixon, had upstaged by calling for U.S. military action against North Korea. In addition, because of the reports of North Korean mischief, Kissinger had had reason recently to review the *Pueblo* case. See Henry A. Kissinger, *White House Years* (Boston: Little, Brown, 1979), I: 247, 318.
8. Philip Shabecoff in the *New York Times,* May 14, 1975.
9. Ford, *A Time to Heal,* pp. 279–80.
10. *New York Times,* May 15–16, 1975.
11. *National Journal,* June 26, 1977, p. 396.
12. Russell Baker, "A Meow in Search of an Enemy," *New York Times,* April 23, 1977.
13. See Richard E. Neustadt, *Presidential Power,* Revised Edition (New York: John Wiley & Sons, 1980), pp. 225–31.
14. *Washington Post,* March 20, 1977.
15. *Ibid.*, Feb. 2, 1977.
16. "Carter's First 100 Days: The Test Is Yet to Come," *National Journal,* April 30, 1977, p. 676.
17. Jefferson is an unclassifiable case, rendered exceptional in part by the nature of the 1800 election, in part by his own deliberate self-deprecation where Congress was concerned, and in part by the newness of President and congressmen alike to the weather and swamps of Washington, D.C.
18. Zbigniew Brzezinski, *Power and Principle: Memoirs of the National Secu-*

rity Advisor (New York: Farrar, Straus & Giroux, 1983), p. 57. Other Carter Administration insiders feel that whatever Brzezinski's cooler judgment may have been, he was actively stimulating the President's penchant for attempting too much too soon.

19. We allude especially to the Brzezinski memoirs cited above and to Jimmy Carter, *Keeping Faith: Memoirs of a President* (New York: Bantam Books, 1982); Hamilton Jordan, *Crisis: The Last Year of the Carter Presidency* (New York: G. P. Putnam's Sons, 1982); and Cyrus Vance, *Hard Choices* (New York: Simon & Schuster, 1983).

Chapter 5: Dodging Bothersome Analogues

1. The text of Bundy's memorandum is in "The War in Vietnam: Classified Histories by the National Security Council: Deployment of Major U.S. Forces to Vietnam: July 1965" (University Publications of America Microfilm), vol. IV, frames 0563–0572. Alternatively, "Vietnam Documents," Kennedy School of Government Case No. C15–80–271S. To a greater extent than footnotes can indicate, what appears here owes a debt to Larry Berman, *Planning a Tragedy* (New York: Norton, 1982); Richard Betts and Leslie Gelb, *The Irony of Vietnam: The System Worked* (Washington, D.C.: Brookings Institution, 1979); George C. Herring, *America's Longest War: The United States and Vietnam, 1950–1975* (New York: John Wiley & Sons, 1979); and Stanley Karnow, *Vietnam: A History* (New York: Penguin Books, 1984).
2. Kenneth P. O'Donnell and David F. Powers, *Johnny, We Hardly Knew Ye* (Boston: Little, Brown, 1970), p. 13. There is, however, newly available evidence showing the strength of Kennedy's early skepticism. "He questioned the wisdom of involvement in Vietnam since the basis thereof is not completely clear. By comparison he noted that Korea was a case of clear aggression. . . . The President said that he could even make a rather strong case against intervening in an area 10,000 miles away against 16,000 guerrillas with a native army of 200,000, where millions have been spent for years with no success." McNamara, Rusk, and the Chairman of the JCS urged support of South Vietnam even though McNamara said, "in all probability U.S. troops, planes and resources would have to be supplied in additional quantities at a later date." According to the record, "The President again expressed apprehension on support of the proposed action by the Congress as well as by the American people." Notes on National Security Council Meeting, November 15, 1961 (declassified in 1982), Vice President's Security File, Box 4, Folder "NSC (II)," Lyndon Baines Johnson Library, Austin, Texas.
3. Karnow, *Vietnam*, pp. 277–311, offers the best analysis likely to be written for a long time of the coup and assassination.

4. *Public Papers of the Presidents of the United States: Lyndon B. Johnson, 1963–1964,* 2 vols. (Washington, D.C..: Government Printing Office, 1965), II: 1164, 1391.
5. Bundy to the President, January 27, 1965, quoted in Lyndon B. Johnson, *The Vantage Point: Perspectives on the Presidency, 1963–1969* (New York: Holt, Rinehart & Winston, 1971), p. 123.
6. In an interview with Neustadt on June 27, 1983, General Maxwell Taylor expressed himself as convinced that the civilians involved in the missile crisis retrospectively attributed its successful outcome, not unreasonably, to Kennedy's graduated use and threat of force, starting with the low, controllable level of naval quarantine, and that this impression undoubtedly shaped optimism about the usefulness of "slow squeeze" with reference to Hanoi in 1965–66. U. Alexis Johnson, also a participant in ExComm, made the same point in the mid-1970s to an Australian journalist. Denis Warner, *Not with Guns Alone* (n.p.: Hutchinson of Australia, 1977), p. 132. At the time, almost everyone in the presidential circle favored some kind of reprisal. George Ball said, "We are all in accord that action must be taken. . . . We must make clear that North Vietnam and the Viet Cong are the same. We retaliate against North Vietnam because Hanoi directs the Viet Cong, supplies arms, and infiltrates men." Mike Mansfield said, "The North Vietnamese attack has opened many eyes. We are not now in a penny ante game." Summary Notes of NSC Meeting, February 6, 1965 (declassified in 1982), Presidential Papers, Meeting Notes File, Box 1, LBJ Library.
7. Herring, *America's Longest War,* p. 139.
8. George W. Ball, *The Past Has Another Pattern: Memoirs* (New York: W. W. Norton, 1982), p. 392. Ball's memorandum was originally published as "Top Secret: The Prophecy the President Rejected," *Atlantic Monthly,* CCXXX (July 1972): 35–49.
9. Ball, *The Past Has Another Pattern,* p. 400; Jack Valenti, *A Very Human President* (New York: W. W. Norton, 1975), pp. 319–52, gives a first-hand account of the July debates. The quotation here is from p. 349.
10. For texts, see "The War in Vietnam: Classified Histories by the National Security Council—Deployment of Major U.S. Forces to Vietnam: July 1965" (University Press of America Microfilm), frames 0573–0578 and 0629–0631.
11. For reference, see note 1.
12. The quotation from Bundy is from U.S. Department of Defense, *The Pentagon Papers: The Defense Department History of United States Decision Making on Vietnam,* 4 vols., Senator Gravel edition (Boston: Beacon Press, 1971), III: 311; that from Rusk is from "The War in Vietnam: Classified Histories—Deployment of Major U.S. Forces . . .," VI, frames 0605–0609; that from McNamara is *ibid.*, frames 0556–0562;

that from the JCS is *ibid.*, V, frames 0215–0219, and VI, frames 0742–0755.

13. *Pentagon Papers,* IV: 622. On Tet, see Karnow, *Vietnam,* Chapter 14.
14. *Pentagon Papers,* III: p. 625.
15. Arthur M. Schlesinger, Jr., *Robert F. Kennedy and His Times* (Boston: Houghton Mifflin, 1978), p. 730.
16. Doris Kearns, *Lyndon Johnson and the American Dream* (New York: Harper & Row, 1976), pp. 252–53. Contemporaneous evidence includes the line, "*The President* felt that our mission [in Vietnam] should be as limited as we dare make it." Summary Notes of NSC Meeting, July 21, 1965 (declassified in 1984), Presidential Papers, Meeting Notes File, Box 1, LBJ Library.
17. Hubert H. Humphrey, *Education of a Public Man: My Life and Politics* (Garden City, N.Y.: Doubleday, 1976), pp. 322–24.
18. Berman, *Planning a Tragedy,* p. 371. After LBJ decided to Americanize the war, Clifford reiterated his opinion even more strongly. The following appears under the heading, "Views of Clark Clifford on Viet Nam," subscribed as "taken down by Jack Valenti, Camp David," July 25, 1965, Office Files of the President, Clark Clifford File, LBJ Library:

    "I don't believe we can win in South Viet Nam. If we send in 100,000 troops, the North Vietnamese will match us. And when they run out of troops, the Chinese will send in 'volunteers.' Russia and China don't intend for us to win this war. If we lose 50,000 men there, it will be catastrophic in this country. Five years, billions of dollars, hundreds of thousands of men—this is not for us.

    "At the end of the monsoon season, let us QUIETLY probe and search out with other countries—even if we have to moderate our position—a way for us to get out. I cannot see anything but catastrophe for our nation in this area."
19. Chicago Council on Foreign Relations, *American Public Opinion and U.S. Foreign Policy 1983* (Chicago: Chicago Council on Foreign Relations), p. 29. According to Gallup polls commissioned by the Chicago Council, 72 percent of 1,546 respondents surveyed in 1982 believed that "the Vietnam war was more than a mistake; it was fundamentally wrong and immoral."
20. Berman, *Planning a Tragedy* p. 59; *Pentagon Papers,* III: 352–53.

Chapter 6: Inspecting Issue History

1. Zbigniew Brzezinski, *Power and Principle: Memoirs of the National Security Advisor* (New York: Farrar, Strauss & Giroux, 1983), p. 346. The

fullest secondary account of the episode is Gloria Duffy, "Crisis Mangling and the Cuban Brigade," *International Security,* VIII (Summer 1983): 67–87.

2. *Newsweek,* July 23, 1979, pp. 20 ff., and July 30, 1979, pp. 21–22.
3. Brzezinski, *Power and Principle,* p. 347.
4. Cyrus Vance, *Hard Choices* (New York: Simon & Schuster, 1983), p. 362; *Newsweek,* October 9, 1979, p. 24.
5. *Washington Post,* September 1, 1979.
6. Vance, *Hard Choices,* p. 362.
7. *Ibid.*
8. Don Oberdorfer *et al., Washington Post,* September 9, 1979; *Newsweek,* September 10, 1979, pp. 18–19.
9. Duffy, "Crisis Mangling," pp. 79–82.
10. Frank Freidel, *Franklin D. Roosevelt,* 3 vols., in progress (Boston: Little, Brown, 1952–), II, *The Ordeal:* 263, and III, *Triumph:* 41–42, 100, 139.
11. From a campaign speech in Detroit, October 2, 1932. Samuel I. Rosenman, ed., *The Public Papers and Addresses of Franklin D. Roosevelt,* (New York: Random House, 1938), I: 774–75.
12. Frances Perkins, *The Roosevelt I Knew* (New York: Viking Press, 1946), p. 280.
13. Perkins, *The Roosevelt I Knew,* p. 281. Except where otherwise noted, our account follows that in Perkins, pp. 281–95.
14. Arthur M. Schlesinger, Jr., *The Age of Roosevelt* 3 vols., in progress (Boston: Houghton Mifflin, 1957–), III, *The Politics of Upheaval:* 29 ff.
15. *Ibid.*, III: 36–37.
16. Perkins, *The Roosevelt I Knew,* p. 294. Perkins probably had a lapse of memory in using "1980" as the year her staff in 1935 predicted problems for the trust fund as initially conceived. The predicted year then was 1965. In 1939, when the Social Security Act was being amended, staff studies did suggest 1980 as the year when reserves might run out in the trust fund as then contemplated. Perkins presumably recalled 1939 as 1935 when she wrote those lines in her memoir. See Edwin E. Witte, *The Development of the Social Security Act* (Madison: University of Wisconsin Press, 1962), p. 74.
17. William E. Leuchtenburg, *Franklin Roosevelt and the New Deal, 1932–40* (New York: Harper & Row, 1963), p. 131.
18. Interview with Luther Gulick by Michael McGeary, Institute of Public Administration, New York, February 28, 1980. Quoted with Mr. Gulick's permission.

19. *Public Papers of Governor Franklin D. Roosevelt, 1929* (Albany, N.Y.: L. B. Lyons, 1930), p. 44.
20. Lyndon Baines Johnson, *The Vantage Point* (New York: Holt, Rinehart & Winston, 1979), p. 110.
21. Doris Kearns, *Lyndon Johnson and the American Dream* (New York: Harper & Row, 1976), p. 90.
22. See Freidel, *Roosevelt,* vol. IV, *Launching the New Deal,* chapters 7–8, 21–22, and 27.
23. See Hugh Heclo, *A Government of Strangers* (Washington, D.C.: Brookings Institution, 1977).
24. See Richard E. Neustadt, *Alliance Politics* (New York: Columbia University Press, 1970), chapter 3.

Chapter 7: Finding History That Fits

1. Except where otherwise noted, we rely here on Strobe Talbott's authoritative *Endgame: The Inside Story of SALT II* (New York: Harper & Row, 1979).
2. *Newsweek,* May 2, 1977, p. 48.
3. Cyrus Vance was general counsel for the Department of Defense in 1961, Secretary of the Army from 1962 to 1964, and Deputy Secretary of Defense from 1964 to 1967. Paul Warnke served as general counsel to the Department of Defense from 1966 to 1967, and as Assistant Secretary of Defense for international security affairs from 1967 to 1969. Leslie Gelb was deputy director of the policy planning staff of the Department of Defense in 1967, director in 1968, and acting Deputy Assistant Secretary of Defense for policy planning and arms control staff from 1968 to 1969.
4. Joseph A. Pechman, ed., *Setting National Priorities: The 1978 Budget* (Washington, D.C.: Brookings Institution, 1977), pp. 95–99.
5. Joseph Kraft, *Washington Post,* February 1, 1977.
6. Murray Marder, *Washington Post,* January 21, 1977.
7. Jimmy Carter, *Keeping Faith: Memoirs of a President* (New York: Bantam Books, 1982), p. 218.
8. Zbigniew Brzezinski, *Power and Principle: Memoirs of the National Security Advisor* (New York: Farrar, Strauss & Giroux, 1983), p. 159.
9. Cyrus Vance, *Hard Choices: Critical Years in American Foreign Policy* (New York: Simon & Schuster, 1983), p. 49; Brzezinski, *Power and Principle,* p. 159; Brzezinski, letter to the authors, August 3, 1984.

10. Brzezinski, *Power and Principle,* p. 160; Vance, *Hard Choices,* p. 52.
11. Brzezinski, *Power and Principle,* p. 160.
12. In an entry in his journal, Brzezinski actually mentioned the Vienna summit as a warning precedent. *Ibid.,* pp. 155–56.
13. *Newsweek,* April 4, 1977, p. 21.
14. The issues are summarized more or less in layman's language in 96th Cong., 2d sess., House Permanent Select Committee on Intelligence, "Hearings: CIA Estimates of Defense Spending." CIA: National Foreign Assessment Center SR 80-10005, "Soviet and US Defense Activities, 1970–1979: A Dollar Cost Comparison—A Research Paper" (Washington, D.C.: Central Intelligence Agency, 1980) provides a baseline. Anyone fascinated with the subject can go on to Steven Rosenfielde, *False Science: Underestimating the Soviet Arms Buildup: An Appraisal of the CIA's Direct Costing Effort, 1960–1980* (New Brunswick, N.J.: Transaction Books, 1982), a much more professional piece of analysis than its title would suggest, and literature therein cited.
15. In a large body of literature, the best informed and most concise survey is Michael Mandelbaum, *The Nuclear Question: The United States and Nuclear Weapons, 1946–1976* (Cambridge: Cambridge University Press, 1979). Anyone wishing to dig more deeply should look first at David A. Rosenberg, "The Origins of Overkill: Nuclear Weapons and American Strategy, 1945–1960," *International Security,* VIII (Spring 1983): 3–71, and Harland B. Moulton, *From Superiority to Parity: The United States and the Strategic Arms Race 1961–1971* (Westport, Conn.; Greenwood Press, 1973).
16. See Lawrence Freedman, *U.S. Intelligence and the Soviet Strategic Threat* (Boulder, Colo.: Westview Press, 1977).
17. David Holloway, *The Soviet Union and the Arms Race* (New Haven: Yale University Press, 1983); Robert P. Berman and John Baker, *Soviet Strategic Forces* (Washington, D.C.: Brookings Institution, 1982); and Mark E. Miller, *Soviet Strategic Power and Doctrine* (Miami: Advanced International Studies Institute, 1982), are three recent works that approach the subject historically. The most up-to-date survey (reporting much that was not known in 1977) is U.S. Department of Defense, *Soviet Military Power,* 3d ed. (Washington, D.C.: Government Printing Office, 1984).
18. Talbott, *Endgame,* p. 73.
19. Carter, *Keeping Faith,* p. 217.
20. George H. Gallup, *The Gallup Poll: Public Opinion, 1972–1977* (Wilmington, Del.: Scholarly Resources, 1978), pp. 664–66. These figures are from the spring of 1976. By the summer of 1977 Gallup found

about a quarter of the public to be on each side of this question, with the rest undecided, but that was after the failure of the Vance mission. Pp. 1164–66.

21. James Fallows, "The Passionless Presidency," *Atlantic Monthly,* May 1979, p. 44.

Chapter 8: Probing Presumptions

1. Richard E. Neustadt and Harvey V. Fineberg, *The Epidemic That Never Was* (New York: Vintage Books, 1983) p. 46.
2. See note 6 in Chapter 5.
3. See "Bombing for Peace," in Ernest R. May, *"Lessons" of the Past: The Use and Misuse of History in American Foreign Policy* (New York: Oxford University Press, 1973), pp. 125–42.
4. Peter Wyden, *Bay of Pigs: The Untold Story* (New York: Simon & Schuster, 1979).
5. *Ibid.,* p. 89. Evidence for early Defense support and intra-State opposition is in McGeorge Bundy to President Kennedy, February 18, 1961, and Thomas Mann to Dean Rusk, February 15, 1961, University Press of America, *Declassified Documents* (1984), nos. 555 and 943.
6. McGeorge Bundy to President Kennedy, March 15, 1961, *ibid.*, no. 556.
7. Richard E. Neustadt, *Presidential Power,* revised edition (New York: John Wiley & Sons, 1980) p. 278.
8. Dean Rusk to the authors, August 22, 1984.
9. See Jorge L. Dominguez, *Cuba: Order and Revolution* (Cambridge, Mass.: Harvard University Press, 1978).
10. Arthur M. Schlesinger, Jr., *A Thousand Days: John F. Kennedy in the White House* (Boston: Houghton Mifflin, 1965), p. 249.
11. Richard H. Immermann, *The CIA in Guatemala* (Austin: University of Texas Press, 1982), pp. 162–68.
12. Neustadt and Fineberg, *Epidemic,* p. 43.
13. *Ibid.*. pp. 12–14 *et seq.*
14. See Richard M. Bissell, "Reply to Lucien S. Vandenbroucke, 'The Confessions of Allen Dulles: New Evidence on the Bay of Pigs,'" *Diplomatic History,* VIII (Fall 1984): 378. Elsewhere in this article Bissell makes the trenchant point that while he was an enthusiast for his plan, which he does not in the least deny, that is what the people charged with making plans and carrying out operations have to be and ought to be. In the American governmental system it is up to

their critics and competitors (and superiors) to counter them with equal zest (and better persuasiveness). Regarding the Bay of Pigs, we think this a fair defense on the part of the planner-operator.

Chapter 9: Placing Strangers

1. Rufus Miles was a senior civil servant in the Federal Budget Bureau in the 1940s. His law has been erroneously attributed to various others.
2. "He had a secure and uncluttered concept of the Presidency, inspired by his mythic remembrance of Franklin Roosevelt. . . . Reagan's idea of a President was of a leader who could rally the country to a cause with the power of his voice and use public opinion as a catalyst for change." Lou Cannon, *Reagan* (New York: G. P. Putnam's Sons, 1982), p. 417. Cannon had observed Reagan closely during the gubernatorial years in Sacramento.
3. For an analysis of the spread of American views on the "lessons of Vietnam," see Ole R. Holsti and James N. Rosenau, "Vietnam, Consensus, and the Belief Systems of American Leaders," *World Politics,* XXXII (October 1979): 1–56.
4. See Doris Kearns's excellent account of Johnson's Senate years in *Lyndon Johnson and the American Dream* (New York: Harper & Row, 1976), chapters 4 and 5. For further information on others mentioned above, along with additional biographical sources on them, see "Vietnam Advisers," Kennedy School of Government Case No. C14-80-272.
5. Ball's October 5, 1964, memorandum was originally published in his article "Top Secret: The Prophecy the President Rejected," *Atlantic Monthly,* July 1972, pp. 35–49. Also, see Ball's retrospective comments in George W. Ball, *The Past Has Another Pattern: Memoirs* (New York: W. W. Norton, 1982), pp. 380–85.
6. A comment to the authors, October 24, 1984.
7. See John Steinbruner's authoritative account in *The Cybernetic Theory of Decision* (Princeton, N.J.: Princeton University Press, 1974), especially chapter 9. See also Philip Geyelin, *Lyndon B. Johnson and the World* (New York: Frederick A. Praeger, 1966), chapter 7.
8. See Hugh Heclo, *A Government of Strangers* (Washington, D.C.: Brookings Institution, 1977), especially pp. 103–4. The average does not seem to have changed much, if at all, since Heclo wrote.
9. For summary versions of their biographies, see "Frances Perkins, Secretary of Labor," Kennedy School of Government Case No. C14-81-369, and "Mary Anderson and the Women's Bureau," Case No. C14-81-368. (See Appendixes.) Those are the summaries we use in

class. Both those cases draw extensively on material in the Schlesinger Library at Radcliffe College. For more detail on Perkins, see George Martin, *Madame Secretary: Frances Perkins* (Boston: Houghton Mifflin, 1976.

10. Martin, *Madame Secretary,* pp. 145–47. This refers to relative strangers of the male sex. With intimates of both sexes she could be relatively unbuttoned, we are told, even gossipy (except about her private life, a never mentioned subject).
11. Mary Anderson and Mary N. Winslow, *Women at Work: The Autobiography of Mary Anderson as Told to Mary N. Winslow* (Minneapolis: University of Minnesota Press, 1951), p. 183.
12. Their careers had touched at Hull House, although not at the same time. Among their mutual friends was Margaret Dreier Robins of Chicago, a constant friend to women's causes and to unionization, yet socially impeccable, at home with Easterners of her own class. Among the interests Anderson and Perkins seem to have had in common was concern for unorganized workers in mass production industries. Anderson's private view of stand-pat AFL leadership, including Green's, seems to have been much like Perkins's. Understandably, Anderson hoped for more from organization than did Perkins, who placed her faith more in regulation.

Chapter 10: Placing Across Barriers

1. See David L. Lewis, *King: A Critical Biography* (New York: Praeger, 1970), and Lerone Bennett, *What Manner of Man* (Chicago: Johnson, 1965). These and other sources are summarized in "Martin Luther King," Kennedy School of Government Case No. C14–81–365 (see appendixes).
2. Malcolm X and Alex Haley, *The Autobiography of Malcolm X* (New York: Grove Press, 1964), This and other sources are summarized in "Malcolm X," Kennedy School of Government case no. C14–81–366 (see Appendixes).
3. Marion Dönhoff, ed., *Hart am Wind: Helmut Schmidt's politische Laufbahn* (Hamburg: Albrecht Kraus, 1979), p. 18.
4. Zbigniew Brzezinski, *Power and Principle* (New York: Farrar, Straus & Giroux, 1983), p. 293.
5. See Richard E. Neustadt, *Alliance Politics* (New York: Columbia University Press, 1970), especially chapter 3.
6. The President's remarks were made in the course of his famous year-end TV interview with four correspondents. Skybolt arose only incidentally. The PM only learned of it the next day as he deplaned at

Nassau to be quizzed by British journalists. He then obtained and read a transcript of the President's remarks. That occasioned his comment that "the lady" had been "violated in public."

7. This summary of Macmillan's personal history is drawn in the main from his own sparkling *Memoirs,* 6 vols. (London: Macmillan, 1966–73), and Anthony Sampson, *Macmillan: A Study in Ambiguity* (New York: Simon & Schuster, 1967). In addition, there is in progress an authorized biography by Alistair Horne, fragments of which we have been privileged to see.
8. See Neustadt, *Alliance Politics,* pp. 50–55. Charles de Gaulle, then President of the French Republic, accused the British of being insufficiently European and of being too entangled with the Americans. He used the Nassau agreement as contemporary evidence. By it Macmillan gave up Skybolt, which de Gaulle, along with many Englishmen, interpreted as a defeat, and got instead Polaris pledged to NATO except in "supreme emergency." Macmillan saw the exception as a victory for "independence"; de Gaulle cited the pledge as an entanglement. The latter's desire to keep the British out of Europe for the time (until they should grow weaker, more remote from world position, more in *need* of France) already had been signaled to Macmillan privately. Nassau gave de Gaulle a good excuse for going public.
9. For elaboration see Neustadt, *Alliance Politics,* pp. 89–96. See also Anthony King, ed., *The British Prime Minister* (London: Macmillan, 1969), esp. pp. 44–69, 119–50.

Chapter 11: Noticing Patterns

1. When Stalin died in March 1953, Brezhnev's age was forty-six; Soviet Foreign Minister Andrei Gromyko's was forty-three; Dobrynin's was thirty-four. Brezhnev's most rapid career progress had occurred during the Great Purge. Briefly in eclipse after Stalin's death, he then resumed his rise in the mid-1950s when Khrushchev consolidated control. Gromyko's career had a similar pattern. He had also been a premier specialist on the United States from at least 1939 onward and thus called upon to give opinions during periods of volatile change in relationships. Dobrynin had entered the diplomatic service just after World War II and served as an American specialist through all the frosts and thaws of the Cold War.
2. Cyrus Vance, *Hard Choices* (New York: Simon & Schuster, 1983), p. 51.
3. Available on bookshelves were William W. Prochnau and Richard W. Larsen, *A Certain Democrat: Senator Henry M. Jackson, a Political*

Biography (Englewood Cliffs, N.J.: Prentice-Hall, 1972), and Peter J. Ognibene, *"Scoop": The Life and Politics of Henry M. Jackson* (New York: Stein & Day, 1975). Another useful reference work, available in manuscript, would have been Paula Stern, *Water's Edge: Domestic Politics and the Making of American Foreign Policy* (Westport, Conn.: Greenwood Press, 1979), a study of Jackson's successful efforts to curtail trade with the Soviet Union, whose author was close at hand. She was on the list of bright young ex-congressional aides whom Carter's people wanted to slot into executive agencies. Still nearer at hand was an even better human source, White House energy adviser James Schlesinger, who had been on close terms with Jackson for years.

4. Ognibene, *"Scoop"*, p. 200.
5. *Ibid.*, p. 166.
6. See Strobe Talbott, *Deadly Gambit* (New York: Alfred A. Knopf, 1984), pp. 15–18 *et seq.*
7. Scoop's use of this tactic in connection with the Limited Test Ban Treaty is sketched in Harold Karan Jacobson and Eric Stein, *Diplomats, Scientists and Politicians: The United States and the Nuclear Test Ban Negotiations* (Ann Arbor: University of Michigan Press, 1966).
8. See Robert Jervis, *Perception and Misperception in International Politics* (Princeton, N.J.: Princeton University Press, 1976).
9. The allusion is to the generally valuable manual by Roger Fisher and William Ury, *Getting to Yes: Negotiating Agreement Without Giving In* (Boston: Houghton Mifflin, 1981).
10. "Marxism-Leninism," Kennedy School of Government Case No. C94–80–284, and "U.S. Analyses of the Soviet Economy," Kennedy School Case No. C94–81–373 (see Appendixes). The latter case-study includes CIA data and a stimulating article by Alec Nove, "The Economic Problems of Brezhnev's Successors," excerpted from the Georgetown University *Journal of International Affairs,* Fall/Winter 1978, pp. 201–9.
11. S. Shatalin, "The Economy of the USSR—A Single National Economic Complex," translation in *Problems of Economics,* XXI (August 1978): 24–43. The language on the other side of the debate is illustrated by the following quotation from N. Fedorenko, Secretary of the Economics Division of the Academy of Sciences, an arch defender of centralized planning, from "Long-Range and Current Problems of Economic Science," *Problems of Economics,* XXIII (December 1979): 3–20. Fedorenko said the goal should be "comprehensive intensification of social production through accelerated scientific and technical progress and the implementation of appropriate social and economic policies." We sometimes read our students these quotations from

Shatalin and Fedorenko and then ask them to guess which represents which position in the debate over planning alternatives. A good general work on the subject is Alex Nove, *The Soviet Economic System* (London: Allen & Unwin, 1980).

12. See Daniel S. Hirshfield, *The Lost Reform: The Campaign for Compulsory Health Insurance in the United States from 1932 to 1943* (Cambridge, Mass.: Harvard University Press, 1970), and Monte M. Poen, *Harry S. Truman Versus the Medical Lobby* (Columbia: University of Missouri Press, 1979).
13. Samuel I. Rosenman, ed., *The Public Papers and Addresses of Franklin D. Roosevelt, I: The Genesis of the New Deal, 1928–1932* (New York, Random House, 1938), pp. 742–56. Alternatively, "Economic Growth (B) Four Statements," Kennedy School of Government case no. C94-83-515 (see Appendixes).
14. Summarized very briefly in "Economic Growth (A) Three Theories," Kennedy School of Government Case No. C94–77–186 (see Appendixes).
15. *Economist,* Aug. 22, 1959, p. 511 (*a propos* of a prepublication summary of Rostow's book), and *New York Times Book Review,* May 8, 1960, p. 6.
16. Arthur M. Schlesinger, *A Thousand Days: John F. Kennedy in the White House* (Boston: Houghton Mifflin, 1965), pp. 10–11.
17. Eric Goldman, *The Tragedy of Lyndon Johnson* (New York: Alfred A. Knopf, 1969), p. 62.

Chapter 12: Placing Organizations

1. By "personnel system" we mean accustomed routines and standards, whether codified or not, for recruitment, training, socialization, compensation and other incentives, promotion, and removal or retirement.
2. 94th Cong., 2d sess., Senate Select Committee to Study . . . Intelligence Activities, *Final Report,* Book 4: "History of the Central Intelligence Agency" (by Anne Karalekas), and Thomas Powers, *The Man Who Kept the Secrets: Richard Helms and the CIA* (New York: Alfred A. Knopf, 1979).
3. See Ernest R. May, ed., *Knowing One's Enemies: Intelligence Assessment Before the Two World Wars* (Princeton, N.J.: Princeton University Press, 1984).
4. See Ronald Lewin, *The American Magic: Codes, Ciphers and the Defect of Japan* (New York: Farrar Straus Giroux, 1982).
5. Powers, *The Man Who Kept the Secrets,* p. 31.

6. Except where otherwise noted, what follows comes from Richard E. Neustadt and Harvey V. Fineberg, *The Epidemic That Never Was* (New York: Vintage Books, 1983). See also General Accounting Office, *The Swine Flu Program: An Unprecedented Venture in Preventive Medicine,* June 27, 1977. Note that we designate the then "Health Division" of HEW as the "Public Health Service," its current title, which was not adopted formally until 1977. The same title is and traditionally has been carried by the commissioned corps of doctors who man many but by no means all the posts in PHS.
7. In 1980 Sencer's successor changed the name further to Centers for Disease Control. That produced parallelism with the PHS's great research arm, the National Institutes for Health; as in the case of "institute," it gave every disease (and its legislative sponsors) the prospect of a "center" of its own. The change did not perceptibly affect CDC operations at the time. Neither had Sencer's earlier change.
8. Hale Champion, quoted on p. 19 of "Social Security (B)," Kennedy School of Government Case No. C14–77–198 (see Appendixes).
9. Interview by Richard E. Neustadt with Hale Champion, May 3, 1982.
10. Joseph A. Califano, Jr., *Governing America* (New York: Simon & Schuster, 1981), pp. 372–3. For context see pp. 368–401.

Chapter 13: What to Do and How: A Summary

1. Thucydides, *History of the Peloponnesian Wars,* trans. Rex Warner (London: Penguin Books, 1954), p. 24.
2. Arthur M. Schlesinger, Jr., *The Crisis of the Old Order* (Boston: Houghton Mifflin, 1957), p. 408.
3. See appendixes.
4. E. J. Kahn, Jr., *The China Hands: America's Foreign Service Officers and What Befell Them* (New York: Viking Press, 1975), pp. 242–43.
5. Jacques Barzun and Henry F. Graff, *The Modern Researcher,* 4th ed. (New York: Harcourt Brace Jovanovich, 1985).
6. Frank Freidel, ed., *The Harvard Guide to American History,* 2 vols. (Cambridge, Mass.: Harvard University Press, 1974). A more recent but more specialized bibliography is Richard Dean Burns, ed., *Guide to American Foreign Relations Since 1700* (Santa Barbara, Calif.: ABC Clio, 1983).

Chapter 14: Seeing Time as a Stream

1. Forrest C. Pogue, *George C. Marshall,* vol. III: *Organizer of Victory, 1943–1945* (New York: Viking Press, 1973), pp. 458–59. Pogue's is

the biography of Marshall. Leonard Mosley, *Marshall: Hero for Our Times* (New York: Hearst Books, 1982), summarizes the three Pogue volumes extending through World War II and sketches Marshall's later years. We benefited from having draft "cases" on the lives of Marshall and George Washington prepared by Megan Jones, a former student and also a veteran of service in state government. These are listed with the case-studies in our appendixes.

2. United States Department of State, *United States Relations with China, with Special Reference to the Period 1944–1949* (Washington, D.C.: Government Printing Office, 1949), pp. 380–84. This was the famous "White Paper" that caused Truman and Acheson so much grief. It was reprinted by the Stanford University Press in 1967 and can still be found in bookstores. The whole episode is summarized in greater detail, with specific comparisons to Vietnam, in Ernest R. May, *The Truman Administration and China, 1945–1949* (Philadelphia: J. B. Lippincott, 1975), and in still greater detail, with later documentation, in William Whitney Stueck, Jr., *The Road to Confrontation: American Policy Toward China and Korea, 1947–1950* (Chapel Hill: University of North Carolina Press, 1981).
3. Joseph M. Jones, *The Fifteen Weeks (February 21–June 5, 1947)* (New York: Viking, 1955) is a basic narrative written by an insider. The detail about Marshall's not sharing an advance text with the Department comes from Dean G. Acheson, *Present at the Creation: My Years at the State Department* (New York: W. W. Norton, 1969), chapter 26.
4. The most lively and up-to-date account of the subject is Peter Grose, *Israel in the Mind of America* (New York: Alfred A. Knopf, 1983). The quotation from Clifford is on pp. 292–93.
5. John F. Melby, *The Mandate of Heaven: Record of a Civil War, China 1945–1949* (Toronto: University of Toronto Press, 1968), p. 69. The information on Marshall's in-flight reading comes from Pogue, *Organizer of Victory,* p. 36; "avoid trivia" from George F. Kennan, *Memoirs, 1925–1950* (Boston: Little, Brown, 1967), p. 326. The label was not Marshall's own choice. Robert J. Donovan, *The Presidency of Harry S Truman,* vol. I: *Conflict and Crisis* (New York: W. W. Norton, 1977), p. 287, quotes Clark Clifford as saying that in an election year a Marshall Plan would get more votes in Congress than a Truman Plan.
6. Harry S. Truman, *Memoirs,* vol. I: *Year of Decisions* (Garden City, N.Y.: Doubleday, 1955), pp. 119–21.
7. Ernest R. May, *"Lessons" of the Past: The Use and Misuse of History in American Foreign Policy* (New York: Oxford University Press, 1973), chapter 1, says more about FDR's use of analogies.
8. Samuel I. Rosenman, ed., *The Public Papers and Addresses of Franklin*

D. *Roosevelt*, vol. I: *The Genesis of the New Deal, 1928–1932* (New York: Random House, 1938), pp. 742–56. See Chapter 11 above.

9. Eliot Janeway, *The Struggle for Survival* (New Haven: Yale University Press, 1951), p. 158.
10. Larry Berman, *Planning a Tragedy: The Americanization of the War in Vietnam* (New York: W. W. Norton, 1982), pp. 38–39. See Chapter 5 above.
11. *Newsweek*, (January 24, 1977, p. 19.
12. Pogue, *Organizer of Victory*, p. 315.
13. The documents are all in "Secession A: Foreign Reports," Kennedy School of Government Case No. C14–82–435 (see appendixes). The hypothetical option to purchase bonds is set forth in the Teaching Note available with that case.
14. "The Great Crash," Kennedy School of Government case no. C14–81–376 (see appendixes).
15. The most recent edition is Francis Parkman, *France and England in North America*, 2 vols. (New York: Library of America, 1983). Still in print is Samuel Eliot Morison, ed., *The Parkman Reader* (Boston: Little, Brown, 1955).
16. The liveliest versions of all of these are in the series of Penguin Classics, available in good bookstores in paperback. The translators and dates are: Thucydides (Rex Warner: 1954); Livy, in four volumes (Aubrey de Selincourt, 1960 and 1965; Henry Bettenson, 1976; Betty Radice, 1982); Polybius (Ian Scott-Kilvert, 1979); Plutarch, in four volumes (Rex Warner, 1958; Ian Scott-Kilvert, 1960, 1968, and 1973); Tacitus, *Annals* (Michael Grant, 1956), *Histories* (Kenneth Wellesley, 1964).
17. George Bancroft, *A History of the United States from the Discovery of the American Continent*, 10 vols. (Boston: Little, Brown, 1834–74). An abridged one-volume version was published in 1966 by the University of Chicago Press. Albert J. Beveridge, *The Life of John Marshall* 4 vols. (Cambridge, Mass.: Houghton Mifflin, 1916–19). The story about his Anglo-Saxon composition comes from Claude G. Bowers, *Beveridge and the Progressive Era* (Boston: Houghton Mifflin, 1932), pp. 16–17. Bowers himself could well be on our list. A journalist and politician, FDR's Ambassador to Spain during the Spanish Civil War, he wrote a graphic, if ardently pro-Jefferson, trilogy on the early years of the republic: *The Young Jefferson* (Boston: Houghton Mifflin, 1945), *Jefferson and Hamilton* (Boston: Houghton Mifflin, 1936), and *Jefferson in Power* (Boston: Houghton Mifflin, 1939).
18. Theodore Roosevelt, *The Winning of the West*, 4 vols. (New York: G. P. Putnam's Sons, 1889–96). Selections, edited by Harvey Wish,

were published in New York by Capricorn Books in 1962. Of Winston S. Churchill, *Marlborough: His Life and Times,* 6 vols. (New York: Scribner's, 1933–38); a one-volume abridgement was published by the same house in 1968. The other work referred to here is *The History of the English-Speaking Peoples,* 4 vols. (London: Cassell, 1956–58). Also worth reading, though it conceals more than it discloses, is his biography of his father, *Lord Randolph Churchill,* 2 vols. (New York: Macmillan, 1966). There is in progress a marvelous biography of TR, the first volume of which covers his years as a historian: Edmund Morris, *The Rise of Theodore Roosevelt* (New York: Coward McCann, 1979).

19. The Penguin Classics has an updated version of the Leslie J. Walker translation of the *Discourses* (1983). Another lively though abridged version, translated by Frank Bordanella and Mark Musa, appears in *The Viking Portable Machiavelli* (New York: Viking, 1979). Thomas Babington Macalay, *The History of England from the Accession of James the Second,* was reprinted in New York by the AMS Press in 1968 in six volumes and then revised by the same house in 1980 as half of a twelve-volume *Complete Works.* Henry Adams's full *History* was reprinted in 1962 in New York by the Antiquarian Press. In 1967 the University of Chicago published a one-volume abridgement. The other work referred to here is Arthur M. Schlesinger, Jr., *The Age of Roosevelt,* 3 vols., in progress (Boston: Houghton Mifflin, 1957–).

20. John G. Nicolay and John Hay, *Abraham Lincoln,* 10 vols. (New York: Century, 1890). The University of Chicago published a one-volume abridgement in 1966. Ulysses S. Grant, *Personal Memoirs,* 2 vols. (New York: Webster and Co., 1885–86). Winston S. Churchill, *The World Crisis,* 5 vols. (New York: Scribner's, 1923–29) was also published in a one-volume abridgement (New York: Scribner's, 1949). Of his *The Second World War,* 6 vols. (Boston: Houghton Mifflin) there is a one-volume (Boston: Houghton Mifflin, 1959) and also a two-volume (New York: Time, Inc., 1959) abridgement. Among Harold Nicolson's works are *Portrait of a Diplomatist, Being the Life of Sir Arthur Nicolson, First Lord Carnock, and a Study of the Origins of the Great War* (Boston: Houghton Mifflin, 1930); *Peacemaking 1919* (Boston: Houghton Mifflin, 1933); *Curzon: The Last Phase* (Houghton Mifflin, 1934); *Dwight Morrow* (New York: Harcourt Brace, 1935); and *The Congress of Vienna* (New York: Harcourt Brace, 1946). See also Lord David Cecil, *Melbourne* (Indianapolis: Bobbs-Merrill, 1954); Robert E. Sherwood, *Roosevelt and Hopkins* (New York: Harper, 1950); Arthur M. Schlesinger, Jr., *Robert F. Kennedy* (Boston: Houghton Mifflin, 1978); and Henry A. Kissinger, *The White House Years,* 2 vols. (Boston: Little, Brown, 1979–82).

21. Daniel D. McGarry and Sarah Harriman White, *World Historical Fiction Guide* (Metuchen, N.J.: Scarecrow Press, 1973), and the fourth edition of A. T. Dickinson, *Dickinson's American Historical Fiction* (Metuchen, N.J.: Scarecrow Press, 1981), can help in locating titles.
22. Theodore C. Sorensen, *Kennedy* (New York: Harper & Row, 1965), p. 309.

Index